CLAIM

— OF —

PRIVILEGE

ALSO BY BARRY SIEGEL

FICTION
The Perfect Witness
Actual Innocence
Lines of Defense

NONFICTION
A Death in White Bear Lake
Shades of Gray

CLAIM
— OF —
PRIVILEGE

A MYSTERIOUS PLANE CRASH, A LANDMARK SUPREME COURT CASE, AND THE RISE OF STATE SECRETS

BARRY SIEGEL

HARPER

An Imprint of HarperCollins*Publishers*

www.harpercollins.com

HarperCollins books may be purchased for educational, business, or sales promotional use. For information, please write: Special Markets Department, HarperCollins Publishers, 10 East 53rd Street, New York, NY 10022.

FIRST EDITION

Designed by William Ruoto

Library of Congress Cataloging-in-Publication Data is available upon request.

ISBN: 978-0-06-077702-9

08   09   10   11   12   WBC/RRD   10   9   8   7   6   5   4   3   2   1

To every family touched by the fall of a B-29 over Waycross, Georgia, on October 6, 1948. And to my family as well: Marti and Ally, forever my special girls.

CONTENTS

AUTHOR'S NOTE

THE REPORTS BEGAN AS A TRICKLE, JUST A FEW BRIEF NOTICES. THE TALE they told was a curiosity, a human interest story with a twist: The widow and offspring of three civilian engineers who'd perished half a century before in the crash of an Air Force B-29 were now asking the Supreme Court to reconsider a lawsuit their families had filed at the dawn of the Cold War. The High Court had erred in overturning their damages award back then, the widow and offspring were claiming. The government had lied to the justices. Wrongs must be righted. The petitioners wanted redress.

Yes, human interest with a twist, yet much more. The name of the one surviving widow spoke volumes: Patricia Reynolds Herring. Patricia *Reynolds*. The long-ago case now under challenge carried her name: *U.S. v. Reynolds*. It wasn't as well known as, say, *Miranda*, or *Gideon*, or *Brown v. Board of Education*. Over the years, though, *U.S. v. Reynolds* had wielded comparable influence. In this landmark 1953 ruling, the Supreme Court had formally recognized and established the framework for the government's "state secrets" privilege—a privilege that for decades had enabled federal agencies to conceal conduct, withhold documents, and block civil litigation, all in the name of national security.

Since 1973, the government had been asserting the privilege with increasing frequency, but the ramifications of *U.S. v. Reynolds* reached well beyond those direct assertions: By encouraging judicial deference when the government claimed national security secrets, *Reynolds* had empowered the Executive Branch in myriad ways. Among other

things, it had provided a fundamental legal argument for much of the
Bush administration's response to the 9/11 terrorist attacks. Enemy
combatants such as Yaser Esam Hamdi and Jose Padilla, for many
months confined without access to lawyers, had felt the breath of *Reynolds*. So had the accused terrorist Zacarias Moussaoui when federal
prosecutors defied a court order allowing him access to other accused
terrorists. So had the Syrian-Canadian Maher Arar, like dozens of others the subject of a CIA extraordinary rendition to a secret foreign
prison. So had hundreds of detainees at the U.S. Navy base at Guantánamo Bay, held without charges or judicial review. So had millions
of American citizens when President Bush, without judicial knowledge or approval, authorized domestic eavesdropping by the National
Security Agency.

U.S. v. Reynolds made all this possible. The bedrock of national
security law, it had provided a way for the Executive Branch to formal-
ize an unprecedented power and immunity, to pull a veil of secrecy
over its actions. Yet now here came Patricia Reynolds Herring and
three other women, claiming, in a twenty-eight-page petition, that
U.S. v. Reynolds arose from a willful fraud perpetrated on the Supreme
Court by the government of the United States. By asking the Supreme
Court to "remedy fraud," the four women behind this petition were
taking aim at the very foundation of the state secrets privilege.

Journalists began to scramble. No wonder. Who could ignore the
connections between the apocalyptic anxieties of the Cold War and
post-9/11? Who could ignore the violation of civil liberties, the abuse
of constitutional protections?

Here was history writ both large and small. This story told of
ordinary citizens' lives intersecting with those of the country's most
powerful leaders. The personal and private began with the widows.
Patricia Reynolds, who'd sat tearless in a hotel room on the day she lost
her newlywed husband, finally wept half a century later. Phyllis
Brauner, who never remarried, struggled till her last days with unan-
swered questions. Elizabeth Palya, who sewed, cooked, and nightly
set a formal dinner table, hoped always to make her children's lives
fulfilling.

Now, to those who'd begun to call, Elizabeth's daughter, Judy, said: "This story is all about America. It isn't about a plane crash. It's about my country doing the wrong thing."

It was also about the respectable relatives of civilian engineers finding common ground with enemy combatants such as Yaser Esam Hamdi, then confined in a Navy brig. Enabled by *Reynolds,* unchecked by judges, the federal government had withheld information from them all for national security reasons. The government had essentially said, *believe me.* "Whatever happens," one law professor advised, the new Reynolds petition "is a reminder that even though we have checks and balances, judges have thus far trusted high government officials. . . ."

Whatever happens. Could the new Reynolds petition undo everything *Reynolds* had wrought? Could the petition vacate that landmark 1953 ruling, could it wipe out the whole edifice of national security law? Not likely. But perhaps it could slow the false claims, the abuse of trust. At the least, it could tell the story of how this all came to be—this story about America.

CLAIM
— OF —
PRIVILEGE

PROLOGUE

EARLY ON THE MORNING OF FEBRUARY 26, 2003—A CLOUDY, chilly Wednesday—a determined woman of middle age struggled up the steps that led to the main western portico of the U.S. Supreme Court in Washington, D.C. She had a large purse over her shoulder, a package cradled in one arm, and in her free hand a wheeled black cart that held, by bungee cord, a cardboard box the size of an airplane carry-on. Eight initial steps from the First Street sidewalk, then a large raised plaza paved in gray and white marble, then nineteen more steps to a small plateau. Frances Bisicchia looked up at the building before her. The white marble exterior gave the building a startling radiance. The fluted Corinthian columns topped by American eagles, the bronze flagpoles, the perfect symmetry . . . Fran glanced around, hoping to see a famous politician.

She finally reached the portico. There, on each side, sat two figures carved by James Earle Fraser, *Contemplation of Justice* and *Authority of Law*. In the pediment above, Fran could see the sculptural group by Robert Ingersoll Aitken, *Liberty Enthroned by Order and Authority*. Below the pediment, she could see the inscription, "Equal Justice Under Law." There, before her, were the glorious bronze doors that formed the main entrance to the building.

The doors stood open, protected by a female guard. "I've come to file a petition," Fran said.

The guard studied her. "You can't do that here. You can't bring any packages into the court building." The guard directed her to a sentry station on the far north side.

Fran headed back down forty-four steps. She'd been to Washington just once before, on a chartered-bus day tour. For nearly twenty years, she'd worked as a clerk at the Philadelphia law firm Drinker Biddle & Reath. Inside her cardboard box were forty copies of the petition that her law firm meant to file with the Court clerk's office. This was no ordinary petition but rather a rare request for a writ of error *coram nobis*—a petition that asks the Court to correct an error committed in proceedings "before us."

Once on the plaza, Fran turned right, circling around the building until she reached the sentry station and another female guard. This one would not touch the box of petitions; the aftermath of the late 2001 anthrax scare still lingered. She handed Fran a label for the box and a large plastic bag. "Put the box in the bag," she advised, not at all unpleasantly. "And tie a knot." Fran did as instructed, after pulling one copy of the petition from the box. She held it out to the guard, who time-stamped it—Fran's receipt.

From the Supreme Court, Fran took a taxi to the office of the United States Solicitor General, Theodore B. Olson, at 950 Pennsylvania Avenue. After waiting half an hour in the lobby, she handed one copy of the petition to a messenger from the mailroom. She'd completed her mission. On the taxi ride back to the train station, Fran clutched her copy of the petition, closed her eyes, and rested.

INSIDE THE SUPREME COURT BUILDING, FRAN'S BOX OF PETITIONS WENT to the mailroom of the Court clerk's office, where it joined dozens of similar-looking packages. Only a small fraction of these petitions would make it to the Court's argument calendar; of some eight thousand submitted in a typical year, the Court agrees to hear fewer than 160, about two percent. By the next day, a copy of the *coram nobis* petition sat on the desk of a junior Court clerk named Clayton R. Higgins. His task was to check it for timeliness and conformity with the rules of the Court.

Higgins began to read the petition's preliminary statement: "Three widows stood before this court in 1952. Their husbands had died in the crash of an Air Force plane. The lower courts had awarded them compensation. But the United States was bent on overturning their judgments, and—to accomplish this—it committed a fraud not only upon the widows but upon this Court."

In addition to Patricia Reynolds Herring, this petition spoke for Judy Palya Loether, Susan Brauner, and Cathy Brauner—the other widows' offspring. They had only recently found one another and approached Drinker Biddle & Reath, asking the law firm to take up their cause. Patricia, who was seventy-five, lived outside Indianapolis; Judy and Cathy, both fifty-four, in towns west of Boston; Susan, fifty-eight, on Cape Cod. All had their own children now and homes and careers.

The clerk read on: "At the heart of the case is a set of reports the Air Force prepared on the accident. . . . The Air Force refused to produce these reports, even to the district judge. . . . The United States took the case to this Court . . . contending that the reports contained "military secrets" so sensitive not even the district court should see them. . . . This Court took the government at its word, and reversed. But, it turns out that the Air Force's affidavits were false. . . . It is for this Court . . . in exercise of its inherent power . . . to put things right."

The Court clerk studied the petition's cover sheet. "Petition for a writ of error *coram nobis* to remedy fraud upon this Court." Clayton Higgins had never seen such a petition. He did not think he should now. On Friday, two days after Fran's train journey, he shipped the box of petitions back to Drinker Biddle & Reath. "The above-entitled petition for a writ of error coram nobis was received February 26, 2003," Higgins wrote in a brief cover note. "The papers are returned for the following reason: There are no provisions in the rules of this Court to allow you to file such a document."

That was wrong. At Drinker Biddle, junior associate Jeff Almeida *knew* it to be wrong. After three phone conversations with Higgins on Monday, he convinced the Court clerk to consult others. The next day, March 4, Almeida once again dispatched Fran Bisicchia to Washington. Just before five p.m., Almeida sent an email message to his clients. "I received word that our petition and motion was accepted for filing today," he reported. "At this point I . . . am confident that the clerks won't interfere with this getting where it needs to be. The surprise has probably worn off by now."

In their homes, the women behind the *coram nobis* petition read this news with growing wonder. *Here we go*, they told each other. Patricia was twenty when her husband, Bob, died in the crash of the B-29 on October 6, 1948, near Waycross, Georgia. Susan was four, her sister Cathy unborn, when they lost their father, William Brauner. Judy was seven weeks old, so never knew her father, Al Palya.

For most of their lives, none of them understood what had happened back then, why the B-29 crashed, what Al Palya, Bob Reynolds, and William Brauner were doing on that military plane. Although they knew more now, they still had no idea whether the justices would listen to their plea for the Supreme Court to right a past wrong. They realized it was a long shot; the lawyers had made that clear. At least they had a beginning. Whether they prevailed or not, a door had swung open—to the courthouse, and to their past.

PART ONE

CHALLENGES

June 1946–June 1949

CHAPTER 1

BANSHEE DAYS

June '46–July '47

THE UNION OF BOB AND PATRICIA REYNOLDS HAPPENED IN
an instant. One day in September 1946, Patricia's mother announced
that her friend May had a young man she wanted Patricia to meet. The
young man was renting a room in May's Indianapolis boardinghouse.
He'd just graduated from Purdue with a degree in mechanical engineering and had landed a job at RCA. He'd grown up near Springfield,
Massachusetts, and knew no one in Indianapolis.

No way, Patricia told her mother. She was a year out of high
school, the only child of older working-class parents, a Protestant
growing up in a Catholic neighborhood. Her father, a display-advertising
manager at a Indianapolis newspaper, had died of a heart attack when
she was fourteen, and that had increased her isolation. She was happy
to be alone, watching.

No way, she repeated.

You *are* going to meet this young man, her mother insisted.

Bob Reynolds came over that night. Patricia acted aloof. She was
writing a letter in her room when he arrived, to a Cornell boy she'd
met at a USO dance. Her mother finally came in, giving her the evil
eye. Patricia put down her pen and walked into the living room.

She felt something the moment she saw him. The expression on his face was just so warm and friendly. He *glowed*. They went out that night to a movie. They were an attractive pair—he with a ruddy smiling face, she radiant with shoulder-length hair. After the movie, they sat on the Circle in downtown Indianapolis singing "Tell Me Why" in two-part harmony, her voice a sultry contralto. *Tell me wh-y the stars do shine, / Tel-l me why the ivy twines, / tel-l me why the sky's so blue, / And I will tell you just why I love you.* They sang a lot in those first weeks. She'd been planning to go to art school in New York, but her plans changed. Three months after she met Bob, they married, on November 30, 1946. She was eighteen, he twenty-one.

The world beckoned. That they had started life together in perilous times barely registered. If enemies of America seemed to be rising everywhere—if the United States faced mounting threats despite the surrender of Germany and Japan just months earlier—the Reynoldses did not notice.

That February, Korea had split into U.S.-supported South Korea and Soviet-controlled North Korea. Also that February, the State Department's expert in Moscow, George Kennan, had sent his Long Telegram, warning of the Soviet Union's hunger for "capitalistic encirclement" and "total destruction of rival power." In March, in Fulton, Missouri, Winston Churchill spoke for the first time of an implacable threat to freedom that lay behind a Communist "iron curtain." In May, a civil war erupted in China between Chinese Nationalists and the Communist Chinese forces led by Mao Zedong. Later that month, an FBI confidential memo reported the existence of an "enormous" Soviet espionage ring in Washington, D.C. By autumn, there was consensus in the country that the Kremlin represented a treacherous enemy seeking world domination. The Cold War had begun.

Bob and Pat Reynolds felt the impact only indirectly. What touched them was the United States's need for new, sophisticated ways to defend itself. After World War II, control of the seas would no longer be enough; the country had to master the skies. Driven by a sense of urgency, the military began to focus on the development of long-range guided missiles. A fierce rivalry ensued: The Army Ground Forces, the Army Air Forces, and the Naval Forces all wanted to manage this postwar program. The Air Forces, denouncing the other services' forays as a "flagrant violation," decided to seize the lead by staging a public demonstration—by claiming they had already developed a long-range guided missile. The order came from Commanding General Henry H. "Hap" Arnold: "The purpose of the project is to impress upon the public mind the fact that Army Air Forces have, and can use immediately, some form of guided missile."

So began Project Banshee. Whoever selected the name, whatever its provenance, the term carries an eerie resonance: In Irish mythology, a banshee is a "fairy woman"—sometimes young, sometimes matronly, sometimes an old hag—whose mournful wails herald an imminent death.

RCA, AWARDED A CONTRACT BY THE AIR FORCES IN JUNE 1946, TOOK on a central role in this project. In early 1947, RCA assigned Bob Reynolds to Banshee. For the Reynoldses, this meant moving to Florida, where tests were about to begin. They flew there in an Air Force B-17, Pat smuggled aboard, posing as an Army nurse. The plane had no seats or air pressure; they used oxygen masks. When they were about to land, the pilot asked Pat if she wanted a thrill. She crawled into the Plexiglas nose cone. It was her first plane ride.

In Florida, they lived by the water in Delray Beach, a sleepy coastal town between Palm Beach and Fort. Lauderdale, not for from an Air Force installation in Boca Raton. Home was a garage apartment that did regular battle with mildew. They didn't talk much about Banshee. Pat knew it involved drone planes controlled remotely by mother ships. She knew also that a man named Al Palya was the project supervisor, but she never said more than a hello to him; he was the big shot. Life with Bob—not his work—claimed her attention. She'd traveled outside Indiana only once before and found Florida exotic. She and Bob would rise early and go out walking, watching the sand crabs.

When she looked back on those Florida days, not one single other person came to mind.

AL PALYA CERTAINLY WAS THE BIG SHOT. AN ENGINEER, HE SUPERVISED a team assigned to develop the computerized radar system that would guide drone "missile" aircraft to precision targets thousands of miles away. He'd joined RCA in 1946, after three years at Minneapolis-Honeywell designing an automatic pilot system. At Honeywell, he'd impressed everyone with his ability to solve problems, to build compact analog computers, to put a lot of wires into small boxes. His closest colleagues there, Walt Frick and Bill Ergen, thought Al Palya extraordinary—no one had his type of imagination or drive.

Born in March 1907 on a farm in northern Minnesota to immigrants from what is now Slovakia, he came from "can do" stock. His parents never smoked or drank, his mother never learned to speak English, their home had no plumbing, and their nine children all hated the job of carrying water pails from the well. Al's father was so anxious for his children to get an education—and so troubled by their many missed school days because of winter weather—that he bought a small house close to the school in East Grand Forks.

By high school, Al Palya could play a terrific saxophone, the instrument a gift from his father. At age sixteen, he knew Morse code, held an amateur radio operator's license, and managed a ham radio station; one night he saved a ship at sea by relaying its distress signal. In college (first the University of North Dakota, then the University of Minnesota) he won Charleston dance contests and performed in popular campus bands. One summer he led the orchestra on a ship cruising to the Orient. Later he made travel films in half a dozen of the country's national parks. He was a tournament bridge player, an accomplished photographer, a bandleader, a singer, a carpenter. Although he was also a top engineering student, it took him a good while to graduate, given all his extracurricular activities.

He met his wife, Elizabeth, at his sister Lil's house, while visiting from the University of Minnesota one weekend. He stood five feet nine, weighed 160 pounds, had blue eyes and brown hair. Betty adored his smile and disposition. Their courtship lasted three years. When he turned thirty—by then he'd graduated—Al finally said, "Let's get married." They did so in June 1937, in East Grand Forks, and drove to a Canadian honeymoon in his new red convertible. They settled in Minneapolis. As Al traveled on business for Honeywell, he regularly wrote Betty letters. *Dear Wife . . . It's Saturday, only one week—7 days—till I stand by the railroad tracks waiting for your train . . . Honey I can't start telling you how thrilled I am. Honest I can hardly sit still . . .*

Plenty of others were drawn to Al: Colleagues and relatives appreciated his enthusiasms and optimistic outlook. They enjoyed it when he played his saxophone at social gatherings. Palya's young nephew, David Pope, loved how his uncle filled the Pope home with hilarity. Al paid attention to him, and, most important for a nine-year-old boy who would grow up to be a concert pianist, Al always invited David to play the piano.

At the home of another relative—Betty's sister Jean Perryman—Al talked often about the future. Jean never forgot his visits to her family in Birmingham, Alabama, in the 1930s, the excited predictions he'd make while sitting in their living room. He'd say, they're working on a computer, Jean, that will solve problems in no time. He also told them about television. Jean couldn't imagine that, how they'd be able to bring live pictures into her house. Al seemed like a genius, so musical, so mathematical, always thinking, his mind constantly racing. He had a drawing board at home; when he thought of some notion, he'd go sketch it.

By the early 1940s, Al Palya had spent a lot of time diagramming autopilot systems at this board. From 1943 through 1945, he and his Honeywell colleagues worked in a hangar at the Minneapolis Airport called the "Ghost Room." Al Palya, Walter Frick, Bill Ergen, Bill Culmer—they kept going constantly, all week, a half-day on Saturdays, lots of overtime. When they weren't working, the men and their wives got together socially. There wasn't much to do during World War II; no one had gasoline, and they all had little kids. So they swam, hiked, ate, visited. The women would end up talking about rations, sugar quotas, shoe repairs, recipes, their children—always hoping the war would end soon—while the men sat off by themselves, discussing the problem they were going to tackle the next morning.

Later, when the husbands began traveling—usually to Eglin Air Force Base, in Florida—the wives would gather for the night, often at Betty's house. They never knew in those years what their husbands were working on; it was all so hush-hush during the war. They didn't ask and they didn't gossip. They grew accustomed to the secrecy.

IN EARLY 1947, THOUGH, THE AIR FORCES HAD NO DESIRE TO KEEP Project Banshee a secret. Despite technical problems and daunting shortages of materiel and manpower, the Air Forces—locked in an escalating feud with the other services—kept pushing for a public demonstration. The directives, which assigned responsibility for Banshee to the Air Materiel Command at Wright Field in Dayton, Ohio, usually came from the ever belligerent Curtis LeMay, then a deputy chief of staff, later head of the Strategic Air Command, and, from 1961 to 1965, chief of staff. "Bombs Away" LeMay—"Iron Ass" to his men—made clear the chief purpose of this exercise: publicity and leverage. The mission, he wrote, was "to demonstrate to Congress and to the American Public a long-range guided missile in being." He wanted the project to be given "continuing publicity of the most intelligent and carefully worded nature." He wanted to invite "proper non-partisan news reporters" to fly in the missile airplane. He wanted the demonstration to occur "as soon as possible"—and most certainly "during the then current session of Congress."

At RCA, Al Palya, Bob Reynolds, and their team scrambled to meet severe deadlines. How to guide the missile drone planes to targets without close-range direction from mother ships? How to dive the planes into the targets once there? How—if they chose that option—to drop bombs by remote control from thousands of miles away? It didn't seem possible. Many involved with Banshee thought the project destined to fail. They lacked critical equipment and qualified personnel. They didn't know how to control the missile airplanes from afar. They did not, in truth, have a guided missile to demonstrate.

Al Palya kept refining his part of the project, first out of a RCA plant in Indianapolis, then at RCA headquarters in Camden, New Jersey. He figured he just needed transmitters, receivers, amplifiers, and two computers, one for heading, one for bombing. Couldn't they adapt the principles of Shoran—a short range radar navigation system—to control the drones? With Shoran, an aircraft determined its position by measuring the time required for radar signals to reach and return from fixed responder stations. Why not have the missile aircraft get their bearings that way, by bouncing signals off of ground sites? Yes, that's how they'd do it. At least, that's how they'd try it. By February 1947, Al Palya and Walt Frick had built what they'd imagined: an electrical heading computer that could use Shoran to calculate location, guide the plane, and drop bombs. They and Bill Ergen filed a "Patent Disclosure Data Sheet" with RCA for an invention called "Control of Aircraft or Guided Missile."

Still, the pessimistic assessments about Banshee mounted. In early June of 1947, Bill Ergen and Walt Frick decided to quit the project, despite their admiration for Palya. Frick cited rushed deadlines and inadequate staffing in his resignation letter. "Banshee is a mess . . ." he wrote. "Banshee is generally conceded to be a high level 'boondoggle.'"

Al Palya did not share this view. He never voiced doubt or frustrations about Project Banshee. He loved puzzles, he loved the challenge of figuring out how to make things work. So he remained rooted at RCA and his Haddon Heights, New Jersey, home, where he and Betty now had two young sons. Palya meant to stay at RCA for a long time.

So did Bob Reynolds. In Florida, that summer of 1947, reinforcements finally arrived. Reynolds cheered the assignment to Banshee of much-needed Air Forces personnel—twelve officers and twenty-eight graduates of a radar fundamentals course. For test aircraft, the Air Forces provided seven aging B-29s—four mother ships and three "baby" drones. They were ready to give it a try, no matter all the misgivings. In July 1947, experimental Project Banshee flight tests began out of a military airfield in Boca Raton.

CHAPTER 2

B-29 BOMBERS

Summer '47

THE AIR FORCES HANDED SUPERVISION OF THE BANSHEE flight tests to the newly formed 1st Experimental Guided Missiles Group, based south of Boca Raton at Eglin Air Force Base. Even with the reinforcements, what Bob Reynolds found at Eglin in the summer of 1947 was a skeletal military operation working out of temporary quarters. They had a mission statement, though. Soon after the twenty-eight radar specialists arrived, the Eglin command gathered everyone and spelled it out in a briefing: "We have to prove to the public that we have the ability to deliver long-range bombs. The purpose of this project is to prove to the general public that we have a guided missile and are doing research in this particular field."

Exactly how to prove this remained a puzzle. In those early months, the Guided Missiles Group at Eglin had their hands full just managing to maintain and fly their aircraft. The Group's first major accident came on the morning of May 8, when a B-17 engine caught fire some four miles south of Destin Bridge, out over the Gulf. Smoke filled the cabin, forcing the crew of seven to bail out; three did not survive. Two months later came another fatal accident, this one involving a B-29 that crashed on takeoff and burned one mile north of Eglin Field, leaving nine dead and one seriously injured.

To Bob Reynolds and the Air Force crews, such mishaps had become almost routine with the B-29s. They were always having awful problems with B-29 engines. They regularly had to shut down one engine or another, regularly had to drop down to 1,500 feet with overheating engines and limp home to Eglin.

Indeed, ever since its early development, the B-29 had been experiencing problems with its engines—2,200-hp Wright Cyclone R-3350 twin-row radials. At the start of production, in particular, they had a tendency to leak oil, swallow valves, overheat, and catch fire. That the private contractor, Wright Aeronautical, had made the crankcases of exceedingly light, strong magnesium—to get more horsepower from less weight—didn't help, as magnesium was highly flammable. Nor did it help that the huge engines lacked sufficient airflow to cool the eighteen cylinders packed around a crankshaft core. Rushed development further exacerbated the matter—the Army Air Forces had ordered 250 B-29s before the prototype existed, 1,650 before the first plane flew. Designers, faced with such intense deadlines, tried various stopgaps—air baffles, cowl flaps, propeller cuffs, heat shields—but the engine fires persisted.

There matters stood early on the afternoon of February 18, 1943, when Boeing's legendary chief test pilot, Edmund T. "Eddie" Allen, roared down Boeing Field outside Seattle in the second XB-29 prototype. From the day he'd begun testing this prototype, six months earlier, he'd been facing engine difficulties. The B-29s had to start flying, though—the Air Forces had already ordered them into production—so Allen took off yet again in a troubled plane. Moments later, engine number one caught fire. Allen shut it down, "feathered" the propeller so it wouldn't rotate in the wind, and turned back to Boeing Field. Before Allen could land, a port wing spar burned through and collapsed, crippling the left wing. From the ground, flames could be seen in the cockpit. Allen lost control just before the giant bomber plowed into the Frye meatpacking plant, three miles short of the runway, killing all eleven men aboard and at least nineteen on the ground.

FBI agents descended on the scene, cordoning off the site, seizing amateur photos from a Seattle city bus driver, and imposing strict secrecy. Within days, a furious General Hap Arnold ordered all planes with R-3350s grounded. This disaster only magnified his anger at the manufacturer of the B-29 engines. Relations between the Army and Wright Aeronautical had been contentious throughout the B-29's development.

Still, the Army Air Forces needed Wright—it was the largest producer of aircraft engines in the United States. So modifications continued on the prototypes. The Air Forces both investigated and pushed the manufacturer as Hap Arnold declared the R-3350 "the number one requirement of the Army Air Forces." Even while the military probed and modified, the first B-29s began rolling off production lines at Boeing Wichita in September 1943.

Arnold had reason to exult. The B-29 Superfortress was extraordinary: a huge, striking, ultramodern Art Deco aircraft with a semicircular Plexiglas nose, a lean cylindrical body, and what Curtis LeMay called a "swan-graceful" vertical stabilizer. Pressurized fore and aft (with the bomb bay in between), able to fly uncommonly high and far, computerized and heavily armed—this was one impressive plane. This was also, however, a mechanic's nightmare. Those who'd designed the B-29, an Air Force historical officer would later write, "appeared to forget all about the maintenance of the monster." The Superfortress "was one of the hardest airplanes ever to maintain that ever flew." To keep it flying required skilled mechanics and specialized equipment, with repairs often done in the theaters of operation, if not in the air by the flight crews. Until a design change, a mechanic aiming to conduct a routine engine checkup first had to spend a full day removing the cowling and propeller. Various other design changes followed—they were always tinkering with the R-3350 engines—but still the Superfortress remained full of dangerous problems.

Engine fires continued to erupt. The air-cooling difficulties hadn't been solved, and once an engine caught fire, the magnesium made it nearly impossible to extinguish, especially after the flames burned past the forward section. Sixty years later, Raymond Toliver, a retired Air Force colonel, Pentagon administrator, aviation historian, and B-29 test pilot, still had vivid memories of the Superfortress:

Oh yeah, those engines were bastards. Magnesium engine fronts, overheating all the time. That's why we had them for test flights. We never could figure out why they were getting so hot. Then when I was on Guam, I could see them coming in for miles, coming back from bombing runs with engines on fire. The fire would start in the hub; you could see it glowing for miles out. The magnesium—that made for a white-white light. You could see the white spot way off in the distance, even before you could see the B-29s. One time I was up in a P-51 and I saw a B-29 down close to the water, gear and flaps down, bomb bays open, two engines going, two feathered, and the crew was throwing out everything they could. That plane still went into the water. Once you opened those doors, it wouldn't fly, you'd have a real big drag out there. I didn't like the B-29. It was just a big, loose airplane.

By the time the first Banshee test flights began, modifications had resolved some of the plane's problems—B-29s, after all, had brought the war to Japan and dropped atomic bombs on Hiroshima and Nagasaki. At Eglin Field, though, crews working on Banshee still held their breath when flying a B-29 and still found themselves shutting down overheated engines as they limped home. "What else could you do?" one radar technician recalled. "You had a job to do. At least you had a parachute."

During the summer of 1947, Air Force officers scrambled to modify B-29s for Banshee. Telegrams flew back and forth—constant pleas for equipment. Although masked in the controlled language of a bureaucracy, they suggested urgent need. Sometimes those needs went unfilled, and occasionally military documents chronicled the results. One such document records a fateful moment in the handling of a particular B-29—a fateful moment where it's possible to say destiny could have been changed. The single sheet of paper is a maintenance report, dated June 19, 1947, from Wright Field in Ohio, concerning a B-29 bearing the serial number 45-21866. A remark scrawled on it, signed by one R. H. Melody, says: "*TO 01-20EJ-177 partially c/w. Exhaust manifold installed. Shields not installed.*"

"TO" was a technical order; "partially c/w" meant "partially complied with." This Air Force technical order called for a heat shield to be installed in front of exhaust collector rings to prevent excessive heat from entering the B-29's engines. There is no record of just why Wright Field engineers only partially complied with this technical order, just why B-29 #866 didn't get the mandated heat shields, but postwar conditions suggest an answer: Most likely, Wright Field simply didn't have the shields in stock.

Five days later, at noon on June 24, a crew took off in B-29 #866, intending to deliver it to Boca Raton for use in the Banshee tests. The crew noted malfunctions of various sorts during takeoff and initial flight. After twenty minutes aloft, they decided to return to Wright Field. The plane landed some fifteen minutes later with "ship on red cross on 3 engines and minor malfunctions on 4th," according to a crew member's report. "Red cross" meant not fit to fly. After some discussion at Wright Field, though, a crew flew B-29 #866 to Boca Raton the next day. There, "maintenance to put ship on safe flight condition . . . required approximately six weeks."

In the postwar demobilization, circumstances compelled the Air Forces to push on like this, whatever the shortages and limits. The threat of the Soviet Union colored every decision. By early 1947, President Truman and his advisors saw the Kremlin as directing a multi-level global campaign—"a new kind of war." To congressional leaders that February, they spoke in apocalyptic terms about three continents being vulnerable to "Soviet penetration." The next month, Truman imposed loyalty oaths on federal employees and announced the Truman Doctrine, formalizing a policy of containment against communism. "A fateful hour" had arrived, Truman told a joint session of Congress. Nations "must choose between alternate ways of life. . . . If we falter in our leadership, we may endanger the peace of the world."

Yet Truman, insisting on tight budgets, placed a higher priority on postwar foreign reconstruction than on domestic rearmament. Military spending remained constrained. This only fueled the Air Forces' already intense competition with the other services, which had never abated despite orders by Truman to resolve their differences. The services fought constantly over appropriations, roles, and missions. "Rivalries Hamper Missiles Program" ran a *New York Times* headline that June. "The Air Forces," the newspaper reported, "knowing that the long-range guided missile may eventually replace the bomber, believe that such missiles ought to be developed and operated by them."

The Air Forces' determination grew even stronger the following month, when President Truman, on July 26, 1947, signed the National Security Act, which among other provisions created the Central Intelligence Agency, the National Security Council, and an independent United States Air Force. On September 18, the Air Force (no longer the "Air Forces") officially became a separate branch of the armed services, with W. Stuart Symington as the first secretary of the Air Force and General Carl Spaatz its first chief of staff. From the start, these men faced a major challenge: On August 3, at an Aviation Day parade over Tushino Airport, outside Moscow, three four-engined planes had appeared during a low-altitude flyover. They looked like B-29s. They weren't B-29s, though—they were bolt-by-bolt copies, built by Soviet engineers, based on three intact B-29s in Soviet hands, the result of emergency landings by American pilots during the war. The Soviets called their cloned B-29 the Tu-4. The new United States Air Force had reason for alarm: Although it possessed sufficient range to reach the United States only on a one-way suicide mission, the Tu-4 clone gave Joseph Stalin an intercontinental threat capable of striking New York City, Washington, D.C., and the industrial heartland.

CHAPTER 3

DELAYS AND PROGRESS

August '47–August '48

AL PALYA NEVER STOPPED PUSHING. ON AUGUST 20, FROM Camden, he wrote to Walt Frick in Minneapolis with encouraging news: "I was very busy ever since you left but managed to get equipment supplied where it was needed on time. All phases are at present going smoothly and expect to complete Banshee sometime in October. I have some results on flight tests of the navigational bridge. The N.B. heads the plane in the proper direction, but the run is by no means a straight line. We have not progressed far enough in the Florida flight tests to determine exactly what the trouble is but when we do I will contact you and possibly ask you for some advice."

Less than a month later, at noon on Wednesday, September 17, a hurricane swept across Florida, disrupting the Banshee flight tests—as well as the Reynoldses' idyllic life. Pat and Bob, along with hundreds of thousands, had to evacuate as 150-mile-per-hour winds bore down on Delray Beach—the strongest storm to strike Florida in ten years. When it hit, the storm spared Eglin, causing no harm or casualties, but both Delray Beach and the Boca Raton airfield suffered severe damage. Palya managed to fly down to Florida early on Thursday morning, September 18, on one of the first planes getting into Miami. He found the hangars at Boca Raton "pretty well ruined." The laboratory housing the Banshee equipment had suffered little, though, so they would only have to make some changes in the flight test plans.

Days later, officers at the Guided Missile Group took stock of the crews available for Banshee. What they saw did not please them. Fourteen pilots and seven navigators had recently arrived at Eglin, assigned to Banshee, but many did not have proper flying credentials. On September 23, the Group commander complained to Air Force Headquarters, sounding a warning about future Banshee flights: "Four of the airplane commanders listed above do not have instrument cards and one is not current in the B-29. Most of the co-pilots have very limited experience in B-29 type aircraft." They needed exceptionally experienced pilots and navigators "due to the highly specialized nature of the Banshee Project." So they wanted AF Headquarters to replace "personnel indicated by asterisk" with much more qualified crews. Out of the fourteen pilots sent, the Eglin officers had rejected eight; out of the seven copilots, three. Five of the rejected pilots were not even acceptable as copilots.

Then came a decision to move the site of Banshee test flights from Boca Raton to the Warner Robins depot at Robins Air Force Base, sixteen miles south of Macon, Georgia. This relocation made sense, for Warner Robins was home to the 3150th Electronics Squadron, which existed exclusively to install radar equipment and "furnish the required flights for the testing of radar equipment." But the 3150th also lacked qualified flight crews. So in late October 1947, an urgent telegram arrived at Eglin: "Commanding Officer Warner Robins desires Eglin crew fly missile at Warner Robins on RCA flight tests. . . . Crew should include pilot/experienced/, co-pilot/experienced/ F-4 autopilot man, radar, and aircraft mechanic with electronics knowledge."

The Soviets seemed to be advancing everywhere. That September, Communists won the general elections in Hungary, and Communist parties in eight countries formed a political alliance, Cominform, a precursor of the Warsaw Pact. Truman contemplated a terrifying prospect—that the Soviet Union would draw Western Europe and West Germany into its orbit, that the Soviets would gain control over all European resources, including skilled labor, military bases, and industrial infrastructure. Such a threat only deepened the Air Force's desire to show the world it had a long-range guided missile. At a press conference on October 1, General Spaatz told reporters that the development of guided missiles was far enough along to warrant "thinking" about tactical doctrine for their use. The next month, at a hearing in Washington on November 17, Spaatz boosted the stakes: Testifying before the President's Air Policy Commission, he reported for the first time publicly that the Soviet Union had made copies of the B-29.

"Do you believe that Russia actually is manufacturing B-29s at this time?" asked Thomas F. Finletter, the commission chairman.

"We believe that they are," Spaatz replied.

IN AN UNDATED HANDWRITTEN LETTER COMPOSED AROUND THEN, PALYA provided Walt Frick a revealing update:

> Now should be a good time to drop you a line. Reason is—I have one hell of a toothache and can't even think straight. . . . I must beg your humble pardon for not answering sooner. . . . [I] felt very bad because you did not decide to come to RCA. I think it could have worked out, at least there would have been quite a large gap filled that we have in the group at present. . . . Well, my boy, can't remember if I congratulated you on your manly efforts. If I did not I want to once more offer you congrats. Three bucks says it's a girl. . . . Betty and the boys are in fine shape. I got promoted with a raise a couple of weeks ago. Am now in a supervisory classification. Whatever that can mean. . . . Drop me a line soon, Walt.
> Your friend, Al

Soon after, on November 5, Palya wrote to Bill Ergen, who was then working at the Oak Ridge National Laboratory in Tennessee. He thanked Ergen for a complex set of computations and offered a summary of his own calculations, but he had nothing promising to report: "Since our flight tests are bogged down and will not be resumed until the Base of Operation has been moved from Boca Raton to Macon, Ga. I doubt very much that we will be able to fly the navigation bridge until some time after the first of the year. At that time I will contact you and give you more information on the bridge itself, and possibly bother you with more questions. . . . Give my regards to Viola. If you were a betting man I would wager you two bucks that it's going to be a girl."

A month later, Palya sounded much more optimistic in another letter to Frick. He traded comments about a side business they both had—designing and building toys for the Christmas season. He offered news about his wife—"I don't believe I told you that Betty took a teaching job at Laurel Springs—teaches sewing one day a week." Then he turned to the Banshee project:

> I very much like it here. Security regulations here are
> getting very tight. From small talk its worse than it was during
> the war. Old Banshee is still ridin hi, with a slightly new turn. It
> seems that all the [GE] boys now have orders to produce an
> interim item that can be used, or demonstrated. . . . The trend
> is to use Shoran as a navigation means for all these schemes. That
> means, Walt, our boxes (improved) are going into production.
> Figures at present sound like a "fairy tale" and believe me, Walt,
> it's a darn nice club and very effective. The news about all
> this is more or less on the confidential side so don't publish it.

Palya finished with a wistful tone: "Drop me a line again, Walt. I enjoy your letters very much. You friend, Al."

THE SHIFT OF RCA'S RADAR FLIGHT TESTS FROM BOCA RATON TO WAR-ner Robins required Pat and Bob Reynolds to move. Although Al Pa-lya remained based in Camden, the Reynoldses relocated to Macon, Georgia, settling in there before the Christmas holidays in 1947. They rented rooms in an antebellum house that had been divided into four apartments, on a wide street in the heart of Macon. Their bed was a hand-carved mahogany four-poster. There was a settee in the living room, very Victorian. Mirrors hung on the walls, ceiling to floor, ten to twelve feet tall, gilt-edged, six feet wide; they came from a ballroom that had once been lined with them.

Years later, Patricia remembered only one of the two couples who shared their house—an Air Force pilot named Charlie and his wife, living in the apartment upstairs from them. The two couples hung out together. Being close to a lake, they spent time there. Pat and the other wife didn't work, so they'd go to lunch, go shopping. They never talked about the Banshee project, not because the subject was being avoided, but because they were just young kids having fun.

Among Bob and Pat's favorite activities, as 1947 drew to a close, was to walk around the Macon switching yard, taking pictures. They were quite drawn to trains, in fact were members of a model railroad club. They had been invited to a New Year's Eve party that year but didn't go. Instead, they stayed home and built a model railroad.

The next month, the Air Force once again publicized Banshee—they gave a Scripps-Howard aviation editor a ride in the nose of a B-29 on a drone "bombing run"—but during January and February, the project remained essentially dormant. The delays persisted that spring and summer. Bob Reynolds complained often to Pat about flights being canceled because of one problem or another.

Still, Al Palya's part of Banshee somehow managed to advance at Warner Robins. In between the cancellations, test flights did take off to test his guidance system. Palya joined one of those flights in late February, then at least two in April and two in May. Bob Reynolds flew six times in August and twice in September. Despite a relentless wave of bad Banshee news elsewhere, Warner Robins in August 1948 reported "good progress" on tests of Palya's system.

Al also had good news on another front: On August 16, his third child and first daughter, Judy, was born. He felt on top of his world. After four merit raises at RCA, he was earning $6,720, the equivalent today of more than $100,000. He had what Walt Frick and Bill Ergen considered the "hottest" part of Project Banshee. Now he had a daughter. In family scrapbooks, there is a photo of Judy as an infant, sitting in her mother's lap. In its way, the picture offers a portrait of Al Palya as well—the eager photographer looking at his daughter through the camera.

ALARM ABOUT THE SOVIET UNION AND NATIONAL SECURITY CONTIN-ued to intensify through that first half of 1948. Increasingly, U.S. citizens, not just alien radicals, were finding themselves targeted as the federal government expanded its reach and power. Loyalty oaths, blacklists, congressional hearings—all were under way. In January, the University of Washington fired three professors suspected of being Communists. In February, Communists seized power in Czechoslovakia in a coup. In June, the Soviet's blockade of West Berlin began, the United States responding with the Berlin Airlift. On July 20, federal agents arrested twelve leaders of the American Communist Party, charging them under the Smith Act with conspiring to "teach and advocate" the overthrow of the United States government. Days later, Elizabeth Bentley—the "Red Spy Queen"—disclosed to the House Un-American Activities Committee (HUAC) that Communists, employed within the federal government, had committed espionage throughout the 1930s and war years. In early August, also testifying before HUAC, *Time* magazine editor and former Communist Whittaker Chambers accused Alger Hiss, a top State Department official, of being a Soviet agent.

Thus began HUAC's pursuit of Communists in government, and the country's anxious preoccupation with secrecy. America alone had the atomic bomb, and it seemed imperative to keep its design secret—in fact, to keep everything secret. The Soviet Union's espionage frightened even the imperturbable. So did the sense, fueled by the Soviet's Berlin blockade, that a global war could be sparked at any time by either miscalculation or provocation. Wanting neither to force a military confrontation nor to back down, America had launched the Berlin Airlift—but Truman had also deployed sixty B-29 bombers capable of delivering nuclear weapons to British air bases. Many American policymakers believed Communist Party members to be conspiratorial fanatics bent as much on sabotage as spying. "Could the Reds Seize Detroit?" *Look* magazine asked that year, in an article offering possible ways the Soviets might afflict industrial America (among them, swarming jails to release violent prisoners).

These matters would eventually have considerable effect on the families of all the civilian engineers involved in Project Banshee, but they hadn't yet. In Macon that spring, Bob and Pat had met a group of students from a nearby musical conservatory, and Bob had started playing in a big band they'd put together. He'd tour Georgia with them, performing at college dances and various school formals. Pat would tag along. One night in a diner, just having fun, the band started singing the Gershwins' "Summertime." *Summertime, and the livin' is easy. / Fish are jumpin' and the cotton is high* . . . On impulse, Pat joined in with her sultry contralto. *Your daddy's rich and your mamma's good lookin'* . . . The bandleader, a fellow named Jesse, liked what he heard. "You can really sing," he told her. He asked the others to be quiet. Pat sang solo—*One of these mornings, you're going to rise up singing . . . So hush, little baby, don't you cry* . . . After that, Pat was the girl singer in the band.

It didn't last for long, only for a while that spring and fall. What has endured from that period is a photo of Bob and Patricia. Pat is wearing high heels and a taffeta suit, as if she were dressed for a ball—though in truth she'd just come from church. Bob is wearing tweeds. Her mom, visiting from Indianapolis, took the picture, but the couple doesn't seem to notice her. Pat is looking at Bob with unguarded adoration.

CHAPTER 4

FINAL EXAM

October '48

AT WARNER ROBINS IN THE FALL OF 1948, AL PALYA'S guidance system stood ready for its final-stage design test, scheduled for October 6. This was a big deal, essentially an Air Force "acceptance" exam. At the start of October, the key civilians involved in the flight test began to make their way to Georgia. Al Palya and Bob Reynolds from RCA would be there. So would Richard Cox, an engineer employed by the Air Force—its man on the Banshee project. So would William Brauner and Eugene Mechler, two engineers from an RCA subcontractor, the Franklin Institute, located in Philadelphia.

Walt Frick, who had rejoined RCA in the summer of 1948—unable to resist Palya's persuasion—also traveled to Macon for this test flight. Fifty years later, he would recall his final hours in Camden with Palya before they started heading for Georgia: "Every morning that we were on laboratory projects together, we had formed the habit of taking ten minutes off work precisely at ten o'clock for coffee in a lunch wagon across the street. On the last morning before moving south for the crucial test flight, Al and I left the lab, as was our custom, for our cup of coffee. Parked in front of the lunch wagon was a truck on which there were two wooden boxes identical to those used for shipping [cadavers]. Walking around the truck, Al said to me, "Well, what do you think of that, Walt? Somebody heard we were going to Georgia, and they're sending this guy down to bring us back.'"

On Friday evening, October 1, Palya flew into Chicago with plans to spend the weekend at his sister Lil's home in Elmhurst, Illinois, visiting his mother and siblings. They needed to discuss the care of their elderly mother and the division of their deceased father's property. The father had lost his cash assets in the Depression, then died in 1933, leaving the family with only farmland. Al's mother no longer had her own home; over the past fifteen years, she'd stayed with one child, then another. This situation made for family tensions that Al, being the only male Palya left, often found himself trying to defuse. That August, just six days before his daughter Judy's birth, he'd written a strained letter to his sister Helen, addressing issues about the family farm and finances.

Now Al and his sisters gathered at Lil's home with matters still unresolved. Al seemed tense and serious, the atmosphere morose. The siblings were not equally interested in taking care of Anna, and that fueled resentment. So did the question of which sibling got what part of the family land. No one smiled. The next morning, Monday, October 4, Al Palya, forty-one years old, boarded a plane for Atlanta.

That same Monday, William Brauner, a thirty-four-year-old engineer-physicist with the Franklin Institute, left his home in Aldan, Pennsylvania. Born in Vienna in 1914, Brauner had been active in the Austrian underground before World War II. Discovered by the Nazis, he'd been given twenty-four hours to flee the country. In 1938, at age twenty-four, he'd crossed the Alps into Switzerland, his mountaineering experience a large asset. Brauner managed to immigrate to the United States, where he earned bachelor's and master's degrees in physics at Purdue University. At Purdue he met Phyllis Ambler, a chemistry instructor with a master's degree from Wellesley. He found himself taken by this petite woman with bright blue eyes who always seemed to be listening so intently. They married in August of 1943, she wearing a white satin dress, a bouquet of white roses and gardenias in her arms. He'd been so happy that day, and so proud to be an American.

Like Palya, Brauner always looked at the positive side of things.

Also like Palya, he loved photography. There was something special about the photos he took of his young daughter, Susan. They would, in later years, be his gift to her, the way he spoke to her. Brauner had not been riding on the test flights out of Boca Raton and Warner Robins. In fact, Brauner had never before flown on a B-29. After walking out the front door, he turned back to wave once more to his family—to his pregnant wife, Phyllis, and to four-year-old Susan. His daughter waved back. Her father didn't travel that much; she wasn't used to seeing him go off like this. Susan couldn't help thinking: *I'll never see him again.*

Eugene Mechler, who was thirty-five, another electrical engineer with the Franklin Institute, left his New Jersey home that same morning. He'd earned a master's degree in electrical engineering from Columbia University and had served in the Army Air Corps during the war. He had expertise in radio and radar systems. Like Brauner, he'd not taken part in any of the test flights. As he walked through his front door, he also turned to wave to a pregnant wife and a young daughter, three-year-old Betsy.

Richard Cox, a slender thirty-three-year-old, had no traveling to do that Monday. He awoke in Macon, where he lived in the upstairs room of a "tourist home," a long way from his family's farm in Farragut, Iowa. He represented the government, running tests on RCA's Banshee project. He was studious, quiet, and reserved, a high school valedictorian and a devout Christian who once served as Sunday School superintendent for his Methodist church. His association with Banshee remained largely a mystery to his family. Yet Cox's early letters home did provide hints. In September 1946, he'd written his parents from the RCA plant in Indianapolis, describing postwar conditions and the special assistance provided by Al Palya:

> Well, the trip to Indianapolis went off on schedule. The hotel situation out here is severe. The only way for me to get a room at all was through RCA. A week ahead of time we called Mr. Palya of RCA and he reserved a room in the Warren Hotel in Indianapolis. I was registered as an RCA representative. . . . The restaurants here haven't shut down yet, as you say they did

in Iowa. Here they merely charge more and serve less. Meat is of course a non-existent item on the menu, or is sometimes there at a terrific price. . . . Since I'm to represent the Gov't on all the bench and type tests I've much to learn and a lot of agreements to negotiate. [RCA's] test equipment is at present inadequate and that has to be changed. There's any number of problems to whip.

In fall 1948, Cox found himself again experiencing a temporary dislocation—this time to Robins Field. Early in September, before moving to Georgia, he'd driven home to Farragut for a week's visit. He spent time there with his younger brother, Gerald, talking little about his work, saying only that he had to go to Warner Robins to conduct tests on something secret. One day, he helped his father dig potatoes and pour cement for a basement shower. When he prepared to leave, his mother grew uncommonly emotional. She had no specific premonition, nothing at least that she put in words. She felt afraid, though—afraid something was wrong with his going.

From Macon, on September 18, Richard wrote Gerald to report he'd arrived safely. "That vacation at home was something I really enjoyed to the fullest. I was sorry that it had to end at all. If only I could be located near enough to see all of our family once in a while. . . . But it seems it just isn't to be. . . . Much love from your brother."

Two days later, Cox and Bob Reynolds took off from Robins Field on a Banshee test flight that lasted over five and a half hours. They flew together again on September 30 and October 1. The team had one flight to go—the final-stage test when Al Palya would join them.

On October 3, Cox wrote once more to his brother, commenting on a friend's recent death in an industrial accident back in Iowa: "Such an accident is so uncalled for if only a little precaution is exercised. . . . My training includes so much of safety precautions that it's almost instinctive for me. Guess I can't begin to understand the sort of carelessness involved in Keith's accident. . . ." Cox closed with a reference to his current work: "From the way things look now I may still be around down here for a time. . . . The work goes slowly. Guess there's no percentage in being impatient unless pressure is exerted from up above. . . . This will be all for now. I hope to hear from you again soon. Love from your brother, Richard."

By October 5, Al Palya and Walter Frick were together in Macon. Palya did not, as it happened, have to ride on the test flight scheduled for the next morning. "He went along," Frick told Al's daughter Judy years later, "as a morale booster for the guys who had to do the dirty work."

Frick planned to be aboard, too, but he missed the flight because at the last minute a colleague, Don Lawler, asked him to review test data. Lawler's request might also explain why Bob Reynolds *was* on that flight. Reynolds, who'd flown nine times since August, wasn't scheduled for this final test. He and Pat were getting ready to move to RCA's Camden plant; days before, they'd flown there and leased an apartment in Haddonfield, New Jersey. Their trunks were packed. Then came a last-minute call. Someone couldn't make the flight. Could Bob replace him?

Sure, no problem. Bob had been flying in B-29s regularly, often three times a week. It was like going to the office. Bob and Pat rose early on October 6—they preferred getting things done before the Georgia air grew too hot. He was twenty-four, she twenty, one month from their second anniversary. They walked the hills at five-thirty, holding hands, watching the dawn. Then Bob drove off to Robins Field.

CHAPTER 5

THE FLIGHT

October 6, 1948

IN SOUTH FLORIDA THAT WEDNESDAY MORNING, ENGINEERS struggled with broken dikes in the wake of a hurricane that had ravaged the region the previous day. Although evidence remains uncertain, this hurricane possibly delayed the scheduled Banshee test flight by twenty-four hours, since the B-29's route would take it to Orlando and back. The mandate now, early on October 6 at Warner Robins, was for the plane to take off at precisely 8:30 a.m.

There had been problems in the past holding to a timetable. In late February, the 3150th Squadron's operations officer had felt compelled to type out a "Standard Operating Procedure" for Al Palya's Banshee radar tests, which regularly flew in B-29 #866. "This procedure has been set up so that B-29 #866 *will* repeat *will* take off on project flights at 0830 hours," he wrote. "In order for this to be effective it must be strictly adhered to." Reading this directive, crews involved in the Banshee tests would have felt a burden, would have grasped the obsessive urgency that Air Force commanders attached to this mission:

Pilot, co-pilot, engineer, radio operator and 2 scanners will be scheduled at least one day in advance. Pilot will check with project officer and operations as to the correct loading list which includes the civilian engineers. . . . Supply will open at 0730 hours so that each individual member of the flight crew and the civilian engineers will be able to secure their individual parachutes. . . . The flight crew will report to the line at 0735 hours with their parachutes, at which time the co-pilot will supervise and aid the crew in pulling the props and pre-flighting aircraft. . . . At 0800 hours, transportation will be available. . . . to transport RCA and Wright Field engineers with their parachutes and equipment to the aircraft. . . . At 0815 hours, complete crew including engineers will line up to the left of the nose of the aircraft with parachutes on . . . for parachute inspection by pilot. Immediately after this inspection, engineers and interested members of the crew will hold a short briefing with the pilot as to what is desired on the mission that day. . . .

Despite these instructions, events did not unfold as planned. Memories differed later, but it seems clear that not everyone made it on time to the 8:15 a.m. lineup at the nose of the aircraft. Copilot Herbert W. Moore Jr., for one, arrived late. The pilot, Captain Ralph Erwin, may or may not have started an inspection, may or may not have started checking names against the flight clearance list. Whatever he did, something interrupted him, and soon word came that the flight was being delayed.

As the copilot explained later, a leaking gasket in engine number four caused the holdup. Yet the flight engineer, Sergeant Earl Murrhee, thought they had put off the flight because the civilian electronics engineers had not yet arrived on the field. Murrhee knew about the problem with engine number four—a leak in the right fuel injection pump—but insisted that they had repaired it immediately by replacing the float seal. At the time they postponed the flight, he knew of no mechanical defect.

The operations officer rescheduled takeoff for 1:20 p.m. At one p.m., the crew again assembled outside their B-29. They would have been tired now, having risen near dawn, yet still faced a more than five-hour roundtrip flight to Florida. Pilot Ralph Erwin checked his clearance list to make sure that each man was present, with his parachute. Down the line he walked: Captain Moore, the copilot; Sergeant Murrhee, the flight engineer; First Lieutenant Lawrence Pence Jr., the navigator; Sergeant Walter Peny, the left scanner; Sergeant Jack York, the right scanner; Sergeant Melvin Walker, the radio operator; Sergeant Derwood Irvin, the bombsight and autopilot repairman. Then to the civilian engineers: Al Palya and Robert Reynolds from RCA; William Brauner and Eugene Mechler from the Franklin Institute; Richard Cox from the Air Force's Air Materiel Command.

Standard procedure next called for the pilot to brief both crew and civilian engineers about escape hatches and emergency exit procedures, but this did not occur. "The Air Force personnel was well-informed in the case of emergency," the flight engineer offered later. "The civilian personnel, I had nothing to do with, do not know what they knew. . . . Some had just come down, whether they had been briefed, I do not know." Two, though, were "the regular men that stay in our squadron all the time, Mr. Reynolds and Mr. Palya."

Air Force policy also required that planes be operated by crew members who regularly flew together, but the shortage of qualified officers made this difficult. The men standing before the B-29 this afternoon were not an established squad, in fact barely knew one another. Some came from the Guided Missile Group in Florida, others from the 3150th at Warner Robins. The pilot, copilot, and engineer had never shared the same cockpit.

The airplane assigned to them for this flight, B-29 #866, had been giving the 3150th Squadron trouble ever since it arrived at Warner Robins. Of the previous 189 days, the plane had been out of commission ninety-seven; fourteen consecutive days was the longest period it had ever remained flyable. Vibration in the tail section had been a recurring problem. There'd been many fuel leaks, requiring the fuel-injection pumps to be replaced numerous times. Those charged with maintaining this B-29, both civilians and enlisted men, thought it required an excessive amount of maintenance. As recently as October 1, the plane had been listed as being on "red cross"—grounded, unflyable.

That was not the first time B-29 #866 had been on red cross. Here was the plane that a flight crew had tried to ferry from Wright Field to Eglin Field in June 1947, only to turn back after twenty minutes with three of its four engines malfunctioning. Here was the plane that carried a June 1947 maintenance note, "TO partially c/w. Exhaust manifold installed. Shields not installed."

Those heat shields had never been installed. Pilot Ralph Erwin had to know this, for as he stood before B-29 #866, he held in his hand an Airplane Flight Report that advised, "See 41B for T.O. N C/W"—technical order not complied with. In fact, eight different technical orders for this plane hadn't been complied with, including one calling for general engine conditioning and another for inspection of the horizontal stabilizer. The most critical stated that "a heat shield will be installed at the rear lower cowl assembly prior to installation of the rear exhaust collector rings, to prevent excessive heat from entering the rear of the engines."

Of course, Erwin also knew that technical orders weren't always implemented. Crews had been flying RCA radar tests in this troublesome B-29 since February; crews had been flying lots of troublesome planes in the postwar era. With B-29s out of production, getting replacement parts had become nearly impossible, forcing mechanics to cannibalize aircraft. The airplane flight report issued to Pilot Erwin this morning included, in a box with the heading "Status Today," a red diagonal warning symbol. Yet it also contained an "exceptional release," signed by the 3150th Squadron commander, A. H. Maresh, allowing the plane to fly. These notations would not have given the pilot much pause—exceptional releases kept a good many planes in the air those days. After checking his flight list, Captain Erwin walked around the plane to inspect the landing gear and engines. Then he climbed into B-29 #866. Shortly after 1:00 p.m., the others followed. They were ready to go.

FOLLOWING A STANDARD PREFLIGHT CHECK, THE CREW FIRED UP THE engines. Before taxiing, the flight engineer reported that the number two engine was running a little hot, not uncommon on a B-29. On engine run-up, number two showed a magneto drop of 100 rpm, within proper range for this measure of ignition spark. On power check, the pilot put number two at full throttle with turbo on for about four seconds. He found no loss of power. That was good enough for him.

The thirteen men were spread out in the two pressurized compartments, one fore and the other aft of the plane's giant bomb bays. The two cabins were connected by a tight (thirty-six-inch-diameter) pressurized crawlway that ran atop the bomb bays. In the rear sat the left scanner, the right scanner, the relief scanner and four of the five civilian engineers—Bob Reynolds, William Brauner, Richard Cox and Eugene Mechler. Cox and Reynolds positioned themselves close to the Banshee equipment on the right side, while Brauner and Mechler remained between the scanners' windows. In the forward cabin's cockpit—called the "greenhouse" because of all the glass—sat the pilot and copilot. Behind them were the engineer, the navigator, and the radio operator. Al Palya, who'd started toward the rear when he first boarded, had ended up strapping himself into the bombardier's seat in the Plexiglas nose, below and in front of the pilots—less crowded and a prize seat for sightseeing. Curving panes surrounded him on all sides but the rear, providing an almost panoramic view. He was eager: To-day's mission involved making a run on a fictitious target using his Shoran automatic guidance system.

They had finished taxiing now. Through the windows, the crew could observe a high 3,500-foot overcast, with a scattering of broken clouds below. Visibility was 15 miles, the temperature 87 degrees, the wind southwest at 6 miles per hour, with "no hazard foreseen to exist along proposed route of flight," according to the flight service report. Pilot Erwin lowered the wing flaps to 20 degrees and asked if all the men were ready. At 1:28 p.m., B-29 #866—a 111,000-pound, 99--foot-long fortress with a 141-foot wingspan—roared down the Robins Field runway. In the rear compartment, sitting on a large pillow, Franklin Institute engineer Eugene Mechler thought the pilot was using up an awful lot of runway. But then again, this was Mechler's first ride in a B-29. Takeoff proved normal, with no loss of power. They retracted the landing gear and climbed through light cumulous clouds, power at a standard 2,400 rpm and 43 inches of manifold pressure. The pilot was holding it steady at 185 mph IAS (indicated air speed) At 4,000 feet, just as the B-29 cleared the clouds, the flight engineer reported that engines numbers one, two, and four were running a little hot. Again, this was not unusual, especially in the Georgia heat. The pilot boosted air speed to 195 mph and reduced power to 40 inches of manifold pressure, which meant the nose dipped slightly and a cooling airflow increased over the engines.

The plane kept climbing. In the rear, Bob Reynolds adjusted the Shoran heading computer, setting a fictitious target and fixing on its guiding-beacon pulses. The plan was to turn the B-29 controls over to the Banshee system as they made their run on this target. While preparing, Reynolds explained the equipment adjustments to Richard Cox and answered questions from William Brauner and Eugene Mechler. Satisfied with what he heard, Mechler sat back down on his pillow and started to read a magazine, waiting for the moment when they'd put the plane on automatic guidance.

The B-29 continued to climb. It was close to two p.m. now. In an instant, at 18,500 feet, the aircraft lost power in engine number one. Manifold pressure inside the engine dropped from 40 to 23 inches—a major loss, meaning air speed would have fallen 10 to 15 miles per hour, down to about 180. Fuel consumption on number one also fell. The pilot asked about other readings. All else normal, the flight engineer advised.

At first, neither the pilot nor the copilot were overly alarmed. They put out their cigarettes, though. Then, a moment later, speaking over the plane's interphone, the pilot advised everybody to strap on their parachute. The civilians rushed to obey. Mechler was sitting on his; he pulled it out, struggled into it, and snapped the buckles. Brauner came over and asked for help with his last buckle. Mechler stood up and fastened it across Brauner's chest. They remained on their feet, quiet, awaiting further orders.

As they'd been scrambling into their parachutes, the plane had continued to climb, from 18,000 to 20,000 feet. Why? It is no small question. Some—not all—of those who later came to study the fate of B-29 #866 would challenge this decision by the pilot. Most agree that Captain Erwin should have shut down engine number one at 18,000 feet, when he lost half its power, but they don't agree on what he should have done next. The more aggressive would have kept flying the mission on three engines—*Sure, you can fly on three, happens all the time on B-29s, there's no reason not to keep going.* Others would have headed back to Robins Field—*I don't like this at all. I'd throttle back, start down, go home. Whatever the cause, I'm not going to keep flying without an engine.*

The evidence suggests Captain Erwin just wasn't ready to give up. It makes sense that he would keep climbing. Erwin was a World War II combat pilot and veteran of the B-29 flying culture, where crews often had to shut down engines on long bombing runs across the Pacific. You don't just turn around and quit—and you don't automatically shut down an engine, either. In Erwin's experience, a balky engine cleared up as many times as it needed to be shut down. Even if it didn't, you still had three engines. Erwin harbored a mental tolerance for problem planes.

He also knew that the Banshee crews were under pressure to get this mission completed. *SOP—this procedure has been set up so that B-29 #866 will repeat will take off on project flights at 0830 hours.* He realized that his engines had been working hard all the way up, that B-29 engines had chronic overheating problems, that this particular B-29 lacked critical heat shields. But they needed to do this final-stage test; they needed to put a Banshee demonstration before the public. The duty to deliver against clear evidence of serious engine trouble—Erwin faced a difficult choice.

Or perhaps not so difficult: At least at the start, Erwin had seen no abnormal engine readings other than the drop in manifold pressure. Oil pressure, temp, rpm, cylinder heat, all okay. Later, it's true, the cylinder-head temperatures began dropping, a sign that the cylinders weren't firing efficiently. But why? How serious was this? Maybe symptoms were hiding behind symptoms—but maybe they weren't.

At 20,000 feet, Erwin leveled off and reduced power on his three

good engines, taking them down to 2,100 rpm and 31 inches of manifold pressure. He asked the flight engineer to try to raise the pressure
manually on number one. The engineer worked the emergency amplifier system until he had engine one at 31 inches. It wouldn't hold,
though; pressure started falling back to 23. Sergeant Jack York came up
front, crawling through the narrow tunnel between compartments, to
replace the amplifier with a spare. They tried again to boost pressure.
Again it wouldn't hold.

Now the crew knew it had a problem. Erwin finally decided to
"feather" engine number one, which meant turning it off after posi-
tioning the propeller so it wouldn't keep rotating in the wind. But
Erwin, looking out his window at number one, accidentally pushed
the feathering control for engine number four. Copilot Moore noticed
immediately and unfeathered four—or at least thought he did; engine
four would later be found in the feathered position. The pilot, meanwhile, unaware that he'd now lost number four as well, pressed and
held the correct control button to shut down number one. The engineer closed number one's fuel valve. They felt the slight vibration that
comes when an engine is turned off in flight.

It was too late. Even before number one stilled, the flight engineer and left scanner saw the engine's access doors turn a light
brown—something was toasting in there. Then the scanner reported
smoke coming from number one. The pilot ordered the flight engineer
to hit the engine's fire extinguisher. That seemed to work—the smoke
dissipated. But five seconds later it came back. This time there was fire,
too. In an instant, the flames engulfed the aft half of the engine, then
the entire engine.

"Engine number one on fire," shouted the left scanner, Sergeant
Walter Peny, over and over. "There is a fire on engine number one."

The civilian engineers in the rear compartment stood calmly,
listening to Peny's reports on the fire, listening to him relay information coming from the cockpit over the interphone. Later, Eugene
Mechler would remember no panic, only Peny doing his job, staying at
his position, cool and efficient, shouting loudly enough for everyone to
know the situation. Al Palya, though, would not have been able to

hear. Sitting alone in the Plexiglas nose, Palya's view would be forward, on an empty sky free of flames.

The wing area behind the engine was now ablaze. Flames flashed past the left scanner's window. The entire left wing had caught fire. Captain Erwin by this point may or may not have started a descent, may or may not have ordered the cabin depressurized so they could open the escape hatches. The civilians tugged at the parachutes on their backs; the crew scrambled for positions.

Copilot Herbert Moore later said that he realized he hadn't heard the cabin pressure being released; he knew it would come with a noise or a feeling of force on his ears. He unbuckled his seat belt and turned to the engineer, asking if he'd released the pressure. Yes, the engineer told him. "Somebody then said to open the [escape] hatch leading into the bomb bay . . ." the copilot would later testify. "Nobody seemed to be doing anything, so I got up, took a step towards the bomb bay hatch."

Here events began to blur, many happening at nearly the same time. Having left his seat in the cockpit, the copilot was moving toward the bomb-bay hatch when it blew open, probably because someone had pulled the emergency pressure release. As he stepped back from the hatch, Moore asked the engineer if he'd dropped the front nose wheel. Yes, the engineer replied. The copilot now bent down and opened the nose-wheel door. Seeing that the nose wheel in fact was still retracted—blocking an alternate path out of the plane—he reached over and pressed the down switch on the pilot's instrument panel. This must have slowed the plane: Extending the immense landing gear on a B-29 doubles its "parasite" drag.

"What's wrong with No. 2?" Pilot Erwin asked just then. Again, events blurred. Everything seemed to be happening at once.

The left scanner yelled back, "Engine two is losing power."

Manifold pressure in number two had dropped to twenty inches. Investigators later surmised that either the engineer inadvertently shut off fuel for this engine during the feathering of number one, or flames on the left wing disabled it. Something had surely happened: In the rear compartment, Mechler could hear Sergeant Peny reporting the loss of power on number two. By that time, Mechler could see the flames shooting past the scanners' windows. He could even feel the heat.

Pilot Ralph Erwin was now flying a huge, lumbering B-29 with one and a half engines. With engines one and four feathered and number two at half power, only number three, on the right wing, gave him full thrust. B-29 #866 had gone into a moderate dive, banking about twenty degrees to the left. Engine number three was elevating the right wing, creating both lift and torque in the direction of the bank, pushing the plane into a sloppy, uncoordinated left turn. At this moment, Erwin had two choices, neither of them good. If he added power to his one fully working engine, he'd just make matters worse—he'd increase the lift and torque, forcing the plane into an even steeper banking turn. The only way out of this asymmetric thrust was to reduce power to engine three. Yet he needed to maintain air speed to avoid a stall; the plane was already yawing. If he reduced number three, he'd have nothing—no speed of air over the wings, no lift. In short, there was no possible resolution.

Or was there? Captain Erwin had only one possible way to maintain lift: He had to convert altitude into speed. In order to accelerate without gunning his one good engine, he had to aim his aircraft at the earth and plunge.

Sixty years later, after studying voluminous reports about the fate of B-29 #866, Ray Toliver, the retired Air Force colonel, B-29 test pilot, and aviation historian—who also served the military as an accident investigator—put it this way: "I don't know if he had the means of recovery at this point. Problem is, he has two engines feathered, but he doesn't know it. But I'd put the nose down, level the wings, retard the engines, and dive. He had 20,000 feet to lose, plenty of space to fall." Once he'd regained speed and level flight, Erwin could have safely ordered an evacuation. "You pull out at eight thousand feet," Toliver observed, "then open the doors and parachute."

Captain Erwin did not do this. He did issue an order: "Stand by to abandon ship."

In the rear, Sergeant Peny noticed that the escape hatch to the bomb bay wasn't open. "Open the escape hatch," he called out. Then he unfastened his buckle and lunged for it himself. He blacked out momentarily as he struggled with the handle. Watching him, Mechler couldn't believe what was happening. He felt safe inside this huge hull. Planes land with an engine on fire all the time, he kept thinking. This pilot will get us down okay. He'd rather stay with the ship than parachute.

On the floor before him, Peny recovered his senses and pulled once more on the escape-hatch handle. Finally the hatch popped up and Peny yanked it back over his head. The hatch led into the huge, empty bomb bay. For the crew to parachute, they would next have to open the bomb-bay doors.

That was standard evacuation procedure, but at this moment, perilous—what Ray Toliver would later call a "colossal mistake." B-29 #866, down to one fully operating engine, was flying only thirty to fifty miles per hour above stall speed. Opening the bomb-bay doors would create enormous additional drag, slowing the plane even more. This aircraft could not fly on one and a half engines with the bomb-bay doors open.

Did Captain Erwin realize this? It appears he must have lost track of his air speed—a common problem during in-flight emergencies. That's the only way to explain what happened. In Ray Tolliver's words, "the pilot forgot to fly the airplane."

Erwin now flipped the bomb-bay door switch on the pilot's panel. Instantly, as the doors fell open, drag forced the aircraft into a violent spin to the left. Centrifugal force pinned the crew down, plastering everyone to the floor, one man atop another, unable to move. In the rear, Eugene Mechler landed on something soft, his pillow maybe, and felt other men—among them Bob Reynolds, William Brauner, and Richard Cox—falling on top of him. Only later would he see the cuts on his face and legs, feel his banged-up arm. What he felt mainly was terror. Plummeting earthward, unable to move a muscle, he thought, *This is it. Poor Alice, what will she do?*

In the forward compartment, Copilot Moore had been thrown against the bombardier's seat; he was facing to the rear, one of his heels caught in the nose-wheel well opening. In that position, it is possible he was blocking Al Palya's escape. Moore saw someone—Pence?—standing by the nose-wheel hatch, holding on to an upright post. No one spoke.

In a moment, the spin and centrifugal pressure eased slightly, enough for some of the men to shift. Up front, the copilot managed to pull himself to the nose-wheel hatch. The plane again banked and dove, throwing the engineer, Earl Murrhee, into that hatch. He stuck there, face up in the well, his parachute on his back. The nose-wheel gear had extended, but not enough. The copilot, standing over Murrhee, stuck a foot down and kicked him through, the nose wheel falling free. The copilot instantly followed, jumping at 15,000 feet—after, he'd later testify, hearing someone behind him say, "Go." Al Palya, finally managing to scramble from the nose cone, also lunged for this escape.

In the rear compartment, at the same time, Peny slid through the bomb-bay hatch and jumped from the plane, pulling his rip cord. Mechler had been waiting for the other men to get off him, but when no one did, he pushed himself up and moved slowly toward the door, crawling after Peny, thinking, *How slowly I'm moving. How do I get out of this thing?* He'd had no instruction in evacuation procedures and didn't know the location of the escape hatch. Following Peny's lead, though, Mechler managed to find the way out. He took a moment to get hold of his parachute release handle. As he jumped, he pulled. *My gosh*, he thought. *I pulled it too soon. The chute will foul on the plane.* It didn't. Mechler plunged, then slowed as his chute opened and streamed out behind him. There was the earth, just below, coming toward him.

What of the other men? Mechler could not say. Floating toward earth, he saw no sign of them.

CHAPTER 6

AFTERMATH

October 6–7, 1948

WHILE STILL ALOFT, THOSE WHO JUMPED HEARD A PUFF IN the sky and saw falling pieces of metal. It was 2:07 p.m. B-29 #866 had been airborne for forty minutes. Witnesses on the ground heard an explosion louder than thunder, more like a bomb. Looking up, they watched the plane disintegrate as it plummeted in a spin, trailing white smoke. A Southern Bell lineman working half a mile away, W. A. Whaley, likely put in the first call for ambulances and fire trucks by tapping a telephone line with his test set. The employee of a local business, Henry Brasington, also made an early call, having seen the plane and heard the explosion while working in his company's yard.

Whaley, Brasington, and at least a half dozen others watched as engine number four came off, then the outer panel of the left wing, then engines one and three. All control surfaces, wing flaps, and portions of the stabilizers tore loose. The fuselage broke in two at the rear bomb bay. Nearly all the parts rained down onto the Zachry family's 340-acre cattle farm, just off the dirt Gibbs Street Extension, two miles south of Waycross, Georgia.

A mix of grazing pastures and marsh, the Zachry farm sat on the edge of the vast, cypress-thick Okefenokee Swamp. In his barn, Robert Zachry dove to the ground when he heard the B-29 explode. Ordinarily, he would have been at his furniture store in town, but this was a Wednesday, when everything in Waycross closed for a communal fish fry, a town tradition since the Depression. Zachry, recovering after a moment, told his four-year-old son, Michael, to run for the house, then jumped on his quarter horse and rode out to open the gate on Gibbs Road, known more commonly as Swamp Road. Zachry was born and raised on the farm, and his father before him. He knew the authorities would need to get onto his land.

Michael was still sprinting past the pump house when the plane hit the ground, some five hundred feet from the Zachry barn. He dropped to the grass, then rose and started running again. His six-year-old brother, Bernard, should have been at the adjacent school, but instead was across the street, playing cowboys and Indians with his buddy Joey and a little girl they'd tied to a tree. Bernard saw it all, the plane falling from the sky, the fire and smoke, the parachutes, one engine knocking over their fence, another landing near the schoolyard. He also saw the school principal shouting at him and coming across the road, a heavyset woman trying to climb a fence to get to the wayward children. Bernard's mother reached them first. She scooped him up as the principal grabbed Joey. Bernard never could recall whether anyone untied the little girl.

He remembered the crowd that gathered, though. Waycross had some 22,000 residents then, and at least 500 of them were already straining against the Zachry family's fence. Bernard, his mother, and his brother tried to keep people from knocking it down. They watched a man climb over the fence, pick up a severed arm, and remove a wristwatch. "Well, I can tell you," Bernard Zachry would say fifty years later, "anyone who lives in Waycross remembers it. Biggest thing that ever happened here."

In Waycross that morning, the local *Journal-Herald* had reported on the mayor's proclamation of "Safety Week," prompted by concern over the mounting number of automobile accidents. The newspaper had paid even more attention to the thirty-eighth anniversary of Churchwell's, the oldest and largest department store in town.

Now the anniversary, Safety Week, and the Wednesday fish fry gave way to the sound of sirens. The police and the State Patrol soon arrived at the Zachry farm, then the ambulances, the Red Cross, the reporters, and photographers.

On the ground, Eugene Mechler began to get his bearings. He'd come down easily, to his surprise, and had quickly shucked his parachute. He felt thankful that it was a calm day with little wind—there'd been no danger of being dragged by the chute. He'd landed in some six inches of water and mud, close to the wrecked tail section of the airplane, maybe twenty feet away. That made him think he'd jumped at quite a low altitude. He could hear small pieces of the airplane falling about him. Although he'd lost his eyeglasses in the airplane, when he looked into the sky, he could see it filled with pieces of wreckage. He spotted one sector of sky that seemed clear, so ran toward its center. He stopped, looked up again, and saw that he was safe. He started thinking about the others.

Mechler walked back toward the main part of the plane's fuselage. He peered inside but could not see or hear anything. He hurried to where he saw a man attached to a parachute, lying face down in the water. Mechler started to turn him over to get his face out of the water, but stopped when he realized the man was dead. He checked the clothing to determine whether this was his colleague William Brauner. It wasn't—it was an enlisted man, unknown to Mechler.

Now people from the town were swarming around Mechler on the marshy field. He moved away from the fuselage, still wondering how many had survived. Copilot Herbert Moore approached. Moore, unharmed, had landed about fifty yards from the wreckage, the first to touch ground. He asked Mechler if he was okay, worrying about his cuts. Mechler told him they weren't bad. "This is a damn shame," Moore said. Then he asked Mechler to "take over" while he went into town to call Warner Robins. He particularly wanted Mechler to keep people away from the classified equipment. A growing number of civilians had started to push closer to the crash site, so Mechler tried to hold them off. His presence, combined with the watery field, deterred people from approaching the main wreckage, but he couldn't keep them from the more widely scattered pieces of the plane, strewn over a two-mile radius.

The fuselage of B-29 #866 sat in a pasture on the Zachry farm, with the tail section, broken off at the rear bomb bay, about a hundred yards away. Three of the four engines were scattered 400 to 800 yards from the main wing section. One sat in a field seeded in oats and wheat, one in a field bearing mature corn and soybeans, one in an un-improved pasture. The fourth engine—number two—remained intact on its wing, with the main wreckage.

After the copilot left to make his call, Mechler looked up to see Sergeant Earl Murrhee, the flight engineer. I escaped, Murrhee declared. He'd landed in a creek about two hundred feet from the fuselage. Mechler eyed this man warily. He hadn't really met the crew members before takeoff, particularly those sitting in the forward compartment, so he asked for some identification. That irked Murrhee a bit, although he did reach for his papers. Mechler, meanwhile, kept talking to him, and from his responses soon realized he indeed was from the plane.

Murrhee joined Mechler in trying to keep the crowds back. According to the Waycross newspaper's account the next morning, they and the authorities faced a considerable challenge:

> Standing by the fence originally erected to keep cows in a pleasant pasture were herds of people intent on viewing a spectacle of twisted metal and twisted bodies. Horrified at the calamity which struck like thunder, thousands of people milled to view in awesome horror the wreckage that gave the Zachry farm the sudden aspect of a battlefield. . . . Fields that once grew sweet grasses were splattered with blood. . . . Such a sight has not been beheld in many years. . . . The shrill sirens of the police, the clang and clamor of the fire department, the state patrol, the National Guard, the US Army recruiting men . . . the Red Cross car, the jeeps, the wrecking equipment, the bustle of reporters and photographers, planes circling overhead, and the brass hats from Warner Robins, all became part of the kaleidoscopic panorama of tragedy in the low marsh land fringing the Okefenokee. . . .

When the local and state police took over, Mechler told them about the confidential equipment and asked that they hold back the civilians. The crowds kept coming, though. The jammed roads made it impossible to get an ambulance in or out—or to determine who needed one. From what Mechler had seen so far, he, Murrhee, and Moore were all safely on the ground, with no serious injuries, and one crew member was dead—that's all he knew. A civilian told him he'd watched a parachute come down over in the woods, so Mechler asked some men to go search there. Then Murrhee reported: They had another survivor out that way—the left scanner, Sergeant Walter Peny.

Peny had landed in a swamp about a mile from the main fuselage, badly spraining his ankle. Leaving his parachute behind, he'd managed to start walking through the water toward the nearest farmhouse. A local resident came to his aid, letting Peny lean on his shoulder. At the farmhouse door, Peny knocked.

It turned out to be the Zachry home. The young Zachry boys, Bernard and Michael, would always remember that knock on the back door. When they opened it, there stood one of the men from the plane. Their mother wouldn't let the local newspaper editor into her house that day until he'd cleaned his muddy boots—*You get back out, get the garden hose, clean off your clothes*—but she took in this stranger right away and gave him a cup of coffee. His parachute hadn't opened all the way, he told them. If he hadn't landed in their gater pond, out near the swamp, he might not have survived.

Soon, uniformed military officers from Warner Robins arrived at the site. They took over the task of holding everyone back—and "everyone" included the local police and firemen. From the B-29's tail section, an engineering officer from the 3150th Squadron removed the Banshee equipment.

Searchers, fanning out, found no more survivors. The realization now set in: Only four had made it; nine had not. The bodies of those who'd perished were lying in and near the wreckage. It appeared that Pilot Ralph Erwin's parachute had fouled on the aircraft as he jumped, preventing him from falling free. The radio operator, Melvin Walker, and the navigator, Lawrence Pence, had jumped at too low an altitude; their parachutes never fully opened. The right scanner, Jack York, had not jumped at all—his body was found pinned in the wreckage of the forward bomb bay with a parachute on, as though he were about to leave the aircraft. The repairman, Derwood Irvin, and the civilian engineers Bob Reynolds, William Brauner, and Richard Cox also had not jumped; their bodies were found in the wreckage of the rear pressurized compartment with parachutes on, in a position, according to a later report, "indicating they were unable to leave due to the centrifugal force." Al Palya had managed to jump—but he either failed to pull his chute's ripcord or jumped at too low an altitude, his exit perhaps slowed by the crowd at the B-29's front escape hatch.

SHORTLY AFTER FIVE P.M., PATRICIA REYNOLDS'S NEIGHBOR CHARLIE knocked on the door of her apartment in Macon. "Pat," he said, "there's been an accident down at Waycross. We don't know who survived." They drove the ninety miles in near silence, Pat gazing out the window. Those last moments with Bob filled her mind. The two of them rising near dawn, walking the hills, holding hands.

Once in Waycross, Patricia found that authorities would not allow her near the Zachry farm. Here she was, the only wife close enough to get to the crash site and they were confining her to the state police headquarters. She and Charlie could only sit and wait. At some point, a man from RCA joined them. Everyone else ignored her. Patricia grew agitated. The state police and military officers wouldn't even look at her—later she could not remember ever seeing the whites of their eyes. She asked no questions, feeling very much in the way, very much that she had no right to inquire. At least three hours passed. Patricia's fear deepened. She knew there were survivors, so there was hope. Finally, the RCA fellow went to call his headquarters in New Jersey. Camden, as it happened, had been informed. They knew; only Patricia didn't. The RCA representative returned. Bob had not survived, he told Patricia.

Bob had not survived. Patricia went blank. She departed immediately after getting the news—still not allowed to the crash site. She did not cry.

After the military officers took over, Eugene Mechler and Earl Murrhee left the crash scene. A local resident drove them to the Waycross hospital, where they met up with Walter Peny and received first aid. The staff served them a meal at about six p.m., but they were too nervous to eat. Both Murrhee and Peny felt sick. Peny had a concussion, and Murrhee's throat hurt so much he couldn't swallow.

The three men talked about the day. Mechler mistakenly thought he heard Murrhee say that he (not the pilot) had opened the bomb-bay doors. At the time, Mechler considered Murrhee's action "fortunate," since no attempt had been made to prepare an alternative escape route through the aircraft's rear entrance door. "Richard Cox was the man nearest this rear escape hatch," Mechler would later write, "and if he didn't have any more experience with B-29s than I did he probably didn't know any more than I did about how to get out of a B-29. . . ."

From the hospital, Mechler reported what he knew to Warner Robins, called his wife to say he was okay, then phoned the Franklin Institute. "I suspect William Brauner is dead," he advised. At seven p.m., he placed another call, to the Hotel Lanier in Macon, to tell Al Palya's close friend Walt Frick what had happened. He learned that Frick had checked out and was on his way to Waycross with Don Lawler; they'd reserved a room there at the Hotel Phoenix.

Near 7:30 p.m., Air Force investigators arrived at the hospital, as did Copilot Moore, who had been at the crash site all afternoon. With them for a time was Jack Williams Jr., editor of the *Waycross Journal-Herald*. "As crowds still milled around the field last night where the giant B-29 crashed yesterday," Williams reported on October 7, "the four survivors sat around in a room in a local hospital and tried to remember what happened, but it was mostly a blur because as the plane dived down from 20,000 feet, things happened fast." Williams's story continued:

Staff Sergeant W.J. Peny thinks "there was a guiding hand" which saved them. The Penys are expecting an addition to their family any day now and he believes a kind of Providence spared him. Peny reports coming out of the hatch tumbling. . . .

Captain H.W. Moore called his wife in Macon to tell her the good news and she was at a neighbor's rejoicing as she had already heard from Warner Robins that he was alive. Moore recalls falling out of the plane like a ball and then he straightened out and everything was fine.

"That was the prettiest piece of cloth I ever saw," mused T. Sgt. Earl W. Murrhee. Murrhee fortunately is a little fellow and did not fall as fast as the captain although they jumped about the same time and a tangling of the parachutes might have been disastrous.

Handsome Eugene A. Mechler, the only civilian aboard the plane to survive, remembers that he hesitated but only briefly before jumping into space from the falling plane. Mechler resembles Freddie MacMurray in appearance and in addition to a few head bruises lost his glasses. . . .

These four men are eligible now for the Caterpillar Club whose exclusive membership is confined to those who bailed out in an emergency and go through the initiation rites.

"Yes," the group agreed, "we'll remember this day a long time."

That night, Mechler asked a Warner Robins military officer if he could remain in Waycross in order to make contact with Frick and Lawler. The officer granted him permission, so he stayed behind when the other survivors left the hospital for a flight back to Warner Robins in a C-47.

Frick and Lawler arrived in Waycross at about one a.m. Mechler briefed them at their hotel, supplementing what they already knew. After listening, Frick and Lawler, two men who'd initially planned to ride on the doomed flight, decided to drive back to Macon rather than stay the night in Waycross. For years to come, they would meet at a bar on the date of the accident, lifting a glass to remember, pay tribute, and, no doubt, give thanks.

LATER, HER ATTEMPTS TO RECONSTRUCT THESE HOURS WOULD CON-found Patricia Reynolds. In her memory of the drive back to Macon from Waycross, she was sitting in the front seat of Charlie's car—in the middle, between Charlie and another passenger. This other passenger, a young, somewhat heavy Air Force man, was—as Patricia understood it—a survivor, one from the crew who had walked away from the accident. He kept babbling the whole ninety miles, rambling, sounding as if he were in shock. He talked about baseball a good deal, other sports, never the crash. He seemed so irrational that Patricia felt concerned for him, but the others in the car didn't appear to notice.

Others in the car. Besides the three of them crammed into the front seat—*why?*—someone else was sitting in the backseat. That's how Patricia would later recall it. It didn't make sense, though, she realized that. Why three squeezed in front, one in back? And who was this young babbling survivor? The records don't seem to bear out her memory—the records place all the survivors in a Waycross hospital, then, except for Mechler, flying back to Warner Robins. Yet, half a century later, Patricia would remember this drive with precision. She could still visualize the inside of the car, the lights on the dashboard, the road ahead . . . and *him*, the survivor. There was no conversation, just this guy babbling. Was it a delusion? Hard to believe . . . But perhaps. Patricia could not say.

Nor could she summon much detail about the hours and days that followed. Rather than take her home, Charlie and the others took her to a hotel in Macon and stayed nearby in adjoining rooms. She sat in her room thinking, *What's wrong with me? I should be crying.*

IN EASTERN PENNSYLVANIA ON THE AFTERNOON B-29 #866 FELL, WIL-liam Brauner's wife Phyllis, thirty-two and pregnant with her second daughter, turned to a colleague at Swarthmore College, where she taught chemistry. "Something has happened to Will," she said. She just knew. They were that close, she and this man who felt so proud to be conducting classified work for the U.S. military. When the news came, she cried out. The Brauners' four-year-old daughter, Susan, sat on the stairs that afternoon, watching her mother sobbing and rocking until a doctor with a black bag arrived to sedate her.

In Maryville, Missouri, at Northwest Missouri State Teachers College, an administrator called Gerald Cox to the college president's office. He was a nineteen-year-old junior then, still amazed to be on a campus of 640 students, having graduated in a class of twenty-two at his Farragut, Iowa, high school. In the president's office, Gerald learned that his brother-in-law, Hilton Griswold, was coming to meet him. When Griswold arrived, he told Gerald about his older brother Richard's death. The drive to Farragut would forever remain a blank for Gerald. Back home, he found his mother being attended to in the downstairs guest bedroom by their family and their local doctor; she had collapsed. Gerald knelt at her bedside and cried with her.

Gerald's father arranged the funeral, but their local mortician asked a reluctant Gerald to identify the body, an experience he would never shake. On some nights following the funeral, alone in the family's apple orchard, Gerald would look up at the sky and ask God why his brother had to be taken from them, why he had to fall twenty thousand feet before meeting his death.

The task of retrieving Richard's car and personal effects from his Macon living quarters also went to Gerald. He took the train—his mother would not let him fly—then drove home through the Smoky Mountains in Richard's 1937 Pontiac coupe, sleeping in the car one night. His family decided he should inherit the car, which replaced his motorized bicycle. They were led to believe that Russian sabotage had caused the crash, and as a result, Gerald came to harbor a deep hatred for anything Russian. When the Army later gave him the opportunity, he chose the Counter Intelligence Corps over medicine, thinking he could avenge his brother's death by becoming an operative. More than half a century would pass before Gerald learned that sabotage had nothing to do with Richard Cox's death.

IN HADDON HEIGHTS, NEW JERSEY, WALTER FRICK'S WIFE, MADELYN, along with another RCA wife, knocked on the door at the Palya home.

This, Madelyn would say later, was the single worst thing she ever had to do. Al's son Bill, six at the time, watched his family sitting in a line on the sofa, uncommonly formal, listening to Madelyn—he, his nine-year-old brother, Bobby, and his mom, she holding Judy, just seven and a half weeks old. Betty was crying the most, then Bobby. Billy cried only a little himself, and Judy didn't cry at all. Billy thought that odd—usually it was the baby crying, but today the oldest cried the most. What it meant, he didn't know.

Just days before, he'd had a strained exchange with his father, as Al Palya prepared to leave. Billy at that age had trouble pronouncing certain words, so his father had him on his lap, helping him to practice. Al would say words, Billy would try to repeat, but he wasn't getting it right. They went back and forth until Al said something like, *Don't worry about it, that's just baby talk.* He was trying to reassure, but the comment upset Billy. He jumped off his father's lap and angrily ran up the stairs. Al followed after him. Billy turned and said, *I hate you and I wish you were dead.* That moment stayed with young Billy. He didn't really believe your wishing someone dead could make it happen, but maybe. Who knew? Perhaps he had something to do with it—not the direct cause, but something.

The next morning, a telegram from Robins Field arrived at the Palya home:

> I regret to inform that Mr. A. Palya has died due to injuries received in an aircraft accident at Waycross, GA. . . . The deceased is now at Mincy Funeral Home, 516 Pendleton St, Waycross, GA. Kindly wire collect whether you desire remains to be shipped direct to your home or to a designated funeral home or mortuary, furnishing the name and address of funeral director selected by you to receive remains. Deepest sympathy is extended. . . .

Betty notified Al's mother, Anna, who was staying at a daughter's home in Chicago. Anna had already lost her husband and two other children; she sat now at the kitchen table, tears in her eyes, saying something in Slovak about God's will. *Death wasn't the end of life*, she always told her family. *We will see each other again.* Betty also called her sister Jean, in Birmingham. Jean's husband, W. J. Perryman, a prosperous insurance man, left for the airport instantly, on his way to his sister-in-law's side in New Jersey.

Betty studied the newspaper photos. One featured a solitary body prone in a field of clover in Waycross, covered by a blanket. Since her husband had been the only civilian found outside the aircraft, this most likely was Al. Next to her, she had all the letters he wrote when he traveled on business. *It's Saturday, only one week—7 days—till I stand by the railroad tracks waiting for your train. Honey I can't start telling you how thrilled I am. Honest I can hardly sit still . . .*

Betty had tried always to be a loving housewife and companion. Now she had to be a loving single mother to three young children. She would still make all their clothes, she vowed, all their draperies, their bedspreads, their slipcovers. She'd still cook big meals each night—a meat, a potato, a vegetable, a salad, a dessert, the colors varied, not all the same. She'd still set the table with a tablecloth, the glasses placed at the tips of the knives. She'd still make pot roast with browned potatoes, Swiss steak, sloppy joes, pork roast, doughnuts, sticky buns, orange rolls. She'd still make fudge every Friday night, spaghetti with meatballs every Saturday night, the sauce simmering in the kitchen all day. Judy would forever remember those meals, those weekend smells, her mother's resolve to shelter them from their loss.

CHAPTER 7

RESPONSE

October-November '48

To most of the country, the crash of a U.S. Air Force B-29 in Georgia remained a mystery. An initial Associated Press dispatch, published on October 7 in newspapers across the country, informed citizens that "the plane had been on a mission testing secret electronic equipment which RCA developed and built under an Air Force contract. . . . Full details of the plane's mission were not disclosed, but it was believed that it may have been engaged in cosmic ray research. The Air Force would say only that the bomber was engaged in 'electronic research on different types of radar. . . .' Captain H.W. Moore, one of the survivors, said he could not discuss the cause of the explosion or how he and the others escaped."

Yet in Georgia, at least, there was less secrecy. The local newspapers, provided a report by a Warner Robins public information officer, told their readers more than the Associated Press. "Nine Killed as B-29 Explodes Over City," announced the page-one banner headline atop the *Waycross Journal-Herald* on October 7, 1948. The subhead amplified: "Four Men Leap to Safety; Plane on Special Mission. Fragments of Bodies and Superfort Scattered Over Acres of Zachry Farm." The article continued:

Two fires in one engine and failure of another preceded a "thunder clap" blast that ripped apart a B-29 Superfortress bomber over Waycross, with the loss of nine lives, survivors said today.

The giant four-engine craft exploded yesterday at an altitude of nearly twenty thousand feet. Fragments of bodies and plane were scattered over twenty acres of the farm of Robert Zachry Jr.

Eyewitnesses said "the whole town" heard a roar "like a terrific thunder clap" and stood frozen as bodies and plane parts hurtled downward.

Three of the four who leaped to safety returned last night to the Warner Robins, Ga., Air Force base and told a tragic story of the disaster and their miraculous escape. They are Capt. H.W. Moore, co-pilot; Tech Sgt E.W. Murthee [sic] and Staff Sgt. W.J. Peny.

The plane was on a special mission testing secret electronic equipment, scheduled to land "somewhere in Florida." The other survivor was E.H. Mechler, a civilian technician from Franklin Institute, Philadelphia, Pa. . . .

The most revealing details came from the surviving copilot, whose account had been relayed to reporters by a military spokesman:

Captain Harold R. Daniels, Public Relations officer at Warner Robins Field . . . said Captain Moore gave this account of the tragedy:

"The No. 1 engine caught fire while the plane was flying at an altitude of 20,000 feet. Fire prevention steps were taken at once and the flames were extinguished. The same engine caught fire again shortly thereafter. A few minutes later, the No. 2 engine failed. The pilot gave orders for all personnel to abandon the aircraft. While the bomb bay doors were being opened, however, the aircraft fell into a violent spin, from which it never emerged."

Guards were sent to recover and protect as much of the confidential equipment as possible. One engine was buried in mud more than 250 yards from the largest fragment of the plane. Flesh and parts of bodies were tossed all over the area. Four bodies were found in the tail section, snapped from the main fuselage. Four other bodies were scattered in two to four feet of water in a swamp at the edge of town.

The *Macon Telegraph*, in a page-one story on October 7, repeated Moore's account of the crash, as relayed through the Warner Robins spokesman, but added to it:

> Capt. Moore and Sgt. Murhee [sic] were in the forward section of the aircraft, Capt. Daniels said, and made their escape through the nose wheel escape door after being ordered to abandon the plane. When Sgt. Murhee was half-way through the door, Daniels said Moore told him, he became stuck. It was necessary for Capt. Moore to push him through the door. The co-pilot then followed through the door. The other two survivors left through the rear of the plane, Capt. Daniels said. Capt. Daniels said the cause of the blast has not been determined. The public information officer said Capt. Moore praised the courage and coolness of all personnel aboard the aircraft when the engine fires were discovered and after the pilot gave orders to abandon the ship.

It's worth noting, given later suggestions of "confusion" in the cockpit, that Copilot Moore's report to the news media differed on a significant point from what he was telling investigators. In his official sworn statement, he said he never heard the pilot "give the word" to abandon ship; he'd been off the interphone, after all, having left his cockpit seat. Of the other survivors, only Earl Murrhee thought he'd heard an order to abandon ship, and he wasn't sure who issued it—he initially said Moore "ordered me to bail out," then later was "not positive." It had, of course, been a traumatic day, so some confusion over details—even important ones—was understandable. The confusion would only grow in the coming days and weeks.

In the wake of the crash, Colonel H. A. Moody, maintenance director at Warner Robins, flew immediately to Waycross with two other investigating officers. So did junior supply officer Edward Mitrani, copiloting a C-47 carrying nine empty caskets. He landed it at the local Waycross airfield. As a courtesy, those running the operation took Mitrani and his fellow pilot to the crash scene, but they weren't allowed onto the site itself. What he saw from a distance—mounds of debris, no semblance of a plane—shocked Mitrani. Twenty-four years old, he'd been in combat, seen planes shot down, but he'd never been this close to a plane crash. He didn't know where the bodies were, couldn't see anything specific. He'd known some of the crew on the doomed B-29. Now there was just this heap of twisted metal. As soon as a crew on the ground loaded the bodies into the caskets, Mitrani took off and returned to Warner Robins.

Hours later, Eugene Mechler reported to the civilian dispensary at Warner Robins for a checkup. The medical staff dressed his cuts, gave his back an infrared treatment, and sent him on his way. That afternoon, he packed up William Brauner's belongings and went to Robins Field to write a report of the accident.

The next morning—two days after the crash—Mechler and others were still struggling with paperwork, trying to obtain death certificates and wind up the affairs of those who had died. There were too many forms to fill out, too many questions to answer. Mechler rushed, fighting the clock. Ten minutes before his scheduled departure, he finished everything and boarded a train for home.

The bodies of those killed in the plane crash also headed home: Richard Cox to Hamberg, Iowa; William Brauner to Clifton Heights, Pennsylvania; Robert Reynolds to Palmer, Massachusetts; Technical Sergeant D. T. Irwin to Potean, Oklahoma; Master Sergeant Jack O. York to Atlanta; Technical Sergeant Melvin T. Walker to Delhi,

Louisiana; First Lieutenant Lawrence Pence Jr., to Suffolk, Virginia; Captain Ralph W. Erwin to Fresno, California; Albert Palya to Haddon Heights, New Jersey.

Mincy Funeral Home's bill to prepare and ship Al Palya's body to New Jersey came to $681.27. On Friday, October 8, Walt Frick escorted the body home. Funeral services were held the next Monday in Haddon Heights. They buried Palya three days later, at 2:30 p.m. on Thursday, in the cemetery at Tabor, Minnesota, the town where he'd been born and raised. His widow and three children stood by as they lowered his casket into the earth. Judy was two days short of being two months old.

LATE THAT MONTH, AL PALYA'S SISTER, LILLIAN, DROVE TO WAYCROSS with her husband and sons, David, nine, and Johnny, three. She wanted to see where Al had died, just wanted to bear witness. The Popes were usually jovial, intrepid travelers, always staying in cabin-motels. But this time, David could sense a difference. The mood in the car was subdued. He couldn't grasp that his favorite uncle had been killed.

When they arrived, the Georgia town looked gray and ugly to him. They spent that first day visiting people at farmhouses, David aware of the pained expression on his parents' faces. The Waycross residents were patient and kind, not hurrying them at all. In one house, a woman put her arms around Lil, hugging her, which David thought strange, since this person didn't know his mom. At another, likely the Zachry home, they stood on the front porch and talked for close to an hour. The crash itself was a terrible mess, everyone told them, and the herd of government people a big bother.

The people in Waycross directed the Popes to several areas where pieces of the plane had fallen. David grubbed around at the crash site, which had been cleared within four days of the accident; there'd been no reclamation, just the sale of scrap, with personnel from Robins Field helping the buyers' crew remove the wreckage. All David saw now was an empty field, swampy and mucky. But walking around, his mother found a broken piece of gasket material, about ten or twelve inches long, in an oval shape. David didn't like the burned smell of that gasket, or all the mud—he and Johnny had to stay in the car more than they wished. After two nights in Waycross, he was ready to leave.

IN NOVEMBER 1948, SOME SIX WEEKS AFTER THE CRASH, ELIZABETH Palya put her three children in a car and set out from Haddon Heights for her sister Jean's house in Birmingham. Along the way she stopped in Tennessee to visit her friend Viola, wife of Al Palya's colleague Bill Ergen, who was still working at the Oak Ridge National Laboratory. Part of their gang had remained together there—the Ergens lived across the street from the Gossicks and the Nelsons were next door. Betty stayed at the Ergen home for three days, trying to find some comfort in being around the people she and Al had known so well in those early stages of the guided-missile project.

To Viola, Betty still seemed in shock. She didn't know how or why her husband had died. She hadn't been given any details. She knew only what she'd read in the newspapers. She understood that the plane had gone down, that some had been able to escape with parachutes. She thought Al didn't have one on. That was about it. She didn't know what they were testing or if that equipment had caused the crash.

Mainly, they just didn't talk about the accident. You didn't tend to question the government in those days, Viola would recall, especially there at Oak Ridge. You always had the FBI at your front door, asking about this or that neighbor. Once, a man who lived down the street disappeared suddenly; word was, they'd found something subversive in his trash. That kind of thing happened. The Ergens were sure the government was asking about them, too. You got used to secrecy after a while.

With the men off working, Viola and Betty and Jean Gossick, who had two little boys of her own, spent hours together. They cooked a good deal of the time. They took the kids on walking trails, letting them play on big rocks. They fussed over Betty's baby. Viola thought Judy at three months was heartbreakingly cute. She made sure to have baby things ready for her—a crib and a bouncy chair—things she'd bought for her own newborn a year earlier.

Mostly, they tried to cheer Betty up; Jean Gossick was particularly good at that. Not good enough, though—Betty couldn't hide
how distraught she felt. She didn't know how she'd go on. Yet she had
to, of course, because of her children. She'd majored in home economics and planned to teach that subject. I will manage, she told
them.

It did not take long for the Air Force to generate an accident
report about the B-29 crash. Investigators from the inspector general's
office at Langley Air Force Base in Virginia interrogated the four survivors on October 10 and 11, while a Warner Robins team took statements from both survivors and witnesses on the ground. The Warner
Robins group also catalogued the damage to the various parts of the
aircraft. They recorded the injuries to the survivors. They noted where
and in what condition the bodies were found. They collected the aircraft's maintenance forms, the day's flight plan, the aircraft clearance
form. They drew maps. They took pictures.

In the end, though, they did not so much investigate the accident
as chronicle it. On October 18, twelve days after the crash, a five-man
Warner Robins investigating board submitted its Army Air Forces
Form 14, "Report of a Major Accident." Section M of that report,
"Description of the Accident," offered a moment-by-moment account
of the disaster, drawn mainly from the survivors' statements: "Climb
was continuing normally to an altitude of 1800 or 1850 feet. At this
time the manifold pressure of No. 1 engine dropped from 39" to
20".... The pilot elected to feather No. 1 but first hit the feathering
switch for no. 4.... The access door to the accessory section was observed to be turning brown...."

While this account of the accident avoided judgment, the investigating board, in the space for "Recommendations," did offer oblique
references to what might have happened. They proposed "that a more
comprehensive training program be instituted for B-29 pilots and crew
members in emergency procedures and proper action in cases of engine
fires." They suggested "that pilots be given more detailed instructions
in control technique and precautions to be taken with two engines

inoperative on the same side." They thought pilots should be made "fully aware of their responsibility for the safety of passengers carried and for the proper briefing and training of passengers . . . in the event of an emergency."

That was all, though. The report did not directly mention the failure to brief passengers on emergency procedures. Nor did the report consider why the plane kept climbing to 20,000 feet after one engine lost half its power, or why the plane went into a spin, or what its speed was when the bomb-bay doors opened. The report made no reference at all to the missing heat shields; the report did not even speculate about the cause of the engine fire.

"Cause of failure of Nos. 1 and 2 engines undetermined," the report concluded, "although failure of No. 2 could possibly have been caused by the accidental cutting off of that engine during the feathering of No. 1 engine. A further investigation is being conducted in an attempt to determine the cause of failure."

One other item the report did not bring up: that the copilot, Captain Herbert W. Moore, happened to be the deputy commanding officer and adjutant of the 3150th Electronics Squadron at Robins Air Force Base, the number-two man in the group that flew the Banshee test missions. He had been appointed adjutant on September 27, 1948, just nine days before the crash. Perhaps this at least partly explains why no one was inclined to focus on Moore's decision to leave his seat in the cockpit during the crisis. In late 1948, the only hint of interest in the copilot's role came when an investigating officer from the Inspector General's office questioned him under oath.

> **Q: Did Captain Erwin give the order to abandon the aircraft?**
> **A:** *I had been off interphone since going back to the rear and did not hear him give the word to abandon the aircraft.*
> **Q: What prompted you to leave?**
> **A:** *I was sitting there doing absolutely nothing and nobody seemed to be doing a thing. I knew you had to get these doors open and thought well, let's do something.*

Q: In actually abandoning the aircraft, why did you leave, did you see fire?

A: *When I was thrown forward and the airplane was in the spin, the centrifugal force, first experience I had had except in training plane, and from the position I was in, I just didn't see what else could be done except to make for it.*

Q: Did you observe Captain Erwin attempting to leave the pilot's seat?

A: *No, sir.*

Q: Was there any smoke or fire in the pilot's compartment?

A: *No sir.*

On October 18, Colonel R. V. Ignico, commanding officer at Warner Robins, received the Waycross accident report. That same day, he forwarded it to the inspector general at Langley with his implicit acknowledgment that errors had been made. The reports "have been reviewed and are concurred in," Ignico advised. "Pilots at this station will be instructed again as to their responsibility for briefing all passengers in emergency procedures before takeoff. The training of B-29 crew members in emergency procedures will also be re-emphasized."

Although indirect and incomplete, the accident report still managed to agitate the Air Force's Air Materiel Command, which retained responsibility for Banshee. On November 12, the Command at Wright Field in Dayton vehemently defended its personnel and rejected the implications of the accident report. In a letter to the inspector general, the chief of the Command's Flight Operations Section advised that "this headquarters does not concur with the Form 14 as submitted by the Aircraft Accident Investigating Board in that no actual findings or facts were submitted, or no record of a Board of Proceedings was included in the final report."

What appeared to most bother Air Materiel Command was the suggestion that its crew had caused the crash by letting the doomed B-29 fall into a spin. "The Form 14 was studied at great lengths by personnel of the Operations Section and the Flying Safety Branch this headquarters," the letter continued, "and there appears to be no logical reasons for the aircraft being allowed to get into a spin other than confusion in the cockpit. This theory lacks foundation in that the operator appeared to be extremely well qualified in B-29 aircraft." In other words, it couldn't be true because it couldn't be true.

The Command wanted instead to blame the spin on the fire: "Informally it was learned in this headquarters that the wing fire as mentioned in the accident report was of such intensity that flames were shooting back as far as the horizontal stabilizer. It therefore appears that the wing fire caused the left wing of the aircraft to stall, thereby resulting in a spin."

Years later, this particular claim, in fact Air Materiel Command's entire position, would cause various veteran aviators to hoot. A fire won't "blank out" a wing, they'd point out. A fire wouldn't cause the stall and spin. Rather, the pilot forgot or didn't know how to handle a B-29 with two engines out on one side. The accident investigators, all veteran command pilots themselves, could not have missed that. You can't fly on one and a half engines with the bomb-bay doors open. You can't get excited, you can't get confused. You can't lose track of air speed.

On the day he read Air Materiel Command's letter, the retired Air Force colonel Ray Toliver said, "I just don't believe this." After his flying days, he'd served tenures as director of Operations Forces and Maintenance Engineering in the Pentagon, so felt he understood the military bureaucracy. "They had civilians on board," Toliver pointed out. "There were political issues. They were trying to protect the services."

That might have been the end of it, but for a letter that arrived at Air Force Headquarters in late November of 1948, addressed to General Hoyt S. Vandenberg, commanding general of the United States Air Force. It came from Frank Folsom, then the executive vice president in charge of the Radio Corporation of America's RCA Victor Division. Of the four civilian engineers killed in the crash of the B-29 near Waycross, Folsom pointed out, two had been employees of RCA, another an employee of RCA's subcontractor, the Franklin Institute. Frank Folsom wished to call General Vandenberg's attention to "some of the circumstances" surrounding this fatal event. Folsom also wished to receive a copy of the Air Force's accident report. "I am sure that you realize," Folsom told the general, "that nothing arouses fear and suspicion as much as the appearance that some . . . information is being withheld."

CHAPTER 8

FOLSOM'S LETTER

November–December '48

FRANK FOLSOM'S LETTER TO GENERAL VANDENBERG ROUSED trepidation among the U.S. Air Force officers who first read it in late November 1948. For good reason: At that time, the fifty-four-year-old Folsom was exceptionally influential and well connected. Although a Democrat, he moved across party lines and had many close friends among powerful people in business, government, the military, and the Catholic Church. Both his colleagues and rivals used the word "miracle" to describe how he'd grown RCA's business. "Folsom plays by ear," one of his former bosses observed around this time. "He couldn't possibly gather enough facts to support his inspired decisions. He has the instinct to be right."

On the morning he wrote his letter to General Vandenberg, Folsom was ten days away from being named president of RCA—number two to the company's pioneering CEO, David Sarnoff. Magazine profiles talked of the "merry twinkle in his eye," the "warm personality," the "ancestral Irish charm," the "penchant for fun." Folsom was also deeply religious—he carried a rosary with him always and wouldn't take a business trip that didn't permit him to attend mass on Sunday. He maintained an ongoing correspondence with "some 2,500 first-name friends around the world," including "those in humble as well as high places." When he walked down Fifth Avenue, "everyone seemed to know him as a friend." His secretary wasn't allowed to screen his phone calls. He was "perhaps the most readily accessible major executive in New York."

A profile in the magazine *Nation's Business* provided a memorable example of Folsom's exuberance:

> Folsom's constant display of buoyant energy is cheerfully endured by his less strenuous intimates, who find his vigor offensive only in the morning. An early (6–6:30am) riser, Folsom is also an obnoxiously noisy one who delights in singing in the bath, clomping around, playing the radio at optimum decibels. . . . Shortly after dawn one morning he was thus engaged in his suite in the Sherry-Netherland Hotel in New York when above the din he heard the door buzzer. Folsom delights in visitors any hour of the day or night and quickly wrapped a bath towel around his freshly showered midriff and expectantly opened the door. He was greeted by three respectful men who bowed in unison. "Mr. Folsom," one of them said politely, "we are the bodyguard of The Queen of Egypt, who occupies the suite across the hall. Her Majesty has had no morning sleep for more than a week now. She asks if you please couldn't be a little more quiet when you arise." For several days thereafter, Folsom crept around on tiptoe.

Before joining RCA, Folsom had been active in department-store merchandising for thirty years, starting as a buyer and eventually becoming marketing vice president at Montgomery Ward. He was general manager at the Chicago department store Goldblatt Brothers when, with war looming, he took a leave and came to Washington. He ended up as chief procurement officer for the U.S. Navy, where he earned the admiration and friendship of David Sarnoff, then serving as a communications consultant to the government. Occupied with helping Dwight Eisenhower plan for the D-Day invasion, Sarnoff was looking for someone capable of running the shop back home. After a five-hour lunch one day in Manhattan, he invited Folsom to direct the Victor Division of RCA. Folsom had been performing with distinction for the military—he would later receive the Navy's Distinguished Civilian Service Award and the Medal for Merit from Harry Truman—but he resigned his position in late 1943.

At RCA, Folsom, being a merchandiser at heart, looked around for something to market. Television, then in its infancy, sparked his imagination. He immediately saw how TV could transform the country. He also saw that this could happen quickly—years before others predicted it might. To spur things, Folsom invited one hundred competitors, actual and potential, to a meeting at Philadelphia's Warwick Hotel in March 1947. There he handed everyone RCA's blueprints and promotion plans for TV, then loaded them on buses for a tour of RCA's Camden plant. *Let them see the future*—that was Folsom's reasoning. He wanted strong competition because he believed it would ensure aggressive selling. He understood that public acceptance of TV—his true goal—was a job for the industry, not a single company.

The coming years would prove him right, but television's great growth still remained in the future when Sarnoff, on December 3, 1948, announced Folsom's promotion to the presidency of RCA. Sarnoff held a party in Folsom's honor on December 13 at the Warwick, then a formal "coronation" at an RCA board luncheon on December 30. At the time, RCA employed 65,000 people and enjoyed an annual gross income of $835 million, making it one of the largest and most dominant companies in the country.

BEYOND FOLSOM'S POLITICAL CONNECTIONS, AIR FORCE OFFICERS HAD an additional reason to worry about the RCA executive's letter: From its content, they could see that Folsom had inside sources, that he knew what had transpired over Waycross.

"Dear General Vandenberg," Folsom's letter began. "I wish to call your attention to some of the circumstances surrounding the crash of Air Force B-29 Serial TV45-21866 on 6 October 1948 near Waycross, Georgia, which resulted in the deaths, among others, of four civilian electronic engineers, two of whom were employees of RCA and

another of whom was employed by the Franklin Institute, our subcontractor. . . ."

After first laying out the history of the RCA's involvement with
Project Banshee, Folsom turned to the most damning details of the
crash:

> Although we have not received authoritative information
> from the Air Force regarding the cause of the accident, it appears
> from available informal information and from the statements of
> one survivor (another employee of the Franklin Institute
> [Eugene Mechler]) that one of the engines caught fire, followed
> shortly by a loss of power in a second engine. At about the same
> time the plane went into a spin or tight spiral, and the resulting
> centrifugal force prevented escape for some time. The civilian
> engineers had received no preflight briefing in emergency
> bailout procedures and therefore probably did not make best use
> of the opportunities available to them. Another factor of great
> concern to us is that this particular airplane had a long history of
> unsatisfactory performance. During the time the flight test
> program was being conducted at Boca Raton and at Warner
> Robins Air Bases, the airplane was unavailable for flight tests
> much of the time because of mechanical difficulties. . . . This
> particular airplane had never, to our knowledge, performed
> satisfactorily for a period as long as one month. In regard to this
> flight crew . . . these men were not accustomed to flying
> together and therefore could not be expected to act as a team,
> particularly in an emergency. . . .

Here Folsom directly addressed the question of flight crew error:
"We cannot escape the thought that there would have been more survivors if the flight crew had been together on many flights and were
thoroughly accustomed to operating as a team. We cannot help feeling
that more prompt action on the part of the flight crew in throttling
back the engines and putting the plane into a glide would have allowed
ample time for more, if not all, of those aboard to bail out. We feel that

it is probable that there was some confusion among the pilot, copilot and flight engineer which delayed actions that might have allowed more time for bailing out."

Folsom then delivered a not-overly-subtle threat: "This accident has firmly impressed upon our engineering staff the danger of flying in military aircraft and it appears that certain steps will be necessary if we are to participate adequately in the future in Air Force flight test programs."

Folsom wanted increased compensation from the Air Force for flight pay and extra-hazardous insurance for its employees. He wanted newer, safer aircraft. He wanted flight test aircraft, wherever possible, to be placed under operation of the contractor, and when that wasn't possible, "we feel it necessary that Air Force Regulations be adhered to rigorously." He wanted first-rate flight and maintenance crews—"the crew assigned to experimental flight tests in the past have not always been of the highest grade." If RCA is to assign its key electronic engineers to flight tests, "it seems necessary for the Air Force also to assign its best men. . . . In particular, the flight crew should have flown together long enough to act as a team."

Folsom also wanted his own independent inspection of Air Force planes: "A factor which will go a long way toward reassuring our engineering personnel is a frank and open disclosure of all facts regarding the maintenance and operation of airplanes for experimental projects. In this regard we recommend that we be given the privilege of having an independent inspector inspect the aircraft from time to time. . . . His responsibility will be to report to us regarding the quality of the maintenance and operation of the aircraft."

Finally, Folsom wanted access to Air Force accident reports: "When a crash has occurred, a copy of the official report . . . must be made available promptly to us. . . . Needless to say, the report will not be disclosed except to those who are directly concerned."

Folsom concluded by returning to his threat of withdrawing RCA from future flight test programs, but now he upped the ante by suggesting that he spoke for other military contractors as well: "Since the crash on 6 October 1948, representatives of several other companies have informed us that their electronic engineers have been very reluctant to undertake flights in military aircraft. . . . Therefore, the above recommendations, in addition to expressing our views, represent to some extent the feeling of other corporations. We urge that prompt consideration be given to the above recommendations since our development programs . . . will be slowed considerably until satisfactory arrangements have been made."

In closing, Folsom advised General Vandenberg that "We shall be glad to discuss further, at your convenience, any of the above topics. . . . In regard to the accident discussed above, we would appreciate receiving a copy of the official Air Force findings as soon as possible."

JUST HOW MUCH FOLSOM'S LETTER RATTLED MILITARY COMMANDERS— who both depended on RCA's technical expertise and feared politicians' interference—can be seen in the volume of routing slips it drew. Copies of Folsom's letter soon were moving up and down the Air Force hierarchy, at each step spawning memos directed at others in the chain of command.

Folsom's letter had to be addressed. On November 30, the deputy chief of staff/materiel sent it to the inspector general with a note saying, "The attached letter from the Radio Corporation of America is believed to be a matter of primary concern to your office." The response came quickly—in an instant, considering the usual pace of military bureaucracy. On December 2, the inspector general—Major General Hugh J. Knerr—ordered a "complete evaluation" of the original accident report "along with such additional investigation as may be required to establish further facts bearing upon the conditions contributing to the accident. This runs the gamut of maintenance, crew proficiency and supervision."

In calling for this sweeping new inquiry, General Knerr observed that "the airplane did crash killing a number of people" and Folsom "believes what he writes." So Knerr recommended that the deputy chief of staff assure Folsom in an "interim reply" that the Air Force would reexamine the accident and correct any unsafe conditions. Upon completion of this new investigation, Knerr wanted a report sent to the chief of staff and a "final reply" sent to Folsom "outlining the action taken by the Air Force to prevent recurrence of accidents." This final reply, he emphasized, should be "a detailed response, item by item," to Folsom's letter.

One day later, the inspector general's staff requested that the Flying Safety Division—part of the Office of Air Inspector—conduct the reopened "supplemental" investigation. Agents from that division began to walk back through the circumstances surrounding the crash of B-29 #866. They gave added consideration to interrogations of survivors and others involved. They reassessed the conduct of the crew. They took a new look at the documents and aircraft parts. They conducted additional interviews.

The original investigators at Warner Robins also stirred. In late October, Colonel H. A. Moody, who'd presided over the initial inquiry, had asked Wright Field for an analysis of a cracked exhaust bracket from the doomed plane. In early December—just as the inspector general ordered the renewed investigation—Moody received this analysis, which, though offering no "definitive conclusions," advised that the crack in the bracket "might have" allowed exhaust gas to leak into the engine number one accessories section, which meant "fuel fumes could have been ignited and caused the fire." Most important, the analysis suggested that "if Technical Order 01-20EJA-177 had been complied with," the result might have been different.

Colonel Moody could not and did not ignore this last comment. On December 17, he wrote a "supplemental aircraft accident report" addressed to his commanding general at Warner Robins. Here, for the first time in the official record, came mention of the missing heat shields and the failure to comply with the technical order mandating their installation. Here, for the first time, came a fairly honest account of how and why a fire had erupted aboard B-29 #866.

The fire "appears to have . . . progressed into the accessory section because of the absence of the heat shields," Moody wrote in his conclusions. If the bracket (part of the exhaust rear manifold assembly) cracked during flight, "exhaust fire could have entered the accessory section because of the absence of the heat shield . . . and would have been the source of this engine fire." The heat shield's purpose was "to prevent excessive heat from entering the rear of the engine." Without the heat shields installed, "there is nothing to protect the accessory section from the intense heat of the exhaust stack."

Moody's concluding recommendation: "Since it appears that the failure to completely comply with T.O. 01-20EJ-177 is the most possible cause factor for this accident, it is recommended that definite instructions be issued that will require complete compliance with this Technical Order and eliminate any possibility of heat shields being omitted when this Technical Order is complied with."

On December 17, the same day Moody delivered this report, Colonel R. V. Ignico forwarded it to the inspector general with the comment that "report has been reviewed and is concurred in as being the best possible explanation for this accident. Action has been taken to insure the complete compliance with T.O. 01-20EJ-177 on all B-29 aircraft assigned to this Station. . . ."

ALTHOUGH MOODY'S REVELATION SHED LIGHT ON THE ACCIDENT OVER Waycross, it also obscured matters by narrowing the explanation for the crash to a single primary factor. It wasn't that simple; lots of B-29s with engine fires made it home. Veteran aviators point out that accidents rarely result from one cause but rather from a chain of events. A rushed wartime aircraft design, a strapped postwar military, inadequate maintenance, the failure to install heat shields—all contributed to an in-flight fire that probably turned fatal once the pilot decided to keep climbing beyond 18,000 feet. Add to this the accidental feathering of engine number four, the failure to maintain airspeed, the general cockpit confusion, the opening of the bomb-bay doors before stabilizing the aircraft, and the failure to brief all aboard about emergency exit procedures—what you end up with is a multitude of linked reasons.

The accident over Waycross was a textbook illustration of the aviation adage "The plane only does what the pilot and mechanics tell it to do." The mechanics and maintenance crew commanded the engine to burn by consistently tolerating a leaky fuel-access system and a nearby cracked exhaust collector ring. The missing heat shields between the two systems provided an additional prompt. Fuel, heat, lots of forced airflow fanning combustion—the engine interpreted this as an "order" to ignite a fire. At 18,000 feet, the crew increased the intensity of the fire by adding fuel and emergency boost.

Consider the commands the B-29 just then was receiving from the flight deck. The aircraft, after a long, slow climb, has lost the power of three engines, with the asymmetric thrust of engine number three on the right wing pushing it into an uncoordinated left turn. There's no airspeed left. Then, all at once, the crew drops the landing gear and bombbay doors to follow standard emergency bailout procedures—thereby introducing enormous, spontaneous drag. B-29 #866 responds perfectly to the commands, spinning left in the direction of the turn. The "high" right wing, moving faster on the outside of the turn, enjoying the power of engine three, is still "flying." The left wing stalls and falls out, while the flying right wing races around in a circle, generating lift. In a smaller plane, a pilot can recover, but not in a big, lumbering B-29 with three engines out.

It's undeniable that B-29 #866 was asked to spin and immediately responded. Yet on December 31, 1948, the deputy commanding general at Air Materiel Command headquarters denied just that. What's more, Lieutenant General B. W. Chidlaw—a celebrated military aviation expert who would later gain great prominence by directing development of the United States's original jet engine and jet aircraft—rejected almost everything claimed in Frank Folsom's letter to General Vandenberg. As he clung to the findings of the initial, incomplete, accident report, Chidlaw displayed little regard for the facts. He went so far as to insist that B-29 #866 was "in compliance" with existing technical orders.

"There is no doubt in our minds that every precaution was exercised to insure the proper safety of all personnel concerned," Chidlaw wrote in a letter addressed to the Air Force's Chief of Staff. . . . "All test aircraft are given the best of service and maintenance, in compliance with existing Technical Orders and Regulations prior to assignment to our test missions. . . . All regulations, in this instance, were complied with. . . . This command exercises every precaution in the selection of competent aircrews for all experimental flight test projects. . . . [The pilot] had operated B-29 aircraft for 931 hours as first pilot. . . . It is reasonable to assume that he was familiar with emergency procedure. . . ."

Lieutenant General Chidlaw, of course, had to protect his people. The inspector general and his investigators in the Flying Safety Division faced a different challenge. Three days after Chidlaw's declaration, on January 3, 1949, those investigators delivered their report to the Air Inspector. Just as they had a different challenge, they had a different story to tell.

CHAPTER 9

SPECIAL INVESTIGATION

January–June '49

THE SECOND INQUIRY INTO THE WAYCROSS CRASH, TITLED "Report of Special Investigation of Aircraft Accident," included documents not contained in the original report, additional witness interviews, and new information about B-29 #866's maintenance problems. Three days before the report's official distribution on January 6, 1949, the Air Force Chief of Staff's office, having received an advance summary, upgraded it and all related documents from "Restricted" to "Secret"—the highest security classification. The chief of staff had a reason: This new inquiry offered, for the first time, an unflinching if not comprehensive account of what happened over Waycross.

The nine-page report, written by Colonel John W. Persons, chief of the Flying Safety Division, began with basic information about the doomed airplane and its crew, followed by a neutral "narration of events." Then came a listing of facts, few apparent in the initial report. Among them: The irregular flight crew, the missing heat shields, the inadvertent feathering of engine four, and the failure to brief on emergency procedures. In a section labeled "Discussion," Colonel Persons advised that breaks in the right exhaust collector ring "probably" caused the fire, "aggravated by non-compliance" with technical orders. He also—most important—allowed that "confusion may have existed among the crew during this accident; however, the period of time from the start of the fire until the aircraft entered a spin was very short."

This mention of "confusion" brought the investigation as close as it would get to assessing the performance of the airplane's crew. The report addressed maintenance issues and noncompliance with technical orders but hesitated when discussing possible causes for the aircraft's entry into a fatal spin. Colonel Persons offered two alternative theories: Either "the large fire in the No. 1 engine may have reduced the lift of the left wing sufficiently to cause the aircraft to fall off into a spin," or "the pilot inadvertently caused the aircraft to stall." Veteran aviators scoff at the first theory, yet the report itself dismisses the second theory. The possibility that the pilot caused the spin "is discredited," Colonel Persons wrote, "by the pilot's experience and by the fact that the copilot observed the aircraft to be in a descending attitude just prior to its entry into the spin." Once again, the pilot couldn't have caused the spin because he couldn't have.

The report's conclusions stuck to the maintenance and equipment failures, and here Colonel Persons didn't waver. He declared that "the aircraft is not considered to have been safe for flight because of noncompliance with Technical Orders 01-20EJ-177 and 01-20EJ-178." Equally striking were Persons's recommendations, similar to those made by Frank Folsom: that the Air Force brief civilian engineers in proper emergency procedures; that the Air Force employ "highly qualified maintenance and flight personnel" and establish "minimum permanent flight crews"; that "wherever feasible" flight test aircraft be temporarily transferred to the contractor conducting the test; that "consistent with normal security measures," the contractor "be given the privilege of satisfying themselves as to the airworthiness of aircraft in which they are flying."

The report's recommendations diverged on only one major point from Folsom's requests. Folsom had asked for a copy of the Air Force's accident report. Colonel Persons advised instead "That copies of official AF accident reports not be sent to civilian agencies."

ON JANUARY 10, THE INSPECTOR GENERAL FORWARDED THIS REPORT TO the deputy chief of staff, along with a memo providing an item-by-item discussion of Frank Folsom's letter—guidance on how to respond to the RCA executive. This "talking points" memo, no doubt drafted by Colonel Persons, echoed his Report of Special Investigation, though now it more fully (if ambivalently) addressed the flight crew's conduct. In one passage it defended their conduct: "Evidence available indicates that the action of the flight crew was as prompt as the situation demanded. . . . The factors causing the spin were beyond the control of the crew." Yet in other passages, it allowed that the crew hadn't flown together before, that there had been confusion in the cockpit, that the copilot got up from his seat, that survivors couldn't recall the pilot ever ordering them to abandon ship.

In the end, the talking-points memo, like the investigative report, embraced most of Folsom's demands—except his request for copies of accident reports. Again came the final words: "It is recommended that copies of official Air Force accident reports not be sent to civilian agencies."

On February 17, with this memo in hand, Major General William F. McKee, Air Force assistant vice chief of staff, finally responded in writing to Frank Folsom. After summarizing the events above Waycross, McKee turned to Folsom's claims. He began by echoing the memo's defense of the crew: "Evidence indicates that even though the crew had not flown together as a team, action taken was as prompt as the situation demanded. . . . The factors causing the spin were beyond the control of the crew."

That's all McKee borrowed from the talking-points memo, though. For the most part, McKee's letter ignored that memo, along with the second investigation's report and all the problems connected with the fatal flight—including the cockpit confusion and missing heat shields. No, McKee advised Folsom, "in the interest of security" the aircraft connected to the Banshee project could not be transferred to RCA's control. No, RCA could not be responsible for aircraft maintenance—"we seriously question the ability of any concern . . . to equal the maintenance standards of the Air Force on its own aircraft." No, the Air Force had not violated safety regulations—"There is no question regarding safety procedures. Constant emphasis is placed on this phase of operations." No, it would not help for RCA to conduct its own aircraft inspections—"it is doubtful whether an outside individual could be considered competent in the case of tactical aircraft." No, the Air Force had not taken undue risks—"the Air Force is most anxious to conserve property and life and under no conditions, except extreme emergency, are aircraft permitted to fly when safety is in question."

McKee, in closing, assured Folsom that his "personal interest in this matter is deeply appreciated." He assured also that "every possible action will be taken to maintain full mutual confidence" with civilian contractors. However, "due to the purpose and nature of the Accident Report, it is impossible to furnish copies."

No written record exists of Frank Folsom's response to this letter. He apparently moved on to other matters. He was not, after all, a government gadfly. Far from it. On March 2, 1949, two weeks after McKee wrote his letter, most of the Washington, D.C., power elite, political and military, paid their respects to Folsom by attending a large gala cocktail party given in his honor at the Carlton Hotel. Hosted by the Washington vice president of NBC, the party included more than three hundred guests, including General Dwight D. Eisenhower; Chief of Staff General Omar Bradley; U.S. Senators William Fulbright, Hubert Humphrey, Lyndon Johnson, Estes Kefauver, Warren Magnuson, and Arthur Vandenberg; six Cabinet members, including Secretary of Defense James Forrestal and Attorney General Tom Clark; five rear admirals from the Navy; the Secretary of the Army and an Army brigadier general; three Air Force officers; and, from the White House staff, President Truman's Air Force aide, Brigadier General Robert B. Landry.

Did Folsom have a word with Landry that evening about the crash of a B-29 near Waycross, Georgia? Did he mention to James Forrestal the dismissive, mendacious letter he'd received from an Air Force assistant vice chief of staff? Did he ask the attorney general whether the Air Force could legally withhold an accident report?

If he did, he must have spoken in a way that avoided alienating anyone, for he continued to be honored for many years. Universities conferred degrees, business magazines profiled him, Cardinal Spellman hailed him. In July 1952, Omar Bradley in a letter would thank him for the installation of an RCA TV at his home just in time to watch the Democratic National Convention (Bradley also proposed a golf game "with Ike" if "his campaign leaves him any time"). In May 1954, President Eisenhower would send a note inviting him to "an informal stag dinner" at the White House—a "reasonably early dinner" followed by "a general chat." The president hoped Folsom could attend, but "I realize that you already may have engagements which would interfere. If so, I assure you of my complete understanding."

By then, Folsom's full attention had turned to the challenge of selling television to America. Under Folsom's leadership in early 1949, RCA launched a major advertising campaign in newspapers and magazines. That year, just nine percent of American households had a television set; within five years, fifty-six percent would. Folsom was leading the way into a new cultural era. Here came what Al Palya predicted to his sister-in-law Jean Perryman years earlier—"live" pictures brought right into her living room. Publicly, RCA demonstrated no further interest in the crash of a B-29 in Georgia.

THE FIGHT TO LEARN WHY FIVE AIR FORCE CREW MEMBERS AND FOUR civilian engineers died over Waycross on October 6, 1948, appeared to be over. In March 1949, Captain H. W. Moore temporarily took over command of the 3150th Squadron at Warner Robins. (Moore would remain on active duty until 1965, retiring as a lieutenant colonel with many honors, including the Distinguished Flying Cross.) In November 1948, an official in the Air Force's Flying Safety Division, on a routing slip attached to a copy of the Report of Special Investigation about the Waycross accident, wrote: "This rather interesting report. Folsom's letter too." In June 1949, the log for the 3150th Squadron recorded that a "shortage of B-29 pilots" had been the greatest obstacle to progress on priority projects during the past six months.

The log provided one other relevant observation. During this period, it noted, "safety, both ground and flying, was stressed by CO [commanding officer]." The squadron had received an Air Force "Letter on Aircraft Maintenance," which the CO and maintenance officer "complied with wholeheartedly." They had, the log advised, made "all mechanics aware of the safety campaign and more conscious of the rate of aircraft accidents where aircraft maintenance is a contributing factor."

PART TWO
COURTROOMS

December 1948–December 1953

CHAPTER 10

THOUGHTS OF REDRESS

December '48–June '49

At his weekly news conference on June 16, 1949, President Truman suggested to reporters that a "wave of hysteria" was sweeping the nation. The *New York Times* ran the president's comments atop its front page, following White House rules that required reporters to give his views only indirectly:

> The President likened the current situation created by the conflict with communism to the troubled atmosphere engendered in the early days of the Republic by the alien and sedition laws. He also recalled what he characterized as the crazy activities of the Ku Klux Klan after World I, and said that every great crisis brought a period of public hysteria.
>
> The present feelings would subside as similar situations had died out after past periods of stress, Mr. Truman contended.
>
> The Chief Executive did express confidence, however, that the hysteria had no part of his Executive Department in its grip. He gave assurance that if this ever happened he would root it out.
>
> The country had not gone to hell in the Washington-Adams-Jefferson era and it would not now, President Truman asserted. . . .

The President's views were mostly implied rather than explicit. That was because they were not voluntary declarative statements but answers to questions. His meaning was none the less clear.

No one had to ask Truman to explain his references to "the current situation" and "the present feelings." By the spring of 1949, the Red Scare had taken hold. Speaking before a congressional committee late the previous October, "Park Bench Statesman" Bernard Baruch, a wealthy investor and Democratic Party political adviser, had coined the term "cold war" to describe growing tensions with the Soviet Union. As those tensions deepened—the Soviets came to be regarded as brutal oppressors not unlike Hitler—so did suspicions about anyone ostensibly connected to communism. That January had seen the start of the protracted *Dennis* trial, a prosecution under the Smith Act of twelve Communist Party leaders on charges of conspiring to "teach and advocate" the "violent overthrow" of the government. In March came the arrest on espionage charges of Judith Coplon, a twenty-seven-year-old analyst in the Department of Justice, after she'd been caught in New York with restricted documents in her purse as she met with a Russian engineer. A month later, New York's governor Thomas Dewey signed a bill aimed at ousting reds and fellow travelers from the public school system. Soon the trial of Alger Hiss, indicted for perjury, would begin. Guilt by association spread, with the University of California imposing loyalty oaths on faculty, and HUAC eventually compiling an index of one million "suspects." Domestic communism had become a national security issue.

Given such a mood in the country, it did not seem likely that a trio of bereft widows would think to challenge the government over matters of military secrecy. Yet they began to do just that in the weeks and months after the crash of B-29 #866. They began even though they were all struggling: In Haddon Heights, Betty Palya worked full time as a high school home economics teacher to support her three children. In Indianapolis, Patricia Reynolds had landed a job at RCA but couldn't sleep. In Pennsylvania, Phyllis Brauner planned to move her family to Wellesley, Massachusetts, where she would teach chemistry at Simmons College while working on her doctorate at Boston University.

It was Phyllis who first thought of redress. Theodore Mattern, a New York lawyer and a friend of William Brauner's from their days in the Austrian underground, offered her counsel. At the same time, W. J. Perryman, the Birmingham insurance executive married to Betty's sister Jean, continued to aid his sister-in-law. Soon Mattern and Perryman began corresponding with each other.

The exchange started with a letter from Mattern. Even in those early weeks after the crash, he and Phyllis had been discussing the notion of suing the federal government. He had researched the possibility, concluding they could file under the new Federal Tort Claims Act of 1946, which permitted private parties to seek damages against the United States in bench trials without juries. For unknown reasons, he also concluded that it would be best to file in Philadelphia rather than Georgia, the site of the crash. He'd started looking for the right attorney to handle the case.

In a letter dated December 29, 1948, Mattern wrote to Perryman, informing him of Phyllis Brauner's plan and inviting Betty Palya to join the action. Perryman talked to Betty about the possibility. She was game but worried that she had no money to pay a lawyer.

"I have discussed this with Mrs. Palya," Perryman wrote Mattern on January 7, "and she would be interested in joining in this suit and having representation of the same attorney that you have in mind if same can be arranged on a contingent basis of a percentage of the settlement." Al Palya, he pointed out, "left no estate and with three small children there is nothing available to advance as attorney's fee at this time."

On the same day, Perryman sent a note to Betty, providing a copy of his letter to Mattern. He also assured Betty that he had filed her Social Security claim. She would, he advised, be getting a monthly payment of $63.34, and her teaching "will not in any way affect the Social Security benefits." (For a time, at least, she'd also be getting RCA worker's compensation, $25 a week for each child and for herself). Keep me posted, he concluded, "on how you are getting along."

Mattern wrote back to Perryman on January 14, identifying a prominent New York law firm, Davis, Polk & Wardwell, as his candidate to handle the case. His friend at that firm "promised me he would take it up with their managing attorney in order to have him agree to take the case without a retainer." The "maximum contingency fee" would be twenty percent. This firm is "one of the best known in the United States." Since Phyllis was expecting her second child that month, "I shall not start this action prior to the birth of the child, but intend to go ahead with it immediately thereafter."

Perryman thought Mattern's choice of a law firm excellent. No doubt, he counseled Betty on January 20, this firm "would have considerable weight and influence before any Federal court and judge." Perryman wrote also to Mattern, asking that the law firm send Betty the necessary paperwork. "I certainly appreciate your interest in this," he told the New York lawyer, "and we are anxious to co-operate in every way possible."

On February 14, Phyllis gave birth to her second daughter, Cathy, more than four months after William Brauner's death. Mattern relayed the news to Perryman and asked for a "short outline" from Betty about Al. He would pass this memo to the New York law firm "or to their Philadelphia representative." Here was the first reference to the possible involvement of a lawyer in Philadelphia, where the lawsuit would be filed.

Perryman wrote Betty two days later, requesting information about Al—details such as his age, his schooling, his length of service at RCA, his salary, his duties and responsibilities, and "the type of work that was being conducted on the plane while in flight." Perryman well understood they were now entering the tricky terrain of military secrets. Of course, he himself knew nothing about Al's work, and Betty didn't either. So he offered his sister-in-law careful advice:

> I would suggest that you talk to Walt [Frick] and let him give you all the information he possibly can concerning the work that they were doing at the time the plane left the field and while in flight. . . . Walt does not have to divulge anything that

would be in the nature of a military secret . . . but the whole
thing would hinge on the fact that Al was a highly specialized
technical engineer, that he . . . was in complete charge of a
project developing instruments which were the work of his own
mind that meant considerable money to the RCA people and
also very valuable to the Government. . . .

Perryman had never finished high school. A workaholic who
traveled constantly as he built a network of insurance agencies, Perryman came from a family that had lost everything in the stock market
crash of 1929. The key to his success lay in his ability to read people,
and he showed that instinct now. "I believe that Walt should not be
concerned as to any information that he might give," Perryman advised Betty. If subpoenaed, "I believe . . . Federal law [permits] testimony in cases such as this."

On April 19, Perryman wrote Betty again. He enclosed an en-
dorsement showing a change in car insurance and a check for $200 to
cover unexplained "railroad expenses"—perhaps the cost to ship
Palya's body home. Perryman also enclosed a second check for $50 to
cover the "necessary advance" owed to a lawyer—"Attorney Biddle of
Philadelphia."

This was pivotal news: Rather than the New York law firm, "Attorney Biddle"—Charles J. Biddle—would be representing the widows. In a letter two days later, Mattern confirmed this to Betty. He had
received the $50 check from her and had forwarded it to the law firm
of Drinker Biddle & Reath in Philadelphia.

This firm, Mattern advised, "will from now on handle your
case."

CHAPTER 11

CHARLES BIDDLE

Spring '49

EVEN MORE UNLIKELY THAN THREE WIDOWS CHALLENGING
the federal government was Charles Biddle taking their case. A member of the establishment, he generally represented the rich. The Biddles—bankers, diplomats, lawyers, politicians, military men, agriculturists and horticulturists—were one of Philadelphia's first families. They had been there since 1814, when Nicholas Biddle, for $17,000, purchased property from his wife's family on the bank of the Delaware River, thirteen miles upstream, in Bucks County.

One of the most powerful financiers of his time, Nicholas Biddle was director of the Second Bank of the United States, in which role he contended with President Andrew Jackson for control of the nation's currency. At the 123-acre family estate on the Delaware, called Andalusia, his guests included John Quincy Adams, Daniel Webster, the Marquis de Lafayette, and Joseph Bonaparte, the former king of Spain. He entertained them in a striking two-story Greek Revival manor with a monumental Doric colonnade and spacious porticoes. Known as the "Big House," it stood high on a rise overlooking the estate's three-quarter-mile of riverfront across a grand sweep of lawn. Over the years, Nicholas Biddle and his descendents would add outbuildings, including a Gothic Grotto, a temple-like Billiard Room, and an expansive guesthouse called the Cottage. Nicholas Biddle also imported Guernsey cattle, filled his stables with fine racehorses, and practiced various forms of experimental farming.

Generations of Biddles continued to call Andalusia home after the deaths of Nicholas Biddle in 1844 and his wife in 1855—one descendent suggested they did so because "there they had a roof over their heads." The estate lay largely dormant, though, for more than sixty years—until Charles J. Biddle moved into the Big House in 1923 with his bride, Katharine Legendre, of a noted New Orleans family. Katharine loved to entertain. Painstakingly restored Empire-style furnishings now filled the mansion; priceless volumes (among others, early editions of Voltaire, Machiavelli, Byron, and Scott) lined the library shelves. Charles and Katharine would make Andalusia their year-round residence for half a century. In the words of their son James, for twelve years president of the National Trust for Historic Preservation, they brought the house, gardens, and grounds to "a peak of immaculate preservation not seen since the days of Nicholas Biddle."

Under Charles and Katharine, Andalusia still clung to customs and codes from the Victorian era. Charles Biddle saw to it that the family and dozens of visitors gathered every week in coat and tie, even in the heat of summer, for a traditional Sunday luncheon of roast beef, rice, and peas—all "cooked to death," according to James. Charles traveled to Scotland every year to hunt grouse. The family summered in Maine, loading suitcases, ice boxes, nannies, gardeners, butlers, and maids onto two private railroad cars (the railroad had an Andalusia spur). As he had as a boy, Charles still often paddled a bark canoe past the Big House, doffing his hat to whichever ladies were sitting outside on the porch. Home from work each evening, he enjoyed his two martinis, then repaired to the dining room. Andalusia anchored Biddle. "We all know where we come from," James later observed. Nodding toward the family mausoleum in the Grotto, he added, "and where we go."

James, once married with his own kids, came to rebel against the coat-and-tie Sunday lunches. His parents eventually agreed to alternate formal lunches in the Big House with informal ones by the swimming pool. The pool itself represented another rebellion and compromise. Charles had grown up swimming in the river and saw no need for a pool. Yet when the tides were down, the family had to wade through mud. Other times, they had to deal with rough currents—and a growing fear of pollution. James wanted a swimming pool. "That caused a great commotion with Father," he recalled. "'What's wrong with the river,' Father would say. 'We've swam in the river for two hundred years.'" James eventually had his way, but not before Charles also fussed over the pool pavilion James bought, a converted Gothic Tarrytown front porch. Then one Sunday lunch at the pool, after they'd all had a couple of drinks, Charles backed his golf cart into the water, forgetting he'd left it in reverse.

Even as Charles began to let James take over Andalusia, he held fast to one instruction: James could never plant a tree on the estate. Planting trees, any trees, would alter forever the land they'd inherited. "Of course I planted hundreds of trees after he died," James said. "But not before."

From his manor, Charles Biddle traveled daily by train to downtown Philadelphia. He had joined the law firm of Dickson, Beitler & McCouch in April 1924, after graduating from Princeton University and Harvard Law School and practicing in his father's law firm until the elder's death. Dickson, Beitler & McCouch represented powerful corporate interests, handling coal and railroad reorganizations, corporate financings, interstate commerce lawsuits, negligence cases, and estate work. Biddle, a Republican to the core, soon brought in additional clients, wooed away from his father's old firm—Philadelphia Rapid Transit, the Philadelphia Saving Fund Society, and the Philadelphia Contributionship for the Insurance of Houses from Loss by Fire, the nation's first successful mutual fire insurance company, organized by Benjamin Franklin. In return for landing these clients, the law firm made Biddle a partner on January 1, 1925. Seven years later, the firm changed its name to Drinker Biddle & Reath, and it has not changed since.

In Charles Biddle's day, the firm's daily routine proceeded at a gracious pace. An in-house history of the firm notes that at lunchtime, "partners might walk east to the Union League or west to the Ritten-house Club." On hot summer days, "life could be miserable in the law firm's unairconditioned offices. The older lawyers coped by taking off their wool suit jackets and working in gray linen jackets [unless clients were present], while the younger ones worked in shirt-sleeves. Open windows brought in soot, and sudden breezes could play havoc with a lawyer's neatly stacked papers. . . ." When the dirt and heat became intolerable, "the firm's senior partners conducted little business, re-treating to their summer homes from June through Labor Day."

One evening every spring, all the firm's lawyers would be invited to Andalusia for a dinner party hosted by the Biddles. "From the steps of the portico," the history recounts, "Charles Biddle would dispense potent mint juleps. After greeting her guests, Katharine Biddle, as was her custom, would retire upstairs, leaving the all-male gathering for the dinner and card games that followed."

Although the mood at these parties was convivial, at the law firm most knew their senior partner as "Mr. Biddle." Only a few contemporaries called him "Charlie." His old-fashioned patrician style, refined and scrupulously courteous yet also easy and self-confident, masked the mind of a tough litigator. He'd wave off settlements and march toward the courtroom—*Why are we even talking?*—until he'd won major concessions. Among his most celebrated cases would be his successful defense in 1957 (alongside Thomas Dewey, representing Eli Lilly) of the pharmaceutical firm Merck Sharp & Dohme, accused of price-fixing in its manufacture of the polio vaccine. In 1965, at the request of Governor William W. Scranton, Biddle (along with William Coleman, later secretary of transportation in President Gerald Ford's Cabinet) achieved the desegregation of Girard College by successfully "breaking" the will of banker Stephen Girard, who in 1831 had left money to establish a school for "fatherless white boys."

None of this, though, constituted the core of Charles Biddle's reputation. Above all, he was known as a World War I flying ace. As a member of the Lafayette Escadrille, he served in both the French Army Air Force and the American Expeditionary Force, shooting down eight German planes. On May 15, 1918, while attacking German two-seaters at low altitude behind enemy lines, he was hit, wounded, and forced down, but managed, under heavy fire, to make his way to an advanced British observation post. His combat awards included the Distinguished Service Cross, the Purple Heart, the French Legion of Honor, the Croix de Guerre (with three palms), and the Belgian Ordre de Leopold.

Trained in French aviation schools in 1917, when he was twenty-seven, Biddle took naturally to flying. Two who served with him in the Lafayette Escadrille—Charles Bernard Nordhoff and James Norman Hall, later authors of *Mutiny on the Bounty*—report that he found flying "the most fascinating of all amusements, and he never lost the zest for it." He "kept steadily before him his purpose, which was to perfect himself in the management of combat planes." When he took command of a newly formed squadron, he would tell more than one inexperienced and overeager pilot, "I admire your courage and damn your judgment."

He mainly flew small single-seat fighting planes, known to the French as *avions de chasse*, to the English as "scouts," and to the American Air Service as "pursuit machines." Armed with one or two unmovable machine guns bolted in front of the pilot above the motor, they had maximum speeds of 100 to 135 miles per hour. Most of Biddle's fights were close up to the enemy, at a range of thirty to two hundred feet. Biddle loved these air skirmishes; he was always first to suggest a voluntary patrol.

Throughout the war, he wrote long letters to his parents that reflected this enthusiasm, though they occasionally expressed a longing for peace and home. (Upon his return, he collected these letters into a book, *The Way of the Eagle,* published by Charles Scribner's Sons.) On June 14, 1917, while still in training in Avord, he confidently reassured his mother that "there is no reason at all why a man of reasonable ability . . . should smash if he keeps his wits about him." Writing from Bergues on July 30, he reported, "My spirits are excellent. The work is interesting and I try to . . . do little thinking about what I might be doing if it were not for this damn war." Then, in mid-August, Biddle's closest friend, Oliver Moulton Chadwick, died in combat. Biddle wrote only a brief note to his parents: "My friend Chadwick has evidently been killed. . . . My heart is sick and I cannot write you about it till later."

Air combat, the edgy thrill of engaging the enemy close-up in the skies, soon enough lifted Biddle's spirits. From Dunkirk the day before Christmas, he wrote at length to his parents about the art of shooting down "Huns." "As I have told you before, *aviation de chasse* resembles in many respects other kinds of hunting; for instance, the pursuit of the festive duck. I have noticed that successful Hun hunters often owe their success to the same qualities which go to make a successful duck hunter, that is, patience and knowing where the birds go, so to speak."

On May 15 came Biddle's most serious brush with death—the day an enemy plane forced him down. "I shall tell you from start to finish what happened," he wrote his parents ten days later, "although you probably know most of it already."

When Biddle spotted it, the enemy machine was flying at about 2,000 feet, over isolated battlefields where the opposing lines consisted of nothing more than linked shell holes. Biddle would later describe it as "the slowest bus I ever saw, with a rounded body, a square tail, and the lower wing much shorter than the upper, like many English two-seater observation planes." Biddle dove down after him, making up his mind to get good and close. This he did, ending up fifty yards behind his tail and slightly below. "But I made one bad mistake," Biddle reported to his parents, "a real beginner's trick which was the cause of all my troubles. I evidently was not quite far enough below him. . . . I got caught in the back draught from his propeller, which joggled my machine about so that anything approaching accurate shooting became an impossibility."

Biddle tried to dive further down, then pull up to shoot, but because of the Hun's slow speed, "I found to my astonishment that I had overshot the mark and was almost directly under him, so much so that it was impossible to get my gun on him. He started swerving from side to side to get me out from under him so that the machine gunner could shoot. . . . The Boche and I were at this time about twenty yards apart and if he had only a trap-door in his bottom he might have brought me down by dropping a brick on my head. However, he did not need it. The Hun gave a twist which took me for an instant beyond the protection of his fuselage. It was only for a second or two, but that was sufficient for the observer, who proceeded to do the quickest and most accurate bit of shooting that I have yet run up against."

The Hun's very first shot came crashing through the front of Biddle's machine above the motor, catching him on top of the left knee. "It felt more like a crack on the leg from a fast-pitched baseball," Biddle told his parents, "than anything else I know of except that there is also a sort of penetrating feeling one gets from a bullet." He could not keep track of how many other bullets hit his plane; he knew only that they had knocked out his motor. Working his machine as a glider now, Biddle dove and twisted, trying to coast back to his own lines. He had little altitude, though, and some distance to cover. Finding all his efforts useless, "I saw that there was nothing for it but to smash up as gracefully as possible." He did not want to land behind Hun lines—"I had most unpleasant visions of spending the rest of the war in Germany, which is not at all my idea of a good time"—but if he came down in no-man's-land, he'd have the German guns turned on him.

German guns it would be. Bracing himself, fighting to slow his machine, Biddle slammed into no-man's-land, his machine flipping over and crashing into a tangle of barbed wire less than seventy yards from the enemy trenches and several hundred from the British. Biddle scrambled out and rolled into a nearby shell hole. As the citation from the Belgian Ordre de Leopold put it, "With remarkable courage and presence of mind, and despite his [leg] wound, he detached himself from his smashed machine and made his way from shell hole to shell hole under intense artillery, machine gun and rifle fire, to an advanced British observation post."

"He certainly got the best of me," Biddle would later say of his opponent, "and I don't feel at all vindictive about it, as it was a perfectly fair fight, but just the same it would give me more satisfaction to bring that boy down than any five others."

After spending that first day with his initial rescuers, a platoon of

Irish infantrymen, and eating supper with the company officers, Biddle began walking the half-mile to battalion headquarters, the nearest point an ambulance could access. Despite his discomfort, he looked around with appreciation. "By the time we were started across the duckboards once more," he wrote his parents, "the last light had faded from the west and a brilliant moon in its first quarter lit up the whole scene. This country is fantastic enough during the day, but by moonlight it becomes more so. . . . I could not help thinking of Andalusia with the same moon sparkling on the river, shining on the great white pillars of the house and throwing the shadows of the stately trees across the lawn on a peaceful spring evening. Quite a contrast to this wreck of Flanders."

Less than a month after being shot down, Biddle found himself again at the front as commanding officer of the Thirteenth Pursuit Squadron. There he brought down his third, fourth, and fifth enemy machines in August, his sixth in late September, his seventh in October. Authorities officially credited him with an eighth victory following armistice, when a returning POW confirmed it. On October 25, Biddle took command of the Fourth Pursuit Group; the next month he won promotion to the rank of major.

There would be no more skirmishes in the sky, though, no more patrols. On November 12, he wrote his parents with the news: "The armistice went into effect at 11 am. . . . It is a wonderful relief to have it over, but it does leave you with a very much 'let down' feeling, as though one had suddenly lost one's job."

In truth, Biddle was ready to come home: "I will admit now that there have been days recently when I did not want to fly a bit, the losses in the squadron were so heavy that it was hard not to let it get on one's nerves. . . . It is almost too good to be true to think that before long we shall be home again. There have naturally been a good many days when the chance of ever getting back again seemed a bit slim, and it is hard to realize that I shall some day be shooting ducks on the river once more."

BIDDLE WAS FIFTY-NINE WHEN THEODORE MATTERN FIRST APPROACHED him in the spring of 1949, asking if he'd be interested in a case involving the mysterious crash of a U.S. Air Force B-29 near Waycross, Georgia. More than thirty years had passed since Biddle chased and dodged the Germans. During that time, Biddle had buried his parents and become patriarch of Andalusia. He had clung to his forebears' ways, raised a family, built an eminent law practice, and, to his great pleasure, continued always to shoot ducks on the river. Yet he had never again been the pilot he was in World War I; he had not quite followed the way of the eagle.

How this case from Teddy Mattern must have intrigued him. A B-29 ablaze in the sky would not have seemed entirely strange; Biddle knew about the B-29's chronic engine-fire problems. Yet a B-29 ablaze that falls from the sky, a B-29 that turns sloppily on its wing into a fatal spin—what was that about? Although it wasn't Charles Biddle's habit to represent cash-strapped widows or challenge the government, the patrician Philadelphia attorney could not resist this case. His colleagues understood what drew him most: the story of a B-29 going down and the secrets it held.

CHAPTER 12

THE COMPLAINT

June–November '49

PATRICIA REYNOLDS COULD RECALL NOTHING ABOUT THE first few days after the crash. Phoning her mom, meeting at the Georgia airport, contacting Bob's family—she had blacked it all out. Pat remembered being in a hotel room the first night. The next thing she remembered was the funeral in Springfield, Massachusetts.

That funeral. Yes . . . Pat recalled standing with Bob's brother Dick and her cousin Jim. They were on the veranda, talking and laughing. Pat was saying, *I can't believe we're laughing . . . I can't believe there's still laughter in us.*

Another memory from that funeral: Bob's mother was a "determined" Catholic, while Bob was not. The mom insisted on having a kneeling bench at his casket. Pat felt offended, for Bob would not have appreciated this. Yet what could she do? Bob's mom was a bantam fighter, always suing people; her husband was a big bear of a man, a railroad engineer.

Pat had a third memory of that day: up on the hill, the cemetery. Trees, lush foliage—a beautiful sight. For a girl from Indiana, hills were incredible.

Pat could not recall retrieving Bob's possessions. What had happened to Bob's trombone? It was so important to him. Where did it go? Pat couldn't say. She was just floating. One morning a cousin told her it would be nice if she had a dog. Pat got a white collie, four months old, with impeccable manners. Pat couldn't sleep those nights, so she'd get up at five a.m. and take the dog for a walk. Manhole covers spooked the dog, so she picked him up, carried him over them.

A human-resources man from RCA came to visit her. He eventually offered her a job in RCA's Indianapolis employment office. She had been working for a commercial laundry, and RCA sounded better. She still walked her dog at five a.m, which meant she'd be in her office by seven, though RCA did not open until eight-thirty. She just couldn't sleep. She also had no interest in dating. She never read newspaper articles about the B-29 crash, never wrote or spoke with the other widows. She felt as if she lived among the walking dead.

Then, in the late spring of 1949, six months after the crash, Pat received a phone call from a Philadelphia lawyer named Charles Biddle. He told her about the two other widows, about their lawsuit. He presented the situation, explained the premise. Pat listened, but said no thank you. She wasn't interested; she just didn't want to face this. She had no children. She was not yet twenty-one. She didn't care about the money.

Biddle didn't push her. Thank you, he said. That was it.

BIDDLE DECIDED TO PROCEED WITH JUST THE TWO WIDOWS. (RICHARD Cox, although a civilian, had been a government employee, so his family didn't have the same legal options). On June 21—five days after Harry Truman had talked about a "wave of hysteria" sweeping the nation—Biddle filed a complaint in the U.S. District Court in Philadelphia titled *Phyllis Brauner and Elizabeth Palya v. The United States of America*. In this suit, a civil action brought under the Federal Tort Claims Act, Biddle spelled out the basic details and made his core claim: "The [aircraft] accident and death" of William Brauner and Al Palya "were caused solely and exclusively by the negligent and wrongful acts and omissions of the officers and employees" of the United States of America. For each widow, Biddle requested a sum of $300,000 ($2,265,169 in current dollars) "or such larger amount to which this Honorable Court may determine she is legally entitled."

A sluggish march through the legal system began. Summonses were issued and returned, stipulations made, time extensions granted. June turned to July, July to August, August to September, still with no answer, no developments. One day in September, Biddle picked up his telephone and again called Patricia Reynolds. He understood, he said, and respected how she felt. However, her involvement in the case would give more credence to the lawsuit; it would help the other families if they acted as a group. Pat listened to Biddle's refined tone, so careful and courteous, yet also so warm. She thought of Bob, of how he just glowed from the minute she met him. Something stirred. Okay, she said. Sign me up.

On September 27, Biddle filed a second complaint in U.S. District Court titled *Patricia J. Reynolds v. The United States of America*. The three widows stood together now, Charles Biddle at their side, facing the federal government.

HARRY TRUMAN'S "HYSTERIA" CONTINUED ON, AS NEW THREATS SEEMED to emerge daily. The Communists took over China that summer of 1949, ending a three-year civil war. On September 23, Truman announced that the Soviet Union had detonated its first atomic bomb. On October 1, Mao Zedong declared the formation of the People's Republic of China—"Red China." Six days later, the German Democratic Republic—East Germany—proclaimed its existence.

These were alarming events. Combined, the loss of China and of the United States's atomic monopoly only fueled the panic. Having sole possession of the bomb had checked Soviet aggression and compensated for weaknesses in America's conventional military, allowing the United States to take diplomatic risks. "This is now a different world," declared Michigan's Senator Arthur Vandenberg, a leading Republican authority on foreign policy. The fall of China, with Mao soon after traveling to Moscow to sign the Sino-Soviet Treaty, raised the specter of a monolithic Communist bloc dominating most of Eurasia. "The red tide," *Time* magazine declared, "threatens to engulf the world."

Intense debates over who "lost" China mounted, as did cries to bolster the nation's arsenal. Genuine anxiety about communism mixed with more calculating impulses as some exploited the threat in order to promote their own interests and go after personal rivals. Those consumed by issues of national security clashed with those most concerned with civil liberties. It remained uncertain just how vulnerable America truly was to military attack, but the prospect alone made the planet feel newly dangerous. An influential, top-secret National Security Council paper (NSC-68) began to circulate widely in Washington, sounding grave warnings about the country's "dangerously inadequate military strength" and the Soviets' intent—driven by "a new fanatic faith, antithetical to our own"—to impose their "absolute authority over the rest of the word." Drafted by Paul Nitze, then head of the State Department's Policy Planning Staff, NSC-68 offered a blueprint for how to rearm America and conduct the Cold War, warning that without a huge increase in defense spending, the country would face "a dangerous situation." Truman, though not inclined to triple military budgets, and not overly concerned the Kremlin would attack America, nonetheless feared for the country's security. The global spread of communism, Truman warned, would leave the United States "isolated from our sources of supply and detached from our friends. Then we would have to take measures that might really bankrupt our economy and change our way of life so that we couldn't recognize it as American any longer."

Against this backdrop, the Air Force faced an uncomfortable possibility—that perhaps it could not deliver on the promise of a long-range guided missile demonstration. Since the Waycross crash, Project Banshee had languished, losing resources and missing deadlines. A last scramble began to prevent its demise.

In May 1949, the Air Force had transferred Banshee operations from Warner Robins to the Eglin Air Proving Ground in Florida. It had also ordered a Banshee test demonstration to be held by the end of the year. So Banshee missions continued to fly that summer of 1949, but with limited results; only four of twenty-one were considered successful, and even they required a pilot's intervention. "Banshee mission failures could hardly be laid to a single cause," wrote the Air Force historical officer keeping the squadron log in those days. "The many variables . . . made each individual mission a rather complicated and necessarily a very precise operation." They were just then overhauling the 1st Experimental Guided Missile Group—renaming it the 550th Guided Missiles Wing—but "in contrast with Banshee difficulties, confusion due to administrative reorganization of the unit was slight indeed!"

The death knell came on October 3, in a memorandum from the new 550th Wing calling for the "discontinuance of Project Banshee." The mandated demonstration date of December 1949 couldn't be met. Whatever the deadline, "it will be almost impossible to stage a successful demonstration due to the unreliability of equipment as evidenced by the number of unsuccessful missions." Banshee just no longer looked to have potential value: The Air Force had come to realize how vulnerable Shoran-guided "missile" drones were to enemy action, be it antiaircraft fire, fighter attacks, or electronic jamming of radar signals. The 550th Wing proposed to end Banshee on November 1.

Air Force Headquarters retroactively granted this request on December 1. A termination report that followed listed a number of Banshee's accomplishments (it proved "the feasibility of B-29 remote controlled flight"), but offered a grim conclusion: "The vulnerability of the director and missile aircraft, limited potential accuracy, high-level maintenance and operating personnel requirements . . . make [Banshee] unsuitable for specialized missions."

ON WEDNESDAY, NOVEMBER 16, 1949, THE DAY THE LAST BANSHEE mission flew, a B-29 crashed in the sea off Bermuda after the pilot reported he was attempting an emergency ocean landing. Two days later, another B-29, taking off to join the search for this doomed plane, crashed into the bay off Tampa, killing five men. In total, six B-29s had gone down that November, killing thirty-five men and leaving twenty others missing. This capped a grim year for the Superfortress—twelve of the big ships had fallen from the sky since the explosion over Waycross the previous October. The Air Force had finally seen enough. Hours after the Tampa crash, General Vandenberg ordered the grounding of all B-29s that had not been modernized or that had been carrying "maximum operating stresses." Vanderberg wanted "all speed possible" in overhauling these planes.

The Air Force made no effort to keep secret its grounding of B-29s—the story ran the next day on page one of the *New York Times* in the top-left corner. General Vandenberg had acted after conferring with Lieutenant General Curtis LeMay, then head of the Strategic Air Command. LeMay, speaking in Fort Worth, called the B-29 crashes "examples of the headache military airplanes can be when you must demand top performance of them all the time." He also said, "The modification and modernization program we have had in progress for some time will now be stepped up because we've been having entirely too many engine fires with unmodified engines."

Four days later, on November 22, the government finally submitted its reply to the claims stated in the two lawsuits filed by Biddle on behalf of Phyllis Brauner, Elizabeth Palya, and Patricia Reynolds. The United States of America "avers that there was no negligence and wrongful acts and omissions on the part of any officers or employees of the defendant," declared U.S. Attorney Gerald A. Gleeson. "The defendant was in no manner responsible for the accident."

CHAPTER 13

JUDGE KIRKPATRICK

January–June '50

NOW BEGAN THE DISCOVERY PROCESS. WITH HIS LAWSUITS filed in the courthouse, Charles Biddle had the right to ask the government questions and demand documents. On November 28, 1949, he submitted thirty interrogatories. From the look of them, it's clear that Biddle already had a solid sense of what happened over Waycross.

He asked for a copy of the accident investigation report. He asked for records about the airplane's mechanical condition and maintenance. He asked for copies of witness and surviving crew statements. He asked if the doomed B-29 had experienced engine trouble before the October 6 crash. He asked for a thorough account of what transpired aboard the plane.

He did not get much in response. The answers filed on January 5 by U.S. Attorney Gerald Gleeson and Assistant U.S. Attorney Thomas Curtin were limited, nearly taciturn. The government lawyers also declined to produce the accident report and witness statements, arguing that such documents weren't "within the scope" of the interrogatory. Still, despite their reticence, it cannot be said the Air Force offered false testimony. Except, that is, when it came to Biddle's final, most critical, question. Biddle had a good source somewhere, or maybe it was a sharp litigator's intuition. His thirtieth interrogatory asked: "Have any modifications been prescribed by defendant for the engines in its B-29 type aircraft to prevent overheating of the engines and/or to reduce the fire hazard in the engines?"

The answer, sworn to under oath by Thomas Curtin, was a succinct "No."

Biddle did not challenge the verity of the government's response. Instead, on January 18, he filed a motion seeking a court order compelling the United States to produce the accident report and the survivor statements by Captain Herbert Moore, Sergeant Walter Peny, and Sergeant Earl Murrhee. Speaking for all three widows—their cases had been consolidated for trial—Biddle argued that the documents contained evidence relevant to the lawsuit and necessary to his clients "in preparation for trial."

Gleeson and Curtin responded on January 25 with a motion to quash Biddle's request for documents. They had several reasons, but none at this point involved claims of "state secrets" or national security risk. Rather, they argued that the accident report and findings "are privileged documents, part of the executive files and declared confidential." So were the statements by Moore, Peny, and Murrhee. If the plaintiffs wished, the government lawyers suggested, they could take these three men's depositions.

In this extended legal battle between the government and three widows, there would be several moments that shaped the outcome. One came this January, as the two sides' competing motions arrived at the federal courthouse at Ninth and Chestnut streets in downtown Philadelphia. Whether by chance or conscious decision, the motions landed in the chambers of the Honorable William H. Kirkpatrick, chief judge of the U.S. District Court for the Eastern District of Pennsylvania. For this case, there could not have been a more appropriate judge.

BY 1950, KIRKPATRICK HAD BECOME A LEGEND TO HIS FELLOW FEDERAL judges. He was large and distinguished-looking, with an imposing demeanor, but this did not stop some colleagues from calling him "Kirky." Born in Easton, Pennsylvania, in 1885, to a prominent family—his father was a congressman, judge, and state attorney general—Kirkpatrick also married into money. He earned an undergraduate degree at Lafayette College but never graduated from law school; after a year studying at the University of Pennsylvania, he opted for a clerkship in his father's law office. He apparently learned enough there to pass the bar exam, for he became an attorney in the fall of 1908. During World War I, he served in the Army as a major and lieutenant colonel, a judge advocate and a member of the board of review of courts-martial.

In 1921, he ran successfully for Congress as a Republican in a Democratic district. When the voters did not reelect him, he returned to his law practice in 1923. That same year, George Wharton Pepper, a faculty member whom Kirkpatrick had befriended during his brief time at the University of Pennsylvania, found himself elected to the U.S. Senate. Pepper soon nominated Kirkpatrick for a vacancy on the federal court. President Calvin Coolidge appointed Kirkpatrick to the bench in 1927.

Kirkpatrick continued to live with his family on College Hill in Easton, more than fifty miles from Philadelphia, and eventually managed to get an Easton branch of federal district court opened in a courtroom over the local post office. When sitting in Philadelphia, he would stay at the city's premier hotel of the day, the Bellevue Stratford, claiming the same room every visit. He would take his meals at the Union League Club, a bastion of WASP Republicanism. There he loved to play cards, especially bridge, every night. One story has it that a regular opponent of Kirkpatrick's at these bridge games, a steady loser, invariably showed in his checkbook register the notation "K-I-R-K"—something he eventually had trouble explaining to an IRS auditor, until the auditor decided they must be contributions to a church, worthy of a deduction.

Besides bridge, Kirkpatrick loved swimming in the secluded bay at the family farm in Cumberstone, on the western shore of Maryland. This farm, known as Parkhurst, had been in his wife's family for generations, and Kirkpatrick spent the warm months there, opening it around Easter and closing it at Thanksgiving. The place resembled a southern manor, full of porches and pillars. In his study, Kirkpatrick piled law books to the ceiling, causing the floor to slant. He kept an ancient horse, explaining to visitors that "we love to ride." He also kept what might have been the largest collection of dachshunds on his reach of the coast.

In Philadelphia, in Courtroom 3 of the Ninth Street courthouse—a chamber richly appointed with wood and marble—Kirkpatrick could terrify young lawyers appearing before him. In reality, he was a gracious, soft-spoken man who never cursed or lost his temper. He cared deeply about his staff and for many years employed a blind law clerk, ordering law books for him in Braille. His fellow judges valued his sense of humor. He'd call them to chortle over particular cases, such as one involving a hunting horse that had swallowed a string of valuable pearls (the insurance company wouldn't pay up, claiming the pearls weren't lost—everyone knew just where they could be found). Yet on the bench, Kirkpatrick would clear his throat, look lawyers straight in the eye, and say, "You're representing the plaintiff? Let me hear your argument." Invariably, he would be wearing a green eyeshade, for the courtroom light bothered his eyes. His size, the eyeshade, his gaze—the combination just undid some attorneys.

Even more unnerving was Kirkpatrick's ability to reduce issues to simple questions of fact, to get right to the core of a case. He seemed able to quickly understand the issue; okay, he'd say, this is what it's all about. In one memorable civil antitrust case, he refused to let electrical manufacturers enter "sham" denials after they'd already pleaded no contest or guilty in criminal trials. He had a photographic memory of precedent cases, knowing exactly where to find them—the volume, the page. He wrote opinions almost off the top of his head. Without fail, they were short, concise decisions—no more than eight pages, often fewer. Well, he'd tell his clerks, we know the law. If the lawyers need to, they can look up the cases. He'd laugh at his colleagues' lengthy opinions. Geez, he'd say, we could have handled that in three pages.

Other jurists thought so highly of his judgment that they regularly came to consult him. Rarely did higher courts reverse him. In 1933, six years after his appointment, he became chief judge for his federal district, a position he would hold until his retirement in 1958.

He could have ended up on the Court of Appeals or U.S. Supreme Court, it was often said, but for bad political timing; with the Democrats in control in Washington, he just happened to serve at the wrong era in the nation's history.

Those who worked for Kirkpatrick recognized in him a good sense of justice, and of people. His opinions often reflected a concern for the protection of individual rights—in one notable case he ruled that private citizens, not just the government, could bring lawsuits to enforce federal law. He also believed in an independent, strong-minded judiciary; he did not shy away from taking stands on issues he thought important. What he seemed to care about most was getting all the facts on the table. For that reason, he often embraced broad rules of discovery. In any discovery dispute, it was a sure bet he'd rule to get the maximum out there.

That certainly was Kirkpatrick's perspective in what became his best-known case, *Hickman v. Taylor.* The case began when, on February 5, 1943, a wooden barge belonging to the Baltimore and Ohio Railroad loaded with freight cars sank in the Delaware River at Pier 12 North, in Philadelphia. During the extended effort to recover it, a tug overturned, drowning five of nine crewmen, including Norman E. Hickman. Three days later, the tug owners and their insurance company hired a law firm to defend them against potential lawsuits. A lawyer with that firm, Samuel B. Fortenbaugh Jr., privately interviewed the four surviving crew members and took their signed statements. Fortenbaugh also interviewed others who had information about the accident and made notes about what they told him. When Hickman's family eventually sued (the other dead crewmen's families settled), they asked for copies of all the statements taken by Fortenbaugh as well as his related investigative reports. The tug owners declined to turn them over, arguing that such requests call for "privileged matter obtained in preparation for litigation."

This fight over disputed documents came before the U.S. District Court in Philadelphia in the summer of 1945. All five of the court's judges listened to the arguments at a hearing. Writing for all five, Kirkpatrick ruled that the tug company must hand over the witness

statements. He recognized that the question was one of balanced judgment rather than a clear rule of law. He also recognized that lawyers,
while representing clients, needed "a certain degree of privacy, free
from unnecessary intrusion." Yet there should be a presumption in favor of disclosure, he concluded. Absent unusual circumstances, such
witness statements should be made available.

> The guiding principle [is that] discovery of all matters
> relevant to a suit should be allowed to the fullest extent
> consistent with the orderly and efficient functioning of the
> judicial system. . . . The mere fact that the statements bear upon
> the possible legal liability of a party does not render them
> unreachable. . . . We think it proper to order the production of
> the written statements. . . . We think that none of the statements
> made by witnesses in the present case are protected by any rule
> relating to the privileged communications between attorney and
> client. . . . In taking down what various witnesses told him
> about the case, Mr. Fortenbaugh was acting primarily as an
> investigator.

Kirkpatrick directed the tug company to produce the witnesses'
written statements and to describe in substance "any fact concerning
this case which it learned through oral statements." Kirkpatrick also
ordered the company either to produce Fortenbaugh's notes or to submit those notes to the court, which would determine what portions to
reveal to the opposing party.

Kirkpatrick meant it. When the tug company's owners and their
lawyer refused to comply with his ruling, he promptly held them in
contempt and ordered them imprisoned until they complied. The
company and their lawyer appealed this contempt ruling to the Third
Circuit Court of Appeals, which sat in the same downtown Philadelphia federal courthouse. The appellate judges knew Kirkpatrick well
and admired him—but in this case, sitting *en banc,* they voted to reverse him. What most concerned them was the impact this matter
threatened to have on the lawyer-client relationship. The best public

policy, they reasoned, is to aid people who have lawsuits and prospective lawsuits. Those people should be free to make full disclosure to their lawyers, and those lawyers should be free to put "their whole-souled efforts" into their clients' cases.

The U.S. Supreme Court, accepting the case on appeal by Hickman's family, agreed with the Third Circuit—with qualification. The justices recognized the "widespread controversy" this issue raised, and they allowed that balancing the competing interests "is a delicate and difficult task." They did not think, as did the Third Circuit, that "all written materials obtained or prepared by an adversary's counsel with an eye toward litigation are necessarily free from discovery in all cases." Yet in the end, the justices, ironically seizing upon Kirkpatrick's own language, recognized a lawyer's need for a "certain degree of privacy, free from unnecessary intrusion." They concluded that Hickman's family had shown no "good cause"—particular, essential need—for the disputed documents, that the plaintiff had simply made a "naked, general demand," which was "insufficient to justify discovery under the circumstances."

Hickman v. Taylor ended up back in Kirkpatrick's courtroom, where, on October 9, 1947, even without the disputed documents, he found the tug company liable and awarded damages to Hickman's estate. Kirkpatrick wasn't nearly finished, though, with the matter of discovery. The next year, in the summer of 1948, another case came before him, *O'Neill v. United States*. This one involved a seaman injured by an explosion on the tanker *Cedar Mills* in an Italian harbor—and this time the respondent was not a private company but the United States of America. The seaman filed interrogatories that included a request for copies of written statements taken by FBI agents. The government declined to turn them over, citing *Hickman* and claiming they were "work product" of lawyers; the government also declared they were privileged, by Justice Department order.

Kirkpatrick scoffed at these arguments. The FBI agents might be lawyers, but their relationship with the government had "nothing remotely in common with the relationship between a lawyer and his client." The claim of privilege likewise had no basis; the government here, Kirkpatrick pointed out, wasn't claiming the common-law privilege—rooted in old British doctrine and customs—protecting state secrets against disclosures that might harm national security. Rather, the government was saying that as a sovereign it could refuse to comply with any order of the court, that the attorney general could refuse disclosure of any evidence for any reason.

Kirkpatrick did not think so. The basis for the attorney general's contention—the constitutional theory of three separate and independent branches of government—involved a question that "has risen many times in our history," Kirkpatrick observed in an opinion dated August 23, 1948. But he didn't believe it applied here. The government, through congressional action (the Federal Torts Claims Act), had consented to be sued. If the government now refused to hand over the disputed documents, Kirkpatrick proposed to issue an order barring it from opposing the seaman's claim.

Again the Third Circuit Court of Appeals reversed him. The five appellate judges, sitting *en banc* and citing *Hickman,* ruled in November 1949 that the seaman first needed to show "good cause" for the documents. The district court judge, before reaching an opinion, must decide if the plaintiffs have "demonstrated that the special circumstances of their cases make it essential . . . for them to see and copy the statements sought." Kirkpatrick hadn't done that, the appellate judges concluded, so "the decree of the district court will be reversed."

These two cases, *Hickman* and *O'Neill*, were much on Kirkpatrick's mind when he presided at a hearing on February 15, 1950, over Charles Biddle's request for the B-29 documents. Not only had Kirkpatrick faced similar issues in these earlier cases, he'd also faced the same government lawyer: U.S. Attorney Gerald Gleeson had stood before him on *O'Neill,* and here he was again, accompanied by Assistant U.S. Attorney Thomas Curtin. Across the aisle sat Biddle and his associate, Francis Hopkinson.

Kirkpatrick heard much that day from the U.S. Attorney about the need to show and find "good cause" for the production of disputed documents. The government's written motion to quash had talked only about a claim of executive privilege, but now, in Courtroom 3 at

Philadelphia's federal courthouse, Gleeson pounded as well on what the higher-court reversals in *Hickman* and *O'Neill* had cued him to emphasize. Kirkpatrick listened and asked questions. He did not rule, though, or show his hand.

BIDDLE AND THE THREE WIDOWS WERE LEFT TO WAIT FOR THE JUDGE'S pivotal opinion. Betty Palya continued to teach home economics in New Jersey. Phyllis Brauner, relocated with her widowed mother and two children to Wellesley, turned down an offer of help from family friends who proposed to adopt her baby Cathy. Patricia Reynolds inched back into the world, starting to date Don Herring, a man she'd met in early January.

More than four months passed. Biddle and the widows grew impatient. On June 26, Biddle wrote to Teddy Mattern. "Mrs. Brauner called me the other day when she was in town," he reported, "and she was naturally anxious to know what had happened to her case. . . . In view of the long delay, I can understand perfectly why she should be concerned about it." Biddle continued, in a letter that he copied to all three widows:

> As I have previously reported to you, we are most anxious to get a copy of the report made by the Investigating Board of the Air Force with regard to the causes of the accident and also the statements of the surviving members of the crew. We asked for these under the Federal Discovery Rules but the Government refused to furnish us with copies on the ground that the report and statements were confidential, etc.
>
> We then applied to the Court for an order directing disclosure of these documents. The matter was argued last February and has been pending for decision ever since, largely on the question of whether or not we must show "good cause" for the production of the documents. We concede that the Rules require a showing of good cause but take the position that such cause exists where the essential information is in the hands of the Government and cannot be obtained elsewhere. If there was

ever a case in which such compulsory disclosure was necessary it would seem to be this one.

I have seen the Judge who has the matter two or three times and explained to him the necessity for trying to get the case disposed of at the earliest possible moment. Unfortunately, however, he has not acted as yet and there is nothing more I can do to hurry it. However, with summer vacation coming on, I feel almost sure that we will have some word before very long. . . .

We will keep the case moving as rapidly as we can and let you know when there is anything to report.

Why was Judge Kirkpatrick taking so long to rule? His heavy workload no doubt played a role, but Biddle's repeated pleas—*I have seen the Judge who has the matter two or three times*—suggest something more. Kirkpatrick did not live only in his courtroom. As he pondered the three widows' challenge to the United States of America, he faced also the mounting turmoil in the country and the mounting threats to the nation's security.

The conviction of Alger Hiss for denying that he passed secret documents to Whittaker Chambers, the order by Truman to develop a hydrogen bomb, the arrest of Klaus Fuchs on charges of atomic bomb espionage, Senator Joseph McCarthy's claim to possess a list of 205 Communists working in the State Department—all occurred over these four months. Then, on June 24, Communist North Korean troops crossed the 38th parallel in an invasion of South Korea. Truman was at his home on North Delaware Street in Independence, Missouri, that Saturday, spending the week with his family and attending to personal business. His plane took off from the Kansas City Municipal Airport at two p.m. the next day. By early evening, he was at a dinner conference in Blair House with his top advisers and defense chiefs.

Among the twenty or so at this dinner was the newly appointed secretary of the Air Force, Thomas Finletter, who had replaced Stuart Symington two months earlier. A New York lawyer who once served as chairman of Truman's Air Policy Commission, Finletter had taken office with concerns about the preparedness of the country's armed forces. Now, as the group sat around a big room on the ground floor of Blair House, Truman asked Finletter and General Vandenberg about the state of the Air Force. Neither he nor Vandenberg, Finletter recalled years later, had much "optimism" at that moment about the capacity of the country's air power. Air Force officials did not hold a belief in the "excessive ability of the Air Force to do everything." They did not think that "air could handle the whole aspect of a military operation."

Four days later, the Soviet Union rejected a United States request to use its good offices to end the conflict in Korea. The next day, June 30, Truman authorized the deployment of United States ground troops to repel the invaders, U.S warships to blockade the Korean coast, and U.S. aircraft to attack north of the 38th parallel.

That same Friday, in Philadelphia, Judge Kirkpatrick finally delivered his decision in the matters of *Reynolds v. United States* and *Brauner et al. v. United States.*

DESPITE THE PERIL FACING THE COUNTRY, IT'S CLEAR FROM HIS OPINION that Kirkpatrick's focus was on the rights of individual citizens and the need for separation of powers in government. It is also clear that he'd given careful thought to the appellate-level reversals of his decisions in *Hickman* and *O'Neill* (on appeal, *O'Neill* had become *Alltmont v. United States*). Right from his opening paragraphs, Kirkpatrick addressed both these cases, and he kept referring to them throughout his ruling.

O'Neill/Alltmont, he began, didn't bar production of the witness statements, it just mandated that "good cause" be shown. So in the present B-29 case, the question of whether there exists "good cause" is "properly before this Court." Then Kirkpatrick added *Hickman* to the discussion. The present B-29 case, he pointed out, did not involve statements obtained by an attorney (protected by *Hickman*) or by others under the attorney's direction (protected by *Alltmont*). So on this issue, neither *Hickman* nor *Alltmont* applied. Therefore it was up to him, Kirkpatrick declared: "In determining what amounts to good cause . . . the trial court has a wide discretion. Every case presents its own

particular problems and any attempt to establish rigid rules would seriously impair the flexibility and efficiency of the federal discovery procedure."

With that, Kirkpatrick began to examine the facts. The surviving
B-29 crash witnesses were at three different Air Force bases in Florida;
the burden, expense, and inconvenience of taking their depositions
were factors for the court to consider—though they were not by themselves "good cause." The government lawyers, during courtroom argument, had suggested that the United States might bring the witnesses
to Philadelphia or pay the expenses of Biddle's travel to Florida, "but I
do not understand that any binding commitment to that effect has
been made nor have I the power to order it." Even if it were possible to
take depositions of the witnesses, "the fact remains that . . . disclosure
of the contents of their written statements is necessary to enable the
plaintiffs to properly prepare their cases for trial"—here Kirkpatrick
mindfully planted the needed words—"and furnishes good cause for
production."

Now Kirkpatrick, in characteristic manner, boiled things down
to their essence:

> The plaintiffs have no knowledge of why the accident
> happened. So far as such knowledge is obtainable, the defendant
> has it. When the airplane crashed, it was wrecked and much of
> the evidence of what occurred was destroyed. Only persons with
> long experience in investigating airplane disasters could hope to
> get at the real cause of the accident under such circumstances.
> The Air Force appointed a board of investigators immediately
> after the accident and examined the surviving witnesses while
> their recollections were fresh. With their statements as a starting
> point the board was able to make an extensive investigation of
> the accident. These statements and the report of the board's
> investigation undoubtedly contain facts, information and clues
> which it might be extremely difficult, if not impossible, for the
> plaintiffs with their lack of technical resources to obtain merely
> by taking the depositions of the survivors.

He wasn't suggesting that these survivors "would not answer the questions asked them truthfully." But in a case like this, "in which seemingly trivial things may, to the expert, furnish important clues," the plaintiffs "must have accurate and precise firsthand information" if they are to examine witnesses and "get at the truth in preparing for trial." This "only the statements can give them." The witnesses wouldn't necessarily be hostile during depositions, but "they are employees of the defendant, in military service and subject to military authority." It's fair to assume "they will not be encouraged to disclose, voluntarily, any information which might fix responsibility upon the Air Force." What's more, "the accident happened more than 18 months ago and what the crew would remember now might well differ in important matters from what they told their officers when the event was fresh in their minds."

Besides his wariness about the surviving witnesses, Kirkpatrick questioned the government's candor. The government's answers to Biddle's interrogatories, he suggested, were "far short of the full and complete disclosure of facts which the spirit of the rules requires." For example, he pointed out, when Biddle asked, *Describe in detail the trouble experienced*, the answer was, *At between 18,500 and 19,000 feet manifold pressure dropped to 23 inches on No. One engine.* "Obviously, the [government], with the report and findings of its official investigation in its possession, knows more about the accident than this."

For all these reasons, Kirkpatrick wrote, "I conclude that good cause appears for the production of all documents which are subject to the motion." He wanted it known that the type of executive immunity asserted by the government had been "fully considered and held not sustainable by this Court in *O'Neill v. United States.*" He also wanted it known—again he pointed to *O'Neill*—that "the government does not here contend that this is a case involving the well-recognized common-law privilege protecting state secrets or facts which might seriously harm the Government in its diplomatic relations, military operations or measures for national security." In effect, "the Government claims a new kind of privilege. Its position is that the proceedings of boards of investigation of the armed services should be privileged in order to allow free and unhampered self-criticism. . . . I can find no recognition in the law of the existence of such a privilege." Kirkpatrick's ruling: "The defendant's motion to quash is denied and the plaintiff's motion to produce is granted."

In this fashion, the judge blocked the government from pursuing one avenue—and pushed it toward another.

WITH THE FOURTH OF JULY FALLING ON A TUESDAY THAT YEAR, FRIDAY, June 30, was getaway day for a long four-day holiday. Pleasant weather in the mid-seventies and congested bumper-to-bumper traffic conditions encouraged an early escape from city offices. Before he departed for Andalusia, though, Charles Biddle wrote to Teddy Mattern and the three widows: "I am glad to be able to advise you that Judge Kirkpatrick of the District Court today at last granted our motion for the production by the Air Force of the report of its investigation of the accident and the statements of the surviving Air Force Personnel. I hope the Government will now produce these papers without further contention. I shall keep you advised."

CHAPTER 14

A CLAIM OF PRIVILEGE

July–August '50

ON JULY 20, 1950, JUDGE KIRKPATRICK ISSUED A FORMAL
Order of the Court requiring the United States to hand over copies of
the B-29 accident report and witness statements. At Charles Biddle's
urging, Kirkpatrick gave the government a deadline of August 7. An
intricate legal dance ensued.

As soon as Justice Department officials heard from the U.S. at-
torney in Philadelphia about Kirkpatrick's order, they notified the
Department of the Air Force. The case began to turn, evolve, and es-
calate. Within days of Kirkpatrick's order, the Air Force informed the
Justice Department that it would not produce the documents—the Air
Force would not hand them over even to the attorney general.

On July 24, Biddle, his associate, Francis Hopkinson, and Assistant U.S. Attorney Thomas Curtin met with Kirkpatrick in his chambers. There Curtin presented Kirkpatrick a letter on behalf of Secretary
of the Air Force Thomas Finletter, signed by an assistant. This letter
confirmed that the Air Force would not release the documents, though
for the moment it still carefully framed the matter as a plea.

Acting under the authority of Section 161 of the Revised
Statutes [the "Housekeeping Statute"] . . . it has been determined

that it would not be in the public interest to furnish this report of investigation as requested by counsel in this case. This report was prepared under regulations which are designed to insure the collection of all pertinent information regarding aircraft accidents in order that all possible measures will be developed for the prevention of accidents. . . . Because this matter is one of such primary importance to the Air Force, it has been found necessary to restrict the use of aircraft accident reports to the official purpose for which they are intended. Under our regulations, this type of report is not available in courts-martial proceedings or other forms of disciplinary action or in the determination of pecuniary liability. It is hoped that the extreme importance which the Department of the Air Force places upon the confidential nature of its official aircraft accident reports will be fully appreciated and understood by your Honorable Court.

As Kirkpatrick read these words, the lawyers waited, studying his expression. There is no doubt he wanted the government to hand over the disputed documents. Yet the Air Force's stance gave him pause; this former Army jurist and lieutenant colonel wasn't inclined to dismiss the military's position out of hand. Instead, he expressed a willingness to hold a hearing to further consider the matter. He offered to convene it either in Philadelphia or in Washington, if that would be more convenient. Washington, as it happened, would be more convenient for *him*—Kirkpatrick was about to retreat to his farm in Maryland, only thirty miles from the nation's capital.

Since the government would not be in default until August 7, the meeting ended without resolution. The next day, July 25, Biddle wrote to Mattern, as usual copying his correspondence to the three widows, and in it this mainstay of the establishment could not hide his exasperation with the government. "So as to compel the Government to act," he reported, "I got the Court to enter an order fixing August 7 as the time within which the Government should produce the Air Force report of the B-29 accident and the statements of the surviving members of the crew." He continued, his ire rising:

The United States Attorney advises me that the
Government flatly refuses to produce the report. . . . To my
mind it is perfect nonsense after all these years when B–29s have
had accidents all over the world and have been forced down
nearly everywhere, including Russia, to say that a report on
what caused this accident is a secret which should not be
disclosed. Obviously we are not interested in any secret devices
which may have been on board but which had nothing to do
with causing the accident. And in any event, the answer, which
has been made several times in similar cases, is to let the Court
look at the report and if there is anything which should not be
made public, the Judge can authorize that it be withheld.

We had a meeting yesterday with Judge Kirkpatrick and
the Assistant U.S. Attorney in charge of the cases here. What we
will do when the Government does not produce the statements
within the time allowed is to move for a finding in our
favor. . . . Before entering such an order, if the Government
wishes to be heard, Judge Kirkpatrick will of course give it an
opportunity. . . . If, upon the Government's refusal to produce
the report, we obtain a finding in our favor on the liability, we
will then at the trial simply prove the damages. Since the
Government is apparently determined to appeal the case to the
Circuit Court, no time will be lost. I am sorry to say, however,
that it looks to me as if it is going to be a long time before we
can finally bring these cases to a conclusion, for the Government
seems to be so determined in its position that I would not be at
all surprised that if we win in the Circuit Court it did not
attempt to appeal the cases to the Supreme Court of the United
States.

Biddle seemed no less determined. He meant to fight for the accident report, even if that caused extended delays in the courts. Its production was not absolutely necessary, he allowed to Mattern. He could
base his case entirely on the presumption that the government was at
fault because the airplane had been under its control. He could add

Eugene Mechler's testimony that no emergency exit instructions were given before the flight. They would, Biddle thought, have a good chance of success on this basis alone. But in his judgment, "it would be a mistake to go to trial without first exhausting every effort to get the report of the investigation."

Biddle obviously sensed something in this accident report. "The violent objection to producing it," he observed in closing, "naturally makes one suspicious that it may contain some conclusions very unfavorable to the Government's case."

LEGAL CALCULATIONS INTENSIFIED INSIDE THE HIGHEST LEVELS OF THE Air Force and Justice Department. Judge Kirkpatrick, more than once in his rulings, had told the Air Force that he wouldn't recognize the kind of executive "housekeeping" privilege they were claiming—a privilege to withhold results of internal investigations and anything else they wanted to keep private. Kirkpatrick, again more than once, had suggested that he would recognize the common-law state secrets privilege if the disputed documents involved national security issues. But that, of course, wasn't being claimed in the B-29 case.

Or was it? Air Force brass, faced with Kirkpatrick's prompts, could not avoid the question. They had two basic options at this stage: to hand over the documents, or to withhold them and argue that judges don't have the authority to force production. If the Air Force brass produced, they would surely embarrass themselves and lose the case, given what the accident report contained. So the second option certainly looked more attractive to the Air Force, and no doubt to the Justice Department. They just needed an effective legal argument, a way to establish their fundamental right to withhold documents. Might they find that in the state secrets privilege? Might they even manage to transform this uncodified common law into established, written law? No longer would they have a run-of-the-mill tort action—this would be a major test case. This would be a way to set a critical new precedent, a way to gain lasting power and immunity for the executive branch. That had not been the Air Force's original goal, but then they ran into Judge Kirkpatrick.

The Air Force's moves, as the August 7 deadline approached, gained traction through the indispensable signatures of two men: Secretary of the Air Force Thomas Finletter and Judge Advocate General Reginald Harmon. Both had impeccable reputations. Both also were willing, at this critical moment, to hand Judge Kirkpatrick sworn statements that in later years would raise all manner of questions.

Finletter, then fifty-seven, the son and grandson of judges, an attorney and student of economics and foreign affairs, a former special assistant to Secretary of State Cordell Hull, was a close friend of Harry Truman and, especially, Adlai Stevenson. (A decade later, his own name would be floated as a possible Democratic candidate for the U.S. Senate from New York.) As chairman of Truman's Air Policy Commission, he'd delivered a report to the president in January 1948 entitled "Survival in the Air Age"—a document informed by the belief that whichever country mastered the skies (as Britain once dominated the seas) would control destiny. In an off-the-record speech that May before the New York State Chamber of Commerce, just after being named secretary of the Air Force, Finletter had warned that the United States could no longer consider itself safe behind its navy: "The air lanes now have to be defended. . . . The possibility of damage to this country by attack through the air is incalculable." Yet in the same speech, saying he'd like to "make a diversion at this point," Finletter went out of his way to caution against using claims of national security to keep secrets. "I believe that there has been a tendency in the past to withhold information about military matters from the people on the basis of security which was not justified," Finletter told the New York gathering. "I believe that in their desire to protect their country, many of the men who had this information were withholding information which is quite well known to other nations and which should be known to the people of the United States but was not known."

Reginald Harmon, who was fifty, presented a decidedly different profile. The judge advocate general—in essence, the Air Force's chief lawyer and legal adviser to the chief of staff—had been born on a farm in Olney, Illinois, his parents direct descendents of the state's earliest settlers. He'd worked first as a schoolmaster at a country school, then enrolled at the University of Illinois to study law. He'd been a Protestant Sunday-school teacher, the youngest mayor in the history of Urbana at age twenty-nine, a high priest of the Urbana chapter of the Royal Arch Masons, commander of the Urbana Commandery of Knights Templar, a member of the Order of the Mystic Shrine, and a ruling elder in the National Presbyterian Church. In a questionnaire, he once listed his interests as "golf, gardening and home construction" and his opinions and tastes as "typically American."

President Truman had appointed Harmon as the Air Force's first judge advocate general in September 1948—one month before the crash of B-29 #866. By then, Harmon had been handling legal duties for the Air Force for nearly a decade, first as a second lieutenant with the University of Illinois ROTC, later as a major in the Army Reserve Corps at Wright Field, Dayton, Ohio.

From 1945 to September 1948, he was the staff judge advocate of the Air Materiel Command at Wright Field. That made him the chief lawyer for the military group responsible for Project Banshee and the Banshee B-29s. The plane that fell from the sky over Waycross had belonged to the Air Materiel Command. This lawsuit filed by Charles Biddle on behalf of three widows, this demand for documents, this order to produce—they most certainly would have caught Harmon's attention.

WHEN AUGUST 7 ARRIVED, ASSISTANT U.S. ATTORNEY THOMAS CURTIN, having no documents to hand over, instead asked for the hearing that Judge Kirkpatrick had offered to hold. The judge scheduled it for 9:45 a.m. on August 9—in the U.S. District Courthouse in Washington, D.C. The Air Force and the Justice Department now knew just what they were going to do.

That same August 7, Reginald Harmon signed a sworn affidavit and gave it to Curtin for use at the hearing. In one passage, Harmon explicitly affirmed "that the . . . three witnesses will be made available at the expense of the United States for interrogation by the plaintiffs at a place and time to be designed by the plaintiffs. That these witnesses will be authorized to testify regarding all matters pertaining to the cause of the accident except as to the facts and matters of a classified nature. . . ."

It's possible to regard this as a wily diversion: If those witnesses were definitely available to depose, then the government could argue that the widows didn't yet have "good cause" for the accident report and statements. Diversion or not, this passage in Harmon's affidavit was a mere prelude.

After it came the critical paragraph. Here, Harmon swore "that such information and findings of the Accident Investigation Board and statements which have been demanded by the plaintiffs cannot be furnished without seriously hampering national security, flying safety and the development of highly technical and secret military equipment."

For the first time in the case—more than a year after Biddle had filed lawsuits on behalf of the widows—the government was suggesting, however vaguely, that the accident report and witness statements contained national security secrets.

One day later, on August 8, again for Curtin's use at the hearing, Thomas Finletter signed a sworn affidavit, as well as a formal claim of privilege. His brief affidavit stated his right to promulgate certain regulations. His carefully worded claim of privilege did more. In this document, Finletter alluded indirectly to the state secrets privilege while leaving it to Harmon to make the actual claim. He began by recapitulating arguments previously rejected by Kirkpatrick—that the widows had failed to show "good cause," that the reports were privileged because they were prepared for interdepartmental use only. Then he inched forward. "The defendant further objects to the production of this report," Finletter wrote, "together with the statements of the witnesses, for the reason that the aircraft in question, together with the personnel on board, were engaged in a highly secret mission of the Air Force. The airplane likewise carried confidential equipment on board and any disclosure of its mission or information concerning its operation or performance would be prejudicial to this Department and would not be in the public interest."

Instead of the state secrets privilege, Finletter in these words seemed to cling still to the power of an executive "housekeeping" privilege. Unlike Harmon, Finletter could not quite bring himself to say that disclosure would "seriously hamper national security." Nor could he say directly that the accident report contained state secrets. But he drew close in one phrase of his conclusion: "For the reasons stated above, I consider that the compulsory production of the Reports of Investigation . . . is prejudicial to the efficient operation of the Department of the Air Force, is not in the public interest, and is inconsistent with national security. Accordingly . . . I assert the privileged status of reports here involved and must respectfully decline to permit their production."

With these documents signed by Finletter and Harmon, the government set the hook. Finletter's "consistent with national security" combined with Harmon's "seriously hamper national security" artfully if ambiguously implied a claim of state secrets—a claim that, as Finletter put it, was "beyond judicial authority." Now came Judge Kirkpatrick's time to respond.

CHAPTER 15

THE HEARING

August 9, 1950

RELATIVELY FAIR, COOL WEATHER HAD GRACED MOST OF the eastern portion of the country in the early part of August, but on Wednesday, August 9, Washington, D.C., sweltered. Even in the morning, driving to the downtown U.S. Courthouse from his Maryland farm, Judge Kirkpatrick could feel the warm, heavy air. He was sixty-five, with twenty-three years on the bench behind him, eight years to go until his retirement—although he'd continue to sit part-time as a senior judge until his death in 1970, at age eighty-five.

Once more he had before him the two civil actions he'd been considering since February, *Phyllis Brauner and Elizabeth Palya v. United States of America* and *Patricia J. Reynolds v. United States of America*. The hearing began, as scheduled, at 9:45 a.m. Thomas Curtin appeared on behalf of the government, accompanied by a Department of Justice lawyer and two Air Force colonels from Reginald Harmon's office. Across the aisle, Charles Biddle's associate Francis Hopkinson represented the widows.

"Court is open," Kirkpatrick said.

Curtin rose to introduce his associates. Then he launched into a summary of the case so far. Kirkpatrick interrupted—he'd left his copy of the case file in the U.S. Marshal's office and wanted somebody to retrieve it. Hopkinson offered his copy of the file, but Kirkpatrick wanted his own—"It has some other things there. Can't you send somebody down?"

Curtin continued with his summary, coming finally to the fact that he wished to file a petition for a formal rehearing on the motions to produce and quash documents. He wanted a transcript of this morning's session to be included in his petition, "so that the record in the Circuit Court [of Appeals] will show the whole proceeding."

Kirkpatrick understood well that the government would be appealing whatever he decided. "That is all right," he said.

"May I proceed?" Curtin asked. Kirkpatrick nodded, so Curtin began.

"On behalf of Thomas K. Finletter, Secretary of the Air Force, I desire to present a claim of privilege by the Secretary . . . in these two cases, and I hand Your Honor herewith the claims."

Kirkpatrick started to scan Finletter's claims. Curtin offered to sit down "while Your Honor finishes reading them." Kirkpatrick instead looked up from the pages.

"You can tell me what they say," the judge invited. "They are too long to read."

Curtin said, "Briefly the gist is he states that in his opinion there has been no showing of good cause."

The same old story. This time, though, Kirkpatrick had made sure to document his finding of good cause. Eyeing Curtin, he said only, "This is all right."

Curtin now chose to invoke the *O'Neill/Alltmont* case, in which the Third Circuit had reversed Kirkpatrick's order to produce written statements because the plaintiff had not shown "good cause" for the documents. Finletter's current claim of privilege, Curtin pointed out, follows "almost identically" the claim made by the attorney general in the *O'Neill/Alltmont* cases. "As a matter of fact, it is practically a paraphrasing of·[that] claim."

Again the same old story. Time to focus on the current case, not *O'Neill.* Kirkpatrick asked, "Is this claim of privilege made out any differently from the claim of privilege that was made at the time of the motion to quash?"

"No, sir."

Kirkpatrick sensed what was coming. In *O'Neill*, he'd told the government lawyers they couldn't claim executive "housekeeping" privilege—they had to produce the documents—but that it would be different if they were claiming state secrets. "I want to know whether it still stands," he said now. "As in the [O'Neill] Alltmont case, the Government does not here contend that this is a case involving the well-recognized common law privilege in regard to secrets . . . which might seriously harm the Government in its diplomatic relations, military operations or the national security?"

Curtin had to stall, because Finletter's claim of privilege did not go that far. They'd left it to Reginald Harmon to make the actual claim. "I might say with regard to that point I wish you would pass that for a minute, because that does come into this case in the second document."

"Very well," Kirkpatrick said.

Next Curtin handed up Harmon's claim that the B-29 documents contained state secrets. "I desire," he said, "to present on behalf of Major General Harmon similar affidavits . . . and this point [state secrets] is in this affidavit of Major General Harmon's. It is not in [Finletter's] claim of privilege. It is embodied in a certain way, but this one gives Your Honor more."

As Kirkpatrick read through Harmon's affidavit, Curtin drew his attention to the fact that the government here was officially offering to produce the three surviving crew members for Biddle to depose. Curtin also wanted the judge to notice Harmon's critical words near the end: "Such information and findings of the accident investigation board which have been demanded by the plaintiffs cannot be furnished without seriously hampering national security."

Why Harmon but not Finletter? Curtin offered an explanation before being asked. "Because the secretary of the Air Force, he, naturally, wouldn't know what mission this particular plane was on, what equipment was upon it. It was only upon investigation by the Judge Advocate General's office into the various things [that] he was able to determine this."

So besides the familiar claim of executive "housekeeping" privilege under statutory law, already rejected by Kirkpatrick, they now—nine months after the widows requested discovery—were making a claim of state secrets privilege under common law. This thanks to information newly unearthed by the judge advocate general.

Kirkpatrick did not sound ready to accept such an obvious maneuver. "That claim has been made in other cases," he pointed out, "and it has been usually met by submission of the matter to the Court to determine whether or not it is data which would imperil the safety of the military position of the United States."

"That procedure was followed in two cases," Curtin allowed.

"Yes, I know."

Now their debate drove to the heart of the matter.

Curtin: We do not believe that is good law. We contend that the findings of the head of the Department are binding, and the judiciary cannot waive it.

Kirkpatrick: It is an important question. I suppose, just to state a wholly imaginary and rather fantastic case, suppose you had a collision between a mail truck and a taxi-cab, and the Attorney General came in and said that in his opinion discovery in the case would imperil the whole military position of the United States, and so forth. Would the Court have to accept that? Is that where your argument leads?

Curtin: I think you could interpret it that way.

Kirkpatrick: I only want to know where your argument leads.

Curtin: Under the statute, we contend it is final.

Kirkpatrick: Assume the statute is out of it, and you are claiming common law [state secrets] privilege. . . . Your argument would lead to the point that I suggested?

Curtin: There is no other interpretation. In other words, I say that the Executive is the person who must make that determination, not the Judiciary.

Kirkpatrick: That is the point.

Curtin: In this particular case, the Executive having made
that determination, I submit, sir, it is binding upon
the Judiciary. You cannot review it or interpret it.
That is what it comes down to.

Kirkpatrick had something else on his mind—that the government, in midstream, had changed its reason for not producing documents. "Of course," he said, "there is another fact, that this
particular claim of privilege is merely delaying. It was not made at
the time [of the motions to quash]. I carefully read the briefs, and it
was not suggested there that there was any claim of [state secrets]
privilege."

Two years after the crash, one year after the lawsuit's filing, Curtin said: "In my motion to quash . . . I didn't even know what the trip
was, or what was even on the plane, as a matter of fact."

"All right," Kirkpatrick said.

For the first time at the hearing, Biddle's associate Francis Hopkinson spoke. "Your Honor, I would like to state that in the Cotton
Valley Operators case, the [Supreme] Court took the position it was up
to the Court to decide whether or not there was privilege."

"They have taken that position," Kirkpatrick agreed. "It is an old
controversy."

Kirkpatrick knew of the recent Cotton Valley ruling. In 1949, a
U.S. District judge had ruled that he would dismiss an antitrust lawsuit
if the government didn't produce documents for his private, in-chambers
(*in camera*) review; the Supreme Court in April 1950 had affirmed.
Kirkpatrick asked Hopkinson for a citation on this—he wanted to
study the case. While Biddle's associate searched, Curtin offered to
provide Kirkpatrick copies of all the regulations cited in Finletter's
claim of privilege.

"Whatever you give me," Kirkpatrick said, "I will take it home
with me."

Curtin handed up a thick pile of documents. "That is a whole
set."

Hopkinson, in turn, provided a cite for the Cotton Valley case, but apparently it wasn't what the judge needed. "That won't help me much," Kirkpatrick said. "I am going over to the Supreme Court library shortly. There are several things I want to look up there. I will look it up there."

Hopkinson wanted it known that "after looking this over, I may like to submit a brief."

That was fine with Kirkpatrick: "I would like to have it. It is a very important point."

"There is no necessity for my filing a brief," Curtin said. "You know we filed that complete brief."

Kirkpatrick agreed: "I am thoroughly familiar with the whole business."

Curtin understood: "I don't think any brief is going to change your mind."

"Whatever you want," Kirkpatrick said. "I will read the brief."

THIS TIME, BIDDLE AND THE WIDOWS WOULD NOT HAVE TO WAIT FOUR months for Kirkpatrick to rule, but the weeks still seemed to drag on. At some point during that summer of 1950, Betty Palya and her three children made a round-trip drive to visit relatives in Grand Forks, Minnesota. Upon her return to New Jersey, she wrote her brother-in-law, W. J. Perryman, enclosing copies of letters she'd been receiving from Biddle.

Perryman wrote back on September 1 with obvious appreciation, saying, "I still admire your courage and spunk and just wish that I had as much." Then he turned to the subject of the lawsuit:

> I think Mr. Biddle is doing everything possible with your case and I am certain that he will bring it to trial as quickly as possible. As I have explained previously, courts of every kind are awfully slow and usually judges and lawyers recognize no other urgency than their own. With a case of this sort against the government the lawyers representing the government will make every effort to stall—then afterwards since time means nothing to them or the expense of re-trial they might try and appeal. I

have written to Mr. Biddle inquiring if there are any facts that I might be able to get for him either at Macon or elsewhere and have also asked that he keep me advised as to further moves by the government. . . . Just keep your chin up as I am certain that before too long you will get something out of this case—and it will be worth the effort and waiting.

In his letter Perryman enclosed a check "for yourself and the boys. I know with school starting there will be shoes and sweaters and coats—then too a new hat for yourself to go with your smile."

TWO WEEKS LATER, ON SEPTEMBER 14, SOMEWHERE IN THE PENTAGON, all the disputed B-29 documents—the accident reports, witness statements, and supporting material—apparently came up for a routine classification review. There is no record of why this happened or who handled it, but the stamped markings on the documents—some crossed out, some added and dated—show that the Air Force at this moment reduced their classification category from top-level "Secret" to third-level "Restricted." According to the military code, the definition of "Secret" was "might endanger national security"; the definition of "Restricted" was "for official use only, or when disclosure should be limited for reasons of administrative privacy."

For only twenty-one months, in other words—between January 3, 1949, and September 14, 1950—would the records of the B-29 crash near Waycross be classified as a national security secret. Of course, no one involved knew this—not the widows, not the judge, not the lawyers. Unaware, they continued their legal battle.

On September 21—one week after this reclassification—Judge Kirkpatrick issued an "Amended Order" regarding the "Production and Inspection of Documents." Despite the new state secrets claim, he wrote, he would not relinquish jurisdiction, he would not agree that the judiciary had no say in the matter. But rather than require the United States to hand over the disputed documents to Biddle and the widows, he now ruled that the government should hand them over to him—far from public disclosure—"so that this Court may determine whether or not all or parts of such documents contain matters of a confidential nature."

Kirkpatrick specified when and where his examination of the documents would take place: "At United States Courthouse, Room 2096, in the City of Philadelphia, Commonwealth of Pennsylvania, on the 4th day of October, 1950, at 2 o'clock, P.M."

Kirkpatrick also advised that after his examination, the United States would have to permit the plaintiffs to inspect and copy the documents, except "any part or parts . . . which may have been determined by this Court to be privileged from discovery."

To no one's surprise, the government did not produce the documents on October 4. Eight days later, Kirkpatrick entered a default judgment in favor of the plaintiffs, finding that the B-29 crash near Waycross, and the resulting deaths of Al Palya, William Brauner, and Robert Reynolds, were "caused solely and exclusively by the negligence and wrongful acts and omissions" of the United States of America.

In a letter, Francis Hopkinson reported the news to Betty Palya: "You will be pleased to learn that the District Court has agreed to enter judgment by default against the United States for the reason that the United States has refused to obey the Court's order to produce the Air Force's investigation. Accordingly, the only matter which must be proved in court is the damages. Although the court's action is subject to appeal, nevertheless we are hoping for the best."

CHAPTER 16

FULL VALUE

November '50–October '51

Over the Thanksgiving weekend in 1950, an unexpected wind, rain, and snowstorm battered the Northeast. Described by the Weather Bureau as "the most violent of its kind ever recorded in the northeastern quarter of the United States," it slammed into the region on Saturday, killing 273. Telephone and utility lines were down everywhere, roads flooded, trains halted. In Pennsylvania, where thirty-five died, officials couldn't even estimate the total havoc. Pittsburgh endured a twenty-eight-inch snowfall—the worst storm in its history—leaving the city in a state of emergency, with banks, courts, and industry shuttered, hotels and hospitals jammed. In the eastern half of the state, everything from coal mines to schools were still shut down as the holiday came to an end on Monday, November 27.

The federal courthouse in downtown Philadelphia, however, was open. Snow flurries continued to fall, with temperatures in the thirties, as Judge Kirkpatrick walked to work from his hotel room at the Bellevue Stratford. Charles Biddle also managed to get to the courthouse, coming from Andalusia. So did Betty Palya, from Haddon Heights. Together with Francis Hopkinson and Assistant U.S. Attorney Thomas Curtin, they gathered in Courtroom 3. Since Kirkpatrick had entered a default judgment in favor of the widows, all that remained to consider at this trial was the amount of the damages to award. Which meant Biddle now had to present evidence of how much the lives of Al Palya, William Brauner, and Robert Reynolds were worth.

This made for a clinical affair. As Kirkpatrick watched from the bench, his green eyeshade in place, Biddle began by offering sheets on each of the three engineers that listed their age, life expectancy, education, previous employment, and prospects for the (unrealized) future.

Exhibit A advised that William Brauner had been thirty-four at the time of his death; that he had an additional life expectancy of 32.50 years. Previously a development engineer at General Electric, he'd joined the Franklin Institute as a research engineer in November 1946, starting at $4,400 a year and ending, after two merit increases, at $5,050 a year.

Exhibit B advised that Albert Palya had been forty-one at the time of his death; that he had a life expectancy of 27.45 years. He'd worked first as a self-employed photographic engineer, earning about $3,000 a year, then, from 1941 to 1945, at Minneapolis Honeywell, earning $4,200 a year. He'd joined RCA in August 1945, starting at $4,992 a year and ending, after four merit raises, at $6,720 a year.

Exhibit C advised that Robert Reynolds had been twenty-four at the time of his death; that he had a life expectancy of 39.49 years. He'd earned a B.S. from the University of Purdue in 1946 and joined RCA the same year, starting at $2,280 and ending, after seven increases, at $3,307 a year.

With these exhibits entered into evidence, Biddle called Douglas Hancock Ewing to the stand. From 1945 to January 1949, Ewing had worked at RCA, where he'd been Palya's direct supervisor. Palya, Ewing testified, had been in charge of an engineering group that was working on the development of "quite highly classified electronic equipment for the United States Air Force." In his estimation, Palya "was a very competent mechanical engineer." He had "quite good capabilities, quite unusual capabilities." He was "responsible for suggesting a number of quite ingenious ideas." His salary likely would have kept increasing by ten percent every two years, "leveling off at about $10,000."

Ewing also offered testimony about Bob Reynolds, who had reported to Palya. Reynolds had come to RCA as a "student engineer." Because he worked in the field, "he wasn't in a position to learn as rapidly from the older members . . . as would have been desirable." As a consequence, his first year of service "was somewhat less than satisfactory." After a diligent course of reading and self-instruction, however, "his performance increased to somewhat better than satisfactory." Palya had rated his performance overall as "good . . . fully competent." The last review before his death "showed a marked improvement." By age forty-five, he likely would have been making about six thousand dollars.

Ralph H. McClarren of the Franklin Institute offered testimony about William Brauner, who worked directly under his supervision. Brauner was an "above average" electrical engineer and physicist. He "accomplished work of an unusual nature." He had the ability to "thoroughly analyze a problem from the fundamental physics and mathematics, see that problem through its experimental stage and to actually devise apparatus which conform to his analysis." He also "showed tendencies toward invention, new ideas." His salary likely would have kept increasing, leveling out at $9,000, the top for his job category.

Biddle had all the necessary information on the record by the time he called Betty to the stand. He wanted her to put a human face on the data—he wanted Kirkpatrick to see and hear her. She was five-two with closely cut brown hair and a sweet, gentle expression. She most likely had made the dress she was wearing. This home economics teacher would have found it jarring to be in downtown Philadelphia, in the federal courthouse; she rarely had dinner out, never smoked or drank, never had adventures—she cooked and sewed and worked all the time.

"Mrs. Palya," Biddle asked, "you are the widow of Albert Palya?"

"I am."

"Where do you live?"

"I live at 16 Station Avenue . . . Haddon Heights, New Jersey."

"And you teach, I think, at the Haddonfield High School now?"

"Yes, that is right."

"Have you got any children?"

"I have three children."

"And how long were you and Mr. Palya married before his death?"

"We were married a little over eleven years."

Thomas Curtin had no questions when it came time for cross-examination. Judge Kirkpatrick did, though. "What is your age, Mrs. Palya?"

"I am thirty-eight."

At the close of the trial that afternoon, Kirkpatrick asked Biddle to state for the record the ages of the other two widows. Phyllis Brauner was thirty-four, Biddle informed the judge. Patricia Reynolds—now Patricia Herring, having married Don Herring on July 29—was twenty-two.

Five days later, on Saturday, December 2, President Truman, along with most of his Cabinet and the country's top military brass, came to Philadelphia to watch the annual Army–Navy football game at Municipal Stadium. In Korea, more than 300,000 Chinese troops had just entered the battle, staggering United Nations forces and prompting Truman to talk about the possible use of atomic weapons. One month earlier, two Puerto Rican nationalists had attempted to assassinate him by shooting their way into Blair House. The president appeared unconcerned, though. This being Navy's "home" game, he sat on the Annapolis side of the field; Thomas Finletter and General Hoyt Vandenberg sat on the Army side.

With them were 101,000 spectators, undeterred by near-freezing temperatures and occasional light rain. Thirty-seven special trains oper- ated by the Pennsylvania Railroad had carried nearly half the crowd to the game. Overhead, three squadrons of U.S. Air Force F-51 Mustangs maintained a constant patrol, protecting the air space within a three–mile radius. On the ground, one thousand Philadelphia policemen guarded all approaches to the stadium, while seventy Secret Service agents guarded Truman. Navy, a three–touchdown underdog, beat Army 14–2.

KIRKPATRICK TOOK NEARLY THREE MONTHS TO DECIDE THE "FULL value" of the lives of Al Palya, William Brauner, and Bob Reynolds at the time of their deaths. In an opinion filed on February 20, 1951, he fixed that value at $80,000 each (the equivalent of $622,972 in current dollars) for Palya and Brauner and $65,000 (the equivalent of $506,165) for Reynolds. (Although Palya's earnings were higher than Brauner's, the men's "value" was the same because Palya, being older, had a shorter life expectancy; Reynolds's "value" was less because his earnings were substantially lower.) A week later, Kirkpatrick formally ordered that judgment in these amounts be entered in favor of the widows and against the United States of America.

"I am enclosing copies of Judge Kirkpatrick's decisions," Biddle wrote Betty on February 26. "As you will see, the Court has fixed the damages in your case at $80,000. I hope that you will feel that this amount, if collected, is satisfactory. . . . As I have previously advised you, it may be quite some time before anything is collected, for I believe that the Government will in all probability appeal the case upon the point that there was no right to compel it to disclose the contents of the Air Force report and statements."

The government waited two months—against a period of rising fear and passion in the country. The trial of Julius and Ethel Rosenberg began early that March, serving uncomfortable notice that spies had been operating in America for years, eavesdropping on the Manhattan Project, providing the Soviets information about the bomb. On March 29, a jury found the Rosenbergs guilty of conspiracy to commit espionage—what J. Edgar Hoover called "the crime of the century." A week later, Judge Irving Kaufman—saying "the issue of punishment" comes at a time when the country is "engaged in a life and death struggle . . . a challenge to our very existence"—ordered the Rosenbergs' execution. Even as he spoke, the Korean War was reaching a state of crisis. Truman, having declared a national emergency, rejected calls both for withdrawal and for retaliatory strikes against China that could spark a global battle. In Korea, though, General Douglas MacArthur wanted authority to attack Chinese bases in Manchuria. He made his desires clear in public denunciations of administration policy, a fundamental violation of Truman's guidelines. On April 11, Truman fired the celebrated general for insubordination. MacArthur returned to an emotional welcome in the United States, defiantly defending himself on April 19 in a speech before a cheering joint session of Congress in which he likened a limited war in Korea to appeasement and concluded with his memorable farewell, "I now close my military career and just fade away . . ." Later that evening, one million New Yorkers and a seventeen-gun salute greeted him when his Constellation *Bataan* landed at New York International Airport. At noon the next day, more than seven million hailed him during a triumphant six-hour, nineteen-mile ticker-tape parade.

That same day, April 20, government lawyers in Philadelphia filed their notice of appeal. As Biddle predicted, the government did indeed mean to challenge Kirkpatrick's ruling. In fact, the government meant to challenge Kirkpatrick's very right to make a ruling.

"As we anticipated," Biddle wrote the widows on April 24, "the Government has waited until the last moment to appeal the judgment in your favor to the U.S. Court of Appeals for the Third Circuit. The appeal being taken so late in the year before the summer vacation of the Court, it will not be heard until the Fall and how long the Court will take to decide it after that no one can say, but they are sometimes quite slow. However, you will have the consolation, if we are finally successful, that your judgment will in the meantime bear interest at 6% until paid."

As time passed, the widows recovered, and even thrived. Betty, still watching over her family on a quiet street in Haddon Heights, had met a man, a butcher named Bill Sacker, a handsome World War II veteran who'd served in the Marines. He worked at the grocery store where she shopped. One day he took notice of her when she came to the store with her little girl—he made a fuss over Judy—and now they were dating. Phyllis, settled with her two daughters and widowed mother in their Wellesley home, rushed about constantly, teaching and making progress toward her doctorate. In June, Patricia, living in Indianapolis with her husband, Don Herring, learned she was pregnant with her first child.

Also that June, the government lawyers—as Biddle predicted—

sought once more to delay the proceedings. Biddle opposed their motion: The government, he wrote, "has already had eight months" to prepare its brief. Since the B-29 crash, the widows have been "left without means of support other than the small amount received under the Workmen's Compensation Law." It is therefore "of great importance" to the widows that this appeal be "promptly heard." But it was not prompty heard: The Third Circuit granted an extension and fixed October 8 as the deadline for Biddle's response.

Five days before this deadline, Truman announced that the Soviets had exploded another atomic bomb, their second in two years. On October 6, Joseph Stalin confirmed that the Soviet Union possessed more than one type of atomic bomb, and that tests of the "various calibers" would continue. Sooner rather than later, as it turned out—on October 18, the Soviets detonated yet another atomic bomb, this time dropping it from a Tu-4.

In Philadelphia the next day, Charles Biddle and the government lawyers rose in the federal courthouse before a three-judge panel from the Third Circuit Court of Appeals. The time had arrived for arguments in the appeal of Judge Kirkpatrick's decision.

CHAPTER 17

JUDGE MARIS

October–December '51

EVERYONE IN THE COURTROOM ON OCTOBER 19 UNDERSTOOD that the Third U.S. Circuit Court of Appeals had twice before reversed Kirkpatrick in cases where he'd ordered defendants to hand over disputed documents. The legacy of *Hickman* and *O'Neill/Alltmont* couldn't be ignored. In fact, the lead judge sitting on the appellate panel this morning, Albert Maris, was the very jurist who'd written the *Alltmont* decision that overturned Kirkpatrick's *O'Neill* ruling.

If Kirkpatrick was a legend among the federal judiciary in Philadelphia, Albert Maris was an icon recognized as among the finest judges in the country. His selection for this panel, his appearance on the bench this morning, represented yet another fateful moment shaping the widows' litigation.

Maris was fifty-seven, tall, thin, of erect bearing. He spoke in a deep, firm voice and considered his words before offering them. He "walked like a farmer," one of his colleagues liked to say, putting his feet down without paying attention to where they were going. He was an avid stamp collector and a naturalist who approached physical challenges with vigor. Once, after slipping on some ice near the federal courthouse and falling on his face, he got up and walked himself to the nearest hospital. He was not unwilling to poke fun at the legal profession, belonging for years to a club that lampooned lawyers and judges. He knew every line of Gilbert & Sullivan. He shunned publicity and did not like the title of Judge, so everyone in the federal courthouse called him Albert. A devout Quaker, he never raised his voice, never smoked or drank, yet he loved fancy desserts. Kind, wise, gentle, tactful, courteous—those words reappear often in the many toasts his colleagues made to him at awards dinners through the years.

Born in 1893 in Philadelphia to a family descended from George Maris, a Quaker who arrived from England in 1683, Albert Maris did not have an easy early life. His father, a druggist, died of a ruptured appendix when Maris was six years old, leaving his mother to raise three young children. A shy schoolboy at the Friends Select School, Maris would occasionally slip away from campus to visit a nearby cobbler named Johnny Fitzpatrick, who talked to him earnestly about the "rights of man" and other matters of social justice. This was Maris's first exposure to political issues, and he absorbed it hungrily, picking up what he'd later call "some rather liberal ideas"—ideas that stayed with him all his life.

Maris could not afford to go on to college after finishing high school—just as Kirkpatrick never graduated from law school, Maris never earned a college degree. Instead, he took a job as a clerk in an insurance company and for a year studied Latin (Cicero and Virgil) at Temple University's night school. This enabled him to pass the Law Preparatory Examination and enroll at Temple Law School. Maris continued working at the insurance company by day, since Temple Law was a night school, located in downtown Philadelphia over a shoe repair shop, with half a dozen faculty members and less than one hundred students. He earned his law degree in 1918, and later an engineering degree from the Drexel Institute of Technology. By 1925 he was a partner at a Philadelphia law firm and active in politics as the Democratic County Chairman for Delaware County. When he ran for the State Senate in 1928, against a Republican incumbent in a heavily Republican district, he lost but received the largest vote ever for a Democrat in that region.

Maris remained exceptionally active in the 1930s, serving as a member of the Pennsylvania Democratic State Committee, as president of the People's Association of Delaware County, as editor of the *Legal Intelligencer* newspaper, as president of the Associated Court and Commercial Newspapers, and as a member of the Society of Friends. In June 1936, Franklin Roosevelt named Maris a U.S. District Judge in Philadelphia. Just two years later, FDR elevated him to the U.S. Court of Appeals for the Third Circuit.

There he joined John Biggs, who would become both a close friend and a jurisprudential comrade. Biggs, named the Third Circuit's chief judge in 1939, had roomed with F. Scott Fitzgerald at Princeton and was himself a highly regarded novelist. He and Maris both had judicial philosophies that Justice William Brennan called "humanitarian liberalism." They were willing, as one historian of the Third Circuit put it, to work as "social engineers," to "promote causes and issues [they] thought important."

From the start, Maris's opinions drew admiration as models of clarity, construction, and legal reasoning. They often reflected a strong feel for history and literature; they also often reflected Maris's concern for the rights and dignity of the individual. As a Quaker, one of his law clerks later observed, he lived by the concept that "there is that of God in every man," but Maris was intolerant of injustice, prejudice, and insincerity.

What may be his best-known decision, the landmark *Gobitis v. Minersville School District,* came in 1937 when he was still a U.S. district judge, and it earned him the Supreme Court's lasting attention. The case (whose title misspells the family's name) began two years before at a Minersville, Pennsylvania, public elementary school, when Lillian Gobitas, age twelve, and her brother William, ten, the children of Jehovah's Witnesses, refused to recite the Pledge of Allegiance and salute the flag. Their parents, who lived in an apartment above their self-service food market, had allowed their children to decide this for themselves; Jehovah's Witnesses strongly believe in the Old Testament's prohibition against graven images and idolatry, and the Gobitas children understood the flag to be such an image.

"The Lord clearly says in Exodus 20: 3, 5, that you should have no gods besides Him," Lillian wrote to the Minersville school board. "According to the dictates of my conscience, based on the Bible, I must give my full allegiance to Jehovah."

"I love my country," Billy added. "I love God more and I must obey his commandments."

Such explanations did not prevent the Gobitas family from being condemned by many in Minersville, who thought the children's actions were un-American. The school board, deeming Lillian and Billy insubordinate, voted in November 1935 to expel them. The Gobitas family had trouble getting a lawyer to represent them but in 1937 finally managed to file a lawsuit in the U.S. District Court in Philadelphia.

The matter first came before Judge Maris in late 1937, when the Minersville school district moved to dismiss the Gobitases' complaint. A neophyte on the bench, Maris knew that a number of courts had upheld mandatory flag-salute policies. Still, he denied the motion to dismiss, explaining that "to permit public officers to determine whether the views of individuals sincerely held and their acts sincerely undertaken on religious grounds are in fact based on convictions religious in character would be to sound the death knell of religious liberty. To such a pernicious and alien doctrine this court cannot subscribe."

The next summer, after a trial, Maris granted the injunction sought by the Gobitas family against the school board's orders. He ruled that it was an unconstitutional violation of the Fourteenth Amendment's due-process protection to require schoolchildren to salute the American flag in violation of their religious beliefs. Law students still study his eloquent opinion, which, in celebrating "individual liberty," took explicit judicial notice of "the current world scene."

> No one who heard the testimony of the plaintiffs and observed their demeanor upon the witness stand could have failed to be impressed with the earnestness and sincerity of their convictions. While the salute to our national flag has no religious significance to me and while I find it difficult to understand the plaintiffs' point of view, I am nevertheless

entirely satisfied that they sincerely believe that the act does have a deep religious meaning and is an act of worship which they can conscientiously render to God alone. . . . Under these circumstances it is not for this court to say that since the act has no religious significance to us it can have no such significance to them. I think it is also clear from the evidence that the refusal of these two earnest Christian children to salute the flag cannot even remotely prejudice or imperil the safety, health, morals, property or personal rights of their fellows. . . . They exhibit sincerity of conviction and devotion to principle in the face of opposition of a piece with that which brought our pioneer ancestors across the sea to seek liberty or conscience in a new land. Upon such a foundation of religious freedom our Commonwealth and Nation were built. We need only glance at the current world scene to realize the preservation of individual liberty is more important today than ever it was in the past. The safety of our nation largely depends upon the extent to which we foster in each individual citizen that sturdy independence of thought and action which is essential in a democracy. . . . Our country's safety surely does not depend upon the totalitarian idea of forcing all citizens into one common mold of thinking and acting. . . . Such a doctrine seems to me utterly alien to the genius and spirit of our nation and destructive of that personal liberty of which our flag itself is the symbol.

In November 1939, a three-judge panel of the Third U.S. Circuit Court of Appeals (where Maris by then sat) unanimously upheld this ruling. The Minersville school board subsequently appealed to the Supreme Court, at a time when Nazi forces were marching across Europe. By a vote of eight to one, the High Court in June 1940 overturned Maris's decision, with only Harlan Fiske Stone dissenting.

School boards can compel a salute to the flag despite religious beliefs, Justice Felix Frankfurter wrote in his majority decision (which he chose to read in full from the bench rather than offer the customary summary). The flag is the "symbol of our national unity, transcending all internal differences." The Pledge of Allegiance helps "to evoke that unifying element without which there can ultimately be no liberties." And "national unity is the basis of national security." The courts cannot deny the legislature "the right to select appropriate means for its attainment."

In the wake of the Supreme Court's ruling, a number of school districts rushed to adopt flag-salute requirements, which led to many Jehovah's Witness children being expelled when they would not submit. In West Virginia in 1942, after the State Board of Education implemented such a flag-salute requirement—embracing the *Gobitis* edict that "national unity is the basis of national security"—Jehovah's Witness families sued in federal court. The case, *West Virginia State Board of Education v. Barnette,* reached the Supreme Court in 1943. Just three years after reversing Judge Maris, the justices had decided to revisit the matter.

This time, the majority concluded that Albert Maris had been right after all. By a vote of six to three, the Supreme Court reversed its own recent decision in *Gobitis.* Justices Hugo Black and William Douglas now allowed that "long reflection" had convinced them that their application of principle "in the particular case was wrong." Justice Robert Jackson's majority opinion echoed Maris: "Freedom to differ is not limited to things that do not matter much. That would be a mere shadow of freedom. The test of its substance is the right to differ as to things that touch the heart of the existing order. If there is any fixed star in our constitutional constellation, it is that no official, high or petty, can prescribe what shall be orthodox in politics, nationalism, religion or other matters of opinion, or force citizens to confess by word or act their faith therein."

Frankfurter, despite writing a twenty-two-page dissent, subsequently sent Maris a friendly note. As time passed, Frankfurter more than once in open court would speak admiringly of Maris, calling him a very able judge. In 1942, the Supreme Court justices would name him to the Emergency Court of Appeals, which adjudicated wartime rationing, price controls, and rent control; later they would appoint him Special Master in a number of critical Court cases. "Yes," Maris would say with an amused gleam in his eye, when asked in his nineti-eth year about the *Gobitis* case, "I recall it."

ALBERT MARIS LOVED TO TRAVEL, OFTEN WITH HIS TWO SONS, WILLIAM and Robert. His journeys eventually took him around the world, but from 1924 to 1954 he mainly toured the United States and Canada. In August 1949, he'd taken William on a horseback trip through the Rocky Mountains. In February 1950, while temporarily sitting with judges of the First Circuit in San Juan, Puerto Rico, he'd slipped in trips to Havana and Haiti. That August, he'd spent a month driving through the western United States, staying in motor courts, visiting Rocky Mountain National Park, the Zuni Pueblo, the Gunnison Na-tional Monument, and Mesa Verde National Park.

During the summer of 1951, with the B–29 cases pending before his court and Charles Biddle pushing government lawyers to file their brief, Maris and his wife spent seven weeks in Guam and the Trust Territory of the Pacific Islands. He went at the request of the Interior Department, to "survey and make recommendations" for the possible revision of Guam's judicial code. He delivered a report on July 26 and left Guam the next day, traveling through Manila, Hong Kong, Wake Island, Honolulu, and Los Angeles before returning home to Philadel-phia on the evening of August 13. Besides his official reports and cor-respondence, he'd written a number of "letters home"—a kind of running journal—about his experience. These he began sharing with friends and colleagues.

On August 31, he sent a sampling to Fred Vinson, chief justice of the Supreme Court. "Dear Chief Justice," he wrote in a note. "As I promised you yesterday, I am enclosing a copy of some excerpts from my letters home during my recent mission to Guam . . . which some of my more enthusiastic friends have been kind enough to say make inter-esting reading. In any event, I am sure they will give you, if you have time to glance through them, a good understanding of the problems with which we were faced and how we succeeded in solving them."

Vinson wrote back on September 5: "Dear Albert, Thanks for your letter of Aug. 31, with which you enclosed a copy of some excerpts from your letters home during your mission to Guam. It is a wonderful job of descriptive prose—both interesting and pleasant. I think you missed your calling. You could easily have a best seller."

NOW, SIX WEEKS LATER, MARIS HAD BIDDLE AND THE B-29 CASE BEFORE him. Sitting with him on the bench on October 19 were two of the Third Circuit's most distinguished jurists, Herbert F. Goodrich and Harry Kalodner. Goodrich—he'd written the appellate opinion reversing Kirkpatrick in *Hickman*—had been dean of the University of Pennsylvania Law School in 1940 when Franklin Roosevelt appointed him to the appellate bench. Kalodner was a former journalist whom FDR had appointed to the district court in 1938, Truman to the Third U.S. Circuit in 1946.

Across the aisle from Biddle, U.S. Attorney Gleeson and Assistant U.S. Attorney Curtin this day had a formidable ally: Samuel D. Slade, chief of the Appellate Section, Civil Division, in the Department of Justice. Slade was an appellate specialist who loved literature—he'd majored in English literature at Yale, specializing in Old and Middle English (he also was expert in Latin, Greek, and French), and could quote *Beowulf* in the original. Slade had the unusual ability to compose an entire brief in his mind and dictate it to his secretary. He could also retain it—in oral argument he didn't need notes, and once, when the wrong briefcase was brought to court, he argued without a single piece of paper before him.

Their correspondence and legal briefs convey the essence of what Biddle and Slade said to the Third Circuit appellate panel on this day. The government contested Kirkpatrick's ruling on a number of issues: whether he could rule against the United States without requiring proof from the widows; whether he could judge the widows' "good cause" need for the documents without considering Finletter's assertion that disclosure was "contrary to the public good"; whether a district judge could penalize Finletter's refusal to disclose records without adjudicating "the validity of the refusal." Most fundamentally, the government now challenged whether any judge could force the executive branch to hand over documents it considered privileged. For the first time in the B-29 litigation, the government directly argued that the judiciary could not review Finletter's claim of privilege: "We believe that all controlling governmental and judicial material . . . clearly supports the view that, in this type of case at least, disclosure by the head of an executive department cannot be coerced. . . . We urge that, in this case, the claim of privilege . . . should have been accepted as valid and binding by the district court. . . . We believe that the determination of what documents should not be disclosed [is] necessarily within the discretion and distinctive knowledge of the executive branch."

Biddle responded on several levels, but saved his sharpest words for an attack on this assertion of unilateral, unbridled executive branch power. Claims of privilege indeed are subject to judicial review, he maintained. If the secretary of the Air Force asserts a claim, he must at least show the documents to the judge in chambers. "Briefly and baldly stated," Biddle wrote in his brief, "the contention of the Government is that anything which any of its Departments sees fit to declare shall not be disclosed, shall be beyond the reach of the discovery provisions of the Federal Rules, and that the Government alone shall be the judge of what it will disclose." Biddle thought this preposterous.

Both sides did agree on one notion, at least: that this case involved significant questions of public policy. The final ruling here, Biddle and Slade recognized, would have a critical effect on the historic division of power between the three branches of government. No doubt, Maris and his colleagues on the bench recognized this as well when they rose at the close of the hearing.

THE NEXT DAY, MARIS RECEIVED AN APPRECIATIVE LETTER FROM THE secretary of the interior, Oscar Chapman, thanking him for his official reports and also his "letters home" from Guam. "The Department and the governments of Guam and the Trust Territory," Chapman wrote, "are very fortunate to have had the benefit of your advice." A week later, President Truman signed HR 3899, a revision of the Guam judicial code based on Maris's recommendations. Maris felt satisfied, but as always started laying new plans. These included a trip to Washington to brief Department of Interior officials about the

Trust Territories and a trip to California to brief Ninth U.S. Circuit judges about Guam.

Maris rarely stopped. A typical day around this time, according to Ida O. Creskoff, his former law clerk and later clerk of the court, would

> see him awake with the birds, mow the lawn, walk several miles to his train, dispose of his mail at the courthouse, lecture to his [Temple University Law School] class on Conflict of Laws [he was an adjunct professor], return to the courthouse to hear arguments in the Circuit Court of Appeals, travel to Washington to dispose of matters in the Emergency Court of Appeals, and return to his home in Landsdowne the same evening with just enough time to get a night's rest and to start the next day with zestful anticipation. He wastes no time waiting for trains or classes or courts, having an uncanny knack of timing his activities to the minute. There is a strong suspicion that he saves these minutes in order to be able to devote them to his little black book, from which he is never separated. In it he records every expenditure, even to the cost of a newspaper. He spends some of his precious time each day balancing the account. He has kept this record without a break for years. He accepts with unruffled composure the good-natured ribbing to which his fellow judges subject him because of his supposed passion for frugality. Actually it is a passion for statistical accuracy since the little black book does not help him to resist the lure of a rare stamp to add to his very fine collection or to refuse any of the innumerable appeals for financial aid for the public welfare.

Maris's "little black book" allows a glimpse at the particulars of his life as he contemplated the B-29 case during the fall and early winter of 1951. In October, for example, the month he heard oral argument, Temple University paid him $158.10 to teach his law class. He collected $12 for the rent of two garages. Someone reimbursed him fifty cents for a phone call made at his home. He spent $17 to get his watch repaired, $2 for a haircut, $6.10 on trolleys, $28.80 on newspapers, periodicals, books, and maps. He paid $5 for a "Chester County Days" ticket, another $7.50 for photo supplies—he was an avid photographer. He made a deposit of $300 to Bartlett Tours for a planned 1952 vacation—not his coming May trip to Fiji and the Samoas but his proposed July trip, sailing on the *Queen Elizabeth*, to England for the World Conference of Friends (part of an intended longer tour to Paris, Venice, Florence, Rome, and Naples that he would have to cancel at the last moment due to pressing judicial business). As always, every month he made a number of charitable contributions—a total of $150 to the Lansdowne Monthly Meeting, the Committee on Race Relations, the American Friends Service Committee, the Friends World Committee, the Pennsylvania Association for the Blind, the Women's Christian Temperance Union, and Community Chest. After payment on principal of a collateral bank loan, Maris had on balance, as of October 31, $3,474.08.

The matter of three widows suing the United States of America occupied his mind now, for it had been decided he would write the appellate panel's decision. He had read the lawyers' briefs and heard oral argument, but during his extended review of the issues, Maris returned time and again to Judge Kirkpatrick's opinion. Yes, Maris had written the decision reversing Kirkpatrick's *O'Neill* ruling, but there Kirkpatrick hadn't considered "good cause" and here he had. Yes, Maris and Kirkpatrick could not have been more different in their origins or politics, but Maris was no nemesis of Kirkpatrick's. They saw each other regularly, in meetings of the federal judiciary for the Eastern District of Pennsylvania, and in the corridors of the Ninth and Chestnut courthouse, where both presided. Late in his life, Maris would single out Kirkpatrick as among the judges he most admired. "Of course," he told his interviewer, "Judge Kirkpatrick was one of the distinguished district judges of the United States. I was very fond of him. We worked together very closely. Really outstanding judge, an outstanding character. An able man." One came from modest origins and a liberal Democratic perspective, the other from affluence and a crusty Republican outlook, but they shared an integrity, a concern for civil liberties, and a belief in the notion of three separate but equal branches of government.

By late November, Maris still had not delivered a decision. Patricia Herring had never paid much attention to the litigation, but at this moment—more than six months pregnant—she wrote to Biddle, asking about the progress of the case. On November 29, he wrote back. "The matter was argued before the Court of Appeals on October 19th," he explained, "and we are now simply waiting for the Court to render its decision. It is impossible to foretell how long that may be. . . . The Judges, of course, have a lot of other cases to decide and are hearing new ones all the time. I can only say that I will let you know the minute we have word."

Two more weeks passed, then word came. On the morning of December 11, Judge Maris filed his unanimous "Opinion of the Court." This time, Maris and the Third U.S. Circuit appellate panel stood firmly beside Judge Kirkpatrick. Ruling in favor of the three widows, Maris offered a resounding affirmation of Kirkpatrick's decision, which he quoted at length.

Maris first addressed the question of whether Kirkpatrick had erred in ruling that the widows had shown "good cause" for the documents—the booby trap in *O'Neill*. Here Maris, with obvious appreciation, directly quoted a great chunk of Kirkpatrick's reasoning. *The plaintiffs have no knowledge of why the accident happened. So far as such knowledge is obtainable, the defendant has it. . . . These statements and the report undoubtedly contained facts, information and clues which it might be extremely difficult, if not impossible, for the plaintiffs . . . to obtain merely by taking the depositions of the survivors.* "We cannot say," Maris concluded, that "the district judge erred" in finding good cause. The district court is "necessarily vested with a wide discretion." The supplying of three witnesses for deposition "is no answer at all to the demand for the production of the investigation report." The district court "has cogently pointed out" the vital importance to the widows of seeing the witness statements.

Maris next addressed the government's claim that disclosure of the accident report would hamper open, honest investigations. He began by pointing out that Congress, in passing the Federal Tort Claims Act, had divested the United States of its normal sovereign immunity; the United States had consented to be sued as a private person, so in such litigation could not claim a privilege to withhold documents without judicial review. "Where, as here, the United States has consented to be sued as a private person, whatever public interest there may be in avoiding disclosure of accident reports in order to promote accident prevention must yield to what Congress evidently regarded as the greater public interest in seeing that justice is done to citizens injured by governmental operations. . . ."

Maris was not inclined to stop at specialized legal reasoning, however. Sounding a strong caution against the executive "housekeeping" privilege, he went even further than Kirkpatrick in addressing the critical underlying issues. He made plain that he saw dangers in what the government sought.

> Moreover, we regard the recognition of such a sweeping
> privilege . . . as contrary to a sound public policy. The present
> cases themselves indicate the breadth of the claim of immunity
> from disclosure which one government department head has
> already made. It is but a small step to assert a privilege against
> any disclosure of records merely because they might prove
> embarrassing to government officials. Indeed, it requires no
> great flight of imagination to realize that if the Government's
> contentions in these cases were affirmed, the privilege against
> disclosure might gradually be enlarged . . . until as is the case in
> some nations today, it embraced the whole range of government
> activities. . . . We need to recall in this connection the words of
> Edward Livingston: "No nation ever yet found any inconve-
> nience from too close an inspection into the conduct of its
> officers, but many have been brought to ruin, and reduced to
> slavery, by suffering gradual imposition and abuses, which were
> imperceptible, only because the means of publicity had not been
> secured." And it was Patrick Henry who said that "to cover with

the veil of secrecy the common routine of business is an abomination in the eyes of every intelligent man and every friend to his country."

Next Maris turned to the government's second basis for a claim of privilege—state secrets. Like Kirkpatrick, he noted that the department had advanced this second argument belatedly, after the first "housekeeping" approach had failed. Also like Kirkpatrick, he found the government's position troubling. What bothered him was not the claim itself—he recognized the state secrets privilege as well-settled in common law—but rather the assertion of unilateral executive power, free from judicial review, to decide what qualified as secret.

Maris pointed out that Kirkpatrick had not ordered any documents to be disclosed publicly; he'd only directed that they be produced for private examination in his chambers.

> The Government was thus adequately protected. . . . [But] the Government contends that it is within the sole province of the Secretary of the Air Force to determine whether any privileged material is contained in the documents and that his determination of this question must be accepted by the district court without any independent consideration. . . . We cannot accede to this proposition. On the contrary, we are satisfied that a claim of privilege against disclosing evidence . . . involves a justiciable question, traditionally within the competence of the courts. . . . To hold that the head of an executive department of the Government in a [law]suit to which the United States is a party may conclusively determine the Government's claim of privilege is to abdicate the judicial function and permit the executive branch of the Government to infringe the independent province of the judiciary as laid down by the Constitution.

This abdication seemed unimaginable to Maris: "The Government of the United States is one of checks and balances. One of the principal checks is furnished by the independent judiciary which the

Constitution established. Neither the executive nor the legislative branch of the Government may constitutionally encroach upon the field which the Constitution has reserved for the judiciary . . . Nor is there any danger to the public interest in submitting the question of privilege to the decision of the courts. The judges of the United States are public officers whose responsibility under the Constitution is just as great as that of the heads of the executive departments."

Maris's conclusions: Kirkpatrick did not err in holding that good cause had been shown; Kirkpatrick rightly rejected the broad claim of privilege made by the United States; Kirkpatrick rightly asked to inspect the disputed documents in chambers; Kirkpatrick rightly took "the facts as established" when the government failed to produce those documents; Kirkpatrick rightly entered a default judgment for the plaintiffs.

"Since we find no error," Maris declared, "the judgments entered in favor of the plaintiffs . . . will be affirmed."

ONE DAY LATER, ON DECEMBER 12, CHARLES BIDDLE WROTE HIS CLIENTS with the news: "The Court of Appeals acted more quickly than I had anticipated. Enclosed is a copy of its opinion, which I think you will find interesting and very satisfactory. The next step is to see whether the Government will attempt to take the case to the Supreme Court of the United States in Washington. I will not be in the least surprised if it does so."

Biddle, of course, knew quite well what was coming.

CHAPTER 18

THE VINSON COURT

March–October '52

MORE THAN THREE YEARS AFTER THE B-29 CRASH, THE PAST remained with Betty, Phyllis, and Patricia, even as they tried to move forward. The start of 1952 saw Betty newly married to Bill Sacker, seven years her junior. Patricia was near full term, her child due in February. Phyllis continued both to teach and study, her daughters admiring her drive while yearning for more time with their mother. They all longed for resolution.

In mid-March, they learned—as Charles Biddle had anticipated—that this was not yet at hand. Three months after Judge Maris delivered his opinion, government lawyers appealed the case to the Supreme Court, filing a petition for a writ of *certiorari*, by which the justices call up records of lower-court proceedings for review. Maris's decision should be reconsidered, argued Solicitor General Philip B. Perlman, because it erroneously interprets the law "so as to permit encroachment by the judiciary on an area committed by the Constitution to executive discretion." The issues were of "far-reaching" importance. The "vital questions" involved whether the judiciary had the power "to order production of documents which the executive chooses to withhold" and whether the judiciary could "substitute its judgment for the judgment of the executive." These questions, Perlman pointed out—openly seeking a precedent now—"have twice recently been before the Court but have not been decided."

While Perlman filed this petition, investigators were probing various corruption charges involving Truman administration figures, including Perlman's boss, Attorney General J. Howard McGrath. Biddle referred to these "scandals" in a March 18 letter to Teddy Mattern outlining his Supreme Court strategy. "I received today from the Solicitor General the Government's petition for a writ of certiorari," Biddle began. "We have thirty days within which to file an answer but my present inclination is that it would accomplish no useful purpose to do so. I think the answer to the Government's petition is about as well stated as it can be in the opinion [by Maris] of the Court of the Appeals, to which the Supreme Court will undoubtedly pay more attention than it will to anything that we can say." He continued:

> Of course, one cannot be sure, but my guess is that the Supreme Court will grant the petition because of the importance of the legal question involved, but that after it hears the case it will affirm the judgement [by Maris]. . . . I suppose it will probably be next fall before the case can actually be reached for argument. It is certainly a slow process but there is no help for it. This is probably as good a time to have the legal question come before the Supreme Court in view of all the scandals about Government officials. If the head of a government department is to be permitted to himself decide whether or not to give out information free from any direction by the Courts, it would indeed furnish a great opportunity to cover up things in the Department which they would rather not have come to light.

Biddle's "guess" proved accurate. The justices took just three weeks to decide they would hear this case. On April 7—the same day Attorney General McGrath stepped down, to be replaced temporarily by Solicitor General Perlman—the Court filed its order.

"As you may have seen in the morning papers," Biddle wrote

Mattern, copying the letter to his three clients, "the Supreme Court of the United States granted the Government's petition. . . . As I think the Court adjourns for the summer early in June, I take it that there is no chance of the case being reached for argument before the Fall Term. However, there is no help for that and we should get a final decision before the end of the year, assuming of course that the Supreme Court affirms the judgment."

BIDDLE'S EXPECTATION THAT THE SUPREME COURT WOULD AFFIRM THE Third Circuit ruling had some foundation, especially considering the Court's demonstrated admiration for Maris. Biddle might have been more prophetic, though, if he'd given greater consideration to the Court's chief justice at that moment—Fred Vinson.

The Vinson Court came to be in 1946 after the previous chief justice, Harlan Fiske Stone, died suddenly of a cerebral hemorrhage. Most in Washington expected Truman to replace Stone either with Associate Justice Robert Jackson, who reputedly had been promised the job by Franklin Roosevelt, or with Associate Justice William O. Douglas. Yet Truman soon ran up against the Court's bitter personal and philosophical schisms. The Court contained two warring groups, one led by Hugo Black, the former senator from Alabama, the other by Jackson, the former attorney general. Representatives from both camps began paying visits to the White House. Points were argued, pleas issued. Matters came to a head when Douglas and Black reportedly told Truman they'd resign if he elevated Jackson; Felix Frankfurter may have similarly blocked Douglas's candidacy.

Hoping to resolve the Court's deep discord, Truman on June 6 nominated his poker and drinking buddy Fred Vinson, then secretary of the treasury. A patient, amiable Kentucky politician, Vinson was known mainly as a fellow who could sooth and achieve consensus. Vinson's easygoing nature, though, didn't stand much of a chance against such powerful personalities as Douglas, Black, Jackson, and Frankfurter. (The others on the Court that heard *Reynolds* in 1952, all lesser lights, were Sherman Minton, a former Senator from Indiana; Tom C. Clark, a former attorney general; Stanley Reed, a former solicitor general; and Harold Burton, a former senator from Ohio). Vinson's challenge grew greater just four days after Truman announced his nomination, when Robert Jackson bitterly censured Hugo Black at a press conference in Nuremberg, where he was on special assignment as the chief American war crimes prosecutor. Vinson never did manage to smooth the differences between the factions—which included conflicting views about judicial restraint—or establish his own strong leadership.

By most accounts, Vinson simply lacked the intellectual weight to guide the Court, or even the justices' weekly conferences. "He blithely hits the obvious points . . ." Frankfurter wrote in his diary of these sessions, "disposing of each case rather briefly, by choosing, as it were, to float merely on the surface of the problems raised by the cases." Frankfurter, again in his diary, described Vinson as "confident and easy-going and sure and shallow . . . he seems to me to have the confident air of a man who does not see the complexities of problems." When, in 1949, Vinson actively supported Tom Clark's appointment to the Court, the joke in Washington was that the chief justice wanted someone on his Court who knew less law than he did. A possibly apocryphal story has Frankfurter, on the train to Vinson's funeral in 1953, quipping that his death "is the only evidence I have ever had for the existence of God."

Yet Vinson had Truman's deep trust. They'd worked together closely in Congress when Truman served in the Senate, Vinson in the House of Representatives. There, Vinson initially had appeared to be a conservative in the southern tradition, but he ended up a moderate New Dealer, supporting most of FDR's policies. In 1937, Roosevelt had appointed him to the U.S. Court of Appeals for the D.C. Circuit. Six years later, FDR had convinced him to take a position in the executive branch, serving as director of economic stabilization. After FDR's death in 1945, Truman had named him his secretary of the treasury.

Vinson was a hefty five-foot-eleven, 190 pounds, with gray hair, deep lines in his face, dark circles under his eyes, bushy eyebrows, and a double chin. A friend once said, "He looks like an extremely dignified sheep with a hangover, but he is not at all like a sheep and he never has a hangover." Truman particularly appreciated his sense of humor, folksy way of talking, and homespun philosophy. In fact, Truman embraced these qualities so much that in 1948, on impulse, he decided it would be a terrific idea to send Chief Justice Vinson to Moscow to negotiate personally with Premier Stalin over the lifting of the Soviet Union's Berlin blockade. (Truman later explained he had wanted Stalin to "unburden himself to someone on our side he felt he could trust fully.") Only after a wave of protest about "appeasement" and "embarrassing our allies"—and the rushed intervention of General George C. Marshall, then secretary of state—did Truman drop the idea. While sitting as chief justice, Vinson functioned essentially as part of the executive branch, advising Truman regularly. He joined Truman on trips to Key West during the winter months and with his family came to the White House for Thanksgiving dinners. The two men, from phones by their bedsides, often talked late into the night. Throughout the Truman administration, Vinson was seen as part of the inner circle and a possible presidential candidate himself. In fact, Washington pundits regarded Vinson as the president's choice to succeed him in 1952 if Truman chose not to run.

Although he described himself as "a little left of center," Vinson more accurately occupied the middle of the Supreme Court. The balancing of interests went only so far, however. What most distinguished this chief justice—in fact, the entire seven years of the Vinson Court—was a pronounced inclination to support the government against any challenge to its power. Given Vinson's experience in the executive branch and his close relations with the administration, it's no surprise that he put the needs of the state ahead of individual freedoms, always accepting government claims about imminent crises and emergencies. Nowhere was this tendency more apparent than in cases involving matters of national security. Vinson favored giving the government unfettered power to defend against the many perils of the postwar world.

The Vinson Court's defining opinion in the months before hearing the B-29 matter was *Dennis et al. v. United States*, where the chief justice, writing for the majority over dissents by Black and Douglas,

upheld the prosecutions under the Smith Act that sent twelve acknowledged U.S. Communist leaders to jail. *Dennis*, decided on June 4, 1951,
is considered the nadir of the Vinson Court—and the case for which
Vinson will be remembered. The native Communists had been jailed
not for what they did or conspired to do, but for what they said and
believed, for talking and writing, for "teaching and advocating," as the
indictment and Vinson's opinion put it. Thus the Vinson Court found
constitutional a law that violated the free-speech guarantee of the First
Amendment. "In calmer times," Hugo Black wrote in his pensive dissent, "when present pressures, passions and fears subside, this or some
later Court will restore the First Amendment liberties to the high preferred place where they belong in a free society."

Most of the big cases decided by the Vinson Court spoke to Cold
War anxieties. A justice's sense of peril inevitably influenced his opinions. Members of the Court were no more able than the military or the
administration to ignore the Soviet threat. They'd heard oral argument
in the *Dennis* case just weeks after Congress had passed the Internal
Security Act, which in its preamble identified world communism's
"sole purpose" as "the establishment of a totalitarian dictatorship in
America, to be brought about by treachery, infiltration, sabotage and
terrorism." The justices kept a watch on the Korean War, where Red
Chinese troops had recently launched a major offensive. They couldn't
ignore the infiltration of atomic spies—first Hiss had been convicted of
perjury, later the Rosenbergs of espionage. In his *Dennis* opinion, Vinson spoke of "the inflammable nature of world conditions" and "the
context of world crisis after crisis." The government need not, he
maintained, "wait until the *putsch* is about to be executed." More than
ever before, Supreme Court justices had their eyes on international
affairs.

Before this concerned group of men Charles Biddle would soon
stand to argue the consolidated case now called *United States of America
v. Patricia Reynolds, Phyllis Brauner, and Elizabeth Palya.*

On April 8, 1952, one day after the Supreme Court agreed to
hear *U.S. v. Reynolds*, President Truman, facing the threat of a nation-

wide strike during the Korean War, ordered the federal seizure of the nation's steel mills. Acting to avert a shutdown involving 600,000 workers in mills that produced ninety-five percent of the country's steel, declaring the industry "vital to our defense efforts," Truman relied not on statutes but on his "inherent power." He believed the Constitution gave him a fundamental authority to protect the national health and safety.

Two steel-mill owners, insisting the president had no such inherent power, promptly filed suit in federal court, seeking an injunction. Within days, the matter (*Youngstown Sheet & Tube Co. v. Sawyer*) was before the Supreme Court, after a federal district judge declared the seizure illegal. On May 12, the justices heard oral argument in a packed courtroom—the rule against standing during sessions of the Court was relaxed, allowing some five hundred people to witness the session, two hundred more than the number of available seats. (Hundreds of others stood outside the marble chambers.) The justices questioned acting attorney general Philip Perlman for more than two hours, demanding to know what statutes he'd relied on for the seizure; his argument, William O. Douglas observed at one point, seemed to be that there was "no apparent need for Congress." Douglas wanted to know if the president could seize oil, food, and other industries as well. Robert Jackson wanted to know what "limitations" there were on the president.

By contrast, the attorney representing the steel industry, seventy-nine-year-old John W. Davis, the Democratic candidate for president in 1924, faced relatively few questions. Speaking for eighty-five minutes, he attacked the government's claim that the president was the "sole judge" of the existence of an emergency—and of the remedy. At one point he quoted Thomas Jefferson: "In questions of power, let no more be said of confidence in man, but bind him down from mischief by the chains of the Constitution."

Near the end of the hearing, Justice Tom Clark did venture to ask if the Court had the ability to judge the merits of the emergency, since so many facts had been left unrevealed due to "national security." For once, though, Vinson couldn't deliver for the executive branch. On June 2, the justices, by a vote of six to three, ruled that the president did not have the inherent power to seize the steel mills. "In the framework of our Constitution," wrote Hugo Black in his historic majority opinion, "the President's power to see that the laws are faithfully executed refutes the idea that he is to be a lawmaker. . . . The Founders of this Nation entrusted the lawmaking power to the Congress alone in both good and bad times. . . . This is a job for the Nation's lawmakers."

If Vinson did not prevail this time, he still managed, in his oft-quoted dissent, to lay out his argument for judicial deference. As usual, his words—*gravity of the emergency*—reflected his sense of peril, but they also reflected his perspective as a former member of the executive branch during critical times. "History bears out the genius of the Founding Fathers, who created a Government subject to law but not left subject to inertia when vigor and initiative are required," read his dissent. "The Framers knew . . . that there is a real danger in Executive weakness. . . . Those who suggest that this is a case involving extraordinary powers should be mindful that these are extraordinary times. A world not yet recovered from the devastation of World War II has been forced to face the threat of another and more terrifying global conflict."

THEN CAME *REYNOLDS*. IN EARLY SEPTEMBER OF 1952, CHARLES BIDDLE wrote to Teddy Mattern: "We have been advised by the Clerk of the Supreme Court of the United States that counsel should be present on Tuesday, October 21, 1952, for the argument of the B-29 case."

In a letter dated September 6, Mattern shared this news with Phyllis Brauner. "I shall be in Washington if at all possible," he wrote, "to hear the argument and would be happy to know that I could see you again on that occasion. If you think you could arrange it, let me know so, and I in turn will keep you informed as to the exact hour and other details of the proposed trip."

After sending his "regards to your Mother and love to the two little ladies," Mattern closed with a hopeful thought: "As to you, I feel confident that this will be your last year of unusual hardship and struggle, but also know that you have the determination and ability to see your goal attained before the summer of 1953. From then on, let us pray, your life will be orderly, calm and secure."

Within days, both sides submitted thick legal briefs arguing their positions and defining what was at stake. The government filed first, in an eighty-one-page document signed by the acting solicitor general, Robert L. Stern (who would later write *Supreme Court Practice*, a bible for lawyers going before the Court). Here, as in lower-court arguments, Stern continued to insist that the widows had not shown "good cause for discovery," since they had declined the opportunity to depose the surviving B-29 crew members.

Yet the government clearly had its sights set far higher than the issue of "good cause." Stern argued that Judge Maris's decision "is an unwarranted interference with the powers of the executive," one that forced the department head to choose "whether to disclose public documents contrary to the public interest" or "to suffer the public treasury to be penalized." The courts, Stern insisted, "lack power to compel disclosure by means of a direct demand." Nor can the courts reach the same result "by the indirect method of an order against the United States, resulting in judgment when compliance is not forthcoming."

To support his position, Stern invoked statutes, the Constitution, and common-law privilege. The privilege, he pointed out, had been successfully asserted against congressional demands for the production of executive documents on numerous occasions—from George Washington's refusal to furnish instructions concerning the Jay Treaty, to Truman's refusal, the previous March, to give HUAC files about the federal employee loyalty program. There weren't many opinions to cite as precedent, though, so Stern invoked a case decided in Britain. This 1942 opinion by the House of Lords, *Duncan v. Cammell, Laird & Co.*, held, in a dispute over the sinking of a submarine, that ministers have sole power to decide whether disclosure of departmental documents should be made. Lawyers for the United States already had tried to press *Duncan* on the Third U.S. Circuit, but Maris had not regarded it as controlling—"Whatever may be true in Great Britain, the Government of the United States is one of checks and balances. One of the principal checks is furnished by the independent judiciary." All the same, Stern now advised the Supreme Court that "great weight" should be given to this British case.

In an audacious passage, Stern also argued that despite Maris's conclusions, nothing in the Federal Tort Claims Act (which permitted private parties to seek damages against the United States) imposes any duty of disclosure on a department head. The government can't be likened to a private party, he maintained, because its claim of privilege is made in the *public* interest: "If a private litigant elects not to disclose, he is in effect determining that his own interests will be best served by preserving secrecy. . . . He therefore elects to pay the penalty. When the Secretary elects not to disclose, on the other hand, he is not considering his own interest but is weighing two opposing aspects of the public interest. And as we have shown, he is the person best qualified to do so."

The secretary, Stern concluded, "has been faced with the inadmissible alternative of surrendering documents which must be kept secret, or of causing the Government to be subjected to a large judgment without any proof of liability."

Biddle responded in forty-one pages, half the length of the government's brief. Early on, he wrote, "We could rest our case with confidence on the clear opinion of Judge Maris. We can add little to his exposition." Biddle did his best, though. If the secretary of the Air Force asserts a claim, he argued, he must show the documents to the Court or at least give the Court sufficient information to judge if they threaten national security. The secretary may not assert that "he alone shall be the judge of whether his own claim is well founded." This is especially true "where there is no showing that the documents in question contain any military secret." Biddle continued:

> The basic question here is whether those in charge of the various departments of the Government may refuse to produce documents properly demanded . . . in a case where the Government is a party, simply because the officials themselves

think it would be better to keep them secret, and this without the Courts having any power to question the propriety of such decision. . . . The position of the Government is that anything that any of its departments sees fit to declare shall not be disclosed . . . and that the department heads alone shall be the judges of what they shall disclose. In other words, say the officials, we will tell you only what we think it is in the public interest that you should know. And furthermore, we may withhold information not only about military or diplomatic secrets, but we may also suppress documents which concern merely the operation of the particular department if we believe it would be best, for purposes of efficiency or morale, that no one outside of the department, not even the Court, should see them.

Again Biddle hammered at what the accident report did and did not contain. The government's own response to his interrogatories, he pointed out, showed that the requested information had nothing to do with military secrets. "Let us pause for a moment," he wrote, "to see exactly what kind of information . . . was requested in these cases."

All that was asked was the Air Force investigation report of the accident and the statements of the surviving members of the crew, in each case as to the cause of the accident only. It has never been claimed that the secret electronic equipment that was being tested on this particular plane had anything to do with the accident. In fact, the proof is to the contrary. In the answers to the interrogatories the only indication of the cause of the accident is that one of the aircraft's engines caught fire and the plane went into a spin. In fact, had the Air Force been frank in its answers to Respondents' interrogatories as to the cause of the accident . . . it might never have been necessary to ask for the investigation report or the statements of the witnesses. The Air Force had the report and knew the answer. . . . The Secretary's formal claim of privilege said that the plane at the time was engaged in a secret mission and that it carried confidential equipment, but nowhere was it asserted that either had anything to do with the accident. The whole purpose of the demand by the Respondents was for the purpose of finding out what caused the accident. . . . They were not in the least interested in the secret missions or equipment.

Biddle cited an array of precedent cases in support of his position. He also quoted Kirkpatrick and Maris—Kirkpatrick in *O'Neill* as well as the B-29 case. He argued for the power of the judiciary, as a third, coequal branch of government, to determine whether specific acts of the legislature or executive are legal. There was "certainly no reason," he pointed, "why federal judges should not be considered as trustworthy as representatives of other branches of Government."

Near the end of his brief, Biddle turned to the government's claim that he had no "good cause" for the documents because he'd declined to depose the offered witnesses. "In answer to this," he wrote, "we cannot improve upon Judge Kirkpatrick's summary." So instead, he, like Maris, quoted Kirkpatrick ("I would not go so far as to say the witnesses would be hostile . . .") at great length. He also pointed out that the government's offer of the witnesses was ambiguously qualified—they could testify "except as to facts and matters of a classified nature." He asked, "With absolutely no knowledge of what caused the accident . . . how else could counsel for the Respondents know how to examine intelligently the witnesses . . . unless he could see their statements given immediately after the accident . . . and unless he could also see the report of the Air Force Investigating Board. When an accident is long past, it is so easy for an unwilling witness, with no fear of a written statement to check him, to give the time-worn answer, 'I don't remember.'"

Biddle came finally to his conclusion: "It is clear that there is no practical danger that the security of the country will be jeopardized by requiring the Secretary to consult the Trial Judge. . . . In such interview the Secretary can either convince the Judge that the documents are so vital to security that they must not be shown even to the Judge, or the Judge, after looking at them, can decide what parts, if any, may not properly be shown to the other side."

Fair but cold winter weather prevailed in Washington, D.C., on October 21, 1952, with an early-morning temperature of thirty degrees. In the news that day, Republican presidential nominee Dwight Eisenhower traded campaign barbs with his Democratic rival, Adlai Stevenson. Reporters were paying little attention to the matter of *United States of America v. Patricia Reynolds, Phyllis Brauner, and Elizabeth Palya*.

Oral argument in the case began at 1:30 p.m. in the Supreme Court's grand marble courtroom. For the occasion, Charles Biddle wore striped pants, black tie, and black frock coat with tails. Time and expense had kept Phyllis Brauner from attending, despite an invitation from Biddle; she was then pushing to finish her doctorate. With Biddle were his wife, Katherine, his associate Francis Hopkinson and his wife, and Henry Drinker, the titular head of their law firm. Across the aisle sat Samuel Slade, a familiar figure to the justices. He'd been appearing continually before the Supreme Court since 1946 and that May had played a central role in the steel-seizure case.

No transcript exists of this hearing, but legal briefs, memos, and correspondence suggest how it unfolded. It's known, from Teddy Mattern, that the Court allotted the government and Biddle one-hour each for argument, with a half-hour recess between the two. It's known, again from Mattern, that "the judges were quite interested and shot questions at the lawyers arguing the case." And it's known, from the justices' tally sheets, that four of the nine looking down at Biddle had voted not to accept this case—four had been willing to let Judge Maris's opinion prevail.

"This case poses important problems deserving of review . . ." William O. Douglas's law clerk had advised him in a memo. "The problem of separation of power lies in the background of this case. But you may not wish to review here if you consider the [Maris] decision correct—since a majority of the Court might not agree with [Maris's] view." Douglas, after reading this, had voted to deny *certiorari*. So had Justices Hugo Black, Felix Frankfurter, and Stanley Reed.

Unlike the recent steel-seizure case before the Supreme Court—which turned on whether Congress had passed a law to empower the president—the issue here pitted the executive branch against the judiciary. Did a government claim of privilege absolutely trump a judge's authority? The justices' questions during oral argument most certainly focused on this assertion.

In a letter to Phyllis Brauner two days later, Teddy Mattern wrote, "The big day in Washington is over. Let me state at the beginning that the outcome is anybody's guess, and my personal opinion is that it will be decided by a small majority in favor of either of the parties. . . . Let's hope for the best—the decision might be down within six to ten weeks and in the meantime, all we can do is sit still, cross our fingers, pray and await the dictum."

Mattern tried to be encouraging. He was "kind of glad" Phyllis had not attended the hearing. "You spared your energy for more important tasks." In applying herself to her studies now, "you are doing the right thing at the right time." Keeping that in mind "should lend you that little more needed additional strength to successfully terminate your studies" and "finally arrive at a stage in life which will guarantee . . . a steady income and freedom from anxieties." In the end, though, Mattern could not sustain this effort. Before signing off, he felt obliged to include a cautionary note about the nine justices: "One never really was quite certain on whose side their sympathies lay; therefore, don't let's take anything for granted at this time."

CHAPTER 19

A NICE OPINION

October '52–December '53

ON OCTOBER 25, 1952, FOUR DAYS AFTER ORAL ARGUMENT IN the B-29 case, the nine Supreme Court justices considered *U.S. v. Reynolds* at their regular Saturday conference. From the scribbled notes taken that day, it appears that Chief Justice Vinson spoke first; beside his name in one memo are the handwritten words: "boils down to Executive branch determine privilege." According to other (nearly illegible) notes taken by William O. Douglas, Vinson apparently suggested that "the judiciary can't get into it" without taking away the privilege from the executive branch; Vinson wasn't "convinced that the U.S. can be forced to pay for exercising its privilege." Hugo Black likely spoke next, saying the United States in this case was the "same as any defendant"—the government "can decline" to produce the documents if it can "stand the consequences." Stanley Reed spoke also, and Felix Frankfurter at length, then Harold Burton and Tom Clark. Robert Jackson indicated he would affirm Judge Maris's decision. So did Douglas.

By the end of the conference that day, a straw vote had five justices in favor of reversing Maris and four (Black, Douglas, Frankfurter, and Jackson) in favor of affirming him. Votes could still change as drafts of the opinion circulated—if just one justice from the majority switched, Maris's ruling would stand.

Vinson assigned himself the task of writing the majority opinion, though that job initially fell to a law clerk, who produced two drafts, one dated December 3, another February 19. Just one day later—four months after oral argument—Vinson circulated his own version among the justices. Within hours, Harold Burton sent Vinson a note saying "I agree with your treatment of this difficult question, and am glad to join your opinion of the Court." Tom Clark also quickly agreed, as did Sherman Minton and Stanley Reed. Vinson had managed to hold his five-justice majority.

He added to it, in fact. On March 6, William O. Douglas scrawled a note to Vinson on the back of his copy of the draft opinion. "I voted the other way," Douglas advised, "but will go along. It's a nice opinion." Vinson now had six justices on his side.

That left three dissenters, three who would vote to affirm Maris, and there was no small irony in who they were: The two rivals Hugo Black and Robert Jackson stood together, along with Felix Frankfurter, normally the High Court's champion of judicial restraint.

"Dear Fred," Black wrote to Vinson on the back of his copy of the opinion, "Please note that I agree with the District Court and the Court of Appeals and would affirm their judgment."

In fact, he, Jackson, and Frankfurter agreed so completely with the Court of Appeals that they saw no need to offer their own dissenting opinion. In an extraordinary action, they advised Vinson that they would adopt Judge Maris's opinion as their dissent.

"Dear Chief," wrote Robert Jackson, "I took the other view in this case, but do not intend to write. Unless someone else does, I would like you to note 'Mr. Justice Jackson would affirm on the opinion of the Court of Appeals.'"

"Dear Fred," Felix Frankfurter wrote, "will you please put at the foot of your opinion in *United States v. Reynolds,* the following: 'Mr. Justice Frankfurter would affirm, substantially for the reasons set forth in Judge Maris's opinion for the Court of Appeals.'"

On March 9, Vinson, from the bench, announced and read from the Supreme Court's decision in the matter of *United States of America v. Patricia Reynolds, Phyllis Brauner, and Elizabeth Palya.* As usual, he had reached in this opinion for a conciliatory balancing act, but in the end he had, also as usual, deferred to the executive branch.

"We have had broad propositions pressed upon us for decision," he wrote. "On behalf of the Government it has been urged that the executive department heads have power to withhold any documents in their custody from judicial review, if they deem it in the public interest. Respondents have asserted that the executive's power to withhold documents was waived by the Tort Claims Act. Both positions have constitutional overtones which we find it unnecessary to pass upon, there being a narrower ground for decision."

That "narrower ground" involved a specialized, lawyer's reading of the Tort Claims Act, most particularly the act's Rule 34, which compels production only of matters "not privileged." Had the government properly asserted privilege under that rule? Yes, Vinson held; the government had made "a valid claim of privilege" against revealing military secrets, a privilege "well established in the law of evidence." The judgment against the government, based on its refusal to produce documents, therefore "subjected the United States to liability to which Congress did not consent by the Tort Claims Act."

By "well established" Vinson meant mainly that the state secrets privilege was rooted in common law—the British system of doctrines, customs, and usages deriving from court decisions rather than from codified statutory law. Kirkpatrick and Maris had recognized this common law tradition as well, evolved from British judicial rulings as far back as the early nineteenth century. But it can't be said such cases specifically defined or established the state secrets privilege. Closer to the mark were a pair of early United States court decisions: Aaron Burr's treason trial in 1808 (Burr sought production of a letter sent to President Jefferson) and the landmark *Totten v. United States* in 1875 (a contract dispute involving a Civil War spy retained by President Lincoln). Yet these, too, did not directly involve or establish the state secrets privilege. In truth, only now was the Supreme Court formally recognizing the privilege, giving the government the precedent it sought, a precedent binding on all courts throughout the nation. Most

important, the Court was also—for the first time—spelling out how
the privilege should be applied.

Before doing so, Vinson felt obliged to recognize that there existed only "limited" judicial experience with the state secrets privilege
in the United States. Experience in England (Vinson, like the government, cited *Duncan v. Cammell, Laird & Co.)* "has been more extensive,
but still relatively slight compared with other evidentiary privileges."
Nevertheless, "the principles which control the application of the privilege emerge quite clearly from the available precedents."

Here Vinson, despite Maris's rejection of it, borrowed heavily
from *Duncan:* The privilege must be asserted by the government, and it
is not to be lightly invoked. There must be a formal claim lodged by
the head of a department "after actual personal consideration by that
officer." The court itself must determine "whether the circumstances
are appropriate for the claim of privilege," and yet do so "without forcing disclosure of the very thing the privilege is designed to protect."

This last, of course, was the tricky part; Vinson acknowledged
that "the latter requirement is the only one which presents real diffi-
culty." To resolve it, Vinson presented a "formula of compromise" that
essentially said the government shouldn't have absolute autonomy, but
courts shouldn't always insist on seeing the documents. You can't abdicate control over the evidence "to the caprice of executive officers,"
Vinson instructed trial judges, but if the government can satisfy you
that "a reasonable danger" to national security exists, you shouldn't
insist upon examining the documents, even alone in chambers.

In each case, Vinson added, "the showing of necessity [good
cause]" for the documents will "determine how far the court should
probe" in determining the validity of a privilege claim. Where there is
a strong showing of need, "the claim of privilege should not be lightly
accepted," but even the most compelling need "cannot overcome the
claim of privilege if the court is ultimately satisfied that military secrets
are at stake."

Next Vinson focused on Biddle's decision not to depose the government witnesses, and here the chief justice chose to disregard Kirkpatrick's thoughts on why such depositions would be useless. There is

nothing to suggest that the electronic equipment in this case had any causal connection with the accident, Vinson wrote. Therefore, it should be possible for Biddle and the widows to determine the cause "without resort to material touching upon military secrets." Biddle was given "a reasonable opportunity to do just that" when the Government formally offered to make the surviving crew members available. "We think that offer should have been accepted."

Surprising as it might seem, Vinson in effect seemed here to be agreeing with Biddle that the Banshee equipment had no connection to the accident. Yet Vinson did not explain just how Biddle could therefore determine the accident's cause by interviewing the surviving crew members—the chief justice's "reasonable opportunity" had looked a good deal less reasonable to Kirkpatrick and Maris.

At best, Vinson's *Reynolds* opinion can be seen as an effort to weigh competing legitimate interests. In theory, it did make a kind of sense. Except, of course, for the tricky final condition Vinson laid down—that the judge must evaluate the claim "without forcing a disclosure of the very thing the privilege is designed to protect." How to know if the disputed documents contain secrets without examining them? Why would a federal judge be "forcing a disclosure" if he read the document in the privacy of his chambers? In the years to come, Vinson's "formula of compromise" would increasingly make more sense on the page than in courtrooms. By instructing judges not to insist upon examining documents if the government can satisfy that "a reasonable danger" to national security exists, Vinson was asking jurists to fly blind.

Three days before Vinson announced this decision from the bench, banner headlines had declared the death of Joseph Stalin, causing a newly sworn-in President Eisenhower to warn that a "definite watchfulness is our policy." Other headlines carried news of the Korean War, Senator McCarthy's latest charges, and the progress of the Rosenberg case toward the Supreme Court. Chief Justice Vinson, near the end of his *Reynolds* opinion, seemed to acknowledge all of the surrounding events.

"In the instant case," he wrote,

we cannot escape judicial notice that this is a time of vigorous preparation for the national defense. Experience in the past war has made it common knowledge that air power is one of the most potent weapons in our scheme of defense, and that newly developing electronic devices have greatly enhanced the effective use of air power. It is equally apparent that these electronic devices must be kept secret if their full military advantage is to be exploited in the national interests. On the record before the trial court, it appeared that this accident occurred to a military plane which had gone aloft to test electronic equipment. Certainly there was a reasonable danger that the accident investigation would contain references to the secret electronic equipment which was the primary concern of the mission.

At bottom, Vinson's opinion represented an act of faith. We must believe the government, Vinson held, when it claims this B-29 accident report would reveal state secrets. We must trust that the government is telling us the truth.

Stalin's death continued to dominate the *New York Times*'s front page the day after Vinson announced the *Reynolds* decision, but the *Times*, on page two, did take notice of the Court's ruling. "High Court Denies Right of Judges to Arms Secrets," reported a small headline atop a four-paragraph Associated Press news item. "The Supreme Court," the article began, "ruled 6 to 3 today that judges were no more entitled to learn real military secrets than any other parties to a lawsuit."

That same day, March 10, Biddle wrote to Betty, Patricia, and Phyllis. "I am indeed sorry to have to report to you that the Supreme Court yesterday handed down an opinion reversing the decision of the District Court and the Court of Appeals in your case." He continued, emphasizing that the Court had not dismissed the case, only sent it back to District Court for retrial:

The reason which they gave for so doing was that the Government did not have to produce the report of the Air Force

Investigating Board with respect to the cause of the accident because to have done so might have disclosed secret military information. The answer to this is that we never asked for any secret information but merely to know what caused the accident. However, the Supreme Court unfortunately has the last word.

I hope you will not be too discouraged because, as you know, this is not the end of the case. . . . It is simply that the case is sent back to the District Court for retrial, at which time we shall have to produce such evidence as we can. . . . For this purpose we have Mr. [Eugene] Mechler and we will probably take the depositions of the three surviving members of the crew. . . . After that I would hope that we would get another judgment in an amount not less than the first time.

A week later, Teddy Mattern wrote to Phyllis, saying "there is very little I could add" to Biddle's letter. Now he could not even try to hide his pessimism. In a singularly perceptive analysis, Mattern (like Vinson) took notice of the times and the context:

Of course, I am having my doubts now, as we are deprived of most essential proof to make out a case. . . . Statements by witnesses might and might not spell out negligence sufficient to base a judgment in your favor; Biddle will have to make the best of them. . . . As you know the issues of the case were never tried and we are really starting all over again except that certain proof has been eliminated by the Supreme Court decision. This decision is very much in line with the present hysterical trend in the Government and in peaceful times is almost unthinkable.

Three of the Supreme Court justices, Mattern pointed out, "went so far as to vote against" the *Reynolds* ruling, "even in our troubled times when disclosures of any sort are so deeply dreaded." All told, during the B-29 litigation, "the problem has been considered by thirteen federal judges (one in the District Court, three in the Court of Appeals, and nine in the Supreme Court)," with "seven of them deciding in our favor, six against us." Unfortunately, "the minority carried a stronger weight, and there we are."

Mattern thought it "more than doubtful" that a judge's sympathies for the widows at trial would be enough to "overcome the emaciated proof available." He advised Phyllis to "not count on a positive decision and make no plans based on a favorable one." She worked too hard, he cautioned, "to permit yourself the luxury of daydreams or wishful thinking. You have carried on so far and you will continue successfully without the expected windfall. Your strength will not falter."

One month later, Judge Maris, in Philadelphia, following the dictates of the Supreme Court, formally withdrew his opinion in the B-29 case. "It is ordered," he wrote, "that the mandate of this court issued January 15, 1952, in the above-entitled case . . . is hereby recalled."

BIDDLE'S INITIAL DECISION NOT TO DEPOSE THE GOVERNMENT WITNESSES had obviously hurt him before the Supreme Court. Yet he had reasons for his choice. Biddle figured that he needed solid documentary evidence before he could pose good questions to the witnesses. He also figured that these surviving crew members knew little compared to the findings in the official accident report. He'd watched the government balk at handing over that report, first claiming a "self-investigative" privilege, then, when that didn't work, claiming state secrets. Why? What was in this report? If he deposed the witnesses, he'd probably lose the chance to find out. It would change the subject of the argument. He'd be agreeing to take half a loaf.

Now he had no choice. On March 27, he served notice of his intent to depose Captain Herbert Moore, Sergeant Walter Peny, and Sergeant Earl Murrhee. At some point the next month he did so in his Philadelphia office. Although no transcripts remain of these interviews, Biddle's correspondence suggests that the witnesses had little to contribute. On April 29, he wrote to his clients and Mattern. "There have been some developments since the decision of the Supreme Court," he reported. "The principal one is that we went ahead and took the depositions of the three surviving members of the crew. As I anticipated, they made it quite clear that the secret equipment on board the plane had absolutely nothing to do with the accident and had not even been put into operation."

He'd be retaining an aviation expert as a witness, Biddle advised. He hoped to try the case in June. He hoped to be able to show "not only that the accident was caused by the negligence of the Air Force but that we can do this without getting ourselves involved in any further legal problems." He would "certainly do my best to keep it moving along."

Yet there wasn't anything to keep moving. The government, having established the precedent it sought, had little remaining interest in battling the widows. At some point after Biddle wrote this letter, he and government lawyers began to negotiate a possible settlement of the case.

It's not hard to see Biddle's interest in settling. The paucity of evidence that so worried Mattern would be one reason. So would the threat of further delays and his clients' pressing need for financial help. Then there was, again, the climate of the times to consider.

Just weeks before, Justice William O. Douglas, in a much-noticed *New York Times Magazine* article titled "The Black Silence of Fear," had felt moved to deplore the "ominous trend" in the country toward a domestic witch-hunt, toward a tolerance "only for the orthodox point of view." The Communist threat inside the country "has been magnified and exalted far beyond its realities," so that "suspicion grows until only the orthodox idea is the safe one." Fear has driven "more and more men and women . . . either to silence or to the folds of the orthodox." Douglas saw in this a greater danger than the threat of atomic warfare. "The mind of man," he reminded, "must always be free." Yet the patterns Douglas deplored only intensified that spring of 1952. At televised hearings of Senator Joseph McCarthy's Senate Permanent Investigating Subcommittee, writers such as Langston Hughes and Dashiell Hammett either spoke defiantly or refused to testify. Subpoenaed by HUAC—which was then holding a second, much larger set of hearings into Communist influence within the film industry—playwright Lillian Hellman famously wrote that she "cannot and will not cut my conscience to fit this year's fashions." In April, two of McCarthy's aides, Roy Cohn and David Schine, created headlines during an extended tour of the State Department's European libraries, which they claimed housed some thirty thousand books by pro-Communist writers.

Throughout this tour, from mid-February to mid-June, officials removed several hundred books by more than forty writers from the shelves of United States libraries abroad, the result of confidential State Department directives. In one instance, in Tokyo, the removed books were not stored but burned or scrapped for pulping. Newspaper accounts at the time remained sketchy, however, because library officials were reluctant to discuss the directives, saying variously that the instructions were "classified," "restricted," "secret," and "entirely internal." The final directive in June, according to a *New York Times* report, "had demanded complete secrecy on the whole subject."

That same month, the Supreme Court addressed the fates of Julius and Ethel Rosenberg. The justices had declined three times to hear an appeal of the Rosenbergs' death sentence, but now came a late plea to stay the execution. On June 13, 1953, at its Saturday conference, the Court voted to deny the stay; after announcing this decision on Monday, the justices adjourned for the summer break. Late that night (or possibly early the next day), defense lawyers brought yet another last-minute appeal to William O. Douglas, after first vainly knocking on the door of Hugo Black's home in Alexandria, Virginia. Douglas listened to arguments in his chambers, consulted other justices, agonized—and then, on Wednesday, June 17, granted a temporary stay until the full Court could reconvene, presumably in the fall. Douglas, at once, left Washington on a cross-country automobile trip, thinking the matter resolved.

Chief Justice Vinson thought otherwise: He promptly scheduled a special session of the Court for noon the next day—neglecting to notify Douglas before the associate justice left on his trip. Douglas, hearing the news on his car radio while driving through Pennsylvania, turned back to Washington. After acrimonious oral argument on the afternoon of Thursday, June 18, the justices retired to their conference room for even more rancorous private debate. Black, like Douglas, was furious at Vinson for attempting to overturn a temporary stay granted by an individual justice during a Court vacation. Frankfurter also felt disturbed, as did Harold Burton. They comprised a minority, though, and in the end only Douglas and Black dissented, with Frankfurter declining to dissent or concur. At noon the next day, Friday, June 19, the Supreme Court announced its decision to vacate the stay granted by Douglas; Vinson delivered the oral opinion from the bench, in what would prove to be his last public act as chief justice. Shortly after eight p.m. that evening—just before sundown, so as to avoid conflict with the Jewish sabbath—Julius and Ethel Rosenberg died in the electric chair at Sing Sing Prison in Ossining, New York.

THREE DAYS LATER, JUDGE KIRKPATRICK, SITTING IN PHILADELPHIA, filed an order approving the "stipulation of compromise" that Charles Biddle and two government lawyers had just signed and submitted to him. After weeks of negotiation, and Biddle's consultations with an aviation expert, both sides had agreed to settle the case for $170,000— seventy-five percent of Kirkpatrick's original award of $225,000. In exchange for signing "full and final" releases of their claim, Phyllis Brauner would receive $49,855.55 (the equivalent of $388,233 in current dollars), Elizabeth Palya Sacker $48,355.55 ($376,552), and Patricia Reynolds Herring $39,299.90 ($306,034). The balance, $32,500 ($253,082), would go to Charles Biddle, who earned a contingency fee of just under twenty percent.

In a letter dated June 26, Biddle sent his three clients copies of the release they needed to sign, along with a copy of the settlement agreement. With that in hand, and the assurance of money to come, Betty on July 9 bought a headstone for Al Palya's grave in Tabor, Minnesota, while Phyllis reported to Mattern that she was feeling much better, was once again "her good old self." On August 5, Biddle and the government lawyers filed an "Order to Dismiss" the B-29 case, asking the clerk of the U.S. District Court in Philadelphia to "kindly mark" the matter "dismissed with prejudice." Within days, Betty, Phyllis, and Patricia received their checks.

As the weeks passed, the three women and their families embraced lives now made more comfortable by the government's payment. If the outcome didn't entirely satisfy, it still felt like a relief. Near the end of 1953, after receiving an appreciative letter from Phyllis—who reported that she was doing fine, that the money had been a comfort—Biddle wrote back on December 7: "As you know, I hated to settle the case because I thought if we had carried it through to a finish we could have gotten substantially more. However, something might have gone wrong and perhaps it was better to be sure of receiving the amount which you did."

They seemed now to be at the end of their quest. Five years after B-29 #866 fell from the sky over Waycross, the efforts to learn why drew to a close. The widows had their money, some of their money at least, and the government had its newly established state secrets privilege. Its privilege—and the B-29 accident report, stored deep in a Pentagon filing cabinet, still hidden from public view.

PART THREE

CONSEQUENCES

July 1953–October 2002

CHAPTER 20

JUDY

July '53–February '77

THE CONCLUSION OF THE B-29 LITIGATION CAME AT A moment when the country seemed on the brink of change. One month after the case settled, triple-deck banner headlines announced the signing of a truce and an end to the fighting in Korea. Although President Eisenhower urged the Free World to "stay vigilant"—the armistice didn't resolve the conflict or produce a peace treaty—it was hard not to exhale and look to the future.

Soon the Supreme Court had a new leader. At 2:15 a.m. on September 8, Chief Justice Fred Vinson, at age sixty-three, died of a heart attack at his Washington apartment. The *Reynolds* opinion was not among those mentioned in his obituaries. The three most often cited were his decisions in the *Denny* case, the steel-seizure case, and the Rosenbergs' execution. Eisenhower, who, like Truman, was a good friend of Vinson's, ordered a thirty-day mourning period. Amid the public tributes voiced, the one from Felix Frankfurter stood out for its curtness: "Chief Justice Vinson's death comes as a great shock to me." Within days, news emerged that Earl Warren, the governor of California, would be appointed the next chief justice. Warren officially assumed that position in early October; the next May, the Warren Court handed down its landmark decision in *Brown v. Board of Education,* ruling that public school segregation was unconstitutional.

By then, Senator Joseph McCarthy's career was collapsing. On March 9, 1954, Edward R. Murrow broadcast his damning portrait of McCarthy on the television show *See It Now.* Six weeks later, the nationally televised Army-McCarthy Hearings began, an inquiry into charges that McCarthy had tried to blackmail the military. For the first time, others dared to confront McCarthy publicly, and through television—now in about sixty percent of homes—Americans were able to see for themselves this senator's offensive, bullying manner. The beginning of the end came on December 2, when the Senate officially censured McCarthy for his behavior at the hearings. He would be dead in less than three years.

The Cold War kept escalating: In August of 1953 the Soviet Union announced the explosion of its first thermonuclear device, and five months later Secretary of State John Foster Dulles announced a new U.S. defense policy, one based on "instant and massive retaliation" against any aggressor. But such retaliation would have to be conducted without the aid of a venerable bomber. On November 1, 1954, the U.S. Air Force withdrew from service the B-29 Superfortress.

Across the country, the soldiers who'd fought in Korea were returning, eager to get on with their lives. The family home became their bulwark. The longing for security intensified; consumer spending mushroomed; the marriage rate rose to record levels. This was the world Betty, Patricia, and Phyllis inhabited at the close of the B-29 litigation. In 1953 they saw Swanson introduce the first frozen TV dinner. The next year they watched the first broadcast of the *Tonight Show.* The most popular movie stars were John Wayne, Jerry Lewis and Dean Martin, Gary Cooper, James Stewart, and Marilyn Monroe, in that order. The highest-ranked TV show, for the third year in a row, was *I Love Lucy.* The best-selling nonfiction book, also for the third year in a row, was *The Holy Bible: Revised Standard Version.*

IN THE FIRST YEARS OF HER LIFE, AL PALYA'S DAUGHTER JUDY DIDN'T know what she was missing, not having a father. She'd been only seven weeks old when her dad perished in the crash of a B-29 near Waycross. By the time she was three, her mom had remarried. So there was always a father in the house, as far as Judy knew.

Betty Palya didn't talk about Al. She kept no photos of him around their home, no scrapbooks. Later, Judy would come to realize that her mother just couldn't let herself grieve, not with three small children to raise. Judy and her brothers never sat around with their mother discussing the good old days before their father died. There was little wallowing in the past, or, for that matter, remembering the past. Still, Judy's older brother Bill did once find his mother crying in the living room. This was so out of the blue, something he'd never seen before. Betty handled things, at least when her kids were around.

For a while, they remained in Haddon Heights. Their home was a Dutch Colonial on a quiet street, with a huge backyard and a detached garage. Betty had decided to "get out of the house" even before Al died, so she continued teaching home economics while her new husband, Bill Sacker, ran a butcher store. When she came home, she'd maybe sit down, have a cup of coffee, watch *General Hospital* with Judy. Then she'd get up and start sewing or cooking. She was always working. She paid the bills, painted the walls, did the gardening. She parented and doctored and repaired. While Judy's friends' mothers sat around at the swim club on hot summer days, Betty was making curtains. Judy used to spend a lot of time with Betty, watching her *do* things. What she did most of all, Judy came to feel, was wave her wand, intent on rendering everything wonderful for her family.

Oh, and her cooking—everything made from scratch. Judy's friends liked to eat at her house. "Try to vary the color of the food on the plate," Betty would advise Judy. "Not fish and corn and mashed potatoes. Pick a green vegetable so the plate doesn't look so pale." Judy loved to watch her mother standing over the fudge each Friday. Betty would stir it, beat it, then lift a big spoonful above the pot and let it cascade down in luscious dark brown ribbons. On Saturdays, when her spaghetti sauce simmered all day, the kids got to sample a little bowl in the afternoon.

Betty may have successfully shielded her family from the past, but it stayed with her, of course. One Christmas in those early years, she sent a holiday card to Al's mother: "Dear Mother Palya, We had our picture taken so you could see how we all look today. Aren't the children growing. . . . I'm sure Al would be very proud of his little family. Bill [Sacker] is a fine man and is making us very happy. You will like him. You are welcome to come to see us anytime. We'd love it. Take care of yourself. Lovingly, Betty."

Her brother-in-law, W. J. Perryman, still wrote to her, offering support and advice. On September 14, 1953, a month after the government's settlement, Perryman sent a renewal policy for her home insurance, along with guidance on how it should be handled. Then he turned to the matter of the big payment she'd just received. The payment and her marriage meant the end of her RCA workers' compensation.

"I am awfully glad to know that Mr. Biddle was able to effect settlement for you and that the case has now been closed . . ." he began. "I do hope that you will keep in mind, first that the amount of money you have received does not represent too great a sum under today's conditions, even though it might appear as an awful lot to you. It can very easily and quickly be dissipated." He cautioned that she'd be offered all kinds of advice. He warned her to be particularly wary of the stock salesmen and investment counselors. Understand, he urged, that there is "no quick money" now. The stock and real estate markets "are falling every day." Take what you need "to get you and the children the clothes and other necessities and comforts which you have had to deny yourself during the past several years." Put the remainder in "some safe investments" that will be available in an emergency. "As I told you many times before," Perryman concluded, "I have the utmost confidence in your ability to think and act and you have shown an unusual amount of courage and determination to hold and carry on for your family. . . . I know that you will continue to do so."

It appears that Betty did not entirely follow Perryman's advice, for the next summer, in July 1954, her family moved to a larger house in nearby Haddonfield. One reason for this move was the imminent arrival of a new baby. Betty and Bill Sacker's daughter, Jeannie, was born that October 4—almost exactly six years after Al's death. The family moved once again in 1957, to yet a bigger house in Cherry Hill, NJ, where you bought a lot and from "samples" picked which home you wanted built.

Judy was nine then, and interested in everything. She kept a stamp collection and joined a stamp club—all boys, much to her delight. She was on a swim team from age nine to seventeen, the champion girl swimmer for most of those years. She loved being the princess at the Barclay Farm Swim Club, loved hanging out with the older lifeguards and guys on the swim team. She also took riding lessons and had her own horse during her senior year in high school. She played the piano, at the insistence of her mother, though she didn't much like it. She was in the Girl Scouts for a bit, and 4-H, and Future Homemakers of America.

Judy did well in high school classes and made the National Honor Society without trying very hard. She'd discovered books while in junior high school and read voraciously. She didn't seek out boyfriends; she just wasn't as aggressive about it as some girls were. From the time she was nine, though, she had a crush on a neighbor who was four years older, a boy named John Loether.

It all seemed so normal, growing up in Cherry Hill. That's how Judy would recall it—*no excessive alcohol, no drugs, no beatings . . . We all got along with each other and with our relatives.* Yet one of Judy's childhood friends in those years sensed something amiss. Susan White felt there was an "elephant in the closet" at Judy's house. She believed that the elephant was Judy's father. One afternoon, she and Judy visited the attic of the Cherry Hill home. There were boxes up there, memories from the past. Only with great reluctance did Judy point out her dad's things.

Bill Sacker just wasn't Al Palya. Her stepfather had an impossible task, as Judy's brother Bill would observe years later. He and his brother, given their ages, would have resisted even their natural father, and they resisted their stepdad even more. Once Sacker's own daughter was born, it seemed like all the home movies were of her. Judy, six at the time of Jeannie's birth, became aware that this new sister had a different last name. Eventually, she also came to feel that in her step-dad's eyes, she and her two brothers weren't the same as his own daughter. How hard is it, she wondered, at least to pretend that you love your kids equally?

JUDY'S OLDEST BROTHER, BOB, ENLISTED IN THE MARINE CORPS AND shipped out to Vietnam while she was still in high school. The memory would always stick with Judy, for her mom cried that day. Bob was wearing his uniform, saying goodbye to Betty. She wept, whimpered really, not a lot of tears. But Judy had never seen her like this.

Soon it was her turn to leave. That neighbor boy she'd always had a crush on, John Loether, had finally started noticing her back. At age twenty, after two years of college, Judy married him and left for Illinois, then Spain, then Massachusetts. John found work as a computer specialist, in an industry just emerging. They eventually settled in Bolton, a small Massachusetts town about an hour west of Boston. In 1975, when Judy was twenty-seven, she gave birth to her first son, Kurt. Loving her own child brought to mind her father. She now began to confront what she'd been missing.

Judy had a second son, Travis, in 1979. With her boys, she started making more and more visits to her mother's home in Cherry Hill. During long summer stays, Judy often found herself climbing up to the attic. It was a comfortable place to visit. One morning, she opened a trunk full of costumes and other intriguing things. By nature, she liked to put things in order, so she set to work.

She came across newspaper articles about her father. She also looked through her dad's notebooks, which were full of arcane terms, diagrams, and computations. She found most of them incomprehensible, but kept going back to them. *Shoran . . . Rheostat.* What did they mean? It depended on how much you wanted to figure out, Judy reasoned.

She knew so little. She didn't know government lawyers had refused to turn over an accident report about her dad's fatal B-29 crash. She didn't know the Air Force had claimed that the accident report contained military secrets so sensitive not even judges should see them.

She knew only that she'd lost her father when she was seven weeks old, that he'd died in an airplane crash while on a secret mission, that there'd been a lawsuit, that Mom had won some money. Once, on Veterans Day, she'd asked Betty if her dad was a veteran. "In a way," she'd replied. Al Palya remained a mystery to Judy. Sifting through documents in her mother's attic, she was not consciously seeking a connection to her father. She just thought this was interesting stuff.

On occasion, in that quiet attic, she held up certain documents, the ones stamped "Secret." That's what truly fascinated her: the word "secret."

IN EARLY 1977, IN HER MOTHER'S ATTIC, JUDY CAME ACROSS AN OLD news article about Eugene Mechler, the civilian engineer from the Franklin Institute who had survived the B-29 crash. It said he lived in Erlton, part of Cherry Hill—right nearby. On impulse, Judy looked him up in a phone book and dialed the number. Mechler's daughter answered. It turned out Mechler now split his time between Maine and Florida. The daughter gave Judy an address.

Mechler wrote first, before Judy did, having heard that she'd called. His handwritten words sprawled across the page.

> I was in a B-29 accident in which Al Palya was also
> involved. Do I have the right Palya? You called my daughter
> Marion to ask for more details on the accident. I can send you a
> copy of the report I made, and if you wish I can look for the
> newspaper accounts. . . . I think you will find my account
> interesting. . . . I didn't see anything of [Al] after the plane began
> to have trouble. But I can tell you what happened to the plane.
> Be glad to answer your questions.

Judy wrote back. Mechler responded, his scrawl interspersed with assorted sketches.

> I am sure the plane was not sabotaged. Quite a few B-29s
> had the same problem about this time. A neighbor of mine who

was a crew member of a B-29 during World War II said that there is a magnesium impeller in the supercharger. Once there is an engine fire, the magnesium catches fire and burns till it is all consumed. No extinguisher can put it out. As a result when our engineer pulled the extinguisher on Engine No. 1, the fire went out but shortly started up again. This was a chronic fault with B-29 planes.

I knew your father only as a business associate. Franklin Institute had a subcontract from RCA to study methods of improving the Shoran bombing equipment. . . . Your father was a capable administrator and engineer. . . . He was in charge of our contract. . . . The only other thing I know is that your father had a woodworking shop in the garage with several power tools. This was one of his hobbies. The [Project Banshee] equipment on the plane was what we were supposed to improve. It was no more or less secret than any other experimental equipment classified as "Secret." . . . Our particular project was probably never declassified.

Judy read Mechler's letters with interest but didn't know what more to ask. So she put it all aside, including an invitation to visit Mechler's family at the summer camp they ran in Maine. She had her own life to live, after all.

CHAPTER 21

THE PROGENY OF
REYNOLDS

July '56–October '02

THE APPLICATION OF *REYNOLDS* STARTED OUT SLOWLY. ONE of the earliest instances where a judge relied on *Reynolds* came in July 1956, in a case that arose when the crews of seven Republic of China (Taiwan) ships defected with their vessels to Communist China. The Republic of China and the United States—which had sold the ships to China and held a mortgage on them—ended up suing insurers to recover their losses. The United States wouldn't answer all the insurers' interrogatories, though; Secretary of State John Foster Dulles filed an affidavit saying such disclosure would be "prejudicial to our foreign relations and contrary to the public interest." A federal district judge, in allowing this claim and refusing to dismiss the case, observed that "when [insurers] issued their . . . policies they knew, or should have known, that where military secrets . . . are at stake, certain information is privileged." Then he quoted from the heart of the *Reynolds* opinion: "Even the most compelling necessity cannot overcome the claim of privilege if the court is ultimately satisfied that military secrets are at stake."

By contrast, two years later an appellate panel balked at letting a claim of privilege block an inventor's lawsuit over a patent application; the panel said the district court instead could hold a private *in camera* trial, since the plaintiff already possessed the secret information and just wanted to present it in court. In January 1963, another appellate panel declined to block a plaintiff from getting at least part of an Air Force accident report—but only because the government had asserted a claim of executive (not state secrets) privilege. In July 1968, yet another appellate panel unequivocally recognized the right of the CIA to invoke the state secrets privilege in a slander suit against an agency employee. This panel both quoted from the *Reynolds* opinion and applied its standards: "The court itself must determine whether the circumstances are appropriate for the claim of privilege, and yet do so without forcing a disclosure of the very thing the privilege is designed to protect."

So it began. From 1973 on—after two decades of relative quiet—there has been a marked increase in court decisions involving the state secrets privilege. Several possible reasons exist: the general increase in lawsuits; a growing awareness of the privilege; repeated revelations of misconduct by federal intelligence agencies; and new statutes that made it easier for private citizens to sue the government over constitutional violations.

In July 1974 came the case that sparked the trend: *United States v. Richard M. Nixon*, the dispute over whether Nixon had to produce tape recordings and documents related to White House conversations about the Watergate scandal. Oddly, this was a case where an invocation of *Reynolds* would fail. In a legal brief, White House counsel maintained that "the principles announced in *Reynolds* have been applied by the lower courts to all claims of executive privilege, whether dealing with military secrets or with other kinds of information." In oral argument, Nixon's lawyers again cited *Reynolds*, declaring that "there are some kinds of documents on which the decision of the executive must be final, and not subject to review by the courts."

The Supreme Court wouldn't accept that, but not because it rejected *Reynolds*. The justices made clear that they were denying Nixon's claim because it was based "merely on the ground of a generalized interest in confidentiality." In other words, Nixon was claiming executive, not state secrets, privilege. "He does not place his claim of privilege on the ground they are military or diplomatic secrets," emphasized Chief Justice Warren Burger in the Court's unanimous opinion, the implicit suggestion being that a state secrets claim would have prevailed. Burger recognized and quoted from the *Reynolds* opinion—"It may be possible to satisfy the court . . . that there is a reasonable danger that compulsion of the evidence will expose military matters which, in the interest of national security, should not be divulged." But no Supreme Court case, Burger pointed out, "has extended this high degree of deference to a President's generalized interest in confidentiality."

By drawing such a sharp distinction between executive and state secrets privilege, the *Nixon* opinion inspired presidents and government agencies forever after to make state secrets claims rather than more general executive privilege claims. They now had a fairly clear reading from the Supreme Court that a state secrets claim provided them an absolute privilege.

This is certainly one reason for the sudden spike in use of the state secrets privilege during President Jimmy Carter's administration. With this increase in use, government lawyers could not avoid noticing a judicial willingness to accept the claims—and this willingness only fueled the trend. Scholars differ when calculating state secrets claims—they apply varying definitions and criteria—but according to one count, in the twenty-three years between the *Reynolds* decision and Carter's election in 1976, there were five cases in which the government invoked privilege; between 1977 and 2001, there were sixty-two.

Along with the numbers, the scope of what constituted state secrets began to expand, as did the definition of the privilege. No cases played a bigger role than *Halkin v. Helms I*, decided in June 1978, and *Halkin v. Helms II*, decided in September 1982. These decisions arose from lawsuits filed by former Vietnam War protestors who'd been subjected to intelligence agencies' surveillance and wiretapping. The district and appellate courts soundly upheld a CIA state secrets claim, which in effect stopped the litigation, since the plaintiffs couldn't get the information needed to prove their case. The D.C. Court of Appeals spoke with a particularly deferential tone, explicitly rejecting a role for the federal courts as "continuing monitors of the wisdom and soundness of Executive action." Citing both *Nixon* and *Reynolds,* the D.C. appellate panel noted that courts "should accord utmost deference to executive assertions of privilege on grounds of military or diplomatic secrets," and "courts need only be satisfied that there is a reasonable danger" that military secrets would be exposed.

What made the *Halkin* opinions even more pivotal was their embrace of the so-called "mosaic theory" about what constituted state secrets. No longer did the state secret have to be momentous, or, for that matter, entirely secret:

> It requires little reflection that the business of foreign intelligence gathering in this age of computer technology is more akin to the construction of a mosaic than it is to the management of a cloak and dagger affair. Thousands of bits and pieces of seemingly innocuous information can be analyzed and fitted into place to reveal with startling clarity how the unseen whole must operate. As the Fourth Circuit Court of Appeals has observed: The significance of one item of information may frequently depend upon knowledge of many other items of information. What may seem trivial to the uninformed may appear of great moment to one who has a broad view of the scene and may put the questioned item of information in its proper context. The courts, of course, are ill equipped to become sufficiently steeped in foreign intelligence matters to serve effectively in the review of secrecy classifications in that area.

The retreat of the judiciary intensified as the years passed. In December 1980, in a lawsuit over a contractual relationship with the Navy, the Fourth U.S. Circuit not only honored the Navy's state secrets claim but also held that the plaintiff could make no further attempt to press his action, even with nonprivileged information: "It is evident that any attempt on the part of the plaintiff to establish a prima facie case would so threaten disclosure that the overriding interest of the United States and preservation of its state secrets privilege precludes any further attempt to pursue litigation." In May 1983, in another case involving warrantless electronic surveillance, the D.C. Court of Appeals again talked of the "mosaic theory" and of "factors that limit judicial competence" to evaluate claims. In November 1984, the D.C. Court of Appeals, besides barring a plaintiff's action because the government couldn't defend itself on the record, also now broadened the definition of state secrets to include "disclosure of intelligence-gathering methods or capabilities and disruption of diplomatic relations." A year later, in a defamation action brought by a scientist accused of espionage, a federal court once more stopped a lawsuit cold, this time within an hour of when the Navy intervened; there just was no way to try the case, the trial and appellate judges agreed, without compromising sensitive military secrets. Nor, in January 1990, was it possible to try a case brought by a sixth-grade boy whom the FBI had investigated for writing to 169 countries, requesting information—part of his "encyclopedia of the world" school project. Because a state secrets claim shielded the FBI from disclosure, wrote an appellate panel, the sixth-grade boy "failed to sustain his burden of proof. . . . Accordingly, the cause of action was properly dismissed."

Over time, it became evident that cases involving claims of state secrets were falling into two groups: those where judges dismissed actions because a successful claim of privilege prevented plaintiffs from obtaining needed evidence, and those where courts refused to hear the matter because a trial might reveal sensitive information. In June 1991 and September 1992 came two rulings—concerning an Iraqi missile attack on the U.S. Navy frigate USS *Stark*—that provided particularly vivid examples of both such results.

The Iraqi attack occurred on May 17, 1987, when two Exocet missiles fired by an F-1 Mirage fighter jet slammed into the *Stark*, which was patrolling the Persian Gulf. Among the thirty-seven crewmen killed was Earl Patton Ryals, whose estate filed a wrongful death action against various military contractors, charging that they had negligently designed, manufactured, tested, and marketed the weapons systems on the frigate, including the Phalanx Anti-Missile system. Soon after, the secretary of the Navy asserted the state secrets privilege, and the government filed a motion to dismiss the complaint. The district court promptly granted this motion, entering judgment in favor of the contractors, because the factual issues "could not be resolved without access to classified information." Even without this reason, the court found, the case still must be dismissed because it presents a "political question" about military decision-making that's not subject to judicial review. An appellate panel, in affirming, would not send the case back to district court even for private *in camera* proceedings.

Following this first *Stark* case (*Zuckerman v. General Dynamics*), the second one (*Bareford v. General Dynamics*) made much the same claims but presented a more complicated situation, since those suing submitted 2,500 pages of unclassified information. To no end: Even if the plaintiffs could make their case using this unprivileged information, the district court ruled, the state secrets doctrine barred the action because a trial would threaten disclosure of state secrets. The case had to be dismissed out of hand, an appellate panel agreed, because "no amount of effort could safeguard the privileged information." Going further, the judges also noted that because "classified and unclassified information cannot always be separated," it was appropriate for courts to restrict access not only to evidence involving state secrets but also to "those pieces of evidence . . . which press so closely upon highly sensitive material that they create a high risk of inadvertent or indirect disclosures."

By then, the progeny of *Reynolds*, so appreciably expanded and evolved, little resembled their parent. As it happened, Judge Albert Maris lived long enough to see this—and to see confirmed his cautionary prophecy about the abuse of the state secrets privilege. In his later years, Maris—who after taking "senior status" in 1959, at age sixty-five, continued to serve as a judge—would hear many legal experts complain about the application of *Reynolds*. He'd read critic after critic argue that *Reynolds* was forcing judges to rule in a vacuum without knowing the contents of requested documents. He'd witness government lawyers invoke state secrets claims in all sorts of cases. He'd watch the impulse to protect military secrets begin to look—just as he'd predicted—more like the impulse to cover up mistakes, avoid embarrassment, and gain insulation from liability.

Maris never talked publicly about all this, but while giving an oral history interview at age eighty-two, he struggled to say something admiring about Chief Justice Fred Vinson.

Q: **There was some feeling his legal background was not sufficient to be appointed Chief Justice. Your thoughts?**

A: *Yes, yes, I remember. . . . He obviously was not one of the greatest Chief Justices, most learned Chief Justices we've had in this country. . . . But on the other hand . . . [pause] . . . I think he was a sound chief justice. He was competent. Particularly competent administrative . . .*

Q: **Many said he was appointed by Truman to bring these divisions together within the Court.**

A: *Harmonize. At least the personal relations. . . . I suspect he had pretty good success in this. This area he really had a gift to operate.*

Q: **How do you evaluate Vinson's overall career as chief justice?**

A: *[Long pause] Well . . . I . . . I . . . this is a very difficult thing for me to comment on . . . because . . . this date, I don't have enough facts to base my opinion on. . . . I think his administration of office was good, an adequate chief justice; functioned acceptably. He was not a distinguished lawyer. He certainly wouldn't be put in the first rank of Chief Justices. . . . As far as his contributions to jurisprudence generally, I think they were . . . [pause] . . . [pause] . . . They were . . . [pause] . . . They were certainly . . . [pause] . . . a . . . It's hard to know how to express it.*

Maris never retired. Besides his work as Special Master on complex cases, the Supreme Court kept him busy for years as chair of critical Judicial Conference committees that focused on modernizing federal court procedures. On the occasion of his eightieth birthday, in

1973, the Third Judicial Circuit presented a tribute to Maris during its annual conference at the William Penn Hotel in Pittsburgh. The next May, Chief Justice Warren Burger and retired chief justice Earl Warren cohosted an extraordinary black-tie appreciation dinner for Maris at the Supreme Court, complete with the U.S. Air Force's "Strolling Strings," an array of speeches, and a six-course meal. In March 1983, at a gathering of the Philadelphia Bar Association when Maris was approaching his ninetieth birthday, his colleagues on the federal courts presented him with the first Edward J. Devitt Distinguished Service to Justice Award. Then, in June 1988, on the occasion of Maris's fiftieth year sitting on the Third U.S. Circuit—the longest tenure of any federal appellate judge—the Third Circuit named its main courtroom in his honor, dedicating the Albert Branson Maris Courtroom.

Maris died seven months later, at age ninety-four, filing one last opinion on February 6, 1989, even as he lay stricken by a stroke, with hours to live. It may be just as well that he missed by only eight days·a singular revelation from a former solicitor general. In 1971, Erwin Griswold had stood before the Supreme Court, representing the United States in the landmark Pentagon Papers case (*United States v. New York Times*), where the government, making national security claims, sought to prevent publication of leaked documents about the Vietnam War. Although Griswold, a former dean of Harvard Law School, had only scanned a summary memo on what the Pentagon Papers contained, his legal brief warned the Court that publication of these papers would pose a "grave and immediate danger to the security of the United States." Now, on February 15, 1989, he stepped forward in a *Washington Post* op-ed piece to write: "I have never seen any trace of a threat to the national security from the publication [of the Pentagon Papers]. Indeed, I have never seen it even suggested that there was such an actual threat. . . . It quickly becomes apparent to any person who has considerable experience with classified material that there is massive overclassification and that the principal concern of the classifiers is not with national security but rather with governmental embarrassment of one sort or another."

By the time Griswold wrote this, not just unclassified but readily available public information, such as newspaper articles, had become subject to national security claims. Judges were requiring private *in camera* review of documents in less than a quarter of cases. (Since 1993, it's been less than one-eighth). Yet direct invocations of the state secrets privilege were by no means the broadest legacy of *Reynolds*. Far more often, *Reynolds* was cited or referred to in courtroom arguments and legal briefs. Merely by waving *Reynolds* in the background for "atmospheric effect," government lawyers had learned they could gain significant judicial deference.

This general judicial deference is the greatest legacy of *Reynolds*. Faced with ominous claims about national security, judges in recent years have found it hard to deny governmental power. Justice Department lawyers now firmly possess—and use—what they sought more than fifty years ago. Attorney General John Ashcroft did not even bother to reply when Senator Charles E. Grassley (of Iowa) and Representative Howard L. Berman (of California) wrote him in late 2002 to express concern about abuse of the state secrets privilege.

Just seven weeks earlier, in fact, Ashcroft had invoked it again, in a case involving an FBI whistle-blower. "To prevent disclosure of certain classified and sensitive national security information," a Department of Justice news release advised, "Attorney General Ashcroft asserted the state secrets privilege. . . . The state secrets privilege is well-established in federal law. . . . This privilege has been applied many times to protect our nation's secrets from disclosure. . . . It is an absolute privilege that renders information unavailable in litigation."

CHAPTER 22

WHAT TO SEARCH FOR

January '95–March 2000

THE YEARS 1979 TO 1994 ABSORBED JUDY PALYA LOETHER. She had two children to raise and volunteer activities to tend at the local schools, the Cub Scouts, the county fair, and a garden association. There was her mother to help as well. Widowed a second time when Bill Sacker died of pancreatic cancer in 1988, Betty struggled to keep going on Social Security and a $12,000 annual pension. In 1992, at age eighty, she ran out of money. She also began acting strangely, arguing, calling repairmen for imaginary problems, eating and shopping without logic—all signs of Alzheimer's disease. She had to give up her Cherry Hill home and move into a nearby assisted-living facility. There she had a nice one-bedroom apartment—Judy had spent a long time looking for it—but Betty missed her familiar world.

Judy never let go of the urge to solve the mystery of her father. She felt deeply proud of him. People who talked about Al went on about his brilliance and enthusiasm. In 1988, Judy had traveled to Czechoslovakia (now Slovakia) with her son Kurt and her cousin David Pope to meet the Palya clan. They stayed for three weeks, going to Marhan, where every other person was a Palya. They hosted a party at a hotel there for all the Palyas. The experience kindled something in Judy. She returned home with a renewed curiosity.

She was forty—in a year she'd be the same age as her father when he died. Dad, she realized, was so *young* then. Whenever Judy was with her aunt Lillian, she would ask questions about Al. She never questioned her own mother, though. Nor did she talk to her brothers about their father. It was just a tender area, something they had put aside. Once you put it aside, you didn't know when or how to bring it up.

Judy found it hard, in fact, to have any intimate conversations with her mother. Betty was Victorian in many ways. She'd always made Judy feel loved, but life becomes more complex as you grow older. The hurts piled up, and Judy felt a void now, a sense of longing. Books provided one form of solace—she read constantly and kept a log of the titles. Movies also helped—she could sit in the dark and lose herself. Then, in 1995, the Internet began to emerge. Her husband, John, worked for Digital Corporation, which owned the Alta Vista search engine; he kept talking about its great power.

Okay, Judy thought. What to type in? What to search for?

She'd been collecting old dog books by the American author Albert Payson Terhune. She loved his tales of raising collies at Sunnybank, his New Jersey estate. But other people were collecting his books, too, making them hard to locate. Judy decided to type in Terhune's name. Bingo—lots of links and leads.

Judy didn't yet think to use the Internet to help learn about her father. Instead, in early 1996, when her mom was eighty-four, Judy wrote a letter to Al's colleague Walter Frick. She wanted the Fricks to know what had happened to her mother, and she wanted to hear Walt's memories of her dad. On March 6, Frick, at age eighty-three, disabled somewhat by two mini-strokes, wrote back.

He thought it "thoughtful and kind" for Judy to send them a letter about her mother. They were "very saddened" by her misfortune. They had last heard from her in late 1991, in an exchange of Christmas cards. They had continued to send Betty cards and notes after that, but had never received a reply. They feared she might have "passed on," but were puzzled because their cards were not returned. Betty, they thought, was fortunate to have "a caring daughter" such as Judy.

Frick then turned to a memory of the B-29 crash.

As you probably know, I was with your father on his fatal trip and escaped being with him on that aircraft only because another RCA employee, Don Lawler, wanted me to review the work he had been doing. I had the sad duty of accompanying him to his final resting place. When I got back and called your mother I remember being overwhelmed with sadness because his little infant daughter would never know her father. . . .

Judy wrote Frick several times after that, always asking about her dad. "I can understand that having grown up in a household in which your mother had remarried, you would not have heard much mention of your father," Frick wrote back in February 1998, "and would want to garner as much information about him as you can." After reviewing his prior letters to see what he could add, he offered the fact that Al was an "avid bridge player and a very good one." At Honeywell in the early days, Al had worked on Shoran equipment, "some sort of analog computer." At RCA, he continued with that type of project. "Al always had time for the peons," Walt concluded. "This characteristic kept morale high among people who worked for him."

By then, Judy was roaming widely on the Internet. Sitting before her monitor one day, she typed in Palya, and also her mother's maiden name, Hiler. She began to trace her family's genealogy. On one screen, she found reference to her mom, to the date she got married. That page had links. Judy clicked and found herself staring at part of her family tree. There were her parents—their wedding day. Surfing around, she made another discovery: A boy she'd liked in high school was a relative. Then one day she typed in the word "Shoran"—the radar guidance system mentioned so often in Al's notebooks, and now in Walt's letters. This looked like a big deal—and it was connected to her dad. On eBay, Judy found an old RCA advertisement for Shoran. She bought it for seven dollars.

The Internet became an enchanting escape for Judy. Sometimes, she'd play solitaire on her computer; other times, she participated in a worldwide "massively multi-player online role-playing game" known as Asheron's Call. She'd learned of this through her son Kurt, who played it well into the night. One day he asked, would you like me to create a character for you—*your* character?

You began, Judy saw, by imagining the person you wanted to play. Your choice—everything your choice—and it all happened on the island of Dereth. Judy laughed but took the bait. She began to log on, usually joining 3,000 others from around the world. Dereth was so *huge*, an island full of beaches, castles, waterfalls, and volcanoes. It was truly a *life* inside her computer, beautiful and awesome and complicated. It was like living in the world of a book. Judy found herself on the computer all the time now, laughing—*Okay, others see this as crazed*—but amazed. On Dereth she could go places, do things, meet people. On Dereth she could *run*. On Dereth she could be someone else.

Yet Judy now sought more than fantasy on the Internet. Even before finding Asheron's Call, her choice of search words had begun to focus more and more on her father.

"Lin Writer"—Dad's old roommate, a bridge expert?

"Crashes"

"Waycross"

"Crashes + Waycross"

One day in February 2000, Judy typed in the words "B-29 + Accident." In an instant, that took her to a website titled, in bold black capital letters, "USAF & USAAF AIRCRAFT ACCIDENT REPORTS 1918–1955." Below that was a second line: "Complete accident reports up to December 31, 1955, now available."

At the bottom of the website (Accident-Report.com), Judy found a fuller explanation: "There were thousands of aircraft accidents in early U.S. Air Force history. . . . The reports of these accidents were filed with the Air Force Office of Flying Safety under its various names. Thousands of pages of documents eventually accumulated and were later converted to microfilm. The microfilmed mishap reports had been maintained by U.S. Air Force for many years. Air Force regulations denied any public access to those records until 1996, when they were changed to allow unlimited access to all reports up to December 31, 1955. It's because of this we're able to offer these complete investigation reports!"

Judy stared at her computer screen. *Oh my God.* She hadn't known there was such a thing as military accident reports. Maybe this could help, though her chief interest wasn't in the cause of the crash. As before—as always—she wanted to know why her father was *on* the plane. She wanted to know what was so "top secret" about his work.

At her computer, Judy typed an email message to the operator of this Accident Report website: *"My dad was killed in a B-29 crash. . . . Might you have the accident report about this crash?"*

IN MILLVILLE, NEW JERSEY, A ONCE-RURAL SUBURBAN TOWN FORTY-FIVE miles southeast of Philadelphia, Michael Stowe watched Judy's email message pop up on the computer screen in his cramped office, a room not much larger than a modest storage closet. It may once have been a storage closet, in fact; it occupied a narrow space in one corner of a small wood-frame home that sat on the edge of an untended four-and-a-half acre lot. The smell of animals saturated the air; Stowe's menagerie included a duck, a lethargic sixteen-year-old golden retriever mix named Duke, a younger beagle mix named Marco, and all manner of cats. Out back, a corral held two horses, one an ancient quarter horse named Macs, the other a former harness racer named Dude, both rescued by Stowe's wife, Bea. Beyond the corral rose a sizable scrap heap—the twisted remains of airplane crashes.

The largest pile featured most of a Republic P-47G, victim of a midair collision in 1944. Jumbled with it were the mangled parts, including one engine, of a Lockheed PV-1 that crashed in a snowstorm in 1974. Adjacent heaps offered the battered remnants of a North American P-51H (crash-landed in trees in 1954); a Boeing B-17F (hit a mountain in 1944); a Douglas C-47A (hit a mountain in 1942); a General Dynamics F-16A (hit terrain in 1991); a General Dynamics F-16A (overshot a runway in 1993); a North American F-86A (pilot lost control in 1955); a Republic P-47D (fire in flight in 1943); a Republic

P-47G (midair collision in 1945); a McDonnell-Douglas F-4E (fire in flight in 1986); a Republic-Fairchild A-10A (lost flight control in 1992); a Beechcraft C-45 (hit mountain in 1950s); and a Curtiss SB2C-3 (hit terrain in 1944).

Airplane crashes had mesmerized Michael Stowe since he was thirteen, and he was now thirty-nine. The Millville Airport was about a mile from his childhood home, but it wasn't the airplanes that first caught his interest. Just south of the field were the remains of an air-to-ground strafing range. Stowe, prowling about the "pillboxes" in the woods, sometimes using a borrowed metal detector, began to find machine-gun shell casings dropped from airplanes many years earlier. Stowe spent much of his youth searching those woods for treasures. Later, his mailman, who'd watched fighter pilots training at the Millville Airport during the war, told Stowe where to find dropped bombs and fired rockets. He also told him about some of the airplane crashes. Soon after, Stowe bought his own metal detector. He attached an old M16 rifle sling to his new gadget and wore it across his back, along with an army duffel bag full of tools. The hunts grew ever more bountiful.

For the topic of a ninth-grade paper, Stowe chose the Millville Airport; he started collecting stories from the airport manager, maps and blueprints from city hall. Using this information, he found all sorts of artifacts in the former aerial gunnery range, including two crates of blasting caps hidden in an old Army storage bunker. As time passed, he began to uncover pieces of wrecked airplanes, and to collect them, along with the stories of the men who died in those crashes. He spent hours in the Millville Library, browsing through the microfilm copies of the local newspaper from the 1940s, hand-copying stories related to the airport. At least twelve pilots, he learned, had lost their lives in training flights in this area. Twelve! It astounded him that military airmen had died right there in Millville, and no one remembered them. It also inspired him.

In 1983, in an unused airport building, Stowe founded the Millville Army Air Field Museum and began to look for the families of pilots killed over Millville. He started attracting attention from local journalists, whose articles about him generated new tips from residents, as well as offers of help from archivists in national agencies. From those offers came, among other things, 500 pages of correspondence and a 500-page *Histories of the Millville Army Air Field*, available for purchase on microfilm. When the state of New Jersey announced plans to drain nearby Union Lake, Stowe knew just what he'd find: the remains of a P-47 fighter, which ended up in his museum. Visitors flocked to see it—at least for a while.

Stowe had failed to appreciate that not everyone would share his passion for the airfield and its past. Then there were the ceaseless maintenance problems. In 1992, with the museum's operation starting to affect his health, Stowe left to pursue what he called "aircraft archaeology" in the southern New Jersey area.

All these endeavors were just hobbies, though. Since 1980 Stowe had held a full-time civilian job in Army and Air Force inventory management, more commonly known as "supply"—everything from issuing clothing to overseeing equipment. That's what he was doing in January 1996, when the Clinton administration made available old aircraft accident reports. "I hereby waive the claim of privilege and authorize unrestricted public release of aviation accident reports dated prior to 25 January 1956," wrote the secretary of the Air Force, Sheila E. Witnall. "The Chief of Safety is authorized to transfer all such reports from their present archive at Kirtland AFB [in New Mexico] to the Air Force Historical Research Agency at Maxwell AFB [in Alabama]."

Stowe happened, at this time, to be on an active duty tour with the New Jersey Air Force National Guard. Learning what military flights were going to Maxwell, he drove down to Andrews Air Force Base outside Washington, D.C., in April 1996 and hitched a ride in the back of a general's plane. With a list of accidents in hand, some seventy pages' worth, he planned to sift through the reports right there at Maxwell. But he found them all jammed together on microfilm reels—2,000 pages per reel. After four days there, Stowe hadn't completed researching even one page of his list. It would take him a lifetime to get through this. So he returned home with a new plan: He would have to spend a lot of money; he would have to buy copies of all the available reels.

That's what he did eventually. On the day Judy e-mailed him in February 2000, the file cabinet in Mike Stowe's cramped office contained some one thousand reels, each bought for about thirty dollars—he "didn't want to know" the total investment. The file cabinet, located just over Stowe's left shoulder when he sat at his computer, contained ten drawers, each with a label identifying a date range: *1918–1942; '42–'43; '43–'44; '44–'45; '45–'46; '46–'48; '49–'51; '51–'53*—two million pages in all. A pair of microfilm readers sat on a counter to the left of the computer—one in active use, the other bought cheap, just to have as backup. Stowe kept several other readers in storage to cannibalize for parts.

Having limited resources, he'd needed to earn back some of what he spent. So he'd gone on the Internet, built a website, and started advertising his accident report research service. He had to support his hobby or else he'd go bankrupt.

Plenty of people appreciated Stowe's service. Most days, he received eight to ten email inquiries. He couldn't help everyone, especially those asking about losses in Vietnam, which were outside the time range of the available reports. But he could help a good number. Stowe soon found himself spending hours in his small office; he was there first thing in the morning and last thing at night. When appeals came in, he'd consult his intricately arranged index of names and dates and pilots. Usually, he could go straight to the requested report, popping just the right microfilm reel into his reader. *Yes, that B-24 crashed in Wyoming. All died. . . . No survivors.* If the inquirer wanted a copy of the report, he'd print it out and send it, along with any requested maps and photos. He didn't charge for calling up the accident report, only for the printout—$25 for a report up to thirty pages, twenty cents a page after that, and five to ten dollars for photos, depending on size.

Looking now at Judy Loether's inquiry on his screen, Stowe typed a response: He asked for the date of the accident and the name of the pilot. He knew he could find it anyway after a search, but with a date and pilot—his main indexes—he could go straight to it.

In Massachusetts, Judy, seeing Stowe's message, checked her old newspaper articles for the pilot's name. *Ralph Erwin*, she typed back.

Stowe no longer needed the name, however. Not wanting to wait, he'd searched for "B-29" and "Georgia" in the years 1946 through 1949. It wasn't complicated, Stowe explained later. "We were able to find the report of your accident inquiry and it's very big!" he messaged Judy on February 11, 2000.

Two-hundred and twenty pages, plus fifteen photographs. Stowe wanted to scare people off if they weren't really interested, before he started printing out hundreds of pages. On his old reader, he had to reproduce each page separately, and it took twenty seconds a page.

"Reproduction cost: $63.00," he advised Judy. "If you would like copies of the report, please send check or money order payable 'MSTOWE' to Accident Reports . . ."

A day later, Judy mailed off her check. By the end of February 2000, she held in her hands the Air Force accident report that three widows and Charles Biddle had so strenuously but vainly sought half a century earlier.

FOR A MOMENT, JUDY HESITATED TO PULL THE REPORT FROM ITS LARGE envelope, fearing what gruesome details it might contain. As she began to read, though, she mainly just felt disappointed. This report didn't say what they were doing on the plane, didn't say anything about the confidential research. Other than a passing reference to removing secret equipment from the crash site, there wasn't anything about her father's project. No secrets at all. Shoot, Judy thought. This doesn't have what I want.

Yet she kept reading, and as she did, her consternation grew. Although this report didn't describe anything secret, it sure did seem to document all sorts of mistakes and negligence. It looked to Judy as if an awful lot of bad things had happened in that plane. She understood human error, such as the pilot turning off the wrong engine. But the maintenance supervisors—why hadn't they complied with those technical orders?

In fact, Judy saw, they'd ignored half a dozen technical orders—not just the one about heat shields. What about that copilot—he was sup-posed to be helping the pilot but he jumped up instead and decided to leave. Judy didn't like that one bit; that made her mad. Then there was the engineer, maybe mistakenly cutting off fuel to engine number two. And poor Eugene Mechler, wondering how to get out of there because he hadn't been briefed. Everyone made so many mistakes—what a sad comedy of errors.

Judy turned through the pages again. Despite all the disturbing elements, something about this accident report gave her great comfort. Reading it provided her a connection to her father. No longer did Al Palya seem so unreachable and mysterious.

On impulse, Judy went back to the old newspaper articles about the crash. She read them once more. What jumped out this time was the name Susan Brauner, daughter of the Franklin Institute engineer William Brauner. According to the papers, Susan was four when her father died in the B-29 crash. It occurred to Judy now that there was a woman out there close to her own age, a woman who'd grown up with the same questions.

At her computer, Judy tried a white pages search, typing in Susan Brauner's name. It probably wouldn't work, but maybe. In an instant, the search yielded twenty hits, twenty possibilities. Judy decided to send postcards to all twenty: *My name is Judy Palya Loether. . . . My dad was killed in a U.S. Air Force B-29 crash in October 1948. . . . I'm looking for the Susan Brauner who lost her Dad in the same plane.*

Days later, Judy found a note in her mailbox from a Susan Brauner: *I am the person you are looking for. Needless to say the family is quite curious as to why.* Susan Brauner lived in Massachusetts, the same state as Judy. She had a sister, Cathy. She had a phone number. Judy, composing her-self, made the call. *I found an accident report online,* she told Susan. *There's lots of negligence.*

CHAPTER 23

HOW TO GET STARTED

March 2000–October '01

At her home in Harwich Port, on Cape Cod, Susan Brauner examined Judy's postcard with curiosity. She was fifty-five. William Brauner had never been the mystery to her that Al Palya was to Judy, for in the Brauner family, they talked openly about the dad and husband they'd lost. They had photos and scrapbooks scattered all over the house. Susan and her sister, Cathy, had an uncle who *looked* like William, who shared stories about him. Once Cathy asked her mom about a bathrobe she'd found in a closet. "Oh," Phyllis said, "that's your father's. . . . I suppose there's no reason to keep it."

Susan also had her own memories, however sketchy. One moment still stuck with her—that final look as he left the house for the B-29 flight, she waving to him, he turning to wave back, and her sense that she'd never see him again.

With Judy's postcard in hand, Susan phoned her mother. Eighty-three years old, Phyllis definitely recalled the name Palya, instantly remembered Betty. So this wasn't a crackpot writing now, Susan realized. Should I contact her, she asked her mother. Phyllis didn't hesitate. With two children to raise and the demands of an academic career, she had, of necessity, let go of William Brauner—but she had never ceased thinking of him, never ceased wanting to know what happened to him. She'd always suspected that an enormous amount of information had been withheld. Once, many years after the settlement with the government, she'd requested the B-29 accident report through the Freedom of Information Act. When it arrived, she'd found that all relevant details had been blacked out. That had made her bitter. Late in life, Phyllis still talked to friends about her frustration. Yes, she told her daughter now. Yes—she wanted Susan to contact Judy.

SETTLING INTO WELLESLEY IN THE 1950S, THE BRAUNER FAMILY— PHYLLIS, her widowed mother, and two little girls—had stood out, for single-parent households were a rarity then. Financial matters set them apart, too; they lived in a relatively prosperous community but didn't have much money themselves. Most unusual of all, the Brauner home featured a mom pursuing an academic career in a field that didn't see many women in its ranks.

All through the 1950s, Phyllis taught at Simmons College while studying for her Ph.D. in analytical chemistry at Boston University. The day she defended her thesis at BU, in 1959, also happened to be the day of the annual fair at her daughters' elementary school—and she was the fair's chairperson. After she presented her thesis to BU professors, they asked her to leave the room so they could discuss it. That's fine, she politely informed them, but you only have fifteen minutes, because I must be back at Wellesley to run the school fair.

As the months and years passed, Phyllis earned a distinguished reputation as a professor of chemistry. She never remarried. After receiving her doctorate, she taught at Simmons for twenty-four more years. Her research focused on water quality, and took her to Sweden and Switzerland during several sabbatical leaves. In 1987, at age seventy-three, she joined the first U.S.-Soviet Earthwatch collaboration, an expedition to study the water at Lake Baikal, in Siberia. At first, the scientists were all hesitant of each other, but by the time it came to depart, the Americans were hugging and kissing their Russians colleagues.

Phyllis had interests beyond chemistry: She represented the United States in cultural People to People missions in the 1970s and took part in projects studying endangered wolves in Poland, and Polynesian monuments in the South Pacific. After leaving Simmons College in 1983, she worked with the Armed Forces School of the University of Maryland, teaching and establishing laboratories in Japan and Guam. Then she moved on to a twelve-year teaching stint at Framingham State University, in Massachusetts. Throughout her career, she remained active in the American Chemical Society, becoming the first woman to chair the Northeast Section. She founded an annual science lecture at Boston's Museum of Science that would later be named the Phyllis A. Brauner Memorial Lecture, in her honor. She joined the first goodwill trip of the American Chemical Society to China. In 1985, she received from the ACS's Northeast Section the Henry A. Hill Award for Outstanding Service.

Her daughters, Susan and Cathy, came to see their mom as quite a remarkable woman. Looking back as adults, they talked often about how determined she was, how wonderful a role model. At the same time, they couldn't avoid talking about their father's death and what it had meant to the family.

Money was always tight when they were young, with several years going by without a family car. They struggled even after the government payment arrived, for a chunk of that went to William's mother. Their mom's schedule also was always tight. "In a lot of ways," Cathy would later say, "we lost our childhood." Phyllis worked all the time, taking them with her during summer research trips and sabbaticals. In an era when most mothers were at home baking brownies, they felt lucky when they saw their mom. "Lots of times," Cathy said, "we would have loved for her to be with us, but she couldn't. There were lots of things we couldn't do."

Once, when her mom had joked about not being able to buy milk, Cathy told this to her kindergarten teacher, who called Phyllis to offer them some. Phyllis heard from another teacher when Susan, in kindergarten, announced that her father was "away on a trip." By the time Cathy reached kindergarten, she had the words down pat: "My father was killed in an airplane crash."

All the same, both Cathy and Susan drew considerable strength from their mother and successfully pursued their own careers. At the time Judy's postcard arrived, Cathy had earned a master's degree in communications from Boston University and was editor of the local newspaper in Wellesley, the *Townsman*. Susan was an accomplished real estate developer, specializing in historic renovations. Like their mother, they felt frustrated that they couldn't learn more about their father's death. Susan had once dated a Yale law school student who knew of the landmark *Reynolds* case, and he suggested trying another Freedom of Information Act request. Cathy had done just that; again they'd received only blacked-out documents. Now came Judy's postcard.

ON MARCH 18, 2000, JUDY AND THE BRAUNER FAMILY—PHYLLIS, SUSAN, and Cathy—met for lunch at the Wellesley Inn, which offered a staid charm in the middle of the college town. The Brauners arrived first, with Phyllis walking slowly. She had some medical problems but was determined to be there. The Brauners took seats at a table in the main dining room, next to a window that overlooked an inner courtyard. Twenty minutes late, Judy bustled in, bearing two large canvas bags. She'd spent a good part of the morning in a photocopy shop, making a duplicate of the 227-page accident report. Besides the documents, she had many photos of her father. She also had presents for everyone— homemade soaps with inset shells.

Judy handed them their copy of the report. The others glanced through it—too long to read at the table—while Judy summarized. She began with a factual account but grew emotional as she spoke about the negligence. The Brauners listened carefully, eager finally to learn how their father and husband died. It was hard, though, to absorb everything over a lunch, just from Judy's summary.

At one point Susan said to Judy, "You know there was a Supreme Court case?"

Judy did not. Unaware of the battle over state secrets, she'd focused only on the apparent negligence in the accident report. Susan's explanation stunned her.

When they rose from the table, Judy and Susan walked out to the parking lot together. There they discovered that they both drove Volvos: a kind of bond.

As soon as Judy returned home, she looked up *U.S. v. Reynolds* on the Internet. It wasn't easy to read all the legalese. Still, it seemed obvious to Judy that the Supreme Court justices were talking about an accident report full of national security secrets. No, she thought. That's not in the report. Not a word.

She was full of new questions. Once more she read through her pile of newspaper articles, court documents, and correspondence. She laid everything out in chronological order. She forced herself to digest the legalese. She tracked the case through the district court, the court of appeals, the Supreme Court. Clearly, the *Reynolds* decision concerned national security. No longer was Judy thinking about negligence. Now she was thinking, *What's going on here?*

So were the Brauners. After the Wellesley Inn lunch, Phyllis took home their copy of the report. She read through it carefully, despite being groggy from the medication she was taking every day. What she read upset her; Phyllis felt she'd been lied to.

When Susan read the report, she, too, felt disturbed. She didn't know what to do, but she did wonder about possible legal recourse—for their two mothers, and also for Patricia Reynolds. We need to explore the legal implications, Susan thought. We need to prepare a summary statement to send to lawyers. We need to track down Patricia Reynolds.

Judy agreed. Everyone also believed they should visit with the Franklin Institute engineer, Eugene Mechler. How to get started on all this?

Susan had an idea. On April 24, she wrote a letter addressed to the chairman of the law firm Drinker Biddle & Reath. "In the early 1950s," she began, "your firm represented three widows in the above landmark case. One of the surviving plaintiffs and several of the children of the victims in that case, of which I am one, are researching the case." She continued:

> We recently obtained a key government report/document that had long been classified concerning the crash that killed

our fathers. The report states definitively that the U.S. Air Force was at fault and specifies mechanical omissions that caused the accident. Charles Biddle of your firm suspected that the government's refusal to hand this report over to the court meant that there was negligence, but without it, it was never proved.

My immediate question is if your firm still has the complete file with the depositions of the military crew crash survivors. . . . We realize the file must be quite large, but is it possible to get just the depositions? Our records reflect the fact that these were paid for by our mothers as part of the eventual out-of-court settlement.

The second issue . . . concerns the viability of reopening the case based on the newly obtained information. The deaths of these men left their families to cope not only with tremendous grief but with years of financial hardship. Had they known the truth about the crash, they might not have accepted the settlement offered. . . .

I look forward to hearing from you.

Charles Biddle was twenty-eight years in his grave—actually, in his grotto at Andalusia—having died at age eighty-two. Yet his name remained on his law firm's door and his outsize reputation still inhabited the firm's corridors. Susan Brauner's letter drew the law firm's attention. No one could find the relevant files, though; the firm had moved twice and thrown out many aging documents. They could find only a file card showing that they indeed had handled the case.

On May 22, the chairman of Drinker Biddle & Reath, James M. Sweet, wrote back to Susan. "I'm sorry to report that we have not retained any records, documents, depositions or any other types of material from this case," he advised. "I suppose that that is not surprising, given the fact that the matter at this point is nearly 50 years old. Nonetheless, I was sorry that we were not able to find anything."

As for the viability of reopening the case, Sweet couldn't say. He referred Susan to a well-known law firm in New York that specializes in "aviation matters," Kriendler & Kriendler. "I'm sorry I couldn't be of more help . . ." he closed.

WITHOUT THE RECORDS FROM THE ORIGINAL CASE, JUDY AND THE Brauners were not certain how—or even whether—they should proceed. That August, Phyllis suffered a heart attack; she was in much pain, and her daughters fixed their attention on her. Judy turned back to the Internet, sending out email messages and conducting searches. One message went to her cousin Jeanie Perryman, the daughter of W. J. Perryman, who had helped Betty so much; Perryman himself had died in an airplane accident, a commercial flight in April 1977, from Huntsville to Atlanta, and Judy wanted to thank Jeanie for her father's many comforting letters. Another message went to her cousin David Pope, who, besides having memories of Al, could advise about the B-29 crash, since he was a licensed commercial pilot. Other messages went to a technician who knew about Shoran, to a radar operator who'd flown B-29 combat missions in Korea, to an attorney she'd met at the local cat shelter, and to a retired Montana prosecutor she'd met in her Internet game.

Judy also turned, once again, to Eugene Mechler, writing him with an update on all they'd learned since she'd contacted him in 1977. Mechler was eighty-seven now. "Dear Judy," he responded, his handwriting even more shaky than before, "I remember your interest in my report and Al Palya. Thanks for your letter and the info it contains." He continued:

> I often lie awake at night thinking over all kinds of problems. Not too many years ago, I was thinking about the B-29 crash. Here are some things I learned. We were flying at 22–23,000 feet. If you jump out at that altitude and pull the parachute ripcord, you will freeze to death before you get to a low enough altitude to survive. You must delay opening your parachute till at least 15,000 feet. And if you are a flatlander like most if not all the civilian passengers . . . [you] didn't know

enough to make a delayed jump. I'd say the military crew knew what to do. [But] I didn't know where the escape hatch in the bomb bay wall was located. . . . I wondered, how do I get out of this thing? . . . All my life God has watched over me and this was one more instance. . . .

In a second letter to Judy, after she and the Brauners had sent him the accident report, Mechler repeated that thought: "I realize that it was only God's looking after me that saved me from the accident. I calculate that if it had taken me 10 more seconds I would be dead."

Judy stared at those words: She couldn't help it, they irritated her. God saved Eugene Mechler? Then why not her father? Did God not watch over Al Palya?

Something else gnawed at her. *Why* did those top government officials lie? There hadn't been a lot of money involved, not for the United States government. The federal district judge had said, If you don't want to show the accident report, pay the money. The government could have just done that. Judy didn't understand why the secretary of the Air Force and the judge advocate general would instead lie to the Supreme Court. Okay, yes, they wanted to set a precedent, they wanted to control the documents. But there was a difference between the pilot making a mistake under stress and these guys sitting in a conference room, deciding—*deciding* to lie to establish a state secrets privilege. Often Judy had an image in her mind of that room, of those two high officers signing false affidavits. She wished she could sue those guys' estates. She didn't know where a person got the wherewithal to lie before the Supreme Court. *U.S. v. Reynolds* was based on a lie; Judy wanted to get that story out there.

Those who knew the story intimately were starting to disappear, though. In October 2000, after a long decline, Betty Palya Sacker died at eighty-eight. That December, after a difficult five months, so did Phyllis Brauner, at eighty-four. Soon word arrived that Eugene Mechler was gone. The passage of time pressed on Judy, Susan, and Cathy.

On September 11, 2001, they, with the rest of the country, experienced the terrorist attack on America. In the days that followed,

Cathy Brauner found herself thinking often about how this attack would affect so many families—just as the crash of a B-29 near Way-cross had affected families half a century before. She was a journalist, editor of her local newspaper, but she'd never even told people about the accident, the widows' lawsuit, the landmark *Reynolds* opinion. Now she felt a need to write about it.

On September 27, she published a personal column, titled "This Is What the Terrorists Really Took," in the Wellesley *Townsman*. It began: "One October afternoon in Pennsylvania, my mother suddenly turned to a colleague and said, 'Something's happened to Will.' Something had happened to him, and to all of us." Cathy's column continued, offering a summary of the crash and the immediate aftermath. She wrote of how "the sympathy cards stopped pouring in" after a time, of how "friends and neighbors went back to their everyday lives." She wrote of how her own family had to relocate, of how her mother "worked late into the night and on weekends, grading papers," of how classmates regarded her with disdain—*That's not very pretty*—for wearing "my hand-me-down dress." She told of the postcard arriving from Judy, of Judy meeting the Brauner family for lunch, of Judy's mother and her own mom dying soon after. What linked these mothers, Cathy wrote, "was the knowledge that when public tragedies occur . . . the rest of the world starts to forget, but there can be no forgetting for the families. The days of public mourning become decades of private pain." Children "grow up with idealized memories . . . never quite sure what they truly remember . . ." Families "live out their lives trying to fill a gap that can never really be filled. . . ."

Cathy then drew the link to the 9/11 terrorist attacks:

> The thousands of men and women who died two weeks ago lost their chance to make a fortune or a great scientific discovery. They will never go to important conferences or teach another class.
>
> But chances are, they wouldn't much care. This is what they would care about: Wiping away a baby's tears or taking photos as a daughter gets on the bus on the first day of school.

Cheering at soccer games or taking photos before the prom.
Dancing the first dance with a daughter at her wedding. Taking
a grandchild to the circus. Lifting a glass of champagne at a
golden-anniversary dinner. Holding a dying wife's hand as she
slips away. Cuddling the first great-grandchild.

A terrorist doesn't take one life. He steals the lives, hopes
and memories of generations.

She received, Cathy later reported, "lots of response to my article."

ON OCTOBER 26, PRESIDENT BUSH SIGNED THE U.S.A. PATRIOT ACT,
which broadly expanded the government's surveillance and investigative powers, the aim being to deter and punish terrorist acts worldwide. Five days later, Bush followed with a much-less-noticed but not
unrelated executive order: It extended to former presidents—and their
heirs—the unprecedented, autonomous power to assert the state secrets
privilege to bar disclosure of records generated during their tenure.
The order, Bush told reporters who asked him about it, "lays out a
procedure that . . . is fair for past Presidents." The process, he assured,
"will enable historians to do their job and at the same time protect state
secrets."

CHAPTER 24

WAYCROSS

January–July '02

As 2001 DREW TO AN END, JUDY PONDERED HOW TO CLOSE the year. She and her husband, John, had spent more than thirty New Year's Eves with another couple. This year, though, their friends were traveling to Orlando for the holidays.

Judy had an idea: Why don't we go with you?

Both families set out for Florida the week after Christmas. Judy ended up driving with her friend Janet Peek while the others flew—Judy did not particularly like flying. Studying the route, it occurred to her that their path would take them close to where her father died. On impulse, Judy asked Janet, "On the way back, can we stop at Waycross?"

They stayed in Florida for almost a month. The notion of visiting Waycross continued to tug at Judy. She'd brought an old news story about the site of the B-29 crash—the Zachry farm. Now, roaming the Internet on her laptop, she looked up the Zachrys of Waycross. She found three. She called Robert Bernard Zachry III. She explained who she was and why she was inquiring about a long-ago B-29 crash. Did he recall the accident?

"Well, ma'am . . ." Bernard Zachry had been the six-year-old boy who saw the plane fall. Now sixty, he sounded so nice. "Oh yes, I saw it. I was on the school playground that day. Part of the plane was falling right nearby. My mom came to get me. We'd tied up a little girl to a tree . . . I'm afraid we just left her tied up there."

Next Judy called Bernard's younger brother, Michael, who had been four that day—the one with his father in the farm shed. He remembered running to the house, crying, thinking his dad had died in the explosion.

At Michael's urging, Judy also called their youngest sister, Millie, who had not yet been born when the B-29 fell. She still lived on part of the family's property, so would be her host if Judy came.

If she came? By then, Judy *had* to come. They fixed on Saturday, January 18, and arranged to meet for lunch at an Applebee's in the center of Waycross. Judy drove up from Orlando with Janet that day. Getting to Waycross, it turned out, required more than a brief detour. Located in southeastern Georgia, at the tip of the Okefenokee National Wildlife Refuge, the town was not close to a major interstate highway or city. Savannah was 110 miles to the northeast, Jacksonville seventy-eight miles to the southeast. After leaving I-95, Judy and Janet traveled west on narrow Route 82 for a good hour before arriving in Waycross.

Incorporated in 1874, after extended conflict with the Creeks, Cherokees, Choctaw, and Chickasaws, Waycross for many years had remained something of a frontier community, a place where a man might get shot dead over a disputed paycheck or the loan of a mule. As late as 1945, a swampland farmer named Oliver Thrift had turned his shotgun on two United States Rangers assigned to protect wild animals. "I was sore at the Government," he explained, "because the Government protected the bears and the bears killed my cattle."

Named for the several railroad lines that met there, Waycross for a while had held the promise of continued growth. In his heyday, Bernard Zachry's granddaddy owned, besides his furniture store, eighty-seven rental houses—homes he bought out in the direction he thought the railroad would be expanding. That expansion didn't come, though. At the time of the B-29 crash, the town's population stood at 22,000; on the day Judy drove into Waycross, the city had 15,000 residents.

Judy and Janet found the Zachrys waiting at Applebee's—all fifteen of them. The whole clan had turned out, from the youngest grandkids to Bernard and Michael's father, Robert, who was nearly ninety. These were warm and easy people to talk to, the men with tanned, lined faces, the women full of bustle. Judy brought out photos and a copy of the accident report, which intrigued them. They had never known anything about the plane's mission or why it crashed; they'd known only that a bunch of scientists were on board. Robert Zachry gave Judy an aerial photo of his farm at the time of the accident, a gift from the family. On it, Bernard drew where the plane's parts had landed. By the time lunch was over, they were all just about crying.

Then Bernard's sister, Millie, took Judy and Janet out to the farm. What in 1948 had been open grazing pastures was now a thickly wooded pine tree farm. Realizing the situation needed to be handled slowly, Millie offered her visitors a golf-cart tour of their land. They stopped at Millie's house for refreshments. Only after that did they climb back on the golf cart and head to the area where the B-29 fell to earth. When they arrived, Judy asked to be alone.

SHE STOOD AT THE EDGE OF THE 438,000-ACRE OKEFENOKEE SWAMP, a shallow, peat-filled wetland straddling the Georgia-Florida border that provided a rich haven for alligators and birds, among them herons, egrets, ibises, cranes, and bitterns. Ages ago, geologists believed, the swamp had been part of the ocean. Now it was a vast labyrinth of shrubs, grasses, reeds, lakes, islands, and moss-draped cypress, all proliferating in soft mulch—*Okefenokke* is an Indian name meaning "trembling earth." Not long before the B-29 crash, the Waycross Chamber of Commerce opened a chunk of the swamp to tourists as a park, complete with souvenir shops, exhibits, long boardwalks, and an observation tower. Still, on the day Judy arrived in Waycross, most of the swamp remained protected.

Turning away from the golf cart, away from Millie and Janet, Judy plunged into the forest. High branches offered a canopy. She did not venture too far, choosing instead to sit down on a tree stump and look around. Moss and vines and trunks and branches. This was a marshy, messy place.

Okay, Judy thought, something big should happen. What's it going to be?

On her mind just then was how nice the Zachry family had been to her. To have a stranger on their farm, sitting out here, her father dead more than fifty years. She had thought maybe they wouldn't care, would just say, "It happened over there." Instead—fifteen Zachrys! Judy felt overwhelmed by the family's warmth.

Sitting on the stump, she looked up at the towering trees. Through their branches she realized she could see the sky. She began to think of her father. Up there, then falling.

It came not as a bolt or an epiphany, only a sense: Judy felt as if she'd found her father. He was no longer a mystery. Al Palya had finally become real to his daughter. She tried to imagine his thoughts in those last moments. *Who will take care of my family?* Yes, Judy just knew. He was thinking of them. He was thinking of her; he loved her. Here she was, fifty-three years old, and she hadn't gotten it until this moment.

Judy was not what she called a "really crying type of person," but her eyes filled with tears. *What should she do?* Behind her, out of sight, she could sense Millie and Janet waiting. Time passed, Judy still on the stump. She now grasped the enormity of the wrong. She recognized the impossibility of challenging a long-ago Supreme Court decision. Still, this wasn't right, this wasn't what she expected of her country.

Okay, then. *Give it a try.*

UPON RETURNING HOME TO MASSACHUSETTS, JUDY ON JANUARY 25 typed an email message to Susan Brauner: "I am back from Florida and guess what! I visited the crash site in Waycross. Let's get together for lunch soon and I can tell you all about it. Hate to hurry the experience in email. AND we can talk about the lawsuit. My brother tends to think this is not really a plane crash issue as much as a point of law issue . . . the government lying to the Supreme Court. . . . Why don't we just take it one small step at a time and see where things lead?"

Judy, Susan, and Cathy met at an Olive Garden and there started to devise their plans. They needed to find a lawyer to represent them. Which meant they needed to draft a letter soliciting one, a letter that would summarize facts and list resources. Susan took on part of the job, and soon came across correspondence from Charles Biddle that yielded new information: In Biddle's letter, Patricia Reynolds had become "Mrs. Donald Herring." Her married name—perhaps now they could find her.

In an email message to Judy on March 15, Susan reported on this, then turned to the matter of finding a lawyer. "I think a one page cover letter with summary of facts would be enough to get us started, i.e., for a firm to determine if it was worth our time or theirs. . . . I have attached a summary of our resources, and the most basic questions we have. I think once Judy is able to get the summary done, and provide any other firms we should send a letter to, we are ready to go." Reviewing the accident documents had deeply affected Susan: "Rereading all the information again," she added, "I was stuck all over with what a terrible injustice was done to our mothers. Well after the fact I hope we can rectify that to some degree."

Throughout much of April, the three women traded drafts, trying to calculate what would most interest litigators—hard facts or passionate words about justice. Hard facts won. Late that month, they were finally ready. Susan wondered "who should be lead in this." Judy nominated Susan—"since you are the oldest." So in early May, Susan mailed their letter to the two lawyers they thought most likely to respond with interest.

At the same time, they reached out to a potential new ally. In early April, Judy had followed up on Susan's discovery that Patricia Reynolds was now Mrs. Donald Herring. Searching the Internet for every Donald Herring in Indiana, she'd found twenty-five. Searching for Patricia Herring, she'd found twenty. For a start, Judy mailed out twenty postcards, ten to Donalds, ten to Patricias. *Hello. I am looking for Patricia Herring who was once Patricia Reynolds. Mr. Reynolds was killed in a B-29 in 1948 along with my dad. I have some interesting information for her.* . . . In the third week of April, Judy found in her mailbox a hand-written response, dated April 18.

"Dear Ms. Loether," it began. "I'm really impressed that you have been able to track me down; I'm sure your information was sketchy. I was married to Bob Reynolds, who was killed in the plane crash you mentioned. I'm sorry, but I wasn't acquainted with most of the personnel aboard and I don't remember your father. If you wish to contact me further, you can reach me in the following ways. . . ." Patricia had signed her note "Patricia (Reynolds) Herring."

AT HER HOME JUST OUTSIDE INDIANAPOLIS, IN THE DAYS AFTER SHE SENT that note, Patricia kept rereading Judy's postcard. *I am looking for . . . who was once Patricia Reynolds.* Pat then was seventy-four. Fifty-four years had passed since Bob Reynolds's death. She had lived a full life, had three grown children and much to be proud of—including art galleries featuring her watercolors. Yet in her house, Bob's ghost had always claimed a place.

After the crash, after the funeral, after she returned home to her mother in Indianapolis, Patricia did not keep in touch with Bob Reynolds's family. Nor did she ever meet, write, or talk to the other two widows. Her numbness wore off slowly, but it did wear off. She'd met Don Herring a year and a half after the crash, in early 1950. She married him six months later, on July 29, 1950.

Don worked in automotive machinery sales. They settled in Indianapolis and started a family, then moved to Michigan in 1960 when Don changed employers, living for thirty years in Birmingham, the prosperous Detroit suburb. Patricia became an active volunteer. She put out her three kids' grade school newsletters, she was the PTA vice president, she was the regional chair for the school millage campaign, she was the senior Girl Scout leader, she helped out at the Children's Hospital hematology department—*You get the idea*, she'd later say. Her main endeavor, though, was to organize a group of women to go into Detroit, after the riots of 1967, to help in the housing projects' new Head Start Program—"quite an eye-opener."

When her youngest child entered middle school, she decided to take her uneducated, inexperienced self out into the paid job market. She tried doing this through an employment agency—and ended up as manager of the agency. That eventually led to her being hired by a county school district to administer a federally funded program aimed at training unskilled people and getting them jobs. She won this position over candidates with advanced degrees because "a tough old chicken" in the district wanted her "nuts-and-bolts" experience. Patricia, the only agency manager without so much as a bachelor's degree, had a wonderful time surpassing all the other programs' achievement levels, but she knew she needed to get a degree.

So she enrolled at Wayne State, taking twelve credits each semester while working fifty hours a week on the job, raising three kids, and—"if he was lucky"—taking care of Don. This worked for five years, until her health failed; the day after Christmas 1971, she started spitting blood. She'd been a two-pack-a-day smoker for thirty years, but in the hospital, the doctors ruled out cancer. They operated on her lungs anyway, removing her lower left lobe despite an unclear diagnosis. Pat took a leave from the district and never returned; she went back to volunteer work, this time at a large hospital, where she eventually became the volunteer coordinator. With the children grown, Pat and Don relocated to Indianapolis in late 1989.

There Patricia, who'd been planning to attend art school when she met Bob Reynolds, became a painter. She worked primarily in watercolor, her subject matter studies of people, often based on photos taken by her son during his time with the Peace Corps in Thailand and Morocco. Despite the late start, she flourished, finding herself "juried" into Indiana's professional shows, where she sometimes won awards. Her work ended up being hung and sold by the Alliance Gallery at the Indianapolis Museum of Art. The Hoosier Salon Gallery also agreed to represent her, though Patricia couldn't get past thinking she was outclassed there.

PAT STARED AGAIN AT JUDY'S POSTCARD. *I AM LOOKING FOR . . . WHO was once Patricia Reynolds.* She felt more curious than excited. What is this about, she wondered. It couldn't be about the crash, the litigation. No, not all these years later. But if not, then what?

Pat had thought about what life with Bob might have been like. They were just kids, of course. Their exciting honeymoon existence inevitably would have become mundane. Still, she had to admit, Bob had been right by her side all this time. She'd talked to Bob in her mind over the years. As she grew older, she became conscious of the age gap. He remained twenty-four.

One morning the phone rang—it was Judy, responding to Patricia's note. They talked for an hour and a half, Judy as always passionate about the negligence. Patricia began to understand something of what this involved. Judy ended up giving her the address of Michael Stowe's website. Patricia ordered a copy of the accident report. It arrived in late May 2002.

As she started to read, Pat was returned to the past, this time facing things she hadn't in 1948. No longer could she block her feelings, no longer was this a dormant issue. Patricia wept. The horror of the missteps. She believed in fate, that we all had a destiny. In her mind, this crash was a prime example. Bob wasn't even supposed to be on that plane.

The factual description of the crash didn't bother her as much as learning about the government's refusal to provide information. Yet one element of the accident did stand out: She'd always thought the plane had instantly exploded. Now she realized that there'd been a period when Bob must have understood what was happening. She hadn't considered that before. She wondered what Bob had thought in those final moments.

All this was painful for Don as well as Patricia. Although involved and caring, he couldn't help but feel uncomfortable. They had to talk things out, discuss how it affected him, and they did. Pat filled in the gaps when he struggled in their conversations; she had no problem talking. In a way, she embraced the pain. Here was a chance to go through a process she had never really started. The crash had demonstrated to Pat how little control she had over her life. That was just too hard, because she, like most people, endured by making herself feel she could determine life. So back then she'd acted as if nothing had happened. Patricia felt a terrible guilt. She had kept nothing, not even the letters from Charles Biddle.

She reread the accident report twice, then started an exchange of emails with Judy, answering questions, posing some herself. She didn't know anything about the state secrets issue, only that something was wrong in this matter. The government's conduct shocked her, especially the sworn affidavits signed by the secretary of the Air Force and the judge advocate general.

Curiosity had evolved to pain, and now came another feeling: the urge for a settling of scores. A quest . . . Patricia considered that an exciting notion. On June 6, 2002, she called Judy. She had much interest in what Judy and the Brauners were doing, she said. She thought she just might want to be a part of it.

ALL THREE FAMILIES WERE TOGETHER ONCE AGAIN. THEY DID NOT, however, have a lawyer to represent them. It had been a month since Susan sent out letters to two attorneys, and she'd not heard back from either, despite leaving email and voice-mail messages. In early June, she wrote to a third law firm. Still, no one stepped forward to take their case.

Then, on Tuesday morning, July 2, while driving to work listening to Boston public radio station WBUR, Susan happened to hear reporter Fred Thys deliver a piece about a 9/11 widow, Ellen Mariani, of Deery, New Hampshire. Her husband, Neil, had been on United flight 175 out of Logan International. Mariani wanted to sue, it seemed, but the federal government had blocked her by invoking the state secrets privilege. On the WBUR broadcast, a law professor was talking about the *Reynolds* case.

Intrigued, Susan tried to track down the law professor. She also called Fred Thys, seeking contact information regarding the Mariani case, and in this conversation she gave Thys the outlines of their own experience. Later that day, he called back to say WBUR wanted to do a story on them. Susan emailed the news to Judy, Cathy, and Pat. "Reporter Fred Thys . . . plans to come to the Cape on Monday,

July 15. . . . I think this is an opportunity to 'get the story out' so a willing attorney might hear it. . . . I am hopeful that both Judy and Cathy can make it—we do owe this to our fathers."

Patricia messaged back from Indiana with her regrets and appreciation. "Obviously I can't make the interview, nor did you probably expect me to, I'm sure. I wish I had information to offer which might be helpful to you but I really have nothing. I was in such a fog at the time of the crash, had no family to support me . . . and was so naive and inexperienced. . . . The efforts which you young women are making to vindicate your fathers is admirable and I wish you well."

Cathy also couldn't attend, so it would be just Susan and Judy with the WBUR reporter. Throughout the early days of July, they exchanged emails in preparation. On July 15, Judy rose early to make the two-hour drive down to Susan's home on Cape Cod. When Fred Thys arrived, the two women talked to him for an hour and a half. "We think we were able to answer all his questions," Susan reported to Pat later that day. "He did seem quite interested in the situation and we sent him along with several pounds of information to review. . . ."

Judy and Susan continued to provide Thys with materials, and he began his own research. One day, he sent them a link to a website about Charles Biddle. Judy, visiting the site, learned for the first time that Biddle had been a World War I flying ace. That impressed her—this was the man her mom had as a lawyer.

Judy next visited the website of Biddle's old law firm, Drinker Biddle & Reath. She just wanted to see what more she could learn about Charles Biddle. He'd been so brilliant before the Supreme Court, she felt, and had lost only because the government lied. If only he could know this, could know he was right.

A thought occurred to Judy: If they couldn't give their case to Charles Biddle, they could give it to his law firm. Maybe to the firm's government-relations specialist, Gregg Melinson—Judy saw his name listed on the website. They needed to move fast, while there was all this talk about the *Reynolds* case being linked to 9/11. They should try, at least. If Charles Biddle's old law firm didn't want the case, if they thought it couldn't be done, she'd believe them. That would be the end.

Judy saw, at the bottom of the firm's home page, a place to type out email messages. It was July 18, 2002. She began to write.

> Dear Mr. Melinson, 50 years ago Charles Biddle, of your firm, successfully represented my mother and two other widows in the above case that was then appealed by the government to the U.S. Supreme Court. The decision was reversed by the Supreme Court in what was to be a landmark decision. As a result, the widows settled and received a fraction of the mathematical "value" the district court had determined the lives of their husbands to be worth. The disputed document that the government worked so hard to hide has recently come to light, and shows no secrets at all, no threat to national security. What it shows is gross governmental negligence. U.S. v Reynolds has recently been the topic of some discussion since the 9/11 attacks and recent lawsuits that are demanding documents that the government deems secret. While the decision of the Supreme Court might have been a good one where secrets ARE involved . . . this landmark case was based on a cover up. . . . Mr. Melinson, we seek to right a wrong done to our mothers by the US Government. We have contacted your firm and you have kindly given us some names of other attorneys. But I can't help but think that if Mr. Biddle were still alive HE would want to right this injustice himself . . . [to] finish the case he started and so passionately tried. The firm with the name of Charles Biddle on it should be the firm that sees that justice is finally done in this case. I thank you for your time. . . .

At Drinker Biddle & Reath, in downtown Philadelphia, Gregg Melinson passed this message to Wilson M. Brown III, the chair of the firm's litigation department. In his corner office on the twenty-fifth floor of One Logan Square, Brown studied Judy's words. He recalled the earlier inquiry from Susan Brauner, he recalled vainly searching for the files, but Judy's message seemed to convey more concrete material about the concealment, not just the negligence. It also helped that Judy wrote on behalf of all the clients, that they'd come together. Brown, then fifty, was about to step down as the firm's litigation chair, so happened to be looking for a fresh legal challenge.

Drinker Biddle & Reath, as in Charles Biddle's time, mainly represented big corporations, asset managers, and investors, employing more than 450 lawyers in Philadelphia and regional offices across the country. Wilson Brown usually represented corporations in commercial disputes over contracts, trademarks, securities, and antitrust matters. His defense of insurance companies, often in cases involving coverage for environmental and toxic tort exposures, had won him particular recognition as a premier trial attorney. Here now was the chance for a different type of achievement: to find a remedy for an apparent wrong. Here also, he had to admit, was a chance to stand before the Supreme Court.

Most enticing of all, though, was the connection to Charlie Biddle. Wilson had not known Biddle, being a teenager when Biddle died. But he knew about the famous parties at Andalusia, the deadly mint juleps, the room lined with Biddle's combat medals. He knew also about Biddle's reputation as a trial lawyer—the warm human face, the guy with a tough-as-nails smile. In the end it all came down to Charlie Biddle. This was his case, a case he'd taken all the way to the Supreme Court. That's what hooked Wilson Brown.

The firm would, nevertheless, move slowly; they would not yet commit. They would need to see all the documents, the accident report and case records stored in the Supreme Court's archives. They would have to determine just when Judy Loether got the accident report—a statute of limitations applied. And they would need, of course, to review Fred Vinson's *U.S. v. Reynolds* opinion.

After reading that opinion, and seeing how much the accident report had been Vinson's focus, Brown wrote to Judy on July 25. "Thank you for your inquiry to my partner via our web site . . ." he began. "I am interested in following up with you about the Reynolds case. This was well before the time of most of us, but the past of this firm means a great deal to all of us who carry on its name, and we are intrigued with the cause you have outlined. Whether we can do something for you remains to be seen, but we'd very much like to explore that further at our expense."

Judy waited just one day before reporting to Pat and the Brauners. "Hold on to your hats!" she exclaimed in an email. "I was visiting the Drinker Biddle & Reath web site to see if I could learn more about Mr. Biddle. . . . I ended up sending an email to their government specialist on the spur of the moment. . . . Well, this is the reply!!! Woot Woot!!! I am going to send him a brief note tomorrow and get the accident report off to him ASAP. We must bone up on all of this so we are more fluent in the facts. . . . Frankly, I think they have responded to the Charles Biddle part of this more than the allure of the case itself . . . and this is good. When it boils right down, wouldn't Mr. Biddle want to do something if HE saw that accident report? Wouldn't he? I hope this law firm has that sense of responsibility to him."

PART FOUR

REVELATIONS

July 2002–September 2007

CHAPTER 25

ON THE SIDE OF RIGHT

July–November '02

ENCOURAGED BY THE POSITIVE RESPONSE FROM WILSON Brown, Judy on July 26 took the opportunity to pour out her feelings to this Philadelphia lawyer. She knew she was being "a bit lengthy and passionate," she later told Pat and the Brauners, "but that's me."

She thanked Brown for his reply. She regretted not keeping a copy of what she wrote to his law firm—"my note was rather spur of the moment. . . . I don't remember exactly what I said." She called Brown's attention to the fact that *U.S. v. Reynolds* just then was getting press attention related to the *Mariani* case. She promised to have the accident report, which "has everything in it Biddle thought he would find," sent directly to Wilson from "my source, M. Stowe of Millville, NJ." She offered to meet at a location of his choice—perhaps Susan Brauner's house on Cape Cod, where "you would be welcome to stay in her guest house if you would like an opportunity to visit this 'jewel' of Massachusetts."

In closing, Judy returned to the consequences of *Reynolds*, to the connection between their case and the government's numerous later uses of the state secrets privilege.

I might add this. . . . U.S. v Reynolds has come to be a landmark case that is used by the government when it claims that documents cannot be turned over to the courts because of national security. Yet this very case is now proven, in my mind, to be based on a lie that did injury to 3 widows and 5 little children. . . . It allowed the government an area of no checks and balances. How many times has the government used this decision, not to protect national security, but for its own purposes?

Judy, in signing her email message, explicitly said she spoke for all the survivors—not just the Brauner sisters but also Pat and her own brothers, Bill and Bob. Three days later, it occurred to Judy that she needed to confirm this claim officially. She needed to ask her brothers and Pat if they truly wanted to be involved.

Pat responded immediately. In messages to Susan and Judy, she expressed her deep appreciation and admiration for all they'd done—"your devotion to this cause would gratify your parents, I'm sure." Reading all the material and following the developments, she acknowledged, "has revived some of the pain of the past," but "that isn't bad. . . . I have been finally getting information I should have had 54 years ago." For that, she wanted to thank Susan and Judy. She also wanted them to know, "I have decided that it would be appropriate for me to be an active part of this project." The more public exposure to this case, the wider the spotlight on the government's conduct—"that alone makes this a worthy project."

Judy's brothers, Bill and Bob, also signed on, though they didn't want to assume active roles. Bill Palya allowed that he wouldn't have acted on his own, being "somewhat cynical," but thought his sister's effort "a good thing." The government had to fight fair, he believed. "If the government can go to the Supreme Court and lie, then it's all over. . . . The government must absolutely tell the truth or none of it matters."

The Brauners and Judy once again set about reviewing documents, assembling packets of information, and laying out time lines. On August 7, back from a vacation, Brown messaged Judy to acknowledge the latest materials she and Susan had sent. His law firm was still searching for other documents, he advised, and still waiting for the accident report from Michael Stowe. Once they had everything in hand, "we can talk."

NOTHING IN WILSON BROWN'S BACKGROUND OR UPBRINGING SUGGESTED that he would respond with a crusader's outrage. Like Charles Biddle, he was a solid member of the establishment. On his mother's side, his forebears had arrived in America from Scotland in the late eighteenth century. His father and grandfather had both been bankers. He'd grown up primarily in Richmond, Virginia, but had also spent some years in Winston-Salem and Charlotte, the family trailing after his father's successful career. He'd attended the University of North Carolina-Chapel Hill as a Morehead Scholar majoring in English and history, had graduated with highest honors, then had ended up in law school—the University of Virginia-Charlottesville—mainly because he wasn't sure what he wanted to do.

Lawyers weren't then the object of so many jokes. In fact, when Brown was growing up in the South, they were highly respected and well regarded, even those who came to clean things up. Brown enjoyed the opportunity the law seemed to offer, the chance to contribute, to engage in an intellectual exchange. He did well in law school, making the law review, and upon graduation, found himself drawn to Drinker Biddle & Reath. He liked the people at that firm, thought they were down to earth—a mix, but largely self-made folks. They offered a system where you could learn from a variety of people, rather than be tagged to one or two. He had the option right off of doing business law or litigation, and without hesitation chose litigation. He relished the endless diversity of challenges he faced in a courtroom.

At a meeting of DBR lawyers over an insurance-company defense matter, Brown happened to mention this unusual situation he might be taking on, an old Charlie Biddle case. A junior associate named Jeff Almeida came up to Brown after the meeting. He was thirty and had been at the firm for six years, coming out of William & Mary Law School in Williamsburg, Virginia, and Trinity College in Hartford, Connecticut, where he majored in history. He'd attended at least one hundred mandatory meetings on insurance litigation by then. He had not found many of them to be terribly exciting. The case Wilson had mentioned sounded different. It promised to involve lots of constitutional issues, which interested Almeida. He knew, in a big firm like DBR, that he had to jump if he wanted in on a case.

I'd like to volunteer for this Biddle case, he told Brown. I'd like to help you.

In early September, the accident report from Stowe finally arrived. Almeida read through it first. As he turned the pages, he kept looking for military secrets. He reread the document, but still could see no secrets. He called Brown. "Hey, Wilson," he said. "I've read this report. There's nothing in there."

At summer's end, while waiting for a decision from Drinker Biddle & Reath, Judy, Pat, and the Brauner sisters decided they should get together—their first gathering as a full group and the first chance for the others to see Pat in person. Plans were made to meet at the Isabella Stuart Gardiner Museum in Boston, an exquisite hundred-year-old institution housed in a fifteenth-century Venetian-style palace where three stories of galleries surround a flower-filled courtyard. "It will be nice to greet all of you in October," Judy messaged everyone on September 13. She wanted Pat to bring a picture of Bob, since "we have had this tradition of having their pictures with us when we get together." Susan, too, should bring photos; Judy would have some of her mom.

As far as the case and DBR's plans, "I guess they are having a tough time deciding what to do," Judy advised the others. "Seems to me that it's not a clearly winnable case with complicated law issues. I was thinking how glad I am that we have Mr. Biddle's words in those letters, and that DBR has seen them. I'll bet they feel an obligation to him, to finish what he tried to do. . . . I wonder if this is the first glimpse many of them have had into who Mr. Biddle was. . . ."

The gathering in Boston did not take place as planned. Pat and her husband, Don, made the long drive to Boston early, to visit art exhibits. One night there, as they were leaving the historic, dimly lit

ON THE SIDE OF RIGHT

Durgin-Park restaurant at the Faneuil Hall marketplace, Pat slipped on the top step of a long, steep stairway. She fell head over heels, the entire length. Prostrate on the landing below, she found she couldn't move, at least for the moment. Her neck and hip hurt badly. An ambulance rushed her to the Mass General emergency room, where they filled her with painkillers.

So instead of a private museum, Pat first met Judy and Susan in the lobby of her hotel, the Boston Marriott, after returning from the hospital. At least Pat could move by then. Sitting on a lobby sofa, she looked strikingly elegant to Judy, who had been expecting more of a grandmotherly type. Don fussed over Pat, clearly attentive and concerned, but Pat displayed little discomfort, despite a painful leg. They all made the best of the situation, even joking that Pat "sure would remember *fall* in Boston." They had brought Pat gifts and family photos to share. Pat found Susan to be a ladylike, sociable woman. What most stood out about Judy was her focus and intensity. Pat appreciated the chance to meet them both. The next day Don drove her home, she stretched out in the back of the car.

AT DRINKER BIDDLE & REATH, BROWN AND ALMEIDA WERE NOW wading through the full file on the *Reynolds* case. They restudied the accident report. They reviewed the "record of case," pulled from the Supreme Court's archives. They looked for documents at the district court, including transcripts of hearings and judges' rulings. They searched for original copies of the affidavits, not retyped versions—they wanted to see Finletter's and Harmon's signatures. They roamed the Internet, seeking websites about B-29s. They began to build a chronology of what was going on in the courts, what was known about the accident. They began to weigh their legal strategy, what options they had, what approaches they might take, what kind of petitions they might file.

Brown considered the challenge that taking on *U.S. v. Reynolds* posed. It was one thing to spot a wrong, but how on earth do you convince the U.S. Supreme Court—so wedded to the legal notion of finality—to *fix* a wrong? More to the point, how do you convince the

Court to fix its own fifty-year-old error? They had the elapsed time to deal with, plus a number of legal hurdles. There was nobody alive but Pat Herring to tell the story. There were no whistle-blowing witnesses or documents. They had only a factual record limited to the accident report, plus their own understanding of the times and circumstances. What's more, Drinker Biddle & Reath had no guarantee of getting compensated; they'd have to take this case on a contingency basis, collecting a percentage of any recovery, which was not the norm at a corporate defense firm accustomed to clients with deep pockets.

Still, Brown felt excited. The history, the interesting set of facts, the intriguing law, Charlie Biddle's connection—here was that chance to do what he'd always wanted, that chance to be on the side of right. He had to laugh at the notion; okay, okay, cases *always* involved right versus wrong, the lawyers just argued over who was right. But this was different. Here they had moral clarity. Here he'd be the one with the sword, leading the charge.

Brown couldn't believe that the solicitor general's representative had stood flat-footed before the Supreme Court, saying the accident report contained national military secrets. The solicitor general's job was to represent the government before the Court. He only had his integrity—on that basis the justices listened to and trusted him. If he lost his credibility, he lost everything. How could he risk that?

Brown kept thinking about the hearing before Judge William Kirkpatrick in August 1950. That was the key, the heart of this whole deal. Kirkpatrick had ordered the government to produce the reports, and the government first responded by saying it had a "housekeeping" privilege to withhold results of an internal investigation. Only after Kirkpatrick said they didn't have that privilege—that such a privilege didn't exist—did the government, months later, suddenly claim a state secrets privilege. Brown could well imagine what Kirkpatrick thought. No way did this judge take those two affidavits by Thomas Finletter and Reginald Harmon at face value. He *knew* what was going on.

Those affidavits—Brown looked at them again. They were so carefully crafted, obviously worded to avoid a perjury rap. "The airplane likewise carried confidential equipment on board and any disclosure of its mission or information concerning its operation or performance would be prejudicial to this Department and would not be in the public interest." Nothing there directly said the accident report contained secrets. Finletter probably just signed it, a piece of paper put before him. But Harmon would have known; he or his staff must have orchestrated this. They had nothing to lose, really. If the false affidavits convinced Kirkpatrick to back down, the Air Force could continue its cover-up. If Kirkpatrick didn't back down, they'd just have to pay the damages they'd owe anyway once the documents came to light. Better yet, they'd have the chance to appeal, to test the state secrets privilege before higher courts at a time of deep concern over national security.

Brown had no doubt that's how this case played out. That's precisely how most such test cases developed. This one involved $255,000, substantial money back then. But in the grand scheme of things, a federal judge's power to order production of documents mattered much more. Evolution, indeed. This case had escalated.

Brown didn't have a precise strategy yet, didn't know exactly how they'd seek relief. But he knew now that he wanted to take this case. He'd be thrilled to seek justice for these families—and for Charlie Biddle. He couldn't say no.

In early November, Brown arranged to hold a phone conference with Judy, Pat, and the Brauner sisters. On Friday, November 8, with everyone on the line, he and Almeida introduced themselves and briefly talked about the firm. In Cape Cod, Susan took notes, as did Pat in Indianapolis. In Massachusetts, Judy wondered what these lawyers meant to do.

A moment later, Brown told her: "We're going to take the case."

THE NEXT DAY, PAT SAT DOWN TO WRITE AN EMAIL TO JUDY AND Susan. She typed "We're on our way" for her subject line. She continued: "Hello, you two. Wow! Susan, if I'd known we had a scribe in our midst on Friday I wouldn't have been so concerned about my own note-taking! . . . Thanks so much for your work. . . . Judy, did you ever dream, when you started your search almost three years ago, that it would lead along such a path? Once again, I want to commend you on the perseverance and passion you have demonstrated in getting this investigation going. I keep a mental list of my ten most-admired women . . . and I've recently added you to the group. . . . I'm sure the next few months are going to be interesting ones for us and we'll have many emails flying (or whatever they do). Fond wishes to you both, Pat."

CHAPTER 26

ROUTES OF RELIEF

November '02–March '03

IN LAWYERS' PARLANCE, WHAT WILSON BROWN NOW HAD TO find were "potential routes of relief." The most obvious would be through the U.S. District Court in Philadelphia where the *Reynolds* case began before Judge Kirkpatrick. Yet Brown and Almeida faced a puzzle: What was there to remedy in District Court? Despite the government lawyers' best efforts, Kirkpatrick hadn't been defrauded, nor had Judge Maris and the Third Circuit Court of Appeals. Kirkpatrick and Maris had rejected the government's claims.

The fraud had succeeded only before the Supreme Court. Could they possibly seek direct relief there? Could they ask the justices to remedy a fraud that had been committed on the Supreme Court itself? That would be tricky, for despite the Court's extensive power, it had limited original jurisdiction in a case. Normally, the justices only considered, on appeal, rulings from lower courts. So somehow, Brown had to find a way to tie the B-29 case into the Supreme Court's jurisdiction.

He could file a piece of paper in the original *Reynolds* litigation, seeking to reopen it. Or he could file a paper in a new case, attacking the 1953 judgment and suggesting Supreme Court jurisdiction. Talking it over, Brown and Almeida concluded that it would be best—since the case was over, judgments entered and settled—to file a paper to the Supreme Court, saying, *Look, this case was based on fraud; we don't want to reopen it but we want a fair, just, "equitable" remedy.* At the same time, they would offer the Court the first option as well: They would invite the Court, if it chose, to treat their petition as a motion for relief filed in the *Reynolds* case itself.

To go directly before the Supreme Court, however, they would need to file not just any piece of paper. They would need to file a petition for an extraordinary writ (court order)—one within the justices' authority because they sat, in a sense, as an extension of the Vinson Court that considered the original 1953 appeal.

The question, then, would be: What sort of writ?

When Supreme Court jurisdiction is unclear, Brown had learned at law school, you should consider the All Writs Act, which gives federal courts the power to use all recognized writs necessary to bring about a just remedy. They'd spent a whole evening in class discussing a particular case where the Supreme Court had intervened in a state matter involving a bribed trial judge. The justices had just reached in and ruled without oral argument. In class, they'd talked about the exceptional powers the Court had to address wrongs with writs.

From a shelf in his office, Brown pulled his copy of *Black's Law Dictionary*, a seldom-used present he'd received when he started law school. He and Almeida began to go through the thick volume, reading about the ancient writs that might apply—writs designed to correct a ruling, writs designed to allow judges to get past the finality of a court decision. In time, one caught Brown's eye: a writ of error *coram nobis*. He knew something about this from law school but read now in Black's to refresh his memory.

A petition for a writ of *coram nobis,* by calling belated attention of the court to facts that were not available in the original trial, essentially provided a means for a court to correct errors of fact made in proceedings "before us." The notion was to submit the plea to the court that had entered the original judgment—not just to help the particular petitioner, but also, as the Supreme Court put it in one case, "to maintain public confidence in the administration of justice."

This was an uncommon remedy—to continue litigation after final judgment and all levels of review. Lawyers rarely used it; indeed, few of the ancient writs really figured in the lives of judges anymore. That's because Rule 60 in the Federal Rules of Civil Procedure, adopted in 1938, abolished such writs in civil lawsuits, providing other ways to correct mistakes and attack judgments. As Brown understood it, though, Rule 60 applied only to civil proceedings in district courts, not in appellate courts or the Supreme Court. *Coram nobis*, he believed, lived on in all criminal cases and in appellate-level civil cases.

"Oh yeah," Brown said to Almeida. "This is it."

There had been, he came to realize, two *coram nobis* cases in the 1980s relevant to the B-29 case—*Hirabayashi v. United States* and *Korematsu v. United States*. They offered obvious parallels: Both derived from original cases involving abject judicial deference to the military and the executive branch; both involved documents discovered forty years later that revealed a shocking fraud on the court by the government.

Brown was quite familiar with the original cases, for the *Hirabayashi* and *Korematsu* rulings are infamous in judicial history. In these cases, in 1943 and 1944, the Supreme Court upheld convictions of men of Japanese descent who'd been prosecuted for violating curfew and relocation orders on the West Coast during World War II. In issuing these orders restricting movements by Japanese-Americans, Lieutenant General John L. DeWitt, head of the Western Defense Command, had claimed "military necessity." Such a claim must be honored, the Supreme Court ruled. "We cannot reject as unfounded the judgment of the military authorities," Justice Hugo Black wrote in his December 1944 *Korematsu* majority opinion—an opinion considered a nadir for both the Court and Black. Then, in 1981, lawyer and legal historian Peter Irons discovered that the government had withheld critical documents from the *Korematsu* Court, documents revealing that Justice Department lawyers had regretted DeWitt's racist attitudes and doubted his claims of "military necessity." In 1982, another researcher, Aiko Yoshinaga, who had been interned at Manzanar just out of high school, found an original, unedited copy of DeWitt's report explaining the basis for his orders.

Here DeWitt didn't claim "military necessity" at all; instead, he declared that because of traits "peculiar to citizens of Japanese ancestry," it would be impossible to separate the loyal from the disloyal.

In January 1983, based on these discoveries, both Fred Korematsu and Gordon Hirabayashi sought writs of error *coram nobis* to vacate their convictions. That November, U.S. District Judge Marilyn Hall Patel granted Korematsu's *coram nobis* petition, writing in her opinion, "[*Korematsu*] stands as a caution that in times of distress the shield of military necessity and national security must not be used to protect governmental actions from close scrutiny and accountability." In February 1986, U.S. District Judge Donald S. Vorhees granted Hirabayashi's *coram nobis* petition and the next September the U.S. Ninth Circuit Court of Appeals affirmed.

Despite these precedents, Brown knew relying on *coram nobis* would be a long shot. *Hirabayashi* and *Korematsu* were criminal cases, which might not apply to civil litigation. It would, at any rate, be hard to overcome the Supreme Court's strong preference for finality. Perhaps equally important, it would be hard to overcome the context of the times.

Brown understood that he, in 2002, faced as troubled a public arena as Charles Biddle did fifty years earlier. The 9/11 terrorist attacks, the mounting fears about international terrorism, the U.S.A. Patriot Act, John Ashcroft's absolutism, Dick Cheney's secrecy, the Bush administration's due-process denials involving "enemy combatants"—all were echoes of the Cold War era when the Supreme Court had decided *Reynolds.* Yet Fred Korematsu and Gordon Hirabayashi had prevailed with *coram nobis* petitions, and maybe they could, too. Discovering the B-29 accident report, after all, was analogous to finding General DeWitt's original statement.

At the least, this type of writ would be an effective way to get the Supreme Court's attention, and that's just what Brown wanted to do—fully engage the Court. This will be our path, he decided. We'll petition for a writ of error *coram nobis.*

WHAT, THEN, WOULD BE THE REMEDY THEY SOUGHT, WHAT RELIEF? Could they possibly ask the Supreme Court to overturn *U.S. v. Reyn-*

olds, to set aside a landmark rule of deference on national security matters? No, that wouldn't help Brown's clients, that wasn't what they had hired him to do. Besides, it wouldn't work—they wouldn't even get through the courtroom door.

A writ of error *coram nobis* called for the correcting of a mistake. That meant they wouldn't be asking to retry the case, either. Rather, they'd be asking the Court to set aside the reduced judgment reached in the settlement between the government and the three widows. They'd be asking the Court to make the widows "whole"—to grant them the balance of the original judgment they didn't get, $55,000 (equivalent to $415,281 in current dollars), plus compounded interest, an estimated $1.14 million in all. Only that goal was within their immediate reach. Their civil action's broader implications would depend on how the families' story affected judges and politicians in the future.

So the narrative here was important. They needed to tell a compelling tale in their opening Preliminary Statement, not just make a legal argument. For this, Brown turned to Jeff Almeida.

Working on the case had been a kick for Almeida. Half of each day he'd had to focus on the firm's insurance defense work, but during the other half, he was immersing himself in state secrets doctrine, Cold War history, and B-29 lore. Now he had a chance to write. Almeida sat before his computer and began.

> *Three widows stood before this court in 1952. Their husbands had died in the crash of an Air Force plane. The lower courts had awarded them compensation. But the United States was bent on overturning their judgments, and—to accomplish this—it committed a fraud not only upon the widows but upon this Court. As a result, what the widows had won was lost. One of the widows and the children of the other two now ask the Court to right this wrong.*
>
> *At the heart of the case is a set of reports the Air Force prepared on the accident that killed the widows' husbands. The Air Force refused to produce these reports, even to the district judge for in camera review. The district court, therefore, ruled for the widows on liability, determined damages, and entered judgment. The Court of Appeals affirmed.*

Undeterred, the United States took the case to this Court and advanced a sweeping claim of executive privilege, contending that the reports contained "military secrets" so sensitive not even the district court could see them. It pointed to affidavits of two of the highest-ranking men in the Air Force in support of this plea. This Court took the government at its word, and reversed.

But, it turns out the Air Force's affidavits were false. The Air Force recently declassified the accident reports. They include nothing approaching a "military secret." Indeed, they are no more than accounts of a flight that, due to the Air Force's negligence, went tragically awry. In telling the Court otherwise, the Air Force lied. In reliance upon that lie, the Court deprived the widows of their judgments. It is for this Court, through issuance of a writ of error coram nobis and in exercise of its inherent power to remedy fraud, to put things right. . . .

Brown loved Jeff's opening passage. Almeida's words, he was sure, would grab the judges. This fleshed things out, made plain why they thought the government had done the widows wrong.

With a preliminary statement in hand, Brown and Almeida next began to lay out the facts and arguments of their petition. Let's get in all we need, Brown urged, but no more. Unlike Charles Biddle, they did not have to speculate; they could declare. *It was in a motion for a rehearing that the United States first invoked "state secrets" protections. . . . Contrary to the Air Force's sworn testimony, the accident reports and witness statements contain no military or national security secrets. . . . The Air Force presumably sought to protect these materials to avoid the embarrassment and public scrutiny their production would have generated. . . .* United States v. Reynolds *stands exposed as a classic "fraud on the court," one that is most remarkable because it succeeded in tainting a decision of our nation's highest tribunal. . . .*

Brown and Almeida labored over their conclusion. Although tempting, they couldn't appear here to be seeking to overturn *U.S. v. Reynolds*. Brown chose his words carefully.

Some may find in this petition reason to doubt the wisdom of this Court's holding in U. S. v. Reynolds. *Others will see this "back*

*story" as merely a sad footnote that takes nothing away from the logic of
the Court's 1953 decision. The merits of the* Reynolds *holding—and
its impact on present-day controversies—present interesting and no doubt
important questions. But petitioners do not come here to raise any of
them. Whether the legal principles established in* Reynolds *are right or
wrong is for another day and another case.*

*For petitioners, the only issue this Court must confront today is
whether it will tolerate a fraud—a fraud that struck at the integrity of the
Court's decision-making process and that cheated three struggling widows
and their children out of that which was rightly theirs. Petitioners pray
that it will not.*

At last they had a draft. Brown and Almeida shared it with their
clients in mid-February 2003. In response, Judy, apologizing for her
"emotional reactions," wrote Almeida to say how "deeply moved" she
was to read it, "to see our case so thoughtfully and cogently laid out."
This case, she continued, "is about all the things human beings are
passionate about, the people we love and our country. . . . In reading
this [petition], I felt you have rushed to our side . . . and drawn your
sword in our defense. . . ."

By the end of that February, Wilson Brown had in hand a final
version. He felt good about their chances of getting heard by the Supreme Court. He believed they had written as powerful an argument
as they could. They were ready to file.

Jeff Almeida placed a call to one of his law firm's most trustworthy clerks—Frances Bisicchia. Can you catch a train to Washington, he
asked. We'd like you to hand-deliver a petition directly to the Supreme
Court.

IN MASSACHUSETTS AND INDIANA, JUDY, PAT, AND THE BRAUNER SISTERS
steeled themselves. For weeks they had been preparing for the media
attention they suspected might be coming their way. "The more I
thought about possibly speaking to the national press . . . the more
concerned I became," Susan wrote to Cathy and Judy. "I wonder if the
two of you feel the same? My solution: Let's nominate Judy to be our

spokesperson. Certainly she would be articulate, and I suspect she would enjoy doing it. Instead of keeping a talking point card by the phone, we could keep Judy's number. What do you think? With anxiety, Susan."

Pat embraced this idea—Judy "would relish the role and do a super job"—but mainly she thought this was "an academic discussion in the long run as major media attention seems unlikely to me."

Susan agreed: "I would be mighty surprised if there is any reaction at all to the story, frankly."

With just hours to go, Pat wrote to Judy and the Brauners: "As we've all agreed, one of the major goals in this petition is to 'shine the light' on the government's misrepresentation to the Supreme Court and us in the past. The way that will be achieved for the general public . . . is through the media. However, I'm REALLY not comfortable in generating that information, as it would seem to me if this story has 'legs' it will run on its own. That doesn't mean, Judy, that it isn't perfectly appropriate for YOU to put out a news release. . . . As I told Wilson . . . this is totally YOUR story, and I like treating it as such. . . . Whatever you want to say—or not say—will be fine. On my part, I'm fine with responding to any inquiries I get—I just don't choose to open the discussion myself. I STILL wonder if we're not overblowing the 'breaking news' value of the story? We'll be finding out soon, now. Let's all take a few deep breaths."

Pat's approach seemed reasonable to Judy—"everyone has their own comfort level"—but for her part, Judy was about to alert the local *Courier Post* in New Jersey and send off a package to the *Waycross Journal Herald* in Georgia. "Here we go!" she exclaimed.

In Philadelphia early the next morning, Wednesday, February 26, Fran Bisicchia hailed a taxicab from DBR's downtown office and made it to the Thirtieth Street train station with only moments to spare. By noon, a box of *coram nobis* petitions sat inside the guard shack just off the far north side of the U.S. Supreme Court building. By early afternoon, the plea rested on a counter in the Court clerk's office.

Now came time to wait—but not, as it turned out, for long.

The only journalist who knew about their petition was the Boston radio reporter Fred Thys, who the previous August had broadcast a pair of stories about their quest. The day after Fran's train trip, he broadcast another report, titled "A Case to Shake the Foundation of National Security Law." In Indianapolis, Pat thought it "a good thing" that Thys got her age right this time, joking that otherwise "I'd get after him with my cane!!" Then, writing to Judy and the Brauners, she turned more serious: "So far I've had no contact from reporters. Will pass the word when and if. . . . As time has passed I have had more of an emotional reaction to our entire process than I would have expected. For fifty years I have accepted the loss of Bob as inevitable destiny, but unbelievably, after all these years, I find myself struggling with it again."

Judy shared that feeling. "I had never grieved for my father," she wrote Pat and Susan. "While it has been difficult to do so, I guess I feel that I am glad that I had the opportunity. . . . It was . . . like . . . for the first time realizing what he meant to my mother, my brothers and me, and how much I had missed him."

By the next day, Friday, February 28, a few reporters had started to call, and one—David B. Caruso of the Associated Press—filed a report. That evening, Judy composed a message to the editors of the *Waycross Journal-Herald*. "You will shortly be getting a packet of information that has at its core the crash of a B-29 bomber just outside Waycross in which my father and eight other men were killed . . ." she began. "I specifically asked that your newspaper get this package because Waycross is at the heart of the story, and I know many of the people of Waycross remember that day. . . . As a side note, it was when I was in Waycross, at the crash site, that I decided to try to sue the government. . . . My country, my America had not done the right thing. I asked my father what to do and he told me to give it a try."

Pat wept when she read Judy's words to the Waycross editors. "You are our spokesperson for good reason (other than the obvious fact it's your story)," Pat messaged her the next day, Saturday, March 1. "Your eloquence and heartfelt feelings convey it all. I'm proud to be your friend."

That same day, Pat felt moved to write her own words about Bob Reynolds. "I've begun to feel very guilty for not presenting Bob's story before," she began, in an email sent to everyone involved in their case. She continued:

> I've felt that it was your story, not mine, but as you said, Judy, the whole case is about YOUR FATHERS AND BOB, not us.
>
> Also, because I felt that the story was more about family tragedy and injustice I have said little about Bob's life and where he fitted into the picture, but I've begun to realize that, by saying nothing, I have been dishonoring his memory.
>
> I don't care if the *Indianapolis Star* or any other local paper wants to talk to me. It's just that this area wouldn't qualify as home territory for Bob. He grew up in a small town near Springfield, Mass., and came to Indiana to attend Purdue University. The job with RCA was his right after graduation and it was shortly after that when we met, fell madly in love and quickly married.
>
> October 6, 1948, ended [our] dream. . . . Although this was not the loss of a father and didn't result in a widow's struggles for her family, it WAS the tragedy of unfulfilled promise. We can only speculate what contributions he might have made to his world. As a young man of musical and creative talent, compassion, intelligence and great humor, we might have expected much.
>
> I hope this gives Bob a little more dimension than my silence has.
>
> —Pat

"Hug . . ." Judy messaged back. "Each of us is traveling this path now."

As Judy and Pat exchanged these messages on Saturday, the box of *coram nobis* petitions was on its way back to Drinker Biddle & Reath, shipped by Clayton Higgins, the junior Court clerk who believed "there are no provisions in the rules of this Court to allow you to file such a document." The box had not yet arrived at DBR, though, so no one knew the Court had already rejected the petition. Not the lawyers, not the clients—and not the news media.

On Sunday, March 2, Fred Thys took his radio report national, broadcasting a new version for NPR's *All Things Considered*. On Monday, more reporters scrambled, some inquiring at the Supreme Court. But by then, of course, the Court no longer had the box of petitions, no longer had the case in any form. Clayton Higgins felt obliged to call Drinker Biddle & Reath.

Brown and Almeida reeled when they heard the news. They'd felt so confident about their petition; they'd felt the justices would grant not only a hearing but also relief. It had never occurred to them that they would not even get through the door.

Arguing on the phone with Higgins that Monday, Almeida invoked the Court's Rule 20, relating to petitions for extraordinary relief. He cited binding Supreme Court cases and other statutory rules. He talked about the All Writs Act. He insisted that the Court clerk did not have authority to send back their petition. That was Almeida's main theme, which he hammered on in three different conversations with Higgins: The clerk's office had exceeded its authority. It was up to the nine justices, not the clerk, to decide whether the Court had jurisdiction.

Higgins finally relented, saying he'd talk to others in the clerk's office. The next morning, Tuesday, March 4, Almeida received a phone call from the more senior chief deputy clerk of the Court, Christopher Vasil. In his twenty-three years there, Vasil also had never seen a *coram nobis* petition. Like Higgins, he did not believe such petitions were allowed. Yet he was willing to let the justices decide: He advised Almeida to resend his plea with a covering "motion to file a petition for writ of error *coram nobis*."

That's definitely improper, Almeida countered. It adds a hurdle that isn't required. He didn't push his argument, though—they had to maintain cordial relations with the Court clerks. Immediately after talking to Vasil, he composed the requested motion. *The writ of error* coram nobis *has come before this Court infrequently. When it has, however, the Court has uniformly upheld its availability. . . . Petitioners believe the writ of error* coram nobis *is perfectly suited to the challenges of this case. . . . A Petition for a Writ of Error* Coram Nobis *is surely a very rare occurrence in the life of the Supreme Court Clerk's Office. . . . But, with all due respect, the Petition submitted to the Clerk last week comports with the Court's rules, and the Clerk's Office ought not to have declined to accept it. . . . For the Clerk's Office,* at the filing stage, *to deny petitioners an opportunity to come before the Court on the serious issues their Petition presents would be the ultimate injustice in the sad story that is* United States v. Reynolds.

On that Tuesday, with this motion attached to the petition, Fran Bisicchia once again hailed a cab to the Thirtieth Street Station in Philadelphia, once again rolled her cardboard box to the Supreme Court's guard shack. Word of her completed mission reached everyone late that afternoon.

In an email message to Brown, Susan Brauner paid homage to Almeida's accomplishment: "Wilson, let me understand this correctly. You work with someone who took on the Supreme Court today and seemed to have handled it quite well. I worked with a carpenter's assistant today who actually managed to walk into the low doorway (yes—it is a very old building) so many times he literally knocked himself out. Can we trade, please . . . ?"

THE FILING OF A *CORAM NOBIS* PETITION SPARKED GROWING MEDIA interest—multiple stories in a range of smaller local newspapers, larger pieces in newspapers such as the *Boston Globe, Philadelphia Inquirer,* and *National Law Journal,* and a stream of requests for television interviews. NBC's New York and Philadelphia TV stations made plans to tape Judy and Susan at Judy's home on Friday, March 7. The day before that, Pat received her own invitation from a local NBC affiliate. "Well-l-l-l-l-l, ladies," she reported to Judy and the Brauners, "I'm beginning to realize that our story really is a bigger deal than I would ever have guessed. I understand the intensity of the interest in the East, but I thought of it as more of a local story. DBR must see it somewhat differently. They are flying Doug Kramer [the firm's chief marketing officer] to Indianapolis and he is escorting me to the NBC-TV affiliate for an on-camera interview in the studio tomorrow a.m. I'm not crazy about the format—will be very nervous staring at a camera, I know. Judy, you present our purpose so eloquently, but I'm not secure in my ability to even be coherent. . . ."

The media attention kept escalating—soon came calls from, among others, the *Los Angeles Times* and *60 Minutes II*—for now their case looked to be getting under way. On March 13, Almeida sent word that the Supreme Court was scheduled to consider their "motion to file" at a conference late that month. "This is good news because we are at least past the clerks and before the Court itself. . . . We know that our petition is not sitting in a box in the corner of a junior clerk's office, and that it is not on the long pony ride back to our offices in Philadelphia."

Indeed it wasn't. By then, the petition had drawn the attention of certain figures in the executive branch. On March 18, Brown received an email from Alison L. Massagli of the President's Foreign Intelligence Advisory Board. The board, Massagli advised, would like a copy of the petition that DBR had recently filed with the Supreme Court regarding *U.S. v. Reynolds*. Massagli had learned of this petition from an article in the *Philadelphia Inquirer*, but she understood from the news story that the Court "sent it back, not knowing what to do with it. . . ." Therefore, "we have had some trouble gaining a copy from the Supreme Court's webpage. Please let us know if this request can be granted and if so, we would appreciate the petition as soon as possible."

Brown couldn't help but notice that Massagli had copied this message to Catherine Lotrionete, a member of the National Security Council. He liked this—attention paid! He promptly sent them a copy of the petition and motion. At the same time, he messaged Judy, Pat, and the Brauners, sharing the communication from Massagli. "I thought you would find it interesting," he wrote, "that at least one arm of the Executive Branch is interested in our case."

Judy liked this, too. To everyone, she wrote: "Just eight months ago I remember pounding my fist on that accident report and saying . . . that I just wanted to tell SOMEONE that what the government did was wrong. . . . While this media frenzy has been difficult . . . many more Americans now have this knowledge. . . . And now, thanks to the article in the Philadelphia Inquirer, someone in the White House itself has taken an interest in this story. All I can say is WOW!"

CHAPTER 27

A CREATIVE TRY

March–June '03

"U.S. Ready to Rescind Clinton Order on Government Secrets," declared a headline in the *New York Times* on March 21, 2003. Wilson Brown read the article by Adam Clymer with interest.

> Making it easier for government agencies to keep documents secret, the Bush administration plans to revoke an order issued by President Clinton that among other provisions said information should not be classified if there was "significant doubt" as to whether its release would damage national security.
>
> The new policy is outlined in a draft executive order being circulated among federal agencies. A final version is expected to be adopted before April 17, when the last elements of the Clinton order would take effect, requiring automatic declassification of most documents 25 or more years old. . . .
>
> Other provisions of Mr. Clinton's order, which was issued in 1995, are already in force. But major changes to them contemplated in the draft would treat all information obtained from foreign governments as subject to classification. . . .
>
> The new policy would also permit reclassification of documents that have already been made public. . . .

Brown and his clients had always been focused on the relevance of their legal challenge to current affairs. The insistence on secrecy and uni-lateral executive branch power had, after all, become a hallmark of the Bush administration. Yet this news report underscored the matter in a striking manner. Clinton's declassification order in 1995 did not directly enable Michael Stowe to buy a thousand reels of aviation accident reports, but its tenor led the Air Force Secretary to "waive the claim of privilege" and "authorize unrestricted public release" of the reports. Now Bush wanted to revoke Clinton's order and reclassify some documents.

"If you didn't think our Petition was timely before," Brown wrote in a message to his clients that included a copy of Clymer's article, "read today's NY Times."

In Indiana, Patricia couldn't believe the words on the page. "Reading this took my breath away," she messaged Brown. "Timely? It's almost as if the issue was being pursued because of this case! At least NOW we know why the White House was interested in the petition. Thank you so much for bringing this to our attention."

In Massachusetts, Judy thought it would be interesting to send copies of their petition to the various folks quoted in the *New York Times* article. "Would stir up the water a bit," she suggested to Brown.

Days later, the issue was still on her mind, so she sent a longer message to Wilson, Pat, and the Brauners, asking, "can we re-visit this article and discuss it a bit?" She continued:

> I am going to suggest a few things here and understand that
> there may be differing opinions. . . . First, I think this is exactly
> why . . . the President's Foreign Intelligence Advisory Board was
> interested in our petition. . . . Our petition clearly causes one to
> question government claims of secrecy and certainly
> demonstrates the government's problems with declassifying once
> secret documents. They must be VERY interested in seeing what
> the Court will do and how the press is reacting to it.

Judy's intention was "not to cause trouble," but "our problem with the government certainly factors into a situation like this one."

The more their case was discussed, "the better it is for us, our cause, and for 'our government.'" Judy wondered: "What do you all think?"

Susan Brauner, believing government on all levels should be "held accountable," said she "would strongly support" wide dissemination of the petition, if Wilson agreed. "I would be glad to pry the secret conference doors open and figuratively toss in a few Petitions. . . . We are all aware that one case, i.e. Reynolds, can have an effect on our legal system for years and years and years. For this reason, I strongly support using whatever current leverage we have to hopefully have a similar impact. . . ."

Brown, as it happened, did not agree. He could not help but think as a lawyer—as his clients' lawyer. They should not be advocates for or against the Bush reclassification scheme, he advised. "If we are seen as rebels with a cause, that might prompt concern on the Supreme Court that we are asking them to revisit the whole subject of national security law—which THIS particular court will have NO interest in doing. So, as a deliberate strategy and for the good of the cause, I do not want us to appear as advocates, or as siding with advocates for the time being. Once the case is decided, we can get on the soapbox if we want."

Once the case is decided. When would that be? That's what they all were now wondering.

The Supreme Court had accepted their "motion to file" petition on March 4, and Almeida had expected a ruling by the end of that month. It did not come. Instead, on April 4, the Court took the unusual step of asking Solicitor General Theodore B. Olson if his office wished to submit a response. The justices, in effect, were inviting the government to comment on whether the Court should grant review.

If it was an unusual step, it was less so than in the past. This was the twenty-third such invitation to the solicitor general in the Court's 2002–3 term, up considerably from an average of sixteen a year. Legal analysts had various theories: Perhaps the Court just had a high regard for Olson, perhaps the Court was taking greater care in screening cases—or perhaps the Court had become overly dependent on the government's views. Whatever the reason, the solicitor general's advice, when sought, appeared to carry considerable weight. In the three previous terms, the Court had followed his guidance seventy-four percent of the time.

It took a while to get that guidance, though. The solicitor general's office, with just twenty lawyers, was inundated with cases to argue and briefs to file. They couldn't ignore a "CVSG"—a call for the views of the solicitor general—but they could put it on a back burner, since CVSGs usually carried no firm deadline.

Brown didn't mind the delay, for he'd taken heart that the justices had invited this response from the government. It meant they were paying attention to the petition. If they were just going to reject it without thought, they wouldn't have bothered to ask the solicitor general to submit. At least he and his clients weren't getting the back of a hand. For a time, Brown even entertained the notion that the solicitor general might share a sense of dismay at what his own office had done fifty years ago.

Ted Olson did not, however. On May 30, almost two months after being invited to comment, he submitted a response asking that the Court reject the motion. Some of his arguments did not surprise Brown. Wilson had expected the government lawyers, to argue, for example, that "the law favors finality," that you can't reopen every case where documents get declassified. He'd expected them to point out that the widows had declined the government's offer to depose the surviving crewmen, instead making a "strategic decision" to settle for $55,000 less than the initial judgment. He'd more than expected them to argue that this matter should not occupy the Supreme Court, that the Court didn't have jurisdiction, that the case should be pursued in lower courts through other "routes of relief." What Brown had not expected was for the solicitor general to insist there'd been no fraud committed—and no claim made that the accident report contained state secrets.

Yet that's precisely what Olson maintained. The government in

1950, Olson argued, never stated that "the particular accident reports or witness statements in this case in fact contained military or state secrets." Rather, the secretary's claim of privilege expressed concern that the report "might lead to disclosure" of classified information. The secretary was "legitimately concerned" that classified information might be embedded, for example, in the Air Force's internal memos and in the letter Frank Folsom of RCA wrote to General Hoyt Vandenberg. What's more, national security was implicated even if there were no Project Banshee secrets involved: There was "a strong national interest" in discovering the cause of military aircraft accidents; the "promotion of flying safety" was "particularly important to the interests of national security."

Like Chief Justice Vinson, Olson in conclusion invoked the context of the times and employed it as a justification:

> [I]n this type of proceeding, it is easy for parties to make hindsight judgments. . . . The proper focus for the courts is to seek to evaluate the claim of privilege from the standpoint of the day and context in which it was asserted. The claim of privilege in this case was made in 1950, at a time in the Nation's history—during the twilight of World War II and the dawn of the Cold War—when the country, and especially the military, was uniquely sensitive to need for "vigorous preparation for national defense." . . . The allegations of fraud made by the petition in the case . . . must be viewed in that light.

In his office, Brown grew agitated as he studied this document. He could counter with so many arguments: That it was absolutely preposterous, despite Finletter's artfully ambiguous language, to suggest the Air Force never claimed the report contained state secrets; that Folsom's letter had made only vague, passing reference to Project Banshee and had not at all been the issue back then; that rather than keep it a secret, the Air Force had heavily publicized its experiments with remote-controlled aircraft. But whatever he did, Brown knew he'd be reduced to disputing factual issues. That's what made Olson's denial so disingenuous. By saying the government had never claimed the accident report contained state secrets, the solicitor general was signaling to the justices that there were factual issues to address. If so, then the matter must go to a lower court, for the Supreme Court justices were not in the business of trying facts.

Such remarkable obfuscation. It was, Brown felt, an effort to scare the justices away.

BROWN AND ALMEIDA FILED THEIR REPLY TWO WEEKS LATER. THEY pointed out that the only documents at issue half a century ago were the accident report and witness statements. The "accident investigation file" and "ancillary" materials in that file were never the object of discovery or court orders—Judge Kirkpatrick confined his order directing a private *in camera* review solely to the report and statements. Secretary Finletter and Major General Harmon did indeed say those specific documents contained state secrets. Judge Kirkpatrick understood the Air Force's affidavits to claim precisely that. So did Judge Maris and the court of appeals. So did the Supreme Court—the affidavits, Chief Justice Vinson wrote, established "a reasonable danger that *the accident investigation report* would contain references to the secret military equipment."

Yet the government, Brown and Almeida argued, now "does not pretend" the report and statements contain military secrets. "Indeed, to defend its actions fifty years ago, the government must look to a file that plaintiffs and the courts did not seek, for an exchange of correspondence with RCA that plaintiffs and the courts did not request, and then suggest that these materials, with their passing reference to 'Project Banshee,' somehow justify the Air Force's conduct. . . . The RCA correspondence was never at issue. . . . What was at issue, as Secretary Finletter and Major General Harmon knew, was the official report and the statements. In their affidavits, these two officials swore to the courts that *those* documents contained state secrets—and this was a lie."

Only the Supreme Court can remedy this fraud, Brown and Almeida continued, for this fraud did not succeed in the lower courts. "It only succeeded in this Court. Even the government concedes that 'only this Court can set aside its own judgment.'" Yes, the Court relinquished jurisdiction when it ruled in 1953, but the Court "did not thereby forfeit all power as a court of equity later to correct its mandate."

Toward the end of their reply, Brown and Almeida slammed the government's claim that any fraud worked on the Court was immaterial because the widows eventually made the "strategic decision" to settle. "It is worth noting how thoroughly disingenuous the government's argument really is. . . . The widows' decision . . . could hardly be called 'informed' much less 'strategic.' The widows were entirely ignorant that their judgments had been vitiated through fraud. Moreover, the discovery the Air Force had offered—depositions of the three surviving crewmembers—could never substitute for the contents of the official accident report. Why? Because . . . not a single one of those crewmen knew that the main cause of the accident was the Air Force's failure to comply with technical orders."

Brown and Almeida closed by arguing that this case "does no violence to any doctrine of finality." Other settlements in other cases, they assured, "will not be vulnerable to attack unless the government has there engaged in a fraud upon the Court. . . . If there is another case anything like this one . . . petitioners will be very much surprised. But if there is, why should there be no remedy?"

As they waited now for the Supreme Court to respond, the feature articles and television interviews multiplied. Increasingly, journalists were trying hard to put Brown and his clients on that soapbox he wanted to avoid. Although Brown kept maintaining that this case is "about three families . . . not about national security law," many news accounts were finding broader meaning beyond the human interest. The reporters, like the litigants, couldn't ignore parallels with current times. The new Reynolds claim offered a clear lesson about the consequences of expanding the government's homeland security powers. It could also be compared to the case of Yaser Esam Hamdi, the American-born Saudi captured in Afghanistan, who was then challenging his enemy-combatant designation after being long confined without access to a lawyer. Judges seeking to evaluate government state secrets claims, appellate panels saying they can't—it all sounded familiar, it all resonated.

If the mounting media attention at times discomfited those involved in the case, it also seemed to inspire them. In a message to Susan Brauner on June 16, Judy expanded on a theme she'd discussed before:

> It goes without saying that ALL of us have a primary interest in winning. But what exactly is winning? Is it just a favorable Supreme Court ruling and money? I have felt it important to talk to the press, so that the People hear this story and know what their government did. Without any press coverage, even if we "win" . . . the People would not be educated . . . and forewarned. . . . If we win, the financial judgment will be relatively miniscule. I believe the biggest hurt we can do to the forces in the government that seek to harm, deceive and do evil is to publicize what they had done. . . . What else is involved in "winning"? For me a VERY important goal that has grown out of this lawsuit is seeing that many people can be blessed by this tragedy. What better way to turn it around on a human basis, and not just a legal basis?

Other voices, however—less optimistic voices—could also be heard in that early summer of 2003. A number of legal experts pointed out that they couldn't recall a petition for this type of writ ever being filed directly to the Supreme Court. The federal rules had essentially supplanted writ practice, George Washington University Law School professor Jonathan Siegel told a reporter. "This is a creative try [but] I would have to guess it's not going to work. It's a basic principle of law that once a case gets decided and the decision is final, that's it." Kate Martin, director of the Center for National Security Studies, scoffed at the importance being given to the discovery of fraudulent government claims. "That the facts of the original case are not true is irrelevant to the state secrets privilege," she said with a shrug. "The idea that it undercuts the privilege is ridiculous. Often in cases, after they're decided, the facts are proven to be not true. That's the nature of the legal system. Sometimes people lie. Sometimes there's new information."

George Washington University law professor Jonathan Turley—whose own office stood sealed by a federal judge concerned that it might contain state secrets—talked to a reporter in a campus conference room: "For the Supreme Court to address the fact clearly that it had been lied to would open difficult issues. It would be like Claude Rains saying, 'I'm shocked, shocked.' . . . The Court used the facts of Reynolds to say the government could be trusted. . . . Reynolds was based on trust, on willful blinders. There's much danger in going back now, in recognizing that the government routinely lies. They're not going to face that. They won't reopen this. I think Reynolds is like discovering an unfaithful wife after fifty years of marriage. You're hurt by the betrayal, but you can't turn back half a century. You preserve the marriage for the children's sake."

Turley spoke those words in Washington on Friday, June 20. The Supreme Court's 2002–3 term ended the following week, and it proved to be a memorable five days, yielding two seminal Supreme Court decisions: One (*Grutter v. Bollinger*) preserved affirmative action in university admissions, the other (*Lawrence v. Texas*) recognized the due-process rights of gay men and lesbians. Amid the cascade of stories, columns, and editorials, few noticed another action by the justices.

On Monday of that week, June 23, the Supreme Court delivered a simple one-sentence ruling in the case titled *In re Patricia J. Herring, et al.*: "The motion for leave to file a petition for a writ of error *coram nobis* is denied."

BROWN AND ALMEIDA HAD NOT EXPECTED SUCH AN OUTCOME. THIS was worse than anything they'd imagined. At the least, they thought, the Court would deny and say, go file it in federal district court. It never crossed Brown and Almeida's minds that the justices would just deny without comment. The Court could at least have sent a message.

Near four p.m. that Monday, Almeida emailed all their clients, arranging for a late afternoon conference call. There he gave them the news and talked about possible next steps—alternative "routes of relief."

Meanwhile, Brown spoke to the journalists: "The denial of our petition is not necessarily the end of the road. . . . We do not believe there is any question but that there was fraud upon the Court here. The question for our clients is whether there is any remedy for this fraud."

When it was over—the conference call and the press interviews—Judy sat at her computer in Massachusetts. "How about a group hug here," she wrote everyone.

> I know . . . for everyone this is a disappointment. But what I am doing at this moment is adding up all our successes and we have had a lot of them. My first goal was to "TRY" to do something about this injustice. How much more we have accomplished than that!!! Just about a year ago we had no attorneys and little hope of finding one. Who knew about the lie the government told except for a few of us? . . . The intellectual community didn't know the facts about US v Reynolds. . . . Onward and Upward, we are still right and we are still standing tall!

On Cape Cod, Susan appreciated Judy's attempted cheer but could not summon quite the same level of optimism. "I am sure you are absolutely right," she wrote Judy. "I am just too drained and too tired to rise to your level of positive thinking. But, said Miss Scarlett, tomorrow is another day."

CHAPTER 28

OTHER TYPES OF COMFORT

September '03–September '04

BY THE END OF SUMMER, THE DESIRE FOR A PARTY HAD overcome feelings of disappointment. Invitations began to arrive in dozens of mailboxes. "The Court Has Decided . . ." they read. "You Have Been Ordered to Appear at a Clam Bake on Cape Cod." Besides a traditional shore dinner, the "docket" promised "Dart Throwing at Justices." All nine targets were depicted right there on the invitation, in eerily convincing sketches drawn by the group's resident artist, Patricia Herring. In Pat's scene, eight justices were dancing; one, Sandra Day O'Connor, was perched on a swing—"a vote swing," the caption explained.

In mid-September, everyone arrived at Susan Brauner's home in Harwich Port. It was the first time they had all gathered as a group. Pat and Don flew in from Indianapolis. Judy and her husband, John, drove from Bolton, an hour west of Boston. So did Cathy and her daughter, Hyacinth, from Wellesley. Susan's daughter, Julianna, and Julianna's husband, Ronald Lovell, showed up with their two children. From Philadelphia came Wilson Brown and his wife, Anne—his clients had never met him in person. A number of Brauner family friends attended, thrilled to honor the memory of Phyllis; among them was Dr. Doris Lewis, the chair of both the Phyllis A. Brauner Memorial Lecture Committee and the Suffolk University chemistry department.

They all stood together in Susan's backyard on Cape Cod, minutes from Nantucket Sound. Susan's house was a classic half-Cape built in about 1750. There were two windows to the side of the front door and a number of the expected features, including a central chimney, a round cellar, and a birthing room. "The Old Landmark," as the house was called, had been owned for a long time by Mildred McKee, Phyllis Brauner's prep school Latin teacher. When Miss McKee died in 1997 at age 101, Susan bought the property, having held right of first refusal for years.

This was a home full of family memories. Phyllis and her parents had visited the property, and Phyllis had honeymooned there. Susan and Cathy had seen it as children. Susan's daughter and son-in-law had honeymooned there, too, and now here were the grandchildren.

On came the food, first homemade clam chowder and samples of Cape Cod wine and Nantucket ale. Then lobster rolls, steamers, corn on the cob, potato salad, fruit salad, and a table full of desserts. Children ran around and scooted off to the beach. Jokes flowed easily about government officials and High Court justices. The partygoers had dropped their dart-throwing idea, but only because they expected their local congressman to show up.

Their fight wasn't over. They were lobbying Congress for a remedy, and within days would file a new "independent action" seeking relief in U.S. District Court. However those efforts turned out, they could take comfort in knowing they'd already realized one type of success: Other lawyers challenging state secrets claims had started to study and use their petition. When the government invoked *Reynolds*, these lawyers could now introduce the story of the landmark case's fraudulent genesis.

Still, an elegiac mood colored the day's celebration. Pat felt that whatever happened "wouldn't be the same as the Supreme Court admitting fault." Susan allowed that the Court's wordless denial had "stung," had been "a kind of revelation." Judy confessed that she'd expected the Department of Justice to be "appalled" at what transpired fifty years ago. She'd had a fantasy, even, that President Bush would call her to say this was wrong, we'll make it right, we're very sorry.

"It didn't happen that way," Judy said, as the clambake wound down. "Maybe the law isn't about right or wrong. The concept that the government lied to the Supreme Court seemed to me a terrible thing to do. It appears that the justices were not as appalled as I was."

All the same, other types of comfort were available to those who'd come to Susan's home. At nightfall, they assembled in the softly lit family room, four generations together, many of them laboring over a mammoth jigsaw puzzle—an image of the globe—brought by Pat as a present for Hyacinth. Pat had never met the other widows. That seemed strange to her, looking back—incredible, really—and she felt regret. Now Pat sat at a table in this family room with the daughters and grandchildren of those women, helping them all to assemble a jigsaw puzzle of the world. "It was our mothers' loss not to have known you," Susan had told Pat earlier, "and our gain." My gain too, Pat thought.

From a corner of the room, Judy watched the others moving pieces of the puzzle. Their fathers and husbands, she believed, would be happy to know they were together. She felt far from devastated. At the clambake that afternoon, she'd risen to say, "I hope we have another chance to gather, to celebrate victory." Yet now she thought: *I would put a higher value on this experience today than on winning a Supreme Court decision.* Not so for Wilson Brown—at least, not entirely so. At the clambake, when Judy had announced she "still wanted victory," a glum Brown had added, "Yeah, me too."

IF CHARLES BIDDLE FACED A TOUGH CHALLENGE IN FIGHTING THE government's national security claims at the height of the Cold War and McCarthyism, so too did Brown in the fall of 2003. In the wake of the 9/11 terrorist attacks, the Bush administration had been relentlessly extending executive branch powers. This was nothing new: In the name of national security, the executive branch during crises has always claimed extraordinary powers, while courts traditionally have deferred—Justice Black's 1944 *Korematsu* opinion being a prime example. Yet the Bush administration's position that national security claims trump everything—including scrutiny by judges—signaled an alarming escalation of executive power. Secrecy enshrouded much of this escalation, justified in courtrooms more than once by invocation of *U.S. v. Reynolds.*

While contemplating how to renew his clients' legal challenge, Brown watched the branches of government engage in a fundamental struggle over the separation of powers doctrine. In late April 2003, Attorney General John Ashcroft, in a private nineteen-page opinion, unilaterally ruled that illegal immigrants could be held indefinitely without bond if their cases presented national security concerns. That same month, federal prosecutors were in court appealing a judge's order allowing defense attorneys to visit enemy combatant Jose Padilla, an American citizen. In late May, the Supreme Court said it would not review government antiterrorism policies that allowed secret deportation hearings for foreigners rounded up after the 9/11 attacks. The next month, a federal appellate court—citing a strong inclination to defer to the executive branch on national security issues—ruled that the Bush administration could conceal the identities of hundreds detained after 9/11. "America faces an enemy just as real as its former Cold War foes," the majority opinion observed, "with capabilities beyond the capacity of the judiciary to explore."

One case that most directly tested the lines of power between the judiciary and executive branch involved Zacarias Moussaoui, the French citizen accused of conspiring with Al-Qaeda in the 9/11 attacks. Sitting in Alexandria, Virginia, U.S. District Judge Leonie Brinkema told prosecutors they had to allow Moussaoui's lawyers to depose a key witness held overseas by the U.S. military. John Ashcroft on July 14 refused, stating that this would result in the "disclosure of classified information compromising national security." In response, Judge Brinkema in early October banned prosecutors from seeking the death penalty against Moussaoui or using any evidence at his trial that linked him to the 9/11 attacks. A month later, Brinkema put the case on hold until appellate courts resolved the matter. Attention now turned to the Supreme Court: Would it join the debate over where to draw the line?

At that moment in November 2003, Jeff Almeida received a phone call from one of the attorneys representing Moussaoui. The attorney wanted to know how DBR's *coram nobis* petition had fared before the Supreme Court. The government lawyers, he reported, had been citing the 1953 *Reynolds* opinion in the Moussaoui conflict, had in fact been waving it around the courtroom any chance they got. He was hoping he could, in response, stick *Reynolds* up Uncle Sam's nose.

Not likely, Almeida explained. They spoke for half an hour, though, sharing research notes and cases that might be helpful. News of this conversation drew responses from Almeida's clients. Pat, with wry amusement, spoke about them all being part of a "dubious circle." Susan found the interest from Moussaoui's legal team "most encouraging. . . . If we eventually walk away with nothing more than one concrete example where the case was of possible use to someone else . . . then I will believe we have done some good in impacting or at least raising the issue."

Fred Korematsu also stepped forward now. In November, at age eighty-four, he filed a friend-of-the-court brief with the U.S. Supreme Court on behalf of the Guantánamo detainees. "It is only natural that in times of crisis our government should tighten the measures it ordinarily takes to preserve our security," Korematsu's brief argued. "But we know from long experience that we often react too harshly in circumstances of felt necessity and underestimate the damage to civil liberties. Typically, we come later to regret our excesses, but for many that recognition comes too late. The challenge is to identify excess when it occurs and to protect constitutional rights before they are compromised unnecessarily."

Korematsu's wife, Kathryn, explained to reporters why he filed this brief: "Fred always says he doesn't want what happened to him to happen to anybody [else]."

Susan found this, like the Moussaoui approach, to be a hopeful development. In fact, after getting and reading Korematsu's brief, she wrote to his attorney, asking if she could send Korematsu a personal letter. It amazed her: "Mr. Korematsu, the enemy combatants, and the six of us," she wrote in an email, "have the same government/secrecy/classified information in common."

On September 30, two weeks after the clambake on Cape Cod, Brown filed the new "independent action" with the U.S. District

Court in Philadelphia. He'd initially avoided this "Rule 60" route because there'd been no fraud successfully committed in District Court before Judge Kirkpatrick. Now, though, stymied by the Supreme Court, he had no choice.

Once again in this petition, Brown walked step by step through the history of the case. Then came the usual trading of motions, with the government seeking to get the action dismissed out of hand, without a trial. Brown's clients weren't qualified to assess the accident report, argued James Gilligan, senior trial counsel at the Justice Department. Not only were the plaintiffs unqualified, Gilligan suggested, so were the courts: "The Executive Branch's familiarity with matters of national security means that it has unmatched expertise and insight. . . . For these reasons, the courts give utmost deference to the government's judgments about the harm that could result to national security from such disclosures. . . ."

What's more, Gilligan added, even if Air Force officials *did* commit perjury, that does not "rise to the level" of being fraud.

After a few more exchanges of this sort between the two sides, U.S. District Judge Legrome D. Davis ordered oral argument on the government's motion to dismiss. At 9:30 a.m. on Tuesday, May 11, 2004, for the first time since they thought to challenge the government over *Reynolds,* Judy Loether, Pat Herring, and Susan Brauner would see the inside of a courtroom.

The three took a taxi that morning from their hotel to the federal courthouse at Sixth and Market streets in downtown Philadelphia. After passing through a metal detector, they rode an elevator to the twelfth floor. They found that floor deserted, Courtroom 12A still dark. A man with a briefcase appeared, and Judy wondered if he was the government's attorney. She felt a strong sense of power just then—for bringing the government to court, for making them bother with her, for making them pay attention. A moment later, Brown arrived. They stood talking outside the dark courtroom. Wilson introduced himself to the man with the briefcase—Tony Wagner, associate general counsel for the Air Force, who said he'd come up from D.C. that morning. Judy couldn't help it; she chuckled inwardly, thinking of all the trouble they'd put this man through. This courtroom experience—this felt real. They weren't just passing legal documents back and forth.

Soon the judge's deputy clerk turned on the courtroom lights. Brown and his clients sat to the left of the bench, the government lawyers to the right. They all rose when Judge Davis entered the room. He was fifty-two, a Princeton graduate who'd studied law at Rutgers, worked as an assistant district attorney in Philadelphia, and sat as a Court of Common Pleas judge for five years. George W. Bush had appointed him to the federal bench in 2002. "Good morning, everyone," he said.

As they took their seats, Pat looked around the plain, small room. White walls, brown paneling, nothing else, no art or murals. Maybe she'd watched too many TV courtroom dramas; she'd expected more in a federal courtroom. She'd also expected a full gallery of spectators, but they had no "watchers" beyond a couple of local reporters. They only had their own crowd, though at least they'd managed an impressive turnout: Wilson and Jeff; Wilson's wife, Anne; Doug Kramer, DBR's chief marketing man; Kate Levering, DBR's head of litigation; and Jim Sweet, then DBR's chairman. Before the judge sat his deputy clerk; to the judge's side, his law clerk.

Gilligan had the floor first. Expanding on his legal brief, he took quick aim at the plaintiffs' reading of the accident reports: "They believe that the Air Force must have been lying when it asserted the military secrets privilege because having read the report they don't understand how disclosure . . . could have been harmful to national security. Well, that in itself is understandable, Your Honor, because as the Courts have long recognized, lay persons lack the experience, the expertise and the knowledge that the executive branch possess, and in particular the military departments possess, when it comes to making judgments as to what . . . might be harmful to national security. And, we can't know today . . . why Air Force officials would have concluded that the disclosure of information, that may strike us as somewhat unremarkable today, may have provided valuable intelligence information to the nation's adversaries . . . in the 1950s."

As Gilligan talked, Judy and Pat and Susan tried to follow the legal jargon. *Plaintiffs never attempted to make a showing of need . . . Rules to strike a balance between the competing demands of equity and respect for the finality of judgments . . . The balance that the law has struck is reflected in Rule 60 . . . Finletter and Harmon were not officers of the Court . . .*

Judy, despite listening carefully, couldn't judge the strength of Gilligan's arguments. The case law Gilligan cited sounded quite strong to her. Yet so much of it involved very specialized legal issues. Was "finality" too big a mountain to climb?

Gilligan was now talking about perjury and fraud, comparing the two. *Perjured testimony, while not to be condoned, does not constitute a fraud on the Court. . . . Perjury, deceit and non-disclosure, while not to be condoned, are nevertheless recognized hazards of litigation and parties are given the tools and opportunities to make their case notwithstanding these foreseeable obstacles. . . .*

So, even if the government did lie, that's not such a big deal, not big enough to make it a fraud? How disturbing, Judy thought. There are lies, then, and there are LIES. Little ones are clearly okay. That's what it boiled down to.

Gilligan next revisited the idea that it wasn't possible in 2004 to determine what secrets the accident report held. *Your Honor . . . my belief is we can't possibly know . . .* Judy had laughed when she read this argument in a written brief. Might a judge really see it this way? Judy fought the urge to raise her hand and tell the judge, "But the Russians already had the B-29! Nothing about the B-29 could possibly have been a secret!"

Then came Brown's turn to talk, much to Pat's relief. So far, she, like Judy, hadn't been too impressed. She'd expected drama but had heard only a government lawyer's rather dry presentation. In fact, she suspected the judge had fallen asleep for a while, as his eyes closed and his head bobbed once. He seemed to wake up when Wilson rose to introduce his clients.

This Wilson did right at the start of his presentation, in the hopes of humanizing the proceedings, of attaching faces to his legal arguments. *Here is the widow of Robert Reynolds, here is the daughter of Al Palya, here is the daughter of William Brauner.* And here is what happened to them, Brown told Judge Davis: "They had judgments taken away from them by the U.S. Government's fraud. They were taken away from them when high Government officials falsely swore to the federal judiciary that pivotal documents they had . . . contained state secrets."

Brown continued, relying throughout on a conversational style rather than legal jargon. *Let's start with the facts . . .* He emphasized that the government had only belatedly switched to a state secrets claim. He emphasized that Finletter and Harmon had clearly sworn the documents contained state secrets. He emphasized that the widows would have learned nothing of value no matter how long they deposed the offered witnesses.

As for the disputed documents: "Your Honor is free to read them as are everyone else. They contain nothing that identifies or discusses the secret mission of the plane. . . . They contain nothing that identifies the secret and confidential equipment that was on board. . . . They basically consist of a forthright acknowledgment by the Air Force that it was its negligence and nothing else that caused this accident and killed these men. . . ."

The government, Brown concluded, argues that "widows and lawyers fifty years after the fact cannot tell whether there were, in fact, national security secrets lurking somewhere in these documents. The Government does not pretend to tell the Court where those would be found. I think the Court would be hard pressed to find them. We don't believe they're there."

Judy wanted to applaud. Wilson spoke with passion and simplicity. He tried to focus the judge on the event itself, on the three widows in the courtroom and a government determined to set a precedent through deceitful means. Wilson was nailing it, Judy thought. Finletter and Harmon had not bribed Kirkpatrick or anything like that, but they'd done just what Wilson said—"subvert the integrity of the judicial process in a rather consciously shocking way." Certainly that rose to being fraud? Wilson, it seemed, had answers for every government question.

Then, however, came questions from Judge Davis, questions that appeared to show his hand a bit.

It was cynical, Brown had maintained—the most cynical element in this whole case—for the government to argue that the widows should have deposed the surviving witnesses.

> JUDGE DAVIS: It was nevertheless the directive of the United
>   States Supreme Court that [Biddle] could proceed in that
>   manner, right?
> BROWN: That's right. But that directive should never have
>   been issued. That's our point. . . .

Next, Judge Davis queried the government attorney: "I think it's important to note for the record that the investigative report contains a very precise description of how this airplane performed under the circumstances that it found itself in. It's somewhat technical but there is very clear information that speaks to the performance capabilities of the aircraft. Do you agree or disagree with that?"

> GILLIGAN: I agree with that, Your Honor. There are refer-
>   ences to—there are references to the fact that the plane
>   had to be capable of flying at 20,000 feet. And other
>   references . . . Don't get me wrong, Your Honor, I don't
>   know why the—why Air Force officials fifty years ago
>   thought it was important for purposes of national security
>   to avoid public disclosure of this document. My belief is
>   that we can't possibly know.
> JUDGE DAVIS: It's a fair statement that none of us know?
> GILLIGAN: It's a fair statement that none of us know.

A moment later, it was over. The entire proceeding had lasted slightly under an hour. Leaving the courtroom, Judy couldn't help but think about the two federal judges sitting here in Philadelphia fifty

years before. William Kirkpatrick and Albert Maris had not let the
government put one over on them. Maybe this judge won't either.
Maybe he sees what this case is about.

BY THAT SPRING OF 2004, THE SUPREME COURT HAD JOINED THE DEBATE
over separation of power. The justices had on their docket no less than
five cases involving the Guantánamo and enemy combatant detainees,
including Jose Padilla and Yaser Esam Hamdi. Taken together, the decisions in these cases would help define the power of the executive branch
in times of crisis—and the power of the courts to review the executive
branch. Solicitor General Olson, who'd opposed Brown's *coram nobis* petition, now also opposed all these other cases coming before the Court.
In his brief, he complained about "judicial interference with military affairs" and the "truly dangerous precedent of judicial second-guessing of
quintessentially military decisions." Just as the government lawyers in
Reynolds argued that judges had no right to see classified "state secrets"
documents, they now argued that the Supreme Court had no authority
even to hear the cases about the detainees. Here was a direct challenge to
judicial power and responsibility. The executive branch, observed one
attorney opposing the government's stance, "treats the rule of law and
the judicial system as if they are the enemy of good social order."

Brown could not avoid noticing the parallels. Even as he'd been
preparing for the hearing before Judge Davis, a squadron of other lawyers had been gearing up for Supreme Court hearings. The detainee
cases lurked in the background of everything Brown did. The first round
of oral arguments had unfolded at the Supreme Court on April 20, a
second round on April 28—less than two weeks before Brown and his
clients rose in Judge Davis's courtroom. Brown now waited for the out-
comes in these two different but related tests of executive and judicial
power.

The Supreme Court acted first, and dramatically. On June 28, in
a pair of historic decisions, the justices rejected President Bush's claim
that the war on terrorism gave him unchecked power to imprison enemy combatants. "We have long since made clear that a state of war is
not a blank check for the president when it comes to the rights of the

nation's citizens," Justice Sandra Day O'Connor wrote. Even in wartime, the Constitution "assuredly envisions a role for all three branches [of government] when individual liberties are at stake." The writ of *habeas corpus* "allows the judicial branch to play a necessary role in maintaining this delicate balance, serving as an important check on the executive's power. . . ."

The cases before the Court applied to specific issues: in *Rasul v. Bush*, the right of Guantánamo Bay detainees to challenge their imprisonment in an American court; in *Hamdi v. Rumsfeld*, the right of a U.S. citizen captured in Afghanistan to a lawyer and hearing. They concerned the state's prerogative to detain individuals, and involved criminal, not civil, law. Yet the underlying theme resonated beyond the particulars: Echoing the steel-seizure case of 1952, the Court had asserted its own powers while rejecting the executive branch's. The president's conduct in the fight against terrorism, the Court declared, was not exempt from judicial review.

Days later, Theodore Olson, at sixty-three, stepped down as solicitor general. On his last day in office, in a speech before the Federalist Society, he took a parting shot at a Court he felt had sided with foreign terrorist suspects over the president. One reason the justices did so, Olson suggested, was the specter of *Korematsu v. U.S.* "The justices of this Court," Olsen said, ". . . are keenly sensitive that the Court's human rights precedents have not, in retrospect, been perceived as the Court's finest hours. . . . This Court is determined not to go down in history as the court that turned its back when asked to help."

In Philadelphia that summer, Brown felt heartened by these Supreme Court rulings, even while understanding they involved situations that differed from his case; the Constitution guaranteed bedrock civil liberties but not the absolute right to secure damages for negligence. Might these decisions, all the same, influence Judge Davis's consideration of the case now before him? Brown, hearing Davis's softball questions to the government, had consoled himself with the fact that many times at argument a judge will signal one way, then decide the other way. Brown felt he had the law on his side, so remained hopeful—just as Charlie Biddle likely felt when he walked out of the Supreme Court hearing in October 1952.

ON SEPTEMBER 10, IN A MEMORANDUM AND ORDER, JUDGE DAVIS DID not meet Wilson Brown's expectations. The judiciary, Davis ruled, owed the executive branch much deference in the name of national security. In support of this view, Davis, as if in a hall of mirrors, quoted repeatedly from among the dozens of *Reynolds* "progeny" cases that had sprung up over the decades. What *Reynolds* begat, in other words, would now be used to support *Reynolds*.

Despite the plaintiffs' allegations, Judge Davis did not see anything to suggest that the Air Force "intended to deliberately misrepresent the truth or commit a fraud on the court." But on that matter, he bowed, at any rate, to those who made the initial decision. Fifty years ago, the government "in all likelihood . . . had a more accurate understanding 'on the prospect of danger' . . . than lay persons could appreciate or than hindsight now allows." The mosaic doctrine made it "proper to defer . . . to governmental claims of privilege" even over information that standing alone may seem harmless. A "broader reading" of Secretary Finletter's affidavit "suggests that beyond the mission itself, disclosure of technical details of the B-29 bomber, its operation, or performance would also compromise national security." Although the accident report offered no "thorough exploration" of the secret mission, it provided "a detailed account of the technical requirements imposed by the Air Force to remedy engine and mechanical difficulties." The report "made specific reference to Air Force technical orders geared to . . . eliminating a definite fire hazard." Combined, the affidavits, reports, and orders "implicate far more than the particulars of the secret equipment aboard the flight. . . . Details of flight mechanics, B-29 glitches, and technical remedies in the hands of the wrong party could surely compromise national security." Protecting "the chronic mechanical and technical deficiencies of the B-29 bomber" alone gave the Air Force "sufficient cause to claim the state secrets privilege."

For all these reasons, Davis concluded, "it is hereby ORDERED that the Motion to Dismiss is granted."

★   ★   ★

In Indiana, Pat could not avoid calling this "a sad turn" for their case. "The judge, in his opinion, put on a better case for the government than they did. Oh well."

In Massachusetts, Judy tried to say she didn't feel "enormously distressed." But the meaning of Judge Davis's opinion gnawed at her. If only he'd denied them on legal terms, because of "finality" or a problematic "fraud upon the court" definition. Instead, he'd flat out rejected their assertion that the report didn't contain state secrets. That disturbed Judy. That seemed to invalidate her original analysis.

Wilson Brown shared Judy's dismay but not her sense of being invalidated. On November 8, two months after Davis ruled, he filed a notice of appeal with the U.S. Third Circuit Court of Appeals—Judge Albert Maris's old domain.

CHAPTER 29

THE ALBERT MARIS COURTROOM

January–July '05

FOR ALL OF THEM, THERE REMAINED ONE MYSTERY, EVEN AFTER their many years plumbing the past: Who was R. E. Cox, the fourth civilian to perish in the crash of B-29 #866 on October 6, 1948? He had not worked at RCA with Al Palya and Bob Reynolds, or at the Franklin Institute with William Brauner and Eugene Mechler. His family had not been part of the lawsuit filed by Charles Biddle. There seemed to be no record of R. E. Cox at all, other than his name on a long-ago crew list.

Then, late on the morning of Monday, February 21, 2005, an email message arrived in Wilson Brown's office. It came from someone named Richard A. Cox—a nephew of R. E. Cox. This nephew had read press accounts about the renewed litigation. "My uncle Richard E. Cox," he wrote, "was killed in the 1948 crash. He is survived by my father, Gerald A. Cox, and his sister, Neva Cox Strawhacker. My uncle was working out of Dayton but I believe at the time he was a civilian. . . . Obviously I can't speak for my father, but even if he does not wish to join any potential litigation I would be greatly interested in learning anything I can about the accident. My father was in his teens at the time and has never been provided with much information from the military. Perhaps if nothing else, you could provide my name and contact information to your clients. . . ."

Brown, who was traveling when this message arrived, responded three days later. He described the current litigation, attaching a copy of the *coram nobis* petition and accident-report documents. He could not, however, offer a role in the current litigation. "The Cox family was not a party to the original suit," Brown explained "so it does not have these sorts of claims, and joining in the present case is not an option." Nonetheless, "I am forwarding your email to my clients. I'm sure they would be very interested to follow up with you. They can share with you the general public information they have assembled. . . . They would be interested to know what information, if any, your family may have about your uncle and the crash."

That same day, Brown sent Richard A. Cox's message to his clients, with a comment: "One of you will undoubtedly want to pursue with Mr. Cox what information his family may have. I . . . suspect they have dealt with the same pain you all have suffered."

So began the introduction to yet another family affected by the Waycross airplane crash. Pat was the first to reach out, just hours after receiving Brown's message. "Mr. Cox," she wrote in an email, "my name is Patricia Reynolds Herring. My husband Robert (age 24) was one of the civilians killed in the Waycross crash that took the life of your uncle. Wilson Brown notified us all of your contact and I'm amazed. How did you happen to hear of the case?" She would message her fellow litigants, Pat promised, and coordinate the compilation of information they might send him. She would also be happy to speak to him by phone. "I know the last 2+ years have been an amazing journey of discovery for me, and have often created outrage. We are still moving forward. Will wait to hear from you."

Soon after, Susan also messaged Richard A. Cox, and Judy called him. The mystery of R. E. Cox's identity began to emerge. Susan wondered if it would be possible for Richard to scan in a photo of R. E. Cox and email it to her. "I think I speak for all of us that we would very much like to see him," she wrote. "I hope your father and aunt are pleased with having contact—even if just electronically at this point—with the families of the other civilian victims as well."

Two weeks later, Richard sent the requested photo, along with one of his father (Gerald) and mother. Judy, in turn, sent him a copy of the report about the crash that Mechler prepared for the Franklin Institute, since it contained mention of R. E. Cox. "I hope your family is well," Judy wrote, "and that the information you have learned has given you some closure."

As it happened, Gerald Cox's feeling just then, at age seventy-six, had more to do with connection than closure. To answer everyone's questions, he'd been poring over letters and other memorabilia of his older brother and had not found it at all difficult. "I must say," he wrote in April 2005, "that this time of probing into the life of Richard has been a pleasurable experience for both my sister Neva and me. I have not felt this close to my brother in a long time."

The repeated courtroom setbacks were weighing on Wilson Brown, though it didn't show. Golf, classical music, church, and his family occupied him when he wasn't at his law firm. One son was about to earn his master's degree from Brown University, then go off to work in a production studio in São Paolo, Brazil. The other was majoring in environmental science and religion and playing on the lacrosse team at Gettysburg College. Brown made sure to find time for them and his hobbies. Yet he couldn't shake his concerns, couldn't stop reevaluating the choices he'd made in pursuing *Patricia Herring et al. v. United States of America*. Now was not the time to stop, he told himself, not the time to give up.

He thought this despite the increasing likelihood that his law firm would never see a penny from the B-29 case. He'd fixed DBR's contingent share of any recovery at twenty percent, well below the customary thirty-three percent, but it was what Charlie Biddle had agreed to in 1949. There'd been no opposition from his colleagues; DBR's chairman and financial partner had enthusiastically supported him, however uncommon contingency deals were for corporate defense firms. This enthusiasm endured despite all the costs DBR had incurred—well over half a million dollars, by Brown's estimate. Even if they won now, their share wouldn't cover those costs. As a practical matter, this had become a *pro bono* case. At least they could afford it at a law firm with some $200 million in annual revenues. Brown had heard no grousing.

He found Judge Davis's order maddening. Davis, he believed, had read the Finletter and Harmon affidavits in a way contrary to their language, their purpose, and their context—and in a way that no other federal court had read them, including the Supreme Court in 1953. In making his claim of privilege, Finletter had specifically said the accident report and witness statements were "concerned with secret and confidential missions and equipment." Harmon had sworn that the report and statements "cannot be furnished without seriously hampering national security." And the Supreme Court in 1953 had understood them to say precisely that: *Certainly there was a reasonable danger that the accident investigation report would contain references to the secret electronic equipment which was the primary concern of the mission.*

Judge Davis proposed a theory that not even the government had argued. Davis had treated a footnote in Brown's brief, one that referred to the B-29's engine problems, as an invitation to do his own independent research into the B-29 and the Russian Tu-4. From his research, Davis surmised that it was "at least conceivable" that the accident report "might have alerted the otherwise unaware Soviets to a technical problem in the Tu-4." Davis had decided it would be "hardly shocking to contemplate an Air Force eager to protect from public view the accident investigation report that mentions modifications needed for the B-29, and by extension the Tu-4." Yet the government in 1950 had never suggested anything like this as a basis for its state secrets claim. The government had never once mentioned the Tu-4, although its existence was public knowledge.

What's more, the Soviets did not need to be "alerted" about a technical problem. It would not have been news to them or anyone that a B-29 engine had caught fire—or that this was a perennial problem for B-29s. As Charlie Biddle noted half a century before, B-29s with engines ablaze had been falling from the skies for years. The *New York Times*, in its front-page story about the grounding of B-29s after a spate of accidents in November 1949, had openly announced this—as had Curtis LeMay, who in the *Times* article said, "we've been having entirely too many engine fires" in B-29s. Indeed, the Soviets had been having too many engine fires as well in their copycat Tu-4.

Judge Davis also worried that the accident report described "the mission in question as an 'electronics project' and an 'authorized research and development mission.'" Even more troubling to him, "the report states that the 'projects . . . require aircraft capable of dropping bombs and operating at altitudes of 20,000 feet and above.'" But that wasn't secret information either. First, because the Air Force had been publicizing this program all along, publicity being a central purpose of Project Banshee. Second, because the front-page story in the *Waycross Journal-Herald* on the day after the crash had reported that "the plane was on a special mission testing secret electronic equipment" and "was flying at an altitude of 20,000 feet" when the number-one engine caught fire. Which would not have surprised anyone, since the B-29 had been built as a bomber that could fly above 20,000 feet—something the public knew well before the United States used it in August 1945 to drop the atomic bombs over Japan.

Nothing Judge Davis had isolated from the accident report and witness statements remotely resembled secrets. A foreign agent would need only read the newspapers to learn of them. Davis's speculations were just that—speculation. After first saying we can't ever know the Air Force's reasons for concern, Davis proceeded to surmise what they *might* have been thinking. He didn't have to surmise, though. The Air Force had told the courts that the documents contained "secrets" about the plane's mission and the equipment it carried. This claim was bogus, of course, but the courts ultimately had relied on it to recognize an official state secrets privilege.

That's what had happened. So that's what Wilson Brown would argue before the U.S. Third Circuit. He worked on his brief for more than two months, then filed it on January 19, 2005. Judy celebrated as she read Wilson's words late that month. "I feel like we have a strong case again," she wrote in an email. "I must say [Judge Davis's] opinion looked so bad I began to doubt what I believed to be true. So when I read [our brief], I felt strong in my heart again."

Brown's arguments also had an effect on the appellate judges. In late May, after reviewing all the briefs, the Third Circuit took the relatively uncommon step of ordering oral argument for the afternoon of July 15, 2005. This hearing, according to the clerk of court's notice, would be held at 1:00 p.m. at the Philadelphia federal courthouse—in the Albert Branson Maris Courtroom.

So many at Drinker Biddle & Reath had been following this case, so many wanted to meet the clients and hear their story. No wonder, Brown thought. They were lovely people, not a corporation or an in-house counsel. Why not hold a reception for them on the day before the Third Circuit hearing? This would be good for the clients; it would let them see the people behind the firm, let them see inside DBR. It would also be good for the law firm; it would bring this case alive for the young summer associates.

"The firm would like to host a reception for those of you who can attend on Thursday, July 14, at 4:00 p.m. in our offices in Philadelphia," Brown wrote to his clients. "If any of you wish to speak, you will have a little chance to do so. There will be refreshments and nibbles and quiet chat thereafter. Be done around 5 or 5:30."

It was exceedingly hot and humid in Philadelphia that July 14. Pat and Don Herring attended, as did Judy Loether, Susan Brauner, and Cathy Brauner with her daughter, Hyacinth. In the lobby at One Logan Square, the tony high-rise at Eighteenth and Cherry streets housing DBR's offices, they all had to check in with security officers and get name tags. They then rode elevators to the twentieth floor. A receptionist led them to a conference room where a long table occupied the center space. One wall was all windows, offering a view of downtown Philadelphia, the other all food—fruits, antipasto, cheeses, spreads, crackers, cucumber rounds, vegetables, desserts. Quite a spread, Judy thought. She turned and looked out the window. Down below was Logan Square, until 1823 the setting for burials and executions, later transformed by the French architect Jacques Griber, who made it the gem at the midpoint of the city's Benjamin Franklin Parkway. Far down that parkway, Judy could see the beautiful, rust-colored Philadelphia Museum of Art. They were just blocks from where Kirkpatrick and Maris had heard their case a half-century ago. And there—Judy could see it from the window—stood the Franklin Institute, where William Brauner and Eugene Mechler had worked on their part of Project Banshee. She had been there several times as a kid, on class trips to see the exhibits. She felt as if she were looking down on the past.

With them in the conference room were Wilson, Jeff, Lori Rapuano (another associate who'd recently joined the case), a few DBR partners, and about twenty summer associates. Wilson, preparing to talk, stood at one end of the room, with interns seated at the table and standing against the walls. He first introduced everyone. Next, he spoke a bit about how these clients had come to DBR, offering details of the case and the accident report. He spoke also about Charles Biddle, the law firm's eminent-name partner and host at Andalusia. Then he invited their guests to talk.

Susan went first. She expressed appreciation for the law firm's efforts on their behalf. She talked also about her family, about how her father and Teddy Mattern had come over from Austria before the war. Judy thought her so gracious and well-spoken, a tough act to follow. Pat did quite well, too, thanking the firm and offering touching words in memory of Bob Reynolds. When her turn came, Judy, rather than talk about the case itself, spoke about the principles that had brought her to this room. One was the French motto at her son Trav's college, *Essayons*—"Let us try"—her thought as she sat on a tree stump in Waycross. The other was the old television series *Superman* that she loved watching as a kid—Superman, whose job was to uphold "truth, justice, and the American way."

Cathy had brought a recording of her father talking to Susan a month before the crash, the two of them playing and singing nursery rhymes. Tears filled everyone's eyes. You need to understand, Cathy said. You talk about the law, but this is ultimately about the family.

After that, they mingled and ate and drank, the mood warm and generous—not a businesslike atmosphere at all, though the lawyers were all dressed in dark suits. Wilson Brown appreciated that his clients had spoken kindly about the law firm; he appreciated also that they had helped impart the human meaning of this case to the summer associates. Judy, in turn, valued how much the firm so clearly cared about them. This is the case of a lifetime for me, Jeff Almeida told her.

WHEN THE THIRD CIRCUIT NAMED ITS MAIN COURTROOM FOR ALBERT Maris in a special dedication ceremony on June 27, 1988, Supreme Court Justice William J. Brennan Jr., had presided. Brennan spoke that day of taking "the greatest pride in my cherished friendship with Judge Maris over more than 31 years." Others read letters of acclaim (one from President Reagan, another from Chief Justice Rehnquist) and told stories, among them an account of Maris exuberantly snorkeling and sailing in the Virgin Islands in his late eighties. He was ninety-four on the day of the ceremony, some seven months from his death. "I'm deeply touched by this outpouring of friendship and regard," he told the gathering. "It's really been worth living ninety-four years to have such an occasion. Although I'm not sure I'd recommend to anyone living this long. . . ."

The Albert Maris Courtroom was modern, with dark wood and carpeting but no marble and no windows. The room formed something of an oval, about sixty feet at its widest, rising twenty feet to a flat ceiling. It featured a wooden high bench for the judges, with three comfortable chairs. Albert Maris's portrait hung above the judges' bench; he seemed to be looking down on the courtroom, his expression both inquisitive and dignified. For spectators there were rows of black armchairs and, in the back, three long wooden benches spanning the width of the room.

Wilson Brown and his clients had arrived at twelve-thirty, he being required to register with the court crier thirty minutes before the court convened. With them were Wilson's wife and son, as well as Jeff Almeida, Lori Rapuano, and some twenty summer associates from

DBR. Also present, from New Jersey, were Michael Stowe and his wife, Bea. Ever since he'd helped launch the case by providing Judy with the long-sought B-29 accident report, Stowe had assisted by analyzing various documents. In September 2004, Judy drove to Stowe's home in Millville to meet him in person. Now he couldn't bear to miss this hearing.

At 12:55 p.m., two of the three judges sitting on the appellate panel this day entered the room, Judge Samuel A. Alito Jr., and Judge Franklin Stuart Van Antwerpen. The third, Judge Ruggero J. Aldisert, would be participating by way of videoconference from his chambers in Santa Barbara. Of the three, Aldisert easily had seniority—he'd been appointed by President Johnson in 1968 and was nearing his fortieth year on the bench. As a young judge, he'd been "starstruck" by his colleague Albert Maris, whose opinions he'd read in law school; he considered Maris a "judicial immortal," a "man of historic proportions," and "probably the best opinion writer" ever on the Third Circuit. Aldisert had been a major in the Marines during World War II, and later a prolific author of legal texts; now eighty-five, he'd recently published a memoir, *Road to the Robes.*

Although the two other judges could not claim equivalent experience, Samuel Alito, fifty-five, was much in the news—rumored to be a White House favorite to fill the Supreme Court vacancy created by William Rehnquist's recent death. Smart, talented, and conservative, he'd been appointed to the Third Circuit by George H. W. Bush in 1990. Franklin Van Antwerpen, sixty-three, had started his legal career in Easton, Pennsylvania—William Kirkpatrick's hometown. He'd been appointed by Reagan to the district court in 1987, then by George W. Bush to the Third Circuit in 2003.

Van Antwerpen sat on the left as lawyers faced the bench, Alito on the right. The television monitor offering Aldisert's image was below, in the well, in front of and on the same level as the lawyers. Brown thought the TV hookup a bit weird. Moreover, Aldisert was rather soft-spoken, so it was hard to hear him when he didn't talk right into the mike.

The court clerk had scheduled their matter—now titled *Herring et al. v. United States of America*—fourth on a docket of four cases, so Brown and his clients had plenty of time to observe. The lawyers had to be brief and on point, they could see that much: In all four cases, each side had just fifteen minutes to present their case. Brown didn't think any of the three cases preceding theirs was particularly sexy. One had to do with the cost of something, literally dollars and cents. The next involved a dispute over whether Comcast could amend its subscriber agreement to include arbitration charges. The third was so esoteric, Brown couldn't make himself focus.

Judy, rather than follow the legal issues, studied the judges and lawyers. From the very start, it surprised her to see how the judges began interrupting the appellant lawyer almost as soon as he started talking. When the other side's lawyer stood, he got more of the same, lots of nonstop questions. The matter they were debating seemed pretty open-and-shut to Judy, but by now she knew that the law could take simple issues of right and wrong and make them much more complex.

Finally, it was their turn. "We will hear argument in *Patricia J. Herring et al. versus the United States*," Judge Alito announced. Wilson Brown rose to speak.

HE DIDN'T GET TOO FAR—"THE DISTRICT COURT REACHED FAR OUTSIDE the record that was before him to find facts and use those facts to bolster his conclusions"—before Judge Van Antwerpen interrupted, asking what standard they should follow to define fraud. That pulled Brown into weighing "intentional falsity" against "reckless disregard" for the truth—which he thought was enough to constitute a fraud. Judge Van Antwerpen came back at him again, this time over what constituted a "grave miscarriage of justice." Brown answered, but now had his guard up.

They weren't letting him talk, they were peppering him with questions. That by itself wasn't surprising, but from the questions, you usually learned what was troubling the judges. The signs weren't good here. The questions being asked had already been addressed in the briefs. Brown waited and prepared himself. Something was coming.

On the TV monitor, Judge Aldisert leaned forward and hunched over the mike. "Well, Counsel, as to the actual assertion against the Secretary and the Judge Advocate General, aren't you accusing them of perjury?"

Brown tried to answer but Aldisert interrupted: "Excuse me. Excuse me, Counsel. Then you have to show that there was no reasonable interpretation of their statement that would not meet the accusation of, what did you say, reckless disregard for the truth . . ."

Judge Van Antwerpen jumped in a moment later: "Would you say that the 1949 affidavits, that they may have exaggerated, but weren't there also some elements of truth or at least ambiguity?"

Brown got in one sentence before Judge Aldisert interrupted again: "You're saying you don't believe that they could claim that the workings of the B-29 airplane in 1949, that that was secret?"

Brown: "I don't believe they were claiming that. I not only don't believe they could, I don't believe they were and let me tell you why—"

Judge Aldisert: "Don't you interpret it that they're referring to both the plane, and its contents and problems with the plane?"

Brown could read the situation now. Going into this hearing, he thought winning over Aldisert would be his best shot. Aldisert had been a major in the U.S. Marines, but he'd spent most of his legal career fighting the government. He'd grown up Italian in Pittsburgh; he had a chip on his shoulder all his life. The word was, of this bunch he'd be the most likely to be adventurous. But no: Even his body language was hostile. Aldisert clearly wasn't buying their story.

Brown tried to answer him: "You can interpret it that way. I don't interpret it that way. Let me tell you why. Put yourself in Judge Kirkpatrick's seat. That's the best way to look at this case, I think. Judge Kirkpatrick is sitting there and he's presented with an accident, request for an accident report and the government moves to quash. Does the government say that this accident report contains state secrets? No. Doesn't mention state secrets at all. The government knows well how to—"

Aldisert again wouldn't let him finish: "The answer is yes, Counselor. The statement of the secretary saying the aircraft in question, together with the personnel on board, were engaged in the confidential mission of the Air Force."

No, no, Brown tried to explain—he was talking about five months *before*, when the government first came to Kirkpatrick, not later, when the government returned with a state secrets claim.

"Well now, Counsel," said Judge Van Antwerpen, "the government frequently takes a long time to make up its mind."

And then, again from Van Antwerpen: "Counsel, you're seeking more money here basically?"

What could Brown say? The courtroom seemed so dark now. The lack of windows, the high flat ceiling—it felt like a cave. It felt like he'd left the world.

Yes, Brown allowed, "the relief we're seeking is more money, yes."

Judge Van Antwerpen: "All right now, is that really a miscarriage of justice that you didn't get as much, all the money you could?"

Watching from the spectator seats, Pat had grown progressively shocked by the judges, by what she considered their rudeness, especially the one on video. That man, it seemed to Pat, was out to get them from the start. Judy shared some of Pat's feelings; the volley of questions just never seemed to end. They never let Wilson talk. Now, though, in response to this question from Van Antwerpen, Wilson broke free finally from the legalese and interruptions.

"No," Brown said, "I think the miscarriage of justice is that the Supreme Court was asked to decide a question of first impression on a bogus record. I think that's the miscarriage of justice. I don't think it has to do with how much money we're entitled to, if any. I think it really has to do with the truth, and the truth of this matter is that this report doesn't talk about state secrets in the sense that they were presented to the Supreme Court and in the sense that the Supreme Court understood them. . . . The Supreme Court was defrauded and that should be regarded as a miscarriage of justice."

A moment later, the red light blinked: Brown had run out of time. As he returned to his table, he glanced up at Albert Maris's portrait. How wise and prescient Maris had been in 1951. *We regard the recognition of such a sweeping privilege as contrary to a sound public policy. It is but a small step to assert a privilege against any disclosure or records merely because they might prove embarrassing to government officers . . .* In his presentation, Brown had tried to invoke this great jurist's ruling, but he'd drawn no response. Aldisert and Van Antwerpen had attended their much-honored colleague's memorial service in March 1989, but Judge Maris just did not seem to resonate with the men sitting on the appellate bench today.

For the government, August E. Flentje now rose, an attorney on the civil appellate staff at the Justice Department. Beside him at the government's table was the briefcase man from the District Court hearing, Tony Wagner, associate general counsel of the Air Force. From the start, Flentje did well—but he faced little challenge. The judges were throwing him softballs.

"Do you think the fraud must be intentional? . . ."

"Under 60 B6 you need a grave miscarriage of justice, would you agree with that? . . ."

"Would the perjury standard be applicable? . . ."

Judge Van Antwerpen did push once: "To get to the heart of this matter, your affidavit said the plane's equipment and mission were secret and that wasn't completely true, was it?

"It was true," Flentje answered. "I mean one of our strongest arguments is that they were true in two respects and the first one is the easiest. They were true in that the accident report did contain some details about the secret equipment. It wasn't the primary focus of the accident report and I think the, if you at this—"

Judge Van Antwerpen helped him along: "What equipment in particular?"

Flentje was off and running after that, speaking at length, laying out the heart of the government's position with no interruption from the judges—"It's really just speculation to wonder 50 years later, well would this have been important to an intelligence analyst in the Soviet Union. . . . We don't know. . . . It's not appropriate to reevaluate the initial claim of classified treatment. . . ."

Still no interruptions, no questions from the judges. Flentje talked on. Brown felt more upset by what the judges weren't asking than by what they were. This was the fourth matter on a four-case docket in an unusual late-afternoon session; the judges were tired, they'd had enough.

"Counselor," Judge Van Antwerpen finally asked, "if we disagreed with your notion of the standard of review, do you think you'd still prevail?"

"I think definitely . . ." Flentje began. Again they let him run without interruption.

Judge Alito, soft-spoken, now offered one of his few questions, and to Brown it sounded like a gift. "Would it be impossible at this date to determine whether the details that you mentioned have any intelligence significance at that time?"

Flentje: "I think it would be, I think it would be almost impossible at this date. I think it would come down to speculation. . . ."

Getting into the spirit, Judge Van Antwepen asked, "Was the [district] court wrong in looking outside the record at the time?"

Flentje: "I think it was OK in these circumstances. . . ."

Moments later, after a hurried two-minute rebuttal by Brown, they were done. "Thank you," said Judge Alito. "Thank you for very helpful arguments. We will take the case under advisement."

OUTSIDE THE ALBERT BRANSON MARIS COURTROOM, BROWN MINGLED with his clients and summer associates. They tried to put the best face on the matter, but Brown understood all too well what he'd just experienced.

He'd not found a soldier on the appellate panel to carry their cause. Someone there had at least wanted oral argument—but no one had stepped forward. Brown couldn't imagine what kind of opinion they were going to write, or whether they'd write anything, given the uniqueness of the case. Who knows, maybe they'd send it back to Judge Davis for something. That would be a long shot, though. Brown had managed to say what he wanted to say. That courtroom was just not buying it.

The sight of all the judges hugging the government, that's what most dispirited Brown. If their case was doomed from the start, it was because of *U.S. v. Reynolds*'s lasting legacy—the deference given to government officials who claim state secrets. Brown saw little skepticism on this appellate panel, even from judges who in other situations might be dubious.

What he did see was a sign of the times. After the 9/11 terrorist attacks, everything—including the layout of Logan International in Boston—implicated national security. In a world with so many enemies and so many worries, all must be kept secret. Judges understandably opted for deference. They *liked* it; deference let them off the hook. No one wanted to be the judge who ruled *X*, which led to a disastrous cataclysmic apocalyptic *Y*. Better to say, *We're not equipped . . . we can't tell whether it implicates national security . . . we need to leave this to those who know . . .*

After the others had gone their separate ways—Wilson ten blocks back to his office, Pat and Don to the airport for a flight to Indianapolis, Susan to the Amtrak station for a train to Massachusetts—Judy met the Stowes for an early dinner at Ly Michael's, a contemporary Asian restaurant near the Pennsylvania Convention Center. They sat at a table by the big front window, in a room with informal modern decor, colorful and boxy.

All afternoon in court they had listened to the judges ask if there was a way to determine whether the accident report contained state secrets—to be more precise, whether the Air Force truly believed it contained state secrets. There was a way, of course. Over dinner, Michael Stowe kept making this point, his eyes bright with a private knowledge. The answer came from the government: By downgrading the classification of the accident documents, the Air Force had declared that they did not contain state secrets.

The entire B-29 file, Stowe reminded Judy, had been reduced to the lowest security level, "Restricted," on September 15, 1950, almost two years after the accident. So at the time the *Reynolds* case came before the Supreme Court, the government considered not one page confidential, secret or top secret. "What the government was protecting," Stowe argued, "was not state secrets but the Air Force's right to keep accident reports secret."

Judy agreed. Like Stowe, she had compulsively read and reread the pages of the accident report. In the courtroom today, it had shocked her to hear the government say the big secrets were about the B–29 itself. The judges certainly were brilliant legal scholars who knew much more than she did about the law. But they just didn't seem to grasp the facts. How could these judges ever buy the government's statement—what Wilson Brown called the government's "snake oil"—about 20,000 feet and bomb-bay doors being the state secrets? Only a lawyer could claim that, and only another lawyer could buy it.

Judy's dismay was warranted. The Third Circuit appellate judges had not absorbed the whole story, had not examined every letter and newspaper article, had not read the memos, had not studied the accident report page by page, over and over. If they had, they could not possibly have missed the government's drive to conceal what happened over Waycross in October 1948.

It had been a long, trying day. After dinner, Judy drove fifteen minutes across the Benjamin Franklin Bridge to her half sister's home in Collingswood, New Jersey. She spent the night there in fitful sleep, her mind filled with the exchanges she'd witnessed inside the Albert Branson Maris Courtroom.

CHAPTER 30

THE FINALITY OF JUDGMENT

September '05–May '06

FROM THE START, THEY HAD BEEN SAILING INTO THE wind—into a fierce gale. Ever since Wilson Brown and his clients began conferring, drafting documents, and filing petitions, the government's assertions of the state secrets privilege had been multiplying. By the best available count, the Bush administration had made thirty-nine claims so far—easily eclipsing all past administrations—and none had been rejected at a final legal stage.

In 2000, not long after Judy came across the B-29 accident report, the CIA successfully moved to dismiss an employee's gender discrimination lawsuit by claiming the state secrets privilege; a U.S. district judge in Virginia found that the mere existence of a trial would jeopardize national security. In 2003, a month before Brown filed his *coram nobis* petition, the Bush administration again blocked a lawsuit, this one brought by a senior engineer who charged that a military contractor had submitted false test results; a U.S. district judge in Los Angeles granted the government's state secrets claim, then dismissed the action because the contractor couldn't properly defend itself without the disputed documents. That same month, the government, while seeking to block publication of a book by a former Los Alamos National Laboratory employee, refused to let the employee's own lawyer see the manuscript—and advised U.S. District Judge Emmet Sullivan that the matter was "not reviewable" in his court. When Judge Sullivan rejected this notion, ruling that the lawyer could read his client's manuscript—"This Court will not allow the government to cloak its violations of plaintiff's First Amendment rights in a blanket of national security"—he found himself reversed by an appellate panel.

The years 2003 through 2005 were filled with such cases. A group of contractors found they could not sue the United States over a contract termination dispute after the government successfully invoked the state secrets privilege. A former Department of Energy official found he couldn't pursue a defamation suit when a district court and appellate panel both upheld the government's claim of privilege. A CIA agent found he couldn't sue the agency for racial discrimination because the courts, according to a Fourth Circuit ruling, "are neither authorized nor qualified to inquire further" when an executive-branch department head claims the state secrets privilege. An FBI translator turned whistleblower—fired after alleging defects in the FBI translation program related to 9/11—saw her lawsuit dismissed "in the interests of national security," even though an internal Justice Department report concluded that she indeed had been fired for whistle-blowing.

In Philadelphia, Wilson Brown read the continual reports of these state secrets cases with a feeling of frustrated resignation. Everywhere he looked now, he saw the consequences of a B-29 crash near Waycross in 1948; everywhere he looked he saw the impact of *U.S. v. Reynolds*. He knew what was coming.

FILED ON SEPTEMBER 22, 2005, THE THIRD CIRCUIT'S OPINION IN THE matter of *Herring et al. v. United States of America* affirmed Judge Legrome Davis and upheld the government's position. Writing for a unanimous panel, Judge Aldisert—the man on the TV screen who so admired Albert Maris—seemed to go out of his way to discourage lawyers from making any future claims about fraud on the court.

"The concept of fraud upon the court," he wrote, "challenges the very principle upon which our judicial system is based: the finality of judgment. The presumption against the reopening of a case that has gone through the appellate process all the way to the United States Supreme Court . . . must be not just a high hurdle to climb but a steep cliff-face to scale." The standard for proof must be "an intentional fraud," one that is "directed at the court itself" and "in fact deceives the court." Even then, a finding of fraud may be justified only by "the most egregious misconduct" and "must be supported by clear, unequivocal and convincing evidence."

In no way, Aldisert declared, did the facts in the original *Reynolds* case meet this demanding standard. Why? Because the claim of privilege by the U.S. Air Force in 1950 "can reasonably be interpreted to include within its scope information about the workings of the B-29." Here Aldisert relied not so much on historical context as on an analysis of how Air Force Secretary Thomas Finletter used the word "its" in his formal claim. Finletter's critical passage read:

> The defendant further objects to the production of this report, together with the statements of witnesses, for the reason that the aircraft in question, together with the personnel on board, were engaged in a confidential mission of the Air Force. The airplane likewise carried confidential equipment on board and any disclosure of **its** mission or information concerning **its** operation or performance would be prejudicial to this department and would not be in the public interest.

Did the pronoun refer only to the electronic equipment on board or to the B-29 airplane itself? Brown and the government, in their briefs, had disagreed. "While both readings are conceivable," Aldisert concluded, "the Government's is more logical." Since there was an "obviously reasonable truthful interpretation" of the Air Force's statements, Brown and his clients could not prove perjury, could not "state a claim upon which relief can be granted."

Thus the entire matter—the faulty engine design, the negligent maintenance, the missing heat shield, the improper and unprepared flight crew, the confusion in the cockpit, the inexplicable rolling of a B-29 into a fatal spin, the cover-up—finally turned on the interpretation of a pronoun. Yet it didn't, really. In a footnote, Aldisert went out of his way to say that even if the Air Force's claim couldn't be read as including general concern about the B-29, he'd be obliged to confer "a certain amount of deference to the Government's position because of the near impossibility of determining with any level of certainty what seemingly insignificant pieces of information would have been of keen interest to a Soviet spy fifty years ago."

Reading this opinion, a person would have little notion what the original *Reynolds* case had been about. Aldisert had left out much of the litigation history—including the Kirkpatrick and Maris rulings. He had managed to cast the problem as being whether the government lied to the widows, not to the Supreme Court.

The message Brown heard in Aldisert's words: *We don't want to go there.* The echoes and impact of *Reynolds* rippled all the way—not the least being that footnote about deference. The current Third Circuit panel had been influenced by generations of judges reading *Reynolds.* A lesson learned, Brown thought: The substantial deference Chief Justice Vinson had proclaimed in *Reynolds* now made it hard to stop the government from abusing the state secrets privilege.

Had Wilson M. Brown III, corporate attorney, son and grandson of southern bankers, become a radical? No, he didn't think so. He, in fact, remained sympathetic to the courts' dilemma in this area. Yet he did think the *Reynolds* rule was too deferential, or rather, had *become* too deferential. They needed an effective, appropriate check on executive power—the daily headlines provided undeniable proof of that. If the government was going to push, someone needed to push back.

Okay, maybe the situation had radicalized Brown in some way. He certainly had no regrets about taking this on, despite the hostile and indifferent judges, despite Aldisert's "steep cliff-face to scale." Above all, he deeply valued the extraordinary chance to look under the cover of a state secrets claim. The public usually can't know the basis for such a claim, but here they could, and it was the big daddy of all claims, the very source of the state secrets privilege. What a sight they had seen by pursuing this case—and what a sight others now could see.

That's what Brown and his clients had accomplished, and it was no small achievement. They had never aimed to repeal *Reynolds* or attack the whole edifice of national security law. They'd wanted only to call out the abuse of trust. They'd wanted to tell the story of how this abuse—this dubious claim of privilege—came to be. They had done that. In so doing, they had changed the terms of the argument. Now when government lawyers waved the *Reynolds* flag, judges had to consider its genesis.

Judges err as often as anyone. Legal history offers plenty of examples, cases where those in the majority have proved less than wise, where a minority opinion has eventually prevailed. The Supreme Court reversed Albert Maris's *Gobitis* ruling by an 8–1 vote, only to recognize three years later that he'd been right. The Supreme Court embraced Hugo Black's *Korematsu* opinion by a 6–3 vote, but it is Justice Robert Jackson's eloquent dissent—*the principle then lies about like a loaded weapon ready for the hand of any authority that can bring forward a plausible claim of an urgent need*—that lawyers now celebrate.

For these reasons, Wilson Brown did not feel like quitting just yet. He considered what he might say in a new petition to the U.S. Supreme Court—a more conventional petition for a writ of *certiorari*, seeking review of Aldisert's Third Circuit decision. He'd be writing, in essence, for one law clerk. The justices (except John Paul Stevens) pooled their clerks, with one writing up the recommendation for any particular petition. He just might catch the right clerk.

The story Brown would tell this clerk—the story he kept coming back to—was the *Korematsu* case. He would need to walk through that decision, to say to the justices, You were misled in *Korematsu*. It took you forty years to straighten that out, why not sort out this other one fifty years later?

Brown wondered whether there was any point in even trying. He'd most likely get only a big yawn from the justices, particularly if they failed to read the affidavits in context. Yet it wasn't really a review he sought now. Brown wanted others, in the future, to understand this case; he wanted to secure its legacy. In time, he hoped their views would prevail. Would putting one more piece of paper together help accomplish that?

As HE PONDERED THIS QUESTION DURING THE LAST MONTHS OF 2005, Brown almost daily watched yet another development in the government's expanding exercise of executive power. Among the most revealing was the Bush administration's decision, on November 22, to remove "enemy combatant" Jose Padilla from more than three years of military custody and indict him in the civilian legal system. This move, coming a month after Padilla's lawyers filed an appeal to the Supreme Court over his detention, represented an obvious attempt to keep the issue from judicial review. The Justice Department, in announcing the criminal indictment, said it now considered Padilla's Supreme Court appeal "moot."

Then came the *New York Times*'s revelation, in mid-December, that President Bush, without judicial approval or knowledge, had secretly authorized the National Security Agency to eavesdrop on Americans and others in the country. During a Saturday radio talk on December 17 and a Monday press conference on December 19, Bush insisted he had the right to assert such sweeping executive powers in the war against terrorism. "The fact that we're discussing this program is helping the enemy," Bush said testily.

The *New York Times* editorial page punched back: "When the government does not want the public to know what it is doing, it often cites national security as the reason for secrecy. The nation's safety is obviously a most serious issue, but that very fact has caused this administration and many others to use it as a catchall for any matter it wants to keep secret, even if the underlying reason for the secrecy is to prevent embarrassment to the White House." The morning Brown read those words, he'd already made up his mind. On December 21, four days after the news of Bush's domestic spying program hit the headlines, Brown filed a petition for a writ of *certiorari* with the U.S. Supreme Court. "It ain't over till it's over," he wrote in an email message.

Yet it was over, of course. In his petition, Brown kept swinging. The court of appeals opinion, he wrote, "establishes a standard that promises only to bring shame on the federal judiciary. A fraud directed squarely at the integrity of this Court's decision-making, as happened in the *Reynolds* case, should be confronted, not excused."

And again: "If the Court of Appeals decision should stand . . . officials intent on fraud will find ways to practice their deceit . . . and equity will turn its back on the consequences. That will be a sad day for the victims and for our courts."

Still again: "The lower courts have gone to extraordinary lengths to dismiss this case. The district court conducted its own 'independent' factual research. . . . The Court of Appeals vowed to put a 'cliff-face' before petitioners, and it did. The lower courts have no sufficient stake in this case. This Court does. . . . The only issue this Court must today address is whether it will tolerate a fraud. . . . Petitioners pray that it will not."

Brown, as he'd intended, once more told their story—but he did not catch that solitary law clerk. On May 2, 2006, the Supreme Court delivered a one-sentence ruling in the case titled *Patricia J. Herring et al. v. United States of America*: "The petitions for writs of *certiorari* are denied." The justices added a bit of explanation this time. Recognizing that their new colleague, Justice Samuel Alito, had heard the underlying case while sitting on the Third Circuit, they noted, "Justice Alito took no part in the consideration or decision of these petitions."

Wilson Brown and his clients had nowhere else to go. "There do not appear to be procedures for further review by the World Court," Brown observed, "so I think the courts are now officially closed."

THE COURTS OF LAW MAY HAVE CLOSED, BUT IN THE REALM OF PUBLIC opinion, the discussion continued. Taken as a whole, Wilson Brown and his clients still had good reason to feel they'd won—that they'd accomplished something real, something significant. Yes, the government's claims of privilege just kept coming. In February 2006, U.S. District Judge David Trager had dismissed a lawsuit brought by a Syrian-Canadian, Maher Arar, who'd been detained by the United States, sent against his will to Syria and tortured for ten months; the matter was a foreign policy question, Judge Trager ruled, not appropriate for court review. On May 12,

U.S. District Judge T. S. Ellis III dismissed a lawsuit brought by Khaled El-Masri, a German citizen of Lebanese descent who'd reportedly been kidnapped and tortured by the CIA; the matter, Judge Ellis ruled, was "not proper grist for the judicial mill." Then came three more claims of privilege, all filed late that May, all in response to lawsuits challenging the National Security Agency's domestic eavesdropping program. Yet no longer could such claims be made with little notice or resistance. All drew attention and loud protest from commentators, lawyers, and citizen groups. Wilson Brown and his clients had gotten the word out. They had raised awareness.

Hard evidence of this could be found in the stack of press clippings Judy now was compiling. In these articles and essays, analysts were not just paying considerable attention to every government claim of state secrets. In each and every one, the writer was making prominent reference to the dishonesty underlying the original *Reynolds* decision. One said the state secrets privilege was "born with a lie on its lips." Another believed the *Reynolds* opinion "now carried with it an asterisk, a taint of suspected fraud."

Brown and his clients had also started to influence the pages of professional journals. There had always been scholarly articles on *Reynolds*, but the latest ones were examining it in light of what the *coram nobis* petition revealed. There were comments about the privilege being "judicially mishandled to the detriment of our constitutional system." There were proposals for change, including mandatory *in camera* judicial review of all claims. There were calls for judges to push back against the executive branch.

There were even a couple of occasions where federal district judges did just that. In the summer of 2006, U.S. District Judges Vaughn R. Walker in San Francisco and Anna Diggs Taylor in Detroit ventured to deny government state secrets claims in domestic eavesdropping cases. "It is important to note that even the state secrets privilege has its limits," Judge Walker wrote, his words echoing those of Albert Maris. "While the court recognizes and respects the executive's constitutional duty to protect the nation from threats, the court also takes seriously its constitutional duty to adjudicate the disputes that come before it. . . . To defer to a blanket assertion of secrecy here would be to abdicate that duty. . . ."

As the months passed, more and more voices started seconding that thought. When Judge Walker's decision came up for review before the Ninth Circuit Court of Appeals, a coalition of nonprofit organizations (the National Security Archive, the Project on Government Oversight, the Project on Government Secrecy, the Public Citizen Inc., and the Rutherford Institute) filed an *amicus* brief that decried the government's "overbroad use of the state secrets privilege." In late May 2007, the Constitution Project in Washington, citing Judy Loether's discovery of an accident report free of military secrets, issued a "Statement on Reforming the State Secrets Privilege" that called for congressional hearings, legislative action, and independent judicial scrutiny. In mid-August, the American Bar Association adopted a resolution calling on Congress to regulate the state secrets doctrine and give federal judges more oversight of its use. Once again, the newly discovered B-29 accident report drove the argument: "The Reynolds decision was based on a lie," a Philadelphia lawyer told the ABA delegates, "that took five decades to unravel."

Then, in late January 2008, came a momentous response from Congress: Senator Edward Kennedy, the Democrat from Massachusetts, and Senator Arlen Specter, the Republican from Pennsylvania, jointly introduced the State Secrets Protection Act—a measure that would require judges to examine the actual evidence, rather than trust affidavits, when the government invoked the state secrets privilege. Representative Jerrold Nadler, a Democrat from New York, said he intended to introduce a similar measure in the House. Soon hearings were being scheduled. On January 29, Judy Loether testified before a subcommittee of the House Judiciary Committee. The Senate Judiciary Committee planned its first hearing for mid-February.

There was no way to deny it: Just as the original 1953 *Reynolds* decision spawned lasting, influential progeny, so, too, had a petition for a writ of error *coram norbis* filed on March 4, 2003. The documents disseminated by this petition offered courts and the public an unprecedented chance to compare the government's claims of privilege with the underlying facts. That comparison could only cast doubt on the deference judges routinely gave to government demands for state secrets protection.

"Doing something about it" had seemed so impossible at the start. Now each time Judy spotted another critical article about the tarnished *Reynolds* decision, she read it with wonder, then emailed copies to Wilson, Pat, Susan, Cathy, and others.

"Thanks much for sending this article out," Patricia Reynolds Herring responded to one such alert. "The interest generated by our case may end up being its legacy."

CHAPTER 31

JUST ONE MORE MISSION

January '07

JUST ONE MORE MISSION WAITED. ON THE MORNING OF January 8, 2007, Judy and her husband, John, loaded their Volvo station wagon, shut their home in Massachusetts, and headed south. Judy meant to visit Waycross again.

The notion had started with Michael Stowe. He'd bring his tools and metal detectors; he'd look for artifacts. He felt sure he'd find parts of the B-29. With publicity about the *Reynolds* case continuing to grow, he feared that scavengers would begin descending on the site. He wanted to get there first.

The idea entranced Judy. She and Mike spent most of the summer of 2006 planning. In late June, Judy started toying with an additional idea: While in Waycross, maybe she'd install a marker commemorating the site. In fact, maybe she'd hold a memorial service. Judy began designing a plaque and drafting the language for a dedication.

The best spot to place the memorial, Stowe suggested, would be where the tail of the B-29 landed, since so many of the men perished in that section. He felt certain he could locate that spot—he'd been studying crash photos and maps. He thought he also could determine just how the plane hit the ground. He'd bought a B-29 plastic model kit, assembled it, then cut it up to match the parts as described in the accident report and news accounts. The forward half of the aircraft would have landed inverted, mostly on its nose. Many small pieces from the cockpit area must have been pushed into the mud as the fuselage collapsed into the nose windows. The tail must have fallen straight to the ground, collapsing from the impact and burying more fragments.

Stowe bought a large aerial photo of the crash site and shared it with Judy over a lunch in New Jersey. Judy ordered a bronze memorial plaque. Better to install it at the side of Gibbs Road, they concluded, than in the forest at the crash site. Judy tracked down the current owner of the land, who'd purchased it from the Zachrys, and gained her permission. In late November, Judy's cousin David Pope decided he would join them in Waycross. So did Gerald Cox, Richard E. Cox's younger brother. Shortly before Christmas, the bronze plaque arrived at Judy's home, packed in a wooden crate. Judy's husband and two sons broke it open, out in the garage. Judy thought the plaque looked beautiful.

Now, on January 8, the plaque rested in the Volvo, swathed in bubble wrap, as Judy and her husband started out. They were hauling a mountain of gear, some in a car-top carrier—shovels, rakes, clippers, cutters, saws, batteries, an ax, a machete, a Makita screwdriver, a cooler, two metal detectors, a bin for mixing cement. They stopped in Deptford, New Jersey, to meet Michael Stowe and transfer his equipment to their car, since he was flying to Georgia. That meant cramming more gear into the Volvo—buckets, tubes, rods, handles. In early afternoon, the overloaded Volvo pulled away, Judy waving to Stowe.

They rejoined on Thursday morning, when Stowe and his son Mike landed at the Jacksonville, Florida, airport. Stowe picked up a rental car and followed the Loethers on the seventy-eight-mile drive west to Waycross. They arrived at three p.m. and headed straight for the crash site—or at least tried to. They couldn't find it at first. They wandered around south of downtown in a region of narrow roads, railroad tracks, and small homes, asking directions until someone led them to Gibbs Street. They passed the school where Bernard Zachry had been playing, then an open field that Stowe recognized from his big aerial photo, and finally what seemed to be the wooded area where the plane had crashed.

Stowe and his son started into the forest. They'd been expecting mud, but found no water, no swamp, no thick underbrush. The maps and photos had told them there'd be a drainage ditch leading to the crash site, and there it was. They walked down the ditch, more like a wide trail, hindered only by fallen trees. They reached the intersection of a second, smaller, ditch. Was this the spot?

Stowe looked about for signs of the crash. It had all been open pasture in 1948; now forest had claimed the land. At first Stowe saw nothing. Then he took a few more steps, glanced down, and noticed a three-inch piece of aluminum. It can't be this easy, he thought. He bent to pick it up, but it wouldn't move. He gripped it with both hands and wiggled it vainly. He planted both feet and rocked it back and forth. Finally, the foot-long piece came out, with the imprint of a part number—a piece of the bomber. He carried it to the road and held it out to Judy. "We can go home now," he joked.

Instead, they drove the two miles to their hotel. In his room, Stowe taped his photos and maps to a door. He and his son joined the Loethers for dinner at a nearby Applebee's—the same restaurant where Judy had met the Zachry family in 2000. Back in their room later that night, Stowe and his son reviewed an illustrated parts manual for B-29s. Soon they found a match: What they'd carried from the forest was the intake vent from the leading edge of the B-29's left wing, between the fuselage and engine number two.

The excavation and discoveries continued for more than two days, until Stowe found it—the spot where the B-29's nose hit the ground. The reading there reflected not one big piece, but rather thousands of small fragments buried in an area twenty feet in diameter. Battling thick roots, Stowe and his son pulled up all manner of artifacts: insulation, electrical components, oxygen equipment, window framing, a sand-filled practice bomb (ballast?), and pieces of

Plexiglas from the B-29's nose, badly degraded but recognizable. Judy joined them for part of the dig. The forest was warm and humid, and silent but for the rustle of leaves in the breeze and the isolated calls of hawks. In time, they started to find larger and larger items—pieces of the cockpit and more Plexiglas. Stowe had always expected to find something, despite everyone's doubts, but not this much. He began sticking orange survey flags into the ground as he passed back and forth through the area, establishing an outline of the B-29's tail section. When his son held up a twelve-inch-long piece of metal, Stowe said, "Okay, silver on one side and cockpit green on the other. What is it? Think about it." His son didn't need to think: "Part of the window frame."

They stopped only to help Judy's husband dig the hole for the memorial plaque along the side of Gibbs Road. Then they mixed concrete in a big plastic tray, carrying pails of water from a nearby house. They lifted the bronze plaque from the back of the Volvo, removed the bubble wrap, set it into the hole, and poured the concrete. A handful of local residents started to gather. Sitting in a chair at the edge of Gibbs Road, Judy told her story more than once, speaking slowly and softly. Most of her listeners were astonished, having no idea what had happened in their neighborhood long ago, but one—a gray-haired man in his early sixties—recalled the accident. He'd been a seven-year-old student then at the elementary school across from the Zachry farm. He'd seen the crowds and parts of the airplane and two survivors walking silently down the dirt road, carrying their parachutes.

Judy ended up inviting him and several other neighbors to the memorial ceremony on Sunday. By then David Pope had arrived, and Judy's son Travis, and Gerald Cox with his son Richard. That morning, as Judy sat in her hotel room, organizing her thoughts for the ceremony, the Coxes visited the crash site, seeing the orange flags, the outline of the B-29's tail section—where R. E. Cox had been trapped. His brother, Gerald thought, would appreciate them finding this spot.

When Judy appeared, she adorned the memorial plaque with pots of flowers and small American flags on two-foot sticks, and set twenty more of the flags along the side of Gibbs Road. On an easel draped with a black blanket, she placed a framed photo of her father. In all, seventeen people gathered for the dedication ceremony, including eight neighbors. Some sat on folding chairs, others stood; all commented on their odd sense of camaraderie. At one p.m. under warm sunny skies, Judy began.

"The placing of this memorial is the culmination of a journey for me," she said. "One that started when I was seven weeks old and my father, Albert Palya, died at this place." She continued, summarizing the steps of that journey. She read poems—Tennyson's "Blow, Bugle, Blow" and Robert Frost's "Nothing Gold Can Stay." She read out the names and ages of all who died in B-29 #866. Then she invited others to speak.

Gerald Cox went first, thanking Judy for this "symbol of closure we otherwise would not have had." Judy's son Travis talked of the memorial's importance for future generations. Michael Stowe offered a history of the B-29 and the Banshee project. One of the local residents recalled his memories of the crash and volunteered to look after the memorial. Another vowed that he would make sure this story was told and retold. Judy's husband read the Twenty-third Psalm.

With that, everyone hugged and began to drift off, some to their homes, others to their hotels, Gerald and Richard Cox to the crash site for one last look. Michael Stowe and his son also lingered in the forest, laboring to fill in their excavation hole and pack up artifacts. Soon all was still along Gibbs Road. Only the bronze memorial plaque remained. Above the names of those who died, it offered an account of what had happened here.

On October 6th, 1948, a B-29 took off from Warner Robins Air Force Base in Georgia heading for Orlando, Florida, to test highly secret electronic equipment called Banshee. At 2:08 in the afternoon the plane caught fire, broke apart in the air and came to rest at this place. Four men parachuted to safety and nine men perished.

Project Banshee . . . was to prove that a pin-point target could be precision bombed, via a B-29 drone, by remote control. The technology was based on the Shoran navigational bombsite computer developed by RCA and Minneapolis Honeywell during WWII.

    This crash resulted in the landmark Supreme Court case US v. Reynolds . . . which gave the executive branch of the government the right to withhold documents it deemed secret from the courts.

    This stands as a memorial to those men who died here. May we ever remember their sacrifice.

NOTES AND SOURCES

Author's Note

ix   **Since 1973, the government**   The discussion here and throughout the narrative about the increasing use and ramifications of the state secrets privilege derives from a wide variety of sources. Among them: interviews and email exchanges with Jonathan Turley, Shapiro Professor of Public Interest Law at George Washington University; Steve Aftergood, director, Project on Government Secrecy, Federation of American Scientists; Mark Zaid, managing partner at Krieger & Zaid in Washington, D.C.; Kate Martin, director, Center for National Security Studies; Peter Raven-Hansen, Glen Earl Weston Research Professor of Law, George Washington University; William Weaver, associate professor of political science, University of Texas at El Paso; and Stephen Dycus, professor of law at Vermont Law School.

x   **The personal and private began with the widows.**   Interviews and email exchanges with Patricia Herring, Judy Palya Loether, Susan Brauner, and Cathy Brauner.

xi   **"Whatever happens," one law professor advised**   Stephen Saltzburg, George Washington University Law School, former Supreme Court clerk and member of the ABA's post–9/11 task force on terrorism. Quoted in "New Light on an Old Defense of 'Secrets,'" Marcia Coyle, *National Law Journal*, March 10, 2003.

Prologue

1   **Early on the morning of February 26, 2003**   This sequence and description of the Court derives from multiple interviews and email exchanges with Fran Bisicchia; a visit to the Court by researcher Lane Demas; *The Supreme Court of the United States,* Fred J. and Suzy Maroon (Charlottesville: Thomason-Grant & Lickle, 1996).

2   **[Higgins's] task was to check it**   Christopher Vasil, Chief Dep-
           uty Clerk, U.S. Supreme Court.

2   **Higgins began to read**   Opening lines, Preliminary Statement,
           Petition for a Writ of Error *Coram Nobis* to Remedy Fraud Upon
           This Court, March 4, 2003.

3   **. . . this petition spoke for**   The petition also spoke for Judy
           Palya Loether's brothers, Robert and William Palya, who joined the
           action belatedly and chose to remain "inactive" participants.

3   **The clerk read on:**   Preliminary Statement, Petition for a Writ of
           Error *Coram Nobis*.

3   **On Friday . . . he shipped the box**   Jeff Almeida interviews;
           copy of Higgins's letter provided by Almeida.

3   **That was wrong.**   Jeff Almeida; Christopher Vasil.

4   **In their homes, the women**   Interviews with Patricia Herring,
           Judy Palya Loether, Susan Brauner, and Cathy Brauner.

Chapter 1: Banshee Days

7   **The union of Bob and Patricia**   This passage and others through-
           out the narrative involving the Reynoldse's derive from multiple
           interviews and email exchanges with Patricia Reynolds Herring,
           2003–7.

8   **That February, Korea had split**   *Cold War America 1946–1990*,
           Ross Gregory, chapter 3, "Chronology 1946–1990" (New York:
           Facts on File, 2003); also, *A Preponderance of Power*, Melvyn P. Leffler,
           chapter 3, "The Cold War Begins" (Palo Alto: Stanford University
           Press, 1992).

8   **After World War II, control of the seas**   Leffler, p. 110; "Off the
           Record Remarks," Thomas Finletter, New York City, May 4 1950,
           in the Thomas K. Finletter Papers at the Harry S Truman Library.

9   **A fierce rivalry ensued**   Archives of the Air Force Historical Re-
           search Agency (AFHRA), Maxwell Air Force Base, Alabama. The
           history of the Banshee project's genesis and evolution, here and
           throughout the book, derives from a wealth of internal Air Force
           documents available on microfilm at AFHRA. Microfilm reels used
           for this account: 1934; 1933; 36493; 39960; 1039; 3969; 14870; 3968;
           10580; 2365; K2019. Included on those reels: Group History, First
           Experimental Guided Missiles Group (Eglin Air Force Base: Janu-
           ary–June 1947, July–December 1947, January–June 1948, July–De-
           cember 1948, January–June 1949, July–December 1949); History of the
           550th Guided Missiles Wing (July–December 1949, October–Decem-
           ber 1950); History of the 550th Guided Missiles Wing (October–
           December 1950, Appendix A); History of the 3150th Electronics

Squadron (Robins Air Force Base: January–June 1948, July–December 1948, January–June 1949, July–December 1949); History of the Development of Guided Missiles, 1946–1950 (Historical Office, Office of the Executive Assistant Commanding General, Air Materiel Command, Wright-Patterson Air Force Base, December 1951).

9   **The order came from . . . "Hap" Arnold**   AFHRA: History of the Development of Guided Missiles, 1946–1950—Correspondence, 1946.

10   **Al Palya certainly was the big shot.**   This section on Al Palya draws from multiple interviews with Judy Palya Loether and from her family's scrapbooks, correspondence, and written memories. Additional sources include interviews and documents provided by Judy's cousin David Pope, by Al's sister-in-law Jean Perryman, and by Viola Ergen, the widow of Al's colleague Bill Ergen.

10   **At Honeywell, he'd impressed everyone**   Walt Frick's letters; Bill Ergen's letters; interviews with Viola Ergen.

11   **Palya's young nephew**   Interview with David Pope.

12   **The directives . . . usually came from . . . LeMay**   This particular call for "continuing publicity" came in a memo written by Curtis LeMay on May 23, 1947, in AFHRA: History of the Development of Guided Missiles, 1946–1950—Correspondence, 1946; "Banshee (Guided Missile) Project."

13   **Couldn't they adapt the principles of Shoran**   AFHRA: History of the Development of Guided Missiles, 1946–1950—Correspondence, 1946; "Study of Banshee Utilizing Shoran"; and "Guided Missile Banshee Project."

13   **They and Bill Ergen filed a "Patent Disclosure Data Sheet"**   Copy of patent sheet provided by Viola Ergen.

13   **. . . Bill Ergen and Walt Frick decided to quit**   Interview with Viola Ergen; email message from Steve Frick (Walt's son) to Judy Palya Loether, February 5, 2003.

13   **"Banshee is a mess . . ."**   Resignation letter by Walt Frick to H. R. Dyson, May 1, 1947; provided by Judy Palya Loether

13   **He loved puzzles**   Email message from Judy Palya Loether, October 30, 2006.

13   **. . . reinforcements finally arrived.**   AFHRA: History of the Development of Guided Missiles, 1946–1950; Group History, 1st Experimental Guided Missiles Group, Eglin AFB, January–June 1947.

Chapter 2: B-29 Bombers

14   **The Air Forces handed supervision**   AFHRA: History 550th Guided Missiles Wing, October–December 1950, Appendix

A—Correspondence; March 11, 1947, memo, "Remotely Controlled
B-29 Flight, Project Banshee."

14   **. . . what Bob Reynolds found at Eglin**   AFHRA: Group
History, 1st Experimental Guided Missiles Group, Eglin AFB, January–June 1947.

14   **They had a mission statement**   Interviews and email correspondence with William O'Brien, Eglin radar technician who took written notes at Eglin in 1947.

14   **The Group's first major accident**   AFHRA: Group History, 1st
Experimental Guided Missiles Group, Eglin AFB, January–June 1947.

15   **To Bob Reynolds . . . such mishaps**   Interviews with William
O'Brien.

15   **Indeed, ever since its early development**   This section about
B-29 development and problems derives from a number of sources:
"Boeing B-29 Superfortress" (www.acepilots.com/planes/b29
.html); Joe Baugher, "Boeing B-29 Superfortress" (http://home.att
.net/~jbaugher2/b29_3.html); William R. "Bill" Corker, "Problems Affecting the B-29 Superfortress," in *Boeing B-29 Superfortress*,
by Steve Pace (Wiltshire, UK: The Crowood Press, 2003); Curtis
E. LeMay, and Bill Yenne, *Superfortress: The B-29 and American Air
Power* (New York: McGraw-Hill, 1988); Wilbur H. Morrison, *Birds
From Hell: History of the B-29* (Central Point, OR: Hellgate Press,
2001); Steve Pace, *Boeing B-29 Superfortress* (Wiltshire, UK: The
Crowood Press, 2003); "Prototype Boeing B-29 Crashes into Seattle's Frye Packing Plant" (Seattle, Washington: King Co., www.
historylink.org); Robert M. Robbins, "Eddie Allen and the B-29,"
in *Boeing B-29 Superfortress*, by Steve Pace (Wiltshire, UK: The
Crowood Press, 2003); "Second Report of the Commanding General of the Army Air Forces to the Secretary of War—The American Superfortress," U.S. Air Force Museum (www.wpafb.af.mil/
museum/), February 27, 1945; Earl Swinhart, "Boeing B-29 Superfortress" (www.aviation-history.com/boeing/b29.html); Jacob Vander
Meulen, *Building the B-29* (Washington, D.C.: Smithsonian Institution Press, 1995); Wilson, Stewart. *Boeing B-17, B-29 and Lancaster
Bombers* (Fyshwick, Australia: Aerospace Publications, January
1996).
At the start of production   Swinhart, "Boeing B-29 Superfortress."

15   **Nor did it help**   Vander Meulen *Building the B-29*; Swinhart,
"Boeing B-29 Superfortress."

15   **There matters stood**   "Boeing B-17, B-29 and Lancaster Bombers," by Stewart Wilson; "Eddie Allen and the B-29," by Robert M.
Robbins; "Prototype Boeing B-29 Crashes into Seattle's Frye Pack-

ing Plant," Seattle/King Co. HistoryLink.org; *Birds From Hell* by Wilbur H. Morrison; *Superfortress* by LeMay and Yenne; "Boeing B-29 Superfortress" by Swinhart.

16 **This disaster only magnified his anger** *Building the B-29*, by Jacob Vander Meulen.

16 **The B-29 Superfortress was extraordinary** "Problems Affecting the B-29 Superfortress" by William R. 'Bill' Corker [in Pace, 89–90]; "Boeing B-17, B-29 and Lancaster Bombers" by Stewart Wilson; photos published in *Boeing B-29 Superfortress* by Steve Pace; my personal inspection of a rebuilt B-29 at New England Air Museum, Bradley International Airport, Hartford, Connecticut.

16 **. . . what Curtis LeMay called . . . "swan-graceful"** *Superfortress*, by LeMay and Yenne, p. 59.

16 **"appeared to forget all about the maintenance"** AFHRA: History of AMC Maintenance Program and Problems 1945–1950, by S. A. Zimmerman.

16 **Engine fires continued to erupt.** *Birds From Hell* by Wilbur H. Morrison.

17 **Oh yeah, those engines were bastards.** Interviews with Raymond Toliver at his home in Oceanside, California, 2005–6.

17 **"What else could you do?"** Interviews and email exchanges with William O'Brien.

17 **During the summer of 1947** AFHRA: Group History, 1st Experimental Guided Missiles Group, Eglin AFB, January–June 1947.

17 **One such document records** "Report of Major Accident—Supplemental Analysis of Exhaust Bracket," December 17, 1948, by Col. H. A. Moody, president, Aircraft Accident Investigation Board.

18 **Five days later** "Special Investigation of Major Accident: Statement of Lt. Francis Backert, December 10, 1948.

18 **In the postwar demobilization** References here and throughout the book to Cold War events and context derive from many sources, there being an abundant literature on this era. Among them: David Cole, *Enemy Aliens: Double Standards and Constitutional Freedoms in the War on Terrorism* (New York: New Press, 2003); Ross Gregory, *Cold War America 1946 to 1990* (New York: Facts on File, 2003); Melvyn P. Leffler, *A Preponderance of Power: National Security, the Truman Administration and the Cold War* (Palo Alto: Stanford University Press, 1992); Elaine Tyler May, *Homeward Bound: American Families in the Cold War Era* (New York: Basic Books, 1988); Daniel Patrick Moynihan, "The Culture of Secrecy," *Public Interest*, June 22, 1997; Robert Nott, "Red Scare at Morning," *Santa Fe New Mexican*, February 21, 2003; Ellen Schrecker, *The Age of McCarthyism*

(New York: Bedford/St. Martins, 2002); Richard Alan Schwartz, *The Cold War Reference Guide* (Jefferson, NC: McFarland Press, 1997); Edward Shils, *The Torment of Secrecy: The Background and Consequences of American Security Policies* (New York: Free Press, 1956); Martin Walker, *The Cold War: A History* (New York: Henry Holt & Co., 1993); Randall B. Woods, and Howard Jones, *Dawning of the Cold War: The United States' Quest for Order* (Athens, Georgia: University of Georgia Press, 1991).

18   **. . . they spoke in apocalyptic terms**   Leffler, chapter 4, "From Truman Doctrine to National Security Act."

18   **"A fateful hour" had arrived**   Ibid.

19   **The services fought constantly**   Ibid.; "Rivalries Hamper Missiles Program," *New York Times,* June 4, 1947.

19   **They looked like B-29s.**   "Tu4 Soviet Copy of the B-29," by Joe Baugher; "The First Soviet Strategic Bomber Bears an Amazing Resemblance to the Boeing B-29," by Von Hardesty, *Air & Space Magazine*, February–March 2001; *Boeing B-29 Superfortress*, by Steve Pace, chapter 7.

Chapter 3: Delays and Progress

20   **"I was very busy"**   Letter provided by Judy Palya Loether.

20   **Less than a month later . . . a hurricane**   "Hurricane Sweeps Near East Coast," *New York Times*, September 16, 1947; "Winds Rake Coast in Hurricane Path Nearing Florida," *NYT*, September 17, 1947; "Resorts Hit in Hurricane over Florida, *NYT*, September 18, 1947; "Damage in Florida Rises to Millions," *NYT*, September 19, 1947.

20   **When it hit**   "Floridians Count $20,000,000 Losses," *New York Times,* September 21, 1947.

20   **Palya managed to fly down**   Letter from Bill Ergen to Tom Eaton, September 22, 1947, courtesy of Viola Ergen.

21   **Days later, officers at the Guided Missile Group**   AFHRA: Group History, 1st Experimental Guided Missiles Group, Eglin AFB, July–December 1947.

21   **Then came the decision to move the site**   AFHRA: Group History, 1st Experimental Guided Missiles Group, Eglin AFB, July–December 1947.

21   **This relocation made sense**   AFHRA: History 3150th Electronics Squadron, Robins AFB, July–December 1948.

21   **"Commanding Officer Warner Robins"**   AFHRA: Group History, 1st Experimental Guided Missiles Group, Eglin AFB, July–December 1947.

22   **At a press conference on October 1**   "Guided 200-mile Missile
        Forecast in Prototype Within a Few Years," *New York Times*, Octo-
        ber 3, 1947.

22   **The next month, on November 17**   "Russian Air Gain Noted
        by Spaatz," *New York Times*, November 18, 1947.

22   **Now should be a good time**   Letter courtesy of Judy Palya
        Loether.

22   **"Since our flight tests are bogged down**   Letter courtesy of
        Judy Palya Loether.

23   **"I don't believe I told you**   Letter courtesy of Judy Palya
        Loether.

24   **. . . the Air Force once again publicized Banshee**   "USAF
        Tests Look Far Into the Future," by Scripps-Howard aviation editor
        Max B. Cook, in AFHRA: Group History, 1st Experimental Guided
        Missiles Group, Eglin AFB, January–June 1948.

24   **In between the cancellations**   "Individual Flight Records" in
        Special Investigation of Major Accident, January 1949.

24   **Warner Robins . . . reported "good progress"**   AFHRA: Group
        History, 1st Experimental Guided Missiles Group, Eglin AFB, July–
        December 1948.

24   **. . . he was earning $6,720**   Transcript of Trial for Damages
        Before Judge William Kirkpatrick, November 27, 1950, Philadel-
        phia.

24   **In family scrapbooks**   Photo courtesy of Judy Palya Loether.

25   **Thus began HUAC's pursuit**   Shils, Edward. *The Torment of
        Secrecy: The Background and Consequences of American Security Policies*
        (New York: Free Press, 1956). Walker; Woods & Jones; Schrecker.
        Moynihan, Daniel Patrick. "The Culture of Secrecy," *Public Inter-
        est* (22 June 1997); Walker, Martin. *The Cold War: A History*.
        (New York: Henry Holt & Co., 1993); Woods, Randall B., and
        Howard Jones. *Dawning of the Cold War: The United States' Quest
        for Order*. (Athens: University of Georgia Press, 1991). Schrecker,
        Ellen. *The Age of McCarthyism* (New York: Bedford/St. Martin's,
        2002).

25   **"Could the Reds Seize Detroit?"**   "Red Scare at Morning,"
        Robert Nott, *Santa Fe New Mexican*, February 21 2003; *The Cold
        War*, by Martin Walker (New York: Henry Holt & Co., 1993).

Chapter 4: Final Exam

27   **At Warner Robins in the fall of 1948**   AFHRA: Group His-
        tory, 1st Experimental Guided Missiles Group, Eglin AFB, July–
        December 1948.

27   **"Every morning . . . on laboratory projects** Undated hand-written note by Walt Frick.

28   **On Friday evening, October 1** Handwritten note from Al Palya to his sister Lil, dated September 26, 1948.

28   **They needed to discuss** Interviews with David Pope and July 2004 email message from David Pope.

28   **That August . . . he'd written a strained letter** Letter provided by David Pope and Judy Palya Loether.

28   **Now Al and his sisters gathered** Interview with David Pope.

28   **That same Monday, William Brauner** Interviews with Susan and Cathy Brauner.

28   **At Purdue he met Phyllis Ambler** "Secrets and Lies," by Jennifer McFarland Flint, *Wellesley Magazine*, June 2004.

28   **. . . Brauner always looked at the positive** Interview with Cathy Brauner.

29   **In fact, Brauner had never** Individual flight records in Special Investigation of Major Accident, January 1949.

29   **His daughter waved back** Interview with Susan Brauner.

29   **Eugene Mechler . . . another electrical engineer**: Interview with Mechler's daughters, Betsy and Marion.

29   **Richard Cox . . . had no traveling** Interviews with Richard's brother Gerald Cox; documents provided by Gerald Cox.

29   **Well, the trip to Indianapolis** All Richard Cox letters provided by Gerald Cox.

30   **In fall 1948, Cox found himself** Gerald Cox interviews and correspondence.

30   **Two days later, Cox and Bob Reynolds** Individual flight records in Special Investigation of Major Accident, January 1949.

31   **"He went along," Frick told . . . Judy** Walt Frick, letter to Judy Palya Loether, February 1998.

31   **Frick planned to be aboard, too** Walt Frick, letter to Judy Palya Loether, March 6, 1996.

Chapter 5: The Flight

32   **In South Florida that Wednesday** "Hurricanes Leave One Dead 6 Injured in South Florida," *Waycross Journal-Herald*, October 6, 1948.

32   **Although the evidence remains uncertain** Eugene Mechler, in "Special Report on Project 2082-1 for RCA," prepared for the Franklin Institute after the crash, wrote that "there was no flight on Tuesday due to hurricane warnings in Florida." But no other available documentation reflects this suggestion of a delay from Tuesday to Wednesday.

32 **In late February, the 3150th** "Standard Operating Procedure for Banshee Project in #866 B29," February 24, 1948, in Special Investigation of Major Accident, January 1949.

33 **Despite these instructions** The account here of the events before takeoff derives from statements and testimony of the survivors (Copilot Moore, flight engineer Murrhee, scanner Peny, Franklin Institute engineer Mechler) in the initial Report of Major Accident and the supplemental Report of Special Investigation of Aircraft Accident; also from Mechler's Special Report to the Franklin Institute; and from the narrative summaries in the Report of Major Accident and the Report of Special Investigation of Airport Accident.

34 **Standard procedure next called for** Conclusions, Special Investigation of Major Accident.

34 **"The Air Force personnel was well-informed** Murrhee's testimony, Special Investigation

34 **The men . . . were not an established squad** Statements and testimony of survivors in Special Investigation and Report of Major Accident; testimony of A. H. Maresh in Special Investigation; "Facts" listed in Special Investigation; Memorandum for Chief of Staff USAF, January 3, 1949.

34 **The airplane assigned to them** Discussion in Special Investigation; testimony of Capt. Johnson of 3150th in Special Investigation; Statement of Sgt. Glenn Carter in Special Investigation; Statement of Edmund Surgrue in Special Investigation.

35 **That was not the first time** Statement of Lt. Francis Backert in Special Investigation.

35 **Those heat shields had never been installed.** "Airplane Flight Report," Attachment 19 in Report of Major Accident; Memorandum for Chief of Staff, January 3 1949; "Facts" in Special Investigation; Supplemental Report—Analysis of Exhaust Bracket, December 17, 1948.

35 **"See 41B for T.O. N C/W"** "Airplane Flight Report," Attachment 19 in Report of Major Accident.

35 **Following a standard preflight check** This extended reconstruction of the accident derives from a variety of sources, including testimony of the survivors and conclusions by investigators, as found in: "Appendix #1, History of the 3150th Electronics Squadron," Robins Air Force Base, July–December 1948 (Air Force Historical Research Agency, Maxwell Air Force Base, Alabama); Eugene Mechler's "Special Report on Project 2082-1 for RCA," Franklin Institute of Technology, October 1948; "Report of Major Accident," submitted October 18,1948; "Report of Special Investigation of Aircraft Accident," released January 6, 1949; and "Supplemental Report—Analysis of Exhaust Bracket," submitted December 17,

1948. It should be noted that much of what we know about events inside the doomed B-29 comes from people hurtling about in a catastrophic emergency—and from people with particular reasons to remember events in a certain way.

37   **As they'd been scrambling into their parachutes** Aviators just don't agree on this issue. At the New England Air Museum adjacent to Bradley International in Hartford, Connecticut, a quartet of veteran pilots and mechanics who'd studied all the documents related to the crash of B-29 #866 sat around a conference table in June 2005 debating the matter without resolution, although Glenn Mirtl, a copilot who flew thirteen missions in B-29s, insisted you "could continue with three engines, there's no reason not to keep going." By contrast, in Oceanside, California, retired Air Force colonel Raymond Toliver, a combat and test pilot, aviation historian, accident investigator, and Pentagon administrator, declared that he'd "start down, go home. . . . I'm not going to keep flying without an engine."

38   **The evidence suggests Captain Erwin** In assessing the crash of B-29 #866, I shared the accident report and related documents with a number of aviators. Among those who provided evaluation and interpretation:

> Air Force Colonel Raymond Toliver, a combat and test pilot, aviation historian, accident investigator and Pentagon administrator
> Rinker Buck, journalist, private pilot, accident analyst, and author of *Flight of Passage* (New York: Hyperion, 1997), a memoir of the cross-country flight he made at age fifteen, with his seventeen-year-old brother, in a rebuilt two-seat Piper Cub
> David Pope, a private pilot (and Judy Palya Loether's cousin)
> Ed Mitrani, a C-47 copilot and supply officer at Warner Robins in 1948
> Dave Santos, B-29 mechanic in early to mid-1950s
> Conrad (Connie) Lachendro, B-29 mechanic
> Glenn Mirtl, B-29 copilot
> Dave Amidon, Navy P2V Neptune pilot

40   **Here events begin to blur** Many critical moments were related later through the particular perspective of Copilot Moore. His statements and testimony come from the Major Report, the Special Investigation and Appendix 1 of AFHRA's History 3150th Electronics Squadron, Robins AFB, July–December 1948.

40   **Extending the immense landing gear**   In *Boeing B-29 Superfortress,* Steve Pace writes, "Aerodynamically, it was so streamlined that its parasite drag actually doubled when its landing gear was extended" (p. 181).

41   **Pilot Ralph Erwin was now flying**   I draw here from analysis by Rinker Buck.

41   **Sixty years later**   Interviews with Ray Toliver, 2005–6.

42   **. . . a "colossal mistake."**   Ibid.

43   **. . . hearing someone behind him say "Go."**   Moore's testimony in Special Investigation.

43   **Mechler had been waiting**   Mechler's Special Report to the Franklin Institute.

Chapter 6: Aftermath

44   **Witnesses on the ground**   Witness statements, Attachments 10–17, in Report of Major Accident.

44   **. . . watched as engine number four**   Section M, Description of the Accident, in Report of Major Accident.

44   **In his barn, Robert Zachry**   Interviews with Robert, Michael and Bernard Zachry, June 2003 in Waycross.

45   **In Waycross that morning**   "Mayor Proclaims Safety Week," *Waycross Journal-Herald,* October 6, 1948, p. 1.

46   **On the ground, Eugene Mechler**   Here and throughout this chapter, the account draws from Mechler's statements and testimony in Report of Major Accident, in Special Investigation of Major Accident and in History 3150th Electronics Squadron, Robins AFB, July–December 1948; also, Mechler's Special Report to the Franklin Institute, October 1948.

47   **The fuselage of B-29 #866**   Report of Major Accident, Attachment 2 and Attachment 5.

47   **Standing by the fence originally erected**   "Reaction of People at the Tragedy," by Laurie Lee Sparrow, *Waycross Journal-Herald,* October 7, 1948.

48   **Peny had landed in a swamp**   Walter Peny's statements and testimony in Report of Major Accident, in Special Investigation of Major Accident and in History 3150th Electronics Squadron, Robins AFB, July–December 1948.

48   **The young Zachry boys**   Interviews with Bernard and Michael Zachry.

48   **Soon, uniformed military officers**   Report of Major Accident, Attachment 2.

48   **The bodies of those who'd perished**   Report of Major Accident, Attachment 4—"Annotations from Section I."

49   **Shortly after five p.m.**   Interviews with Patricia Reynolds Herring.

51   **Staff Sergeant W. J. Peng thinks**   "Crash Survivors Thankful and Say Will Remember 'This Day a Long Time,'" by Jack Williams Jr., *Waycross Journal-Herald*, October 7, 1948.

51   **For years to come**   Steve Frick email to Judy Loether, April 22, 2004.

52   **Later, her attempts**   Interviews with Patricia Reynolds Herring.

52   **In eastern Pennsylvania**   Interview with Cathy Brauner; also "This Is What the Terrorists Really Took" by Cathy Brauner, *Wellesley Townsman*, September 27, 2001.

52   **When the news came, she cried out**   Interview with Susan Brauner.

53   **In Maryville, Missouri**   Interviews and correspondence with Gerald Cox.

53   **In Haddon Heights**   Interview with Bill Palya; email from Steve Frick to Judy Loether, July 2, 2003.

54   **I regret to inform that Mr. A. Palya**   Courtesy of Judy Palya Loether, from her family scrapbooks.

54   **Betty notified Al's mother, Anna**   Interviews with Judy Palya Loether and David Pope; Helen Palya's family history, "The Story of Ando and Anna Palya and Their Clan of Nine."

54   **Anna . . . sat now at the kitchen table**   Helen Palya's family history, "The Story of Ando and Anna Palya and their Clan of Nine."

55   **Betty also called her sister Jean**   Interview with Jean Perryman.

55   **Since her husband had been the only civilian**   Interview with Judy Palya Loether.

55   **It's Saturday, only one week**   Courtesy of Judy Palya Loether, from family scrapbooks.

55   **She would still make all their clothes**   Interview with Judy Palya Loether.

Chapter 7: Response

56   **the plane had been on a mission**   "B-29 Explodes, Killing 9," an abbreviated version of the AP story, appeared on p. 25 of the *New York Times* on October 7, 1948.

58   **Capt. Moore and Sgt. Murhee [sic]**   "Crash Survivor Says Fire in Engine Caused Tragedy," *Macon Telegraph,* October 7, 1948, p. 1.

58 **In his official sworn statement** Survivor statements, Report of Major Accident; survivor testimony, Special Investigation; Earl Murrhee's statement in Report of Major Accident; Earl Murrhee's testimony in Report of Special Investigation (here Murrhee wasn't sure whether the order came from the pilot or copilot).

59 **In the wake of the crash** "Special Orders Number 17," in Report of Special Investigation.

59 **So did . . . Edward Mitrani** Interview with Ed Mitrani, August 2004.

59 **Hours later, Eugene Mechler** Eugene Mechler's Special Report to Franklin Institute.

59 **The bodies of those killed** Report of Special Investigation.

60 **Mincy Funeral Home's bill** Copy of bill provided by Judy Palya Loether, from family scrapbooks.

60 **. . . Walt Frick escorted the body home** Walter Frick letter to Judy Palya Loether, March 6, 1996; Steve Frick email to Judy Palya Loether, July 2, 2003.

60 **Funeral services were held** "Former Resident Dies in Explosion of B-29," in an East Grand Forks newspaper around October 15, 1948 (name and date of newspaper obscured in photocopied clipping).

60 **Late that month, Al Palya's sister** Interview with Dave Pope.

61 **In November 1948** Interview with Viola Ergen, June 2004.

62 **It did not take long for the Air Force** Report of Major Accident, October 18, 1948.

63 **He had been appointed** History 3150th Electronics Squadron, Robins AFB, July–December 1948.

63 **Q: Did Captain Erwin** Testimony of H.W. Moore, October 11, 1948, at Headquarters, Warner Robins Air Materiel Area, Robins Air Force Base, given to Major Robert J. D. Johnson, Investigating Officer, Inspector General, First Region, Langley AFB; in Report of Special Investigation.

64 **On October 18, Colonel R. V. Ignico** Report of Major Accident.

64 **. . . "this headquarters does not concur** Report of Special Investigation.

65 **. . . would cause various veteran aviators to hoot** Among them Ray Toliver, Rinker Buck, Dave Pope, and Ed Mitrani.

65 **On the day he read** Interview with Ray Toliver.

65 **It came from Frank Folsom** Letter dated November 22, 1948, in Report of Special Investigation.

Chapter 8: Folsom's Letter

67   **At that time . . . Folsom was exceptionally influential**   This
        biographical sketch of Frank Folsom derives largely from the Frank
        M. Folsom Papers at the University Archives, Notre Dame Univer-
        sity. In particular: Box 1—Biographical information and personal
        correspondence, 1929–67; Box 2—business correspondence/RCA
        1943–68; Scrapbook 3—1946–48 photos, clippings, letters/RCA;
        Scrapbook 5—1948, RCA salute to Folsom, clippings; Scrapbook
        6—1949; Scrapbook 7—1949–54. Among the documents used:
        "RCA's Frank Folsom," by James C. G. Conniff, *The Catholic Digest*,
        July 1954; "Executive Biography Francis Marion Folsom," RCA
        Department of Pubic Affairs, May 1967; "Along the Highways and
        Byways of Finance," by Robert H. Fetridge, *New York Times*, Janu-
        ary 15, 1950; Sermon ("Francis Marion Folsom") delivered by Rev.
        Theodore M. Hesburgh, January 16, 1970; "Frank M. Folson—A
        Biographical Sketch," Department of Information, RCA; "The Man
        Who Sells Takes the Helm," by Dickson Hartwell, *Nation's Business*,
        November 1949; "The Two-Man Team That Runs RCA," *Business
        Week*, November 17, 1951.

67   **"Folsom plays by ear"**   This comment was made by Sewell Av-
        ery, Folsom's boss at Montgomery Ward, quoted in "Along the
        Highways and Byways of Finance" by Robert H. Fetridge, *New York
        Times*, January 15, 1950.

68   **Folsom's constant display**   "The Man Who Sells Takes the
        Helm," by Dickson Hartwell, *Nation's Business*, November 1949.

69   **Folsom . . . would later receive**   Navy's Distinguished Civilian
        Service Award conferred August 3, 1944 by Secretary of Navy James
        Forrestal "for exceptional services to the U.S. Navy"; the Medal for
        Merit was awarded in January 1946, "for exceptionally meritorious
        conduct in the performance of outstanding service. . . . His skill and
        ingenuity materially speeded up the procurement of the weapons of
        war and saved the Navy millions of dollars."

69   **To spur things, Folsom invited**   Hartwell, "The Man Who
        Sells," and elsewhere—this is an oft repeated story.

69   **. . . Folsom's letter began**   In Report of Special Investigation.

72   **Copies of Folsom's letter**   Ibid.

72   **On November 30, the deputy chief of staff**   Ibid.

72   **On December 2, the inspector general**   "Memo for the Air
        Inspector," December 2, 1938, in Report of Special Investigation.

73   **One day later**   December 3, 1948, in Report of Special Investiga-
        tion.

73   **Agents from that division**   Report of Special Investigation.

73   **In late October, Colonel H. A. Moody**   Exhaust bracket memo, October 28 1948, in Report of Major Accident ("It is requested that an analysis be made of enclosed exhaust bracket to determine whether crack was progressive or resulted from crash").

73   **In early December . . . Moody received**   "Exhaust Bracket" (response), December 3, 1948, in Report of Major Accident.

73   **On December 17, he wrote**   In Report of Major Accident.

74   **On December 17, the same day Moody delivered**   In Report of Major Accident.

74   **Veteran aviators point out**   Discussions and email exchanges with Rinker Buck.

74   **The accident over Waycross was a textbook**   Ibid.

75   **Consider the commands**   Ibid.

75   **What's more, Lieutenant General B. W. Chidlaw**   December 31, 1948, letter from Chidlaw, "Subject: B-29 Airplane, Serial No. TB-21866," in Report of Special Investigation.

76   **Three days after Chidlaw's declaration**   "Memo to Air Inspector," January 4, 1949, in Report of Special Investigation.

Chapter 9: Special Investigation

77   **Three days before the report's official distribution**   An initialed, dated, stamped box on the first page of "Memorandum for the Chief of Staff United States Air Force," January 3, 1949, indicates the upgrade to "Secret." In Report of Special Investigation.

77   **The nine-page report**   "Report of Special Investigation of Aircraft Accident Involving B-29 No. 45-21866."

78   **Veteran aviators scoff**   Among them, Ray Toliver. Also, Rinker Buck, Dave Pope, Ed Mitrani, and the four B-29 veterans who studied the report at the New England Air Museum in Hartford.

78   **On January 10, the inspector general**   Routing and Record Sheet, Subject—Report of Major Aircraft Accident Investigation Involving B-29 No. 45-21866.

79   **This "talking points" memo**   "Information Concerning Comments Contained in Letter from Mr. Frank Folsom, RCA," January 10, 1949. In Report of Special Investigation.

79   **On February 17 . . . Major General William F. McKee**   In Report of Special Investigation.

80   **On March 2, 1949, two weeks after**   Frank M. Folsom Papers at the University Archives, Notre Dame University.

80   **Universities conferred degrees**   Ibid.

81   **Under Folsom's leadership in early 1949**   Frank M. Folsom Papers; "RCA History—Television," at RCA.com; *Cold War America*

1946–1990, Ross Gregory, "Radio and Television," pp. 167ff; *Make Room for TV,* Lynn Spiegel (Chicago: University of Chicago Press, 1992).

81 **In March 1949, Captain H. W. Moore** History 3150th Electronics Squadron, Robins AFB, January–June 1949.

81 **(Moore would remain on active duty** National Personnel Records Center, Military Personnel Records; November 14, 2005, response to my inquiry.

81 **In November 1948, an official** Lt. Col. Murl Estes, Deputy Chief, Flying Safety Division, April 4, 1949; in Report of Special Investigation.

81 **In June 1949, the log** History 3150th Electronics Squadron, Robins AFB, January–June 1949.

81 **The log provided one other** Ibid.

Chapter 10: Thoughts of Redress

85 **The President likened the current situation** "Truman Declares Hysteria Over Reds Sweeps the Nation," *New York Times,* June 17, 1949.

86 **By the spring of 1949** See, for example, Ellen Schreker, *The Age of McCarthyism* (New York: Bedford/St. Martin's, 2002).

86 **A month later, Governor Thomas Dewey signed** "Dewey Signs Bill to Oust Reds and 'Fellow-Travelers' in Schools," *New York Times,* April 2, 1949.

86 **They . . . were all struggling** Interviews with Patricia Reynolds Herring, Judy Palya Loether, Susan Brauner, and Cathy Brauner.

87 **It was Phyllis** Interviews with Susan and Cathy Brauner; "Secrets and Lies," by Jennifer McFarland Flint, *Wellesley Magazine,* Spring 2004.

87 **The exchange started with . . . Mattern** Copies of all correspondence referred to here provided by Judy Palya Loether from family scrapbooks.

89 **Perryman had never finished** Interview with Jean Perryman, September 2004.

Chapter 11: Charles Biddle

90 **Even more unlikely** This biographical sketch of Charles Biddle and account of the Biddle family history draws from an extended visit with James Biddle at Andalusia in June 2003, and a number of additional sources. Among them: Charles Biddle, *Fighting Airmen: The Way of the Eagle* (Garden City, N.Y.: Double-

day, 1968); Dave Bruton (Drinker Biddle & Reath partner), interview, April 2003, at DBR offices in Philadelphia; Dave Maxey
(Drinker Biddle & Reath partner), email exchanges, 2005; Debo-
rah S. Gardner, and Christine G. McKay, *Building a Law Firm
1849–1999, A Sesquicentennial History* (Philadelphia: Drinker Bid-
dle & Reath, 1999); James Norman Hall, and Charles Bernard
Nordhoff, "Biographical Sketch—Charles J. Biddle," in *Fighting
Airmen: The Way of the Eagle*, by Charles Biddle (Garden City,
N.Y.: Doubleday, 1968); Marion Willis Rivinus, and Katharine
Hansell Biddle, *Lights Along the Delaware* (Philadelphia: Dorrance
& Company, 1965); and Nicholas B. Wainwright, *Andalusia,
Country Seat of the Craig and Biddle Family* (Andalusia, Pa: Histori-
cal Society of Pennsylvania, 1976), which includes a "Prologue"
by James Biddle.

90   **One of the most powerful**   Wainwright, *Andalusia.*
91   **Katharine . . . loved to entertain**   James Biddle's "Prologue," in
     Wainwright, *Andalusia.*
91   **"a peak of immaculate preservation**   Ibid.
92   **He had joined . . . Dickson, Beitler**   Gardner and Mckay, *Build-
     ing a Law Firm.*
92   **In Charles Biddle's day**   Ibid.
93   **One evening every spring**   Ibid.
93   **Although the mood**   David Maxey, email, August 2004.
93   **His old-fashioned patrician style**   Interview with David Bur-
     ton, April 2003.
93   **He'd wave off settlements**   Ibid.
93   **Among his most celebrated**   Ibid.
93   **. . . at the request of Governor . . . Scranton**   "Scranton
     Picks 2 Phila. Lawyers for Girard Court Test," *Philadelphia Inquirer,*
     September 24, 1965; Gardner and Mckay, *Building a Law Firm.*
93   **Above all, he was known as**   Hall and Nordhoff, "Biographical
     Sketch—Charles J. Biddle"; Gardner and Mckay, *Building a Law
     Firm;* "Charles J. Biddle, Ace in World War I, Dies," *Philadelphia In-
     quirer,* March 24, 1972.
94   **Trained in French aviation schools**   Hall and Nordhoff, "Bio-
     graphical Sketch—Charles J. Biddle."
     . . . "I admire your courage   Related by Murray K. Guthrie,
     Flight Commander, 13th Pursuit Squadron, in "Preface" to Biddle,
     Fighting Airmen.
94   **Throughout the war, he wrote**   All passages from Biddle's let-
     ters quoted here come from his book *Fighting Airmen: The Way of the
     Eagle,* which is a republication of *The Way of the Eagle* (New York:
     Charles Scribner's Sons, 1919).

95 **When Biddle spotted it** Hall and Nordhoff, "Biographical Sketch—Charles J. Biddle."

96 **German guns it would be.** Ibid.

96 **"With remarkable courage** Belgian Ordre de Leopold (Chevalier) by Royal Decree of February 27, 1920, preserved in a Biddle family scrapbook at Andalusia.

97 **Authorities officially credited him** Hall and Nordhoff, "Biographical Sketch—Charles J. Biddle."

Chapter 12: The Complaint

99 **Patricia Reynolds could recall nothing** Interview with Patricia Reynolds Herring.

100 **On June 21 . . . Biddle filed a complaint** Copies of this and all other legal documents, provided by Drinker Biddle & Reath, come from the official Transcript of Record, Supreme Court of the United States, *United States of America, Petitioners v. Patricia Reynolds, Phyllis Brauner and Elizabeth Palya.*

101 **One day in September** Interview with Patricia Reynolds Herring.

101 **On September 27, Biddle filed a second complaint** Transcript of Record, Supreme Court.

101 **These were alarming events.** Among other sources for this discussion, see *A Preponderance of Power,* by Melvyn Leffler (Palo Alto: Stanford University Press, 1993), *Dawning of the Cold War,* by Randall Woods, and Howard Jones (Chicago: Ivan R. Dee, 1991); *The Cold War,* by Martin Walker (New York: Henry Holt & Co., 1993).

101 **"This is now a different world"** *Dawning,* by Woods and Jones, p. 249

101 **"The red tide,"** *Time* **. . . declared** *Walker, p. 62 ff*

102 **. . . "dangerously inadequate military strength"** Leffler, p. 331.

102 **. . . "isolated from our sources** *Leffler p. 13*

102 **In May 1949** Group History, 1st Experimental Guided Missiles Group, Eglin AFB, January–June 1949 and July–December 1949; History of the Development of Guided Missiles, 1946–1950.

102 **So Banshee missions continued to fly** Ibid.

103 **The death knell** Group History, 1st Experimental Guided Missiles Group, July–December 1949, Appendix #4—Letters and Study, Request for Termination Project Banshee.

103 **Air Force Headquarters retroactively granted** Ibid.

103 **A termination report** "Project Banshee Termination Report,"

July 19, 1950, in History 550th Guided Missiles Wing, October–
December 1950.

103   **On Wednesday, November 16, 1949**   "U.S. Grounds B-29s as
Another Crash Kills 5 in Florida," *New York Times*, November 19
1949.

104   **. . . the story ran the next day**   Ibid.

104   **Four days later**   Transcript of Record, U.S. Supreme Court; copy
from Drinker Biddle & Reath.

Chapter 13: Judge Kirkpatrick

105   **. . . he submitted thirty interrogatories**   Transcript of Record,
U.S. v. Reynolds; "Interrogatories Propounded by Plaintiffs Under
Rule 33," filed November 28, 1949.

105   **He did not get much in response.**   "Answer to Interrogatories
Propounded by Plaintiffs Under Rule 33," filed January 5, 1950.

106   **Instead, on January 18 he filed a motion**   "Motion for Production of Documents Under Rule 34," filed January 18, 1950.

106   **Gleeson and Curtin responded**   "Motion to Quash Order and
Motion for Production of Documents," filed January 25, 1950.

106   **By 1950, Kirkpatrick**   This biographical sketch of Judge William
Kirkpatrick derives from a variety of interviews and documents.
Most of the written material is available in the Archives of the Law
Library at the U.S. Courthouse in Philadelphia and the Archives of
the Historical Society of the U.S. District Court for the Eastern District of Pennsylvania, in Philadelphia. Among the documents and
interviews: *Biographical Directory of the U.S. Congress;* Steve Dittmann,
"William H. Kirkpatrick," profile written for the Historical Society
of the U.S. District Court for the Eastern District of Pennsylvania
(Philadelphia); Joseph B. G. Fay, "The Judicial Legacy of Hon. William H. Kirkpatrick: A Snapshot"; John Francis Goldsmith, Address
at memorial services for Judge William Kirkpatrick, June 14, 1971;
"Judge William H. Kirkpatrick, U.S. District Court," Event program, Northampton County Bar Association tribute to Judge William Kirkpatrick, September 21, 1966; "Socialegal Club Presents
Portrait of Kirkpatrick to the District Court," *Philadelphia*, vol. 138,
April 30, 1958. Interviews at the U.S. Courthouse in Philadelphia,
June 2005, with: Dolores Slovitor (U.S. circuit judge), Edward Mullinix (Philadelphia-based lawyer), John Fullam (U.S. district judge),
Joseph Coffey (Judge Kirkpatrick's last law clerk), and Michael Kunz
(clerk of court for the U.S. District Court in Philadelphia).

106   **. . . from calling him "Kirky"**   Dittmann, "William H. Kirkpatrick."

107　　**When sitting in Philadelphia**　Dittmann; interview with Joseph Coffey.

107　　**One story has it**　Circuit Judge John Biggs, Jr. in "Socialegal Club Presents Portrait."

107　　**Besides bridge**　Dittmann; interview with Joseph Coffey.

108　　**. . . the largest collection of dachshunds**　Biggs in "Socialegal Club Presents Portrait."

108　　**Invariably, he would be wearing**　Interviews with Joseph Coffey, Michael Kunz, Edward Mullinix, Judge John Fullam, and Judge Dolores Slovitor.

108　　**Even more unnerving**　Biggs in "Socialegal Club Presents Portrait."

109　　**He could have ended up**　Biggs in "Socialegal Club Presents Portrait"; Goldsmith, Address.

109　　**Those who worked for Kirkpatrick**　Interview with Joseph Coffey.

109　　**. . . his best-known case, *Hickman v. Taylor.***　"The Judicial Legacy of Hon. William H. Kirkpatrick: A Snapshot," by Joseph B. G. Fay; *Hickman v. Taylor et al.,* Civil Action No. 3511, District Court, Eastern District of Pennsylvania, July 30, 1945.

109　　**Writing for all five**　*Hickman v. Taylor et al.,* District Court, July 30, 1945.

110　　**The appellate judges**　*Hickman v. Taylor et al.,* Circuit Court of Appeals for Third Circuit, December 10, 1945.

111　　**The U.S. Supreme Court**　*Hickman v. Taylor,* U.S. Supreme Court, January 13, 1947; 329 U.S. 495, 67 S.Ct. 385.

111　　**. . . he found the tug company liable**　*Hickman v. Taylor,* District Court for Eastern District of Pennsylvania, October 9, 1947.

111　　**. . . in the summer of 1948**　Case No. 287 of 1946, *O'Neill v. United States,* District Court for Eastern District of Pennsylvania, August 23, 1948.

112　　**Again the Third Circuit**　*Alltmont v. U.S. et al.,* U.S. Court of Appeals for the Third Circuit, November 23, 1949.

112　　**These two cases, *Hickman* and *O'Neill***　Transcript of Record, *U.S. v. Reynolds.*

113　　**Phyllis Brauner . . . turned down an offer**　"Secrets and Lies," by Jennifer McFarland Flint, *Wellesley Magazine,* Spring 2004.

113　　**Patricia . . . inched back into the world**　Interview with Patricia Reynolds Herring.

113　　**On June 26, Biddle wrote**　Copy of letter provided by Judy Palya Loether.

114　　**Truman was at his home**　"Mr. Truman's Memoirs: The Attack in Korea," Installment 15 Excerpt from *Years of Trial and Hope,* in *New York Times,* February 7, 1956.

114 **Among the twenty or so** "Mr. Truman's Memoirs"; Oral History Interview with Thomas Finletter, Truman Presidential Museum and Library, Independence, Missouri.

115 **That same Friday . . . Kirkpatrick finally delivered** *Brauner et al. v. U.S., Reynolds v. U.S.,* U.S. District Court for Eastern District of Pennsylvania, June 30, 1950; 10 F.R.D. 468, 1950 U.S. Dist, Lexis 3524.

118 **With the Fourth of July falling on a Tuesday** "Traffic Jam Peak Expected Today as Record Holiday Exodus Begins," *New York Times,* July 1, 1950.

118 **Before he departed** Copy of Biddle's letter provided by Judy Palya Loether.

Chapter 14: A Claim of Privilege

119 **On July 20, 1950, Kirkpatrick issued** Transcript of Record, *U.S. v. Reynolds.*

119 **At Charles Biddle's urging** Letter from Biddle to Mattern, July 25, 1950.

119 **On July 24, Biddle . . . met with Kirkpatrick** Transcript of Record, *U.S. v. Reynolds*; this event is effectively summarized later in Judge Maris's opinion for the U.S. Third Circuit, December 11, 1951.

120 **The next day . . . Biddle wrote to Mattern** Copy of letter provided by Judy Palya Loether.

123 **Finletter, then fifty-seven** This biographical sketch of Thomas Finletter derives from a variety of sources, including: "Thomas Finletter," United States Air Force Biography; Thomas K. Finletter, "The Great Tradition," *Library Journal,* February 1, 1956; "Profile of Thomas K. Finletter," Harry S Truman Presidential Library; "Thomas Finletter, Jurist, 84, Is Dead," *New York Times,* February 5, 1947; Thomas K. Finletter, oral history, Harry S Truman Presidential Library (February 1972); "President Judge Finletter: Thirty Years on Bench," *The Legal Intelligencer,* April 12 1945. Most materials—including appointment books, newspaper clippings, correspondence files, public statements, personal memoranda, and flight logs—are available in the Thomas K. Finletter Papers, Harry S Truman Presidential Library (Independence, Missouri).

123 **(A decade later, his own name** Among other places, evidence of Finletter's name being floated as a candidate for the Senate can be found in a "personal and confidential" memorandum between New York political operatives (Jim Loeb to Milton Stewart) on November 11, 1957, and in "Harriman Silent on Running Mates," *New York*

Times, May 28, 1958. Both are in the Thomas K. Finletter Papers at the Harry S Truman Library.

123 **As chairman of Truman's . . . Commission** Letter from Truman to Finletter, July 18, 1947; response from Finletter to Truman, July 21, 1947; in Thomas K. Finletter Papers at the Harry S Truman Library.

123 **In an off-the-record speech** "Off-the-Record Remarks," New York City, May 4, 1950, in Thomas K. Finletter Papers.

123 **Reginald Harmon, who was then fifty** This biographical sketch of Reginald Harmon derives from a variety of sources, including: his U.S. Air Force Biography; "Reginald Harmon, 92; Led Air Force Lawyers," his obituary in the *New York Times,* October 24, 1992.

124 **When August 7 arrived** Transcript of Record, *U.S. v. Reynolds:* Transcript of Proceedings, U.S. District Court for the District of Columbia, August 9, 1950; Opinion of the Court, Third Circuit Court of Appeals, December 11, 1951.

124 **That same August 7** "Affidavit of the Judge Advocate General, U.S. Air Force," *Patricia J. Reynolds v. United States of America,* subscribed and sworn to August 7, 1950. In Transcript of Record.

125 **One day later** "Claim of Privilege by the Secretary of the Air Force," *Patricia J. Reynolds v. United States of America.* In Transcript of Record.

125 **Instead of the state secrets privilege** My analysis here draws from discussions with Wilson Brown, and from Louis Fisher, *In the Name of National Security* (Lawrence, Kansas: University Press of Kansas, 2006).

Chapter 15: The Hearing

127 **Relatively fair, cool weather** "Weather Throughout the Nation," *New York Times,* August 10, 1950.

127 **The hearing began . . . at 9:45 a.m.** "Transcript of Proceedings" in the United States District Court for the District of Columbia, Washington, D.C., August 9, 1950, *Brauner and Palya v. United States of America, Reynolds v. United States of America;* in Transcript of Record.

131 **In 1949, a U.S. District Judge** *U.S. v. Cotton Valley Operators Committee,* 9 F.R.D. 719 (D La 1949).

131 **. . . the Supreme Court . . . had affirmed** *U.S. v. Cotton Valley Operators Committee,* 339 U.S. 940 (1950).

132 **At some point during that summer** This trip is referred to in a letter from W. J. Perryman to Betty Palya, September 1, 1950. Copy of letter provided by Judy Palya Loether.

132   **I think Mr. Biddle is doing**   Ibid.

133   **Two weeks later on September 14**   The disputed B-29 documents come from Michael Stowe's microfilm archive of U.S. Air Force aviation accident reports. Stowe noticed and deciphered these classification markings.

133   **On September 21 . . . Judge Kirkpatrick issued**   "Amended Order re production and inspection of documents," September 21, 1950. In Transcript of Record.

134   **Eight days later, Kirkpatrick entered a default**   "Order that facts be taken as established," October 12, 1950. In Transcript of Record.

134   **In a letter, Francis Hopkinson**   Copy of letter provided by Judy Palya Loether.

Chapter 16: Full Value

135   **Over the Thanksgiving weekend**   "City Is Repairing Damage of Storm; 206 Dead in Nation," *New York Times*, November 27, 1950; "$400,000,000 Storm Loss Seen; Deaths in 22 States Rise to 273," *NYT*, November 28, 1950; "Pittsburgh Fights to Dig Itself Out," *NYT*, November 29, 1950; "Weather 1," *NYT*, November 27, 1950; "The Weather Throughout the Nation," *NYT*, November 28, 1950.

135   **Since Judge Kirkpatrick had entered a default**   Transcript of Record, U.S. v. Reynolds.

136   **Exhibit A advised that**   Transcript of the Trial Record, *Brauner and Palya v. U.S.A.* and *Reynolds v. U.S.A.*, in the U.S. District Court for the Eastern District of Pennsylvania, before Hon. William H. Kirkpatrick, Philadelphia, November 27, 1950.

137   **She was five-two**   Interview with Judy Palya Loether.

138   **Five days later**   "Army is 3-Touchdown Favorite Over Navy in Classic at Philadelphia Today," *New York Times*, December 2, 1950; "Truman, Under a Wartime Guard, Sees Navy Team Upset the Army," *NYT*, December 3, 1950; "Big Show, Whale of a Game Thrill Truman, Top Brass," *NYT*, December 3, 1950.

138   **Kirkpatrick took nearly three months**   "Opinion on Pleadings and Proof," in U.S. District Court, filed February 20, 1951.

139   **A week later**   "Decree," filed February 27, 1951, in U.S. District Court.

139   **"I am enclosing copies**   Copy of letter provided by Judy Palya Loether

139   **On March 29, a jury**   "Spy Jury Locked Up After Deciding on 2 in Atom Conspiracy," *New York Times*, March 29, 1951; "3 in Atom

Case ·Are Found Guilty; Maximum Is Death," *NYT*, March 30, 1951.

139   **A week later Judge Irving Kaufman**   "Sentencing of Julius and Ethel Rosenberg," excerpted in *The Age of McCarthyism*, by Ellen Schrecker.

140   **"I now close my military career**   "Truman Relieves M'Arthur of All His Posts; Finds Him Unable to Back U.S.-U.N. Policies; Ridgway Named to Far Eastern Commands," *New York Times*, April 11, 1951; "M'Arthur Calls Asia Policy 'Blind to Reality'; Says Joint Chiefs Shared Views on Strategy; Cheered by Congress; Here for Parade Today," *NYT*, April 20, 1951; "Profound Division in Capital Caused by General's Speech," *NYT*, April 20, 1951; "Millions Give Record Welcome to M'Arthur; Tons of Paper Showered on 19-Mile Parade; Files Show General Expected Quick Victory," *NYT*, April 21, 1951.

140   **That same day . . . government lawyers filed**   Transcript of Record, *U.S. v. Reynolds*.

140   **"As we anticipated,"**   Copy of letter provided by Judy Palya Loether.

140   **. . . a butcher named Bill Sacker**   Interview with Judy Palya Loether.

140   **Also that June, the government lawyers**   "Motion to Consolidate . . . And Motion for Extension of Time in Which to File Appellant's Brief," June 21, 1951. In Transcript of Record.

141   **Biddle opposed their motion**   "Answer to Motion for Extension of Time," June 22, 1951.

141   **The Third Circuit granted an extension**   "Order of June 29," in U.S. Court of Appeals for the Third Circuit, by Chief Judge Biggs.

141   **On October 6, Joseph Stalin confirmed**   "Stalin Says Soviet Has Atomic Bombs of Varied Calibers," *New York Times*, October 6, 1951.

Chapter 17: Judge Maris

142   **Maris was fifty-seven, tall**   This biographical sketch of Judge Albert Maris derives from a rich variety of sources. Most material is available in the Albert Branson Maris Personal Papers, Historical Society of the Third Circuit Court of Appeal, U.S. Courthouse Law Library (Philadelphia). Among the sources, there and elsewhere: Albert Maris, videotaped interviews conducted by his son, Robert Maris, 1984; "Appreciation of The Honorable Albert Branson Maris," Supreme Court of the United States, May 20, 1974; John Corr, "A Life Full of Decision," *Philadelphia Inquirer*, May 13, 1985;

Ida O. Creskoff, "Albert Branson Maris," *The Shingle,* Philadelphia
Bar Association, June 1948; "Dedication Ceremony for the Albert
Branson Maris Courtroom," June 27, 1988; Cynthia L. Duffy, "Cut-
ting His Own Path," *The Pennsylvania Lawyer,* October 1988; "Judge
Albert B. Maris '11," *The Westonian,* Winter 1983; Michael E. Kunz
(clerk, United States District Court for the Eastern District of Penn-
sylvania), interview, June 2005, U.S. Courthouse, Philadelphia;
Emilie Lounsberry, "Honoring 50 Years on the Bench," *Philadelphia
Inquirer,* June 28, 1988; "Presentation of Edward J. Devitt Distin-
guished Service to Justice Award to Honorable Albert Branson
Maris," March 23, 1983; Dolores K. Sloviter (U.S. Circuit Judge),
and John P. Fullam (U.S. District Judge), interviews, June 2005,
U.S. Courthouse, Philadelphia; Stephen Presser, *Studies in the History
of the U.S. Courts of the 3rd Circuit 1790–1980.* Bicentennial Com-
mittee of the Judicial Conference of the United States (Washington,
D.C.: U.S. Government Printing Office, 1982); "Proceedings in
Memory of Honorable Albert Branson Maris," March 9, 1989; "Pro-
ceedings of a Special Session of the [Third Circuit] Court of Appeals
Honoring the Honorable Albert B. Maris," January 5, 1959; "The
Albert B. Maris Symposium," videotape and transcript, October 25,
1990; "Tribute to the Honorable Albert B. Maris," Thirty-Sixth
Annual Judicial Conference, Third Judicial Circuit of the United
States, October 16, 1973.

142 **He "walked like a farmer"** Interview with Judge Fullam.

142 **He was an avid** Interview with Judge Sloviter.

142 **Once, after slipping on some ice** Interview with Judge Fullam.

143 **He knew every line of Gilbert & Sullivan** Interview with Judge Sloviter.

143 **A shy schoolboy** This account of Maris's early relationship with the cobbler Johnny Fitzpatrick is repeated in a variety of places, in- cluding "A Life Full of Decisions," *Philadelphia Inquirer,* May 13, 1985. Maris himself talks about the cobbler in videotaped interviews conducted by his son in 1984.

144 **There he joined John Biggs** *Studies in the History of the U.S. Courts of the 3rd Circuit,* by Stephen Presser.

144 **They were willing . . . to work as "social engineers"** Ibid.

144 **As a Quaker** "Albert Branson Maris," by Ida O. Creskoff, *The Shingle,* Philadelphia Bar Association, June 1948. Creskoff, formerly Maris's law clerk, wrote this a year after being appointed chief clerk of the Third U.S. Circuit Court of Appeals.

144 **What may be his best-known decision** *Gobitis et al. v. Minersville School District et al.,* District Court, Eastern District of Pennsylvania.

On motion to dismiss, December 1, 1937; injunction granted June 18, 1938.

144   **The case . . . began two years before**   Apart from the narrative summaries in the court rulings, this account of the *Gobitis* case derives from a variety of articles, including: "Minersville Had Role in High Court's Pledge Ruling," by Dr. Harry M. Bobonich, *The Anthracite History Journal*; "Judge Albert Maris: I Pledge Allegiance," by Burton Caine, *The Temple Review*, Summer 1989; "Compulsory Flag Salute Upheld by Supreme Court in School Case," *New York Times*, June 4, 1940; "Flag Salute Edict Is Ruled Illegal," *NYT*, June 19, 1938; "Court Backs Pupils Refusing Flag Salute," *NYT*, November 11, 1939; "Flag Salute Order Upheld," *Los Angeles Times*, June 4, 1940.

145   **Still, he denied the motion to dismiss**   *Gobitis et al. v. Minersville School District et al.*, on motion to dismiss, December 1, 1937.

145   **The next summer . . . Maris granted the injunction**   *Gobitis et al. v. Minersville School District et al.*, injunction granted June 18, 1938.

146   **By a vote of eight to one**   *Minersville School District et al. v. Gobitis et al.*, Supreme Court of the United States, June 3, 1940.

146   **School boards can compel a salute**   "The Nation—Supreme Court Recess," *New York Times*, June 9, 1940.

147   **In the wake of the Supreme Court's ruling**   "Minersville Had Role in High Court's Pledge Ruling," by Dr. Harry M. Bobonich, *Anthracite History Journal*; "Judge Albert Maris: I Pledge Allegiance," by Burton Caine, *The Temple Review*, Summer 1989.

147   **The case, *West Virginia State***   *West Virginia State Board of Education et al. v. Barnette et al.*, Supreme Court of the United States, June 14, 1943.

147   **This time, the majority concluded**   Ibid.

147   **Frankfurter, despite writing a . . . dissent**   Franklin C. Muse, archivist for the Historical Society of the Third Circuit Court of Appeals, at the Albert B. Maris Symposium, October 25, 1990, U.S. Courthouse, Philadelphia.

147   **As time passed**   Judge Herbert Goodrich, at the Proceedings of a Special Session of the [Third Circuit] Court of Appeals Honoring the Honorable Albert B. Maris, January 5, 1959.

147   **"Yes," Maris would say**   Videotaped interview of Maris, conducted by his son Robert in 1984.

148   **In August of 1949**   Albert Branson Maris Personal Papers.

148   **During the summer of 1951**   Ibid.

148   **On August 31, he sent a sampling**   Ibid.

148   **Vinson wrote back**   Ibid.

149   **Slade was an appellate specialist**   "Philadelphia Barrister: Samuel

D. Slade," *The Shingle*, Philadelphia Bar Association, December 1973.

149   **The government contested Kirkpatrick's ruling** Brief of the United States, *Reynolds v. United States* (Third Circuit, 1951), as quoted in chapter 3 of Louis Fisher's *In the Name of National Security*. Fisher's analysis of this hearing provides a useful perspective.

150   **Biddle responded on several levels** Brief for Appellees, *Reynolds v. United States* (Third Circuit, 1951), as quoted in Fisher, *In the Name of National Security*.

151   **A typical day around this time** "Albert Branson Maris," by Ida O. Creskoff, *The Shingle*, Philadelphia Bar Association, June 1948.

151   **Maris's "little black book"** Albert Branson Maris Personal Papers.

152   **Late in his life** Videotaped interviews, 1984, conducted by Robert Maris.

153   **On November 29, he wrote back** Copy of letter provided by Judy Palya Loether.

153 ·   **On the morning of December 11, Judge Maris filed** "Opinion of the Court" in U.S. Court of Appeals for the Third Circuit, *Reynolds v. United States, Brauner and Palya v. United States;* filed December 11, 1951.

156   **One day later, on December 12** Copy of Biddle's letter provided by Judy Palya Loether.

Chapter 18: The Vinson Court

157   **Phyllis continued to both teach and study** Interviews with Susan and Cathy Brauner.

157   **In mid-March, they learned** "Petition for a Writ of Certiorari to the U.S. Court of Appeals for the Third Circuit," *United States of America, Petitioner, v. Reynolds et al.,* Supreme Court of the United States, October Term 1951; filed March 1952.

158   **Biddle referred to these "scandals"** Copy of letter provided by Judy Palya Loether.

158   **Biddle's "guess" proved accurate.** "Order Allowing Certiorari," *United States v. Reynolds et al.,* April 7, 1952.

158   **"As you may have seen** Copy of letter provided by Judy Palya Loether.

159   **The Vinson Court came to be** This extended discussion of Fred Vinson and the Vinson Court derives from a variety of sources, including: "Chief Justice Vinson Dies of Heart Attack in Capital," *New York Times*, September 8 1953; "Chief Justice Harlan Stone of Supreme Court Is Dead," *NYT*, April 23, 1946; David Cole, *Enemy*

Aliens: Double Standards and Constitutional Freedoms in the War on Terrorism (New York: New Press, 2003); John P. Frank, "Fred Vinson and the Chief Justiceship," *University of Chicago Law Review*, vol. 21, 1953/1954; "Fred M. Vinson," Timeline of the Justices, The Supreme Court Historical Society; "History of the Vinson Court," The Supreme Court Historical Society; "Key Cases Marked Tenure of Vinson," *NYT*, September 9, 1953; Richard Kirkendahl, "Fred M. Vinson," in *The Justices of the United States Supreme Court 1789–1969*, edited by Leon Friedman and Fred Israel, Vol. 4 (New York: Chelsea House, 1995); "New Justice Will Join a Divided High Court," *NYT*, April 28, 1946; "President Asked Jackson Silence," *NYT*, June 15, 1946; Herman C. Pritchett, *Civil Liberties and the Vinson Court* (Chicago: University of Chicago Press, 1954); Ronald Radosh, and Joyce Milton, *The Rosenberg File* (New York: Holt, Rinehart and Winston, 1983); Fred Rodell, *Nine Men: A Political History of the Supreme Court from 1790 to 1955* (New York: Random House, 1955); Bernard Schwartz, *A History of the Supreme Court* (New York: Oxford University Press, 1993); "Split of Jackson and Black Long Widening in Capital," *NYT*, June 19, 1946; "Supreme Court Justices: Fred Vinson," Michael Ariens, www.michaelariens.com; "Truman to Name Member of Court as Chief Justice," *NYT*, April 29, 1946; "Vinson Expected to Bring Supreme Court Harmony," *NYT*, June 9, 1946; "Vinson Named Chief Justice," *NYT*, June 7, 1946.

159   **Yet Truman's plan**   Rodell; Schwartz; Kirkendahl; Ariens; "Chief Justice Harlan Stone of Supreme Court Is Dead," *New York Times*, April 23, 1946; "New Justice Will Join a Divided High Court," *NYT*, April 28, 1946; "Truman to Name Member of Court as Chief Justice," *NYT*, April 29, 1946; "Vinson Named Chief Justice," *NYT*, June 7, 1946; "Vinson Expected to Bring Supreme Court Harmony," *NYT*, June 9, 1946.

159   **Frankfurter may have similarly blocked**   Rodell.

159   **Vinson's easygoing nature**   Rodell; Schwartz; Kirkendahl; Pritchett.

160   **By most accounts**   Rodell; Schwartz; Kirkendahl; Pritchett.

160   **"He blithely hits the obvious points"**   This excerpt from Frankfurter's diary appears in Schwartz, *A History of the Supreme Court*.

160   **When, in 1949, Vinson actively supported**   Rodell; Schwartz.

160   **A possibly apocryphal story**   Ariens.

160   **Vinson was a hefty five-foot-eleven**   Kirkendahl; "Chief Justice Vinson Dies of Heart Attack in Capital," *New York Times*, September 8, 1953.

161   **Truman particularly appreciated**   Kirkendahl.

161 **In fact, Truman embraced** "Chief Justice Vinson Dies of Heart Attack in Capital," *New York Times*, September 8, 1953.

161 **(Truman later explained)** Woods and Jones, *Dawning of the Cold War*, p. 230.

161 **While sitting as chief justice** "Chief Justice Vinson Dies of Heart Attack in Capital," *New York Times*, September 8, 1953; Kirkendahl.

161 **Throughout the Truman administration** Ibid.

161 **What most distinguished this chief justice** Frank; Ariens.

161 **Given Vinson's experience** Schwartz; Frank; Kirkendahl; Schrecker.

161 **The Vinson Court's defining opinion** *Dennis et al. v. United States*, Supreme Court of the United States, 71 S.Ct. 857; decided June 4, 1951.

161 *Dennis* **. . . is considered the nadir** Rodell; Kirkendahl; Pritchett; Schwartz; Cole.

162 **The native Communists** Cole; Pritchett; Rodell.

162 **Thus the Vinson Court** Rodell.

163 **Two steel-mill owners . . . filed suit** *Youngstown Sheet & Tube Co. v. Sawyer*, 103 F.Supp. 569 (D.D.C.) 1952.

163 **The justices questioned . . . Perlman** "High Court Jurists Sharply Question Defense of Seizure," *New York Times*, May 13, 1952.

163 **By contrast, the attorney representing** Ibid.

163 **Near the end of the hearing** Ibid.

164 **On June 2, the justices** *Youngstown Co. v. Sawyer*, 343 U.S. 579 (1952).

164 **As usual, his words** Kirkendahl.

164 **"We have been advised by the Clerk** Copy of letter provided by Judy Palya Loether.

164 **"I shall be in Washington** Copy of letter provided by Judy Palya Loether.

165 **The government filed first** Brief of the United States, *United States v. Reynolds et al.,* in the Supreme Court of the United States, October Term 1952.

166 **Biddle responded in forty-one pages** Brief for Repondents, *United States v. Reynolds et al.,* in the Supreme Court of the United States, October Term, 1952.

169 **Fair but cold winter weather** "The Weather in the Nation," *New York Times*, October 22, 1952.

169 **In the news that day** "Eisenhower Scores Statement on Bias Made by President," *New York Times*, October 21, 1952; "Truman Says G.O.P. Twists Remarks on Religious Bias," *NYT*, October 21, 1952; "Stevenson Taunts Rival for No Plan," *NYT*, October 21, 1952.

169   **. . . Charles Biddle wore striped pants** Letter from Teddy
Mattern to Phyllis Brauner, October 23, 1952. Mattern attended the
Supreme Court hearing.

169   **It's known, from Teddy Mattern** Ibid.

169   **And it's known, from the justices' tally sheets** The votes
of the justices for and against granting *certiorari* are recorded on
tally sheets in the Frederick Moore Vinson Papers, Special Collections Library, University of Kentucky, and in the William O.
Douglas Papers, Manuscript Division, Library of Congress,
Washington, D.C. I have copies of those sheets, obtained from
the Vinson and Douglas archives in December 2005. Reports of
this vote also appear in Louis Fisher's *In the Name of National Security*.

169   **"This case poses important problems** I have a copy of this law
clerk's memo, obtained in December 2005 from the William O.
Douglas Papers. Excerpts from it also appear in Fisher's *In the Name
of National Security*.

170   **In a letter to Phyllis** Letter from Mattern to Phyllis Brauner,
October 23, 1952.

Chapter 19: A Nice Opinion

171   **On October 25, 1952** This account of deliberations by the Su-
preme Court derives largely from documents obtained from the
Frederick Moore Vinson Papers, Special Collections Library, Uni-
versity of Kentucky. Additional source documents come from the
Papers of William O. Douglas, Felix Frankfurter, Hugo Black, and
Robert H. Jackson, Manuscript Division, Library Of Congress,
Washington, D.C. Louis Fisher's *In the Name of National Security*
provides a corroborating source. Fisher, a senior scholar in the
Law Library at the Library of Congress, proves abler than I (and
the handwriting experts I enlisted) at deciphering William O.
Douglas's handwritten notes taken during the Court's Saturday
conference.

171   **. . . "the judiciary can't get into it"** According to Louis Fisher's
reading, Douglas's notes summarize Vinson's remarks this way:
"Should judges have the power to make an inspection? If so counsel
could claim to see it and so eventually you would have a complete
disclosure—Judiciary can't enter into it without taking away a privilege from the Executive—not convinced that U.S. can be forced to
pay for exercising its privilege—reverse."

171   **Hugo Black likely spoke next** According to Fisher's reading,
Douglas's notes summarize Black this way: "Tort Act placed U.S.

in same position as other defs [defendants]—U.S. can decline
to permit [produce?] papers—but if so it must pay the
consequences—affirms."

171 **Stanley Reed spoke also**   According to Fisher's reading, Douglas's
notes summarize Reed: "U.S. can protect itself against disclosure of
secret intelligence."

171 **. . . and Felix Frankfurter at length**   According to Fisher's
reading, Douglas's notes summarize Frankfurter as expressing his
concern that no "body of law" existed on the secrets of the sovereign.

171 **By the end of the conference**   Tally sheets in the Frederick Moore
Vinson Papers, Special Collections Library, University of Kentucky;
and in the William O. Douglas Papers, Manuscript Division, Library
of Congress, Washington, D.C.

172 **Vinson assigned himself**   Frederick Moore Vinson Papers.

172 **"I agree with your treatment**   Ibid.

172 **"I voted the other way,"**   Ibid.

172 **"Dear Fred," Black wrote**   Ibid.

172 **"Dear Chief," wrote Robert Jackson**   Ibid.

172 **"Dear Fred," Felix Frankfurter wrote**   Ibid.

172 **On March 9, Vinson**   *United States v. Reynolds,* 345 U.S. 1 (1953),
decided March 9, 1953.

175 **Three days before**   "Stalin Dies After 29-Year Rule; His Successor
Not Announced; U.S. Watchful, Eisenhower Says," *New York Times,*
March 6, 1953.

176 **Stalin's death continued to dominate**   "Kremlin Guns Roar in
Dirge for Stalin," *New York Times,* March 10, 1953; "Dulles Says
Death of Stalin Enhances Peace Prospects," *NYT,* March 10, 1953.

176 **"The Supreme Court . . . ruled 6 to 3**   "High Court Denies
Right of Judges to Arms Secrets," *New York Times,* March 10,
1953.

176 **That same day, March 10**   Copy of letter provided by Judy Palya
Loether.

177 **A week later**   Copy of letter provided by Judy Palya Loether.

178 **One month later, Judge Maris**   U.S. Court of Appeals for Third
Circuit, *Reynolds v. United States,* Case No. 10,483, filed April 13,
1953. In Transcript of Record.

178 **On March 27, he served notice**   In Transcript of Record.

178 **On April 29, he wrote**   Copy of letter provided by Judy Palya
Loether.

179 **Just weeks before, Douglas**   "The Black Silence of Fear," *New York
Times Magazine,* January 13, 1952. An abridged version is reproduced
in Ellen Schrecker's *The Age of McCarthyism.*

179   **At televised hearings**   "Dashiell Hammett Silent at Inquiry," *New York Times*, March 27, 1953; "Wave of McCarthyism Decried," *NYT*, March 28, 1953.

180   **In April . . . Roy Cohn and David Schine**   "An Annotated Chronology of Important Cold War Events," in Richard Alan Schwartz, *The Cold War Reference Guide.*

180   **Throughout this tour**   "Books of 40 Authors Banned by U.S. in Overseas Libraries," *New York Times*, Junes 22, 1953.

180   **On June 13, 1953, at its Saturday conference**   This summary of the Court's involvement in the Rosenberg case draws from *The Rosenberg File* by Ronald Radosh and Joyce Milton (chapter 27, "The Supreme Court"); *Civil Liberties and the Vinson Court* by C. Herman Pritchett (chapter 1); and "Rosenbergs Executed as Atom Spies After Supreme Court Vacates Stay; Last-Minute Plea to President Fails," *New York Times*, June 20, 1953.

181   **They comprised a minority**   Frankfurter offered a separate opinion, expressing his belief that they needed more time to consider the matter. The next Monday, after the Rosenbergs had been executed, he filed an unequivocal dissenting opinion, saying, "I am clear that the claim had substance and that the opportunity for adequate exercise of the judicial judgment was wanting" (see Pritchett, p. 9).

181   **Shortly after eight p.m.**   "Rosenbergs Executed as Atom Spies After Supreme Court Vacates Stay; Last-Minute Plea to President Fails," *New York Times*, June 20, 1953.

181   **Three days later**   "Stipulation" and "Order," *Phyllis Brauner and Elizabeth Palya v. United States* (Civil Action No. 9793), *Patricia Reynolds v. United States* (Civil Action No. 10142), U.S. District Court, E.D. Penn.; in Transcript of Record.

181   **In a letter dated June 26**   Copy of letter provided by Judy Palya Loether.

181   **With that in hand**   Interview with Judy Palya Loether.

181   **. . . while Phyllis Brauner reported to Mattern**   In a letter to Phyllis dated June 22, 1953, Mattern wrote, "Thanks for your note from which I learned that you are now again your good old self."

182   **"As you know, I hated to settle**   In his letter, Biddle also noted: "I much appreciate your nice letter and I am so glad to know that you are getting along all right and that the money has been a comfort."

Chapter 20: Judy

185   **One month after the case settled**   "Truce Is Signed, Ending the Fighting in Korea; P.O.W. Exchange Near; Rhee Gets U.S. Pledge;

Eisenhower Bids Free World Stay Vigilant," *New York Times,* July 27, 1953.

185   **Soon the Supreme Court** "Chief Justice Vinson Dies of Heart Attack in Capital," *New York Times,* September 8, 1953; "U.S. Mourns Vinson, Delicate Balance of Court at Stake," *NYT,* September 9, 1953.

185   **Eisenhower . . . like Truman** "Eisenhower Leads Tribute to Vinson," *New York Times,* September 9, 1953.

185   **Amid the public tributes** "Other Tributes Voiced," *New York Times,* September 9, 1953.

185   **Within days** "Warren Is Slated for Appointment as Chief Justice," *New York Times,* September 29, 1953.

186   **The Cold War kept escalating** *The Cold War Reference Guide,* Schwartz.

186   **On November 1** "Cold War and Beyond, Chronology of the United States Air Force 1947–97," by Frederick J. Shaw and Timothy Warnock, Air Force History and Museum Program, 1997.

186   **Across the country** See, for example, *Homeward Bound,* by Elaine Tyler May.

186   **In 1953, they saw Swanson introduce** "Chronology 1946–1990" (chapter 3) and "Entertainment" (chapter 17) in *Cold War America,* by Ross Gregory.

186   **In the first years of her life** Judy Palya Loether's memories and perspective here derive from hours of interviews and email exchanges with her, 2003–7.

187   **Still, Judy's older brother Bill** Interview with William Palya, July 6, 2005.

188   **"Dear Mother Palya** Copy of this card provided by Judy Palya Loether.

188   **On September 14, 1953** Copy of letter provided by Judy Palya Loether.

189   **Yet one of Judy's childhood friends** Letter from Susan to Judy, dated February 9, 2003: "When we were growing up and as a child I always felt there was an elephant in the closet of your house and I think I knew the elephant was your father. I remember an afternoon in your attic and an area with your father's things and you very reluctantly pointing them out."

189   **Her stepfather had an impossible task.** Interview with William Palya.

191   **I was in a B-29 accident** Copy of letter provided by Judy Palya Loether.

191   **I am sure the plane was not sabotaged.** Copy of letter provided by Judy Palya Loether.

Chapter 21: The Progeny of *Reynolds*

193   **The application of Reynolds** This discussion about *U.S. v. Reynolds*'s progeny and the decision's public ramifications draws from a wide variety of sources. Among them: Frank Askin, "Secret Justice and the Adversary System," *Hastings Constitutional Law Quarterly*, Vol. 18 (1), Summer 1991, 745–77; David A. Churchill and Elaine J. Goldenberg, "Who Will Guard the Guardians? Revisiting the State Secrets Privilege of *United States v. Reynolds*," *Federal Contracts Report*, Vol. 80, Number 11, 30 September 2003; John W. Dean, "ACLU v. National Security Agency: Why the 'State Secrets Privilege' Shouldn't Stop the Lawsuit Challenging Warrantless Telephone Surveillance of Americans," *FindLaw*, June 16, 2006; Stephen Dycus et al., *National Security Law* (New York: Aspen Law & Business, 2002); J. Steven Gardner, "The State Secret Privilege Invoked in Civil Litigation," *Wake Forest Law Review*, Vol. 29, Summer 1994; Thomas G. Stacy, "The Constitution in Conflict: Espionage Prosecutions, The Right to Present a Defense, and the State Secrets Privilege," *University of Colorado Law Review*, Vol. 58 (2), Spring 1987, 177–254; "The Military and State Secrets Privilege: Protection for the National Security or Immunity for the Executive," *Yale Law Journal*, Vol. 91, 1982; William G. Weaver, and Robert M. Pallitto, "State Secrets and Executive Privilege," *Political Science Quarterly*, Vol. 120, Number 1, Spring 2005; James Zagel, "The State Secrets Privilege," *Minnesota Law Review*, Vol. 50 (5), April 1966, 875–910. I have also interviewed and corresponded with the following: Steve Aftergood (director, Project on Government Secrecy, Federation of American Scientists), interview, June 2003, Washington, D.C.; Stephen Dycus (professor of law, Vermont Law School) email exchanges, 2003–5; Kate Martin (director, Center for National Security Studies), interview, June 2003, Washington, D.C.; Peter Raven-Hansen (Glen Earl Weston Research Professor of Law, George Washington University), interview, June 2003, Washington, D.C.; Jonathan Turley (Shapiro Professor of Public Interest Law, George Washington University), interview, June 2003, Washington, D.C.; William Weaver (associate professor of Political Science, University of Texas at El Paso), interview, Rancho Santa Fe, California, May 2005, and subsequent email exchanges; Mark Zaid (managing partner, Krieger & Zaid), interview, June 2003, Washington, D.C., and subsequent email exchanges.

193   **One of the earliest instances** *Republic of China v. National Union Fire Insurance Co.,* U.S. District Court, District of Maryland, Admiralty Division, July 9, 1956.

194   **By contrast, two years later** *Halpern v. United States*, U.S. Court of Appeals for the Second Circuit, Aug. 4, 1958.

194 **In January 1963** *Machin v. Zuckert,* U.S. Court of Appeals for the District of Columbia Circuit, January 17, 1963.

194 **In July 1968** *Heine v. Raus,* U.S. Court of Appeals for the Fourth Circuit, July 22, 1968.

194 **. . . there has been a marked increase** Interview and correspondence with William Weaver.

194 **Several possible reasons** Robert M. Chesney, "State Secrets and the Limits of National Security Litigation," Wake Forest Legal Studies Research Paper Series, November 2006.

194 **In July 1974 came the case** *United States v. Richard M. Nixon,* U.S. Supreme Court, July 24, 1974.

195 **By drawing such a sharp distinction** William Weaver.

195 **This is certainly one reason** William Weaver.

195 **Scholars differ when calculating** I rely here on Weaver. For an alternate perspective, see Chesney, "State Secrets and the Limits of National Security Litigation."

196 **It requires little reflection** *Halkin v. Helms I,* U.S. Court of Appeals for the D.C. Circuit, June 16 1978; *Halkin v. Helms II,* U.S. Court of Appeals for the D.C. Circuit, September 21, 1982.

196 **In December 1980** *Farnsworth Cannon v. Grimes,* U.S. Court of Appeals for the Fourth Circuit, June 12, 1980.

197 **In May 1983** *Ellsberg v. Mitchell,* U.S. Court of Appeals for the D.C. Circuit, May 10, 1983.

197 **In November 1984** *Molerio v. FBI,* U.S. Court of Appeals for the D.C. Circuit, November 30, 1984.

197 **A year later** *Fitzgerald v. Penthouse International,* U.S. Court of Appeals for the Fourth Circuit, November 7, 1985.

197 **Nor, in January 1990** *Patterson v. FBI,* U.S. Court of Appeals for the Third Circuit, January 8, 1990.

197 **Over time, it became evident** Correspondence with Stephen Dycus, professor of law, Vermont Law School.

197 **In June 1991 and September 1992** *Zuckerbraun v. General Dynamics,* U.S. Court of Appeals for the Second Circuit, June 13, 1991; *Bareford v. General Dynamics,* U.S. Court of Appeals for the Fifth Circuit, September 16, 1992.

199 **Q: There was some feeling** This interview, for the Fred Vinson Archives, was conducted on August 17, 1976. I obtained an audiotape of the interview from the Frederick Moore Vinson Papers, Special Collections Library, University of Kentucky.

199 **On the occasion of his eightieth birthday** The programs and record of proceedings at all Maris tributes mentioned here can be found in the Albert Branson Maris Personal Papers, maintained by the Historical Society of the Third Circuit Court of Appeals at the Law Library in the U.S. Courthouse, Philadelphia.

200   **Maris died seven months later . . . filing one last opinion**   Circuit Judge Dolores K. Sloviter, in remarks at the memorial service for Maris on March 9, 1989, at the U.S. Courthouse, Philadelphia, before a Joint Session of the U.S. Third Circuit Court of Appeals and the U.S. District Court for the Eastern District of Pennsylvania.

200   **In 1971, Erwin Griswold**   John W. Dean discusses this matter in "ACLU v. National Security Agency," *FindLaw,* June 16, 2006. His perspective (quoted below) is particularly useful, since he then was working in the White House. "Serving, at the time, as counsel to the president, I watched as the government sought injunctions against the *New York Times* and the *Washington Post* . . . knowing full well that none of the government's lawyers involved actually knew what was in those documents. The U.S. Attorney in the Southern District of New York had thought it unseemly to argue for a prior restraint upon the press . . . without knowing why. I agreed, and tried to find out what the justification for seeking this extraordinary remedy might be. But the Defense Department refused to explain what was in the papers to anyone. . . . The Solicitor General at the time, Erwin Griswold . . . did not insist on knowing what was actually contained in the Pentagon Papers, and he never found out, even as he insisted on the importance of their continued secrecy."

201   **Judges were requiring private**   According to a tabulation provided me by William Weaver.

201   **Merely by waving *Reynolds***   I first heard the phrase "atmospheric effect" from Peter Raven-Hansen

201   **Attorney General John Ashcroft**   Senator Grassley and Representative Berman were writing Ashcroft about a case involving a whistleblower, Dr. Nira Schwartz, who vainly tried to sue TRW Inc. and Boeing over what she charged were false test results in an antimissile system. She filed her action on behalf of the federal government under the False Claims Act, a law coauthored by Berman and Grassley.

201   **Just seven weeks earlier**   *Sibel Edmunds v. U.S. Dept of Justice,* U.S. Circuit Court for the D.C. District. The Justice Department news release ("Statement of Barbara Comstock, Director of Public Affairs, Regarding Today's Filing in Sibel Edmunds v. Department of Justice") came on October 18, 2002.

Chapter 22: What to Search For

202   **The years 1979 to 1994**   Judy Palya Loether's memories and perspective here derive from hours of interviews and email exchanges with her, 2003–7.

203   **He thought it very "thoughtful"**   Copy of letter provided by Judy Palya Loether.

204   **"I can understand**   Copy of letter provided by Judy Palya Loether.

204   **On eBay, Judy found**   Copy of this ad provided by Judy Palya Loether.

205   **"USAF & USAAF AIRCRAFT**   A printout of this website's home page, as it appeared in February 2000, provided by Judy Palya Loether.

206   **In Millville, New Jersey**   This description of Michael Stowe's home and office draws from my visit there in September 2004.

206   **The largest pile**   This catalogue provided by Michael Stowe.

207   **Airplane crashes had mesmerized Michael**   Michael Stowe's memories and perspective here derive from hours of interviews and email exchanges with him, 2004–7. The passages also draw from numerous local New Jersey newspaper articles about Stowe, from Stowe's personal scrapbook of mementos and press clippings, and from an autobiographical essay written by Stowe.

208   **"I hereby waive**   Copy of this letter provided by Michael Stowe.

210   **"We were able to find**   Copy of this email message provided by Judy Palya Loether.

210   **As she began to read**   The pages Stowe originally provided Judy included all documents from both the initial Report of Major Accident and the second Report of Special Investigation, but they were out of order and not clearly divided into two reports. Later, after studying his microfilm source, Stowe would properly order and divide the pages. I received the first version of the pages from Drinker Biddle & Reath, copied from what Stowe sent Judy in February 2000. I received the second, reordered, version from Michael Stowe.

211   **My name is Judy Palya Loether.**   Copy provided by Judy Palya Loether.

211   **I am the person you are looking for.**   As quoted by Louis Fisher, *In the Name of National Security*, p. 167; note provided to him by Cathy Brauner.

Chapter 23: How to Get Started

212   **At her home**   Susan Brauner's memories and perspective here draw from interviews and email exchanges with her, 2003–4.

212   **Once Cathy asked her mom**   Interview with Cathy Brauner, 2003; "This Is What the Terrorists Really Took," by Cathy Brauner, *Wellesley Townsman*, September 27, 2001.

213   **Settling into Wellesley in the 1950s**   This biographical sketch of Phyllis Brauner and her family derives from interviews with Susan and Cathy Brauner; "Secrets and Lies, What Happened to William Brauner," by Jennifer McFarland Flint, *Wellesley Magazine,* Spring

2004; "Person of the Week: Phyllis Brauner" (wellesley.edu/anniversary/brauner.html); "Phyllis Ambler Brauner, 84, Taught Chemistry at Simmons," by Tom Long, *Boston Globe*, Dec 28, 2000; the Phyllis A. Brauner Memorial Lecture website (http://ase.tufts.edu/chemistry/iacobucci/brauner/index.html); and "This Is What the Terrorists Really Took," Cathy Brauner, *Wellesley Townsman*, September 27, 2001.

214   **"In a lot of ways"**   Interview with Cathy Brauner, 2003.

214   **Once, when her mom had joked**   Ibid.

214   **Phyllis heard from another teacher**   Cathy Brauner, "This Is What the Terrorists Really Took."

215   **On March 18, 2000**   This account of the Wellesley Inn lunch and its aftermath draws from interviews with Susan Brauner, Cathy Brauner, and Judy Palya Loether.

217   **We recently obtained a key government report**   Copy of letter provided by Wilson Brown, Drinker Biddle & Reath.

217   **No one could find the relevant files**   Interviews with Wilson Brown, 2003–7.

217   **On May 22 . . . James M. Sweet wrote back**   Copy of letter provided by Wilson Brown.

218   **Judy turned back to the Internet**   Copies of all email exchanges referred to here provided by Judy Palya Loether.

218   **"Dear Judy," he responded**   Copy of letter provided by Judy Palya Loether.

219   **"I realize that it was only**   Copy of letter provided by Judy Palya Loether.

219   **In the days that followed**   Interview with Cathy Brauner.

220   **On September 27, she published**   Cathy Brauner, "This Is What the Terrorists Really Took," *Wellesley Townsman*, September 27, 2001.

221   **It extended to former presidents**   William G. Weaver and Robert M. Pallitto discuss this in "State Secrets and Executive Privilege," *Political Science Quarterly*, Vol. 120, Number 1, Spring 2005.

Chapter 24: Waycross

222   **As 2001 drew to an end**   Interviews and email exchanges with Judy Palya Loether, 2003–7.

222   **"Well, ma'am . . ."**   This account of Judy's conversations with the Zachrys draws from interviews with both Judy and members of the Zachry family, including Bernard and Michael.

223   **Judy drove up from Orlando**   For this account, I retraced Judy's route, visiting Waycross in June 2003. While there I met the Zachry family for lunch at the same Applebee's where Judy met them.

223   **Incorporated in 1874**   This historical sketch of Waycross draws largely from *History of Ware County, Georgia,* by Laura Singleton Walker (Macon: T.W. Burke Co., 1934).

223   **. . . remained something of a frontier community**   "Two Brothers Shot Dead," *New York Times,* May 19, 1886; "A Farmer Murdered," *NYT,* May 28, 1884.

223   **"I was sore at the Government,"**   "Bears Killed Cows; He Slays 2 Rangers," *New York Times,* June 7, 1945.

224   **She stood at the edge**   This description of the swamp draws from "Okefenokee National Wildlife Refuge," U.S. Fish & Wildlife Service (okefenokee.fws.gov); "Waycross and the Okefenokee Swamp" (swampgeorgia.com); "700 Square Miles of Georgia Swamp," *New York Times,* December 9, 1951.

224   **Not long before the B-29 crash**   "Swamp-Like Glimpses," *New York Times,* March 2, 1947.

225   **Okay, Judy thought**   My account here derives from multiple interviews and email exchanges with Judy Palya Loether. She has told this story to a number of other journalists, so versions of her experience sitting on the tree stump have appeared in several newspapers, including the *Courier Post,* the local New Jersey newspaper that for years landed daily on her family's doorstep.

225   **Upon returning home**   The email exchanges among the plaintiffs and with DBR, here and throughout the narrative, were provided by Judy Palya Loether, Susan Brauner, and Patricia Herring.

226   **. . . Judy mailed out twenty postcards**   Copy of the postcard provided by Patricia Herring.

227   **"Dear Mrs. Loether,"**   Copy of letter provided by Judy Palya Loether.

227   **. . . Patricia kept rereading Judy's postcard.**   Patricia Herring's memories and perspective here derive from hours of interviews and email exchanges with her, 2003–7.

230   **All three families were together**   This sequence draws from interviews with Judy Palya Loether, Pat Herring, and Susan Brauner; also from their email exchanges and from copies of their correspondence.

232   **Dear Mr. Melinson, 50 years ago**   Copy of this message provided by Wilson Brown.

232   **In his corner office . . . Brown**   Wilson Brown's memories and perspective here derive from hours of interviews and email messages with him, 2003–2007.

233   **Drinker Biddle & Reath, as in Charles Biddle's time**   This description of DBR draws from the firm's website (www.dbr.com); Gardner and McKay, *Building a Law Firm 1849–1999* (Philadelphia: Drinker Biddle & Reath, 1999); interviews with Wilson Brown.

233   **"Thank you for your inquiry"** Copy of email message provided by Judy Palya Loether.

Chapter 25: On the Side of Right

237   **Encouraged by the positive response** Copy of message provided by Judy Palya Loether.

238   **Bill Palya allowed that** Interview with William Palya, July 6, 2005.

239   **Nothing in Wilson Brown's background** Brown's memories and perspective here derive from hours of interviews with him, 2003–7. This section also draws from his biography on the DBR website.

239   **At a meeting of DBR lawyers** Interviews with Wilson Brown and Jeff Almeida.

240   **At summer's end** Interviews with Patricia Herring and Judy Palya Loether.

241   **At Drinker Biddle & Reath** Interviews with Wilson Brown and Jeff Almeida.

241   **They looked for documents** DBR provided me a full set of the documents they gathered during their search.

241   **Brown considered the challenge** Besides multiple interviews with Brown, this section draws from his email messages, legal briefs, and petitions to the courts.

242   **. . . no guarantee of getting compensated** Phone conversation with Wilson Brown, November 2, 2006.

242   **Those affidavits** Wilson Brown's reasoning here, spelled out to me in interviews, closely reflects what he wrote in his petition for a writ of error *coram nobis*.

Chapter 26: Routes of Relief

245   **In lawyers' parlance** This account of DBR's legal reasoning and strategy draws from hours of interviews with Wilson Brown, supplemented by additional interviews with Jeff Almeida.

246   **A petition for a writ of *coram nobis*** This discussion about writs of *coram nobis* derives from interviews with Wilson Brown and Jeff Almeida, as well as various cases and law journal articles, including: Marc Hideo Iyeki, "The Japanese American Coram Nobis Cases: Exposing the Myth of Disloyalty," *Review of Law & Social Change*, Vol. 13: 199 (Winter 1984–85); Arval A. Morris, "Justice, War and the Japanese American Evacuation and Internment," book review, *Washington Law Review*, Vol. 59, No. 4 (September 1984); Steven J.

Mulroy, "The Safety Net—Applying Coram Nobis to Prevent the
Execution of the Innocent," *Virginia Journal of Social Policy and the
Law Association* (2003); *United States v. Morgan*, Supreme Court of the
United States, January 4, 1954, 346 U.S. 502, 74 S.Ct. 247.

247   **There had been, he came to realize**   The discussion about the
Hirabayashi and *Korematsu* cases relies on many sources, for this is a
much-examined topic in the annals of law. Among them: "Court
Overturns a War Conviction," *New York Times*, November 11 1983;
Roger Daniels, *Prisoners Without Trial: Japanese Americans in World War
II* (New York: Hill & Wang, 2004); David J. Garrow, "Another Les-
son from World War II Internments," *New York Times*, September 23,
2001; Josh Getlin, "WWII Internees Redress: One Made a Difference," *Los Angeles Times*, June 2, 1988; *Hirabayashi v. United States,*
Supreme Court of the United States, June 21, 1943; *Hirabayashi v.
United States*, U.S. Court of Appeals for the Ninth Circuit, September
24, 1987; *Hirabayashi v. United States,* U.S. District Court for the
Western District of Washington, February 10, 1986; Peter Irons, *Justice at War: The Story of the Japanese American Internment Cases* (Berke-
ley: University of California Press, 1983); Peter Irons, *Justice Delayed:
The Record of the Japanese American Internment Cases* (Middletown,
Connecticut: Wesleyan University Press, 1989); "Japanese-American
Reopens Question of War Internment," *New York Times*, June 17,
1985; *Korematsu v. United States,* Supreme Court of the United States,
December 18, 1944; *Korematsu v. United States,* U.S. District Court for
the Northern District of California, April 19, 1984; Claudia. Luther,
"Fred Korematsu, 86, Fought World War II Internment, Dies," *Los
Angeles Times*, April 1, 2005; Charles McClain, ed., *The Mass Intern-
ment of Japanese Americans and the Quest for Legal Redress* (New York:
Garland Publishing, 1994); "Of Civil Wrongs and Rights, The Fred
Korematsu Story," videotape documentary, NAATA Film Library;
Robert Pear, "A Japanese Relocation Case Tests the Verdict of His-
tory," *New York Times*, June 30, 1985; Ronald J. Riccio, "Subjecting
War to the Law," *New Jersey Law Journal*, July 26, 2004; "U.S. Acts to
Overturn a Wartime Conviction," *New York Times*, October 5, 1983;
Elder Witt, "Japanese-Americans Seek Redress from Court," *Congres-
sional Quarterly Weekly Report*, April 18, 1987.
        "We cannot reject as unfounded   *Korematsu v. United States,*
Supreme Court of the United States, December 18, 1944.

247   **Then, in 1981**   See Peter Irons's two books, *Justice at War* and *Justice
Delayed.*

248   **"[Korematsu] stands as a caution**   *Korematsu v. United States,*
U.S. District Court for the Northern District of California, April 19,
1984. Judge Patel filed her written decision some six months after

granting Korematsu's petition in a dramatic oral opinion delivered from the bench at the close of the hearing in November 1983.

248　　**In February 1986 . . . Vorhees granted**　*Hirabayashi v. United States,* U.S. District Court for the Western District of Washington, February 10, 1986.

248　　**. . . the next September, the U.S. Ninth Circuit**　*Hirabayashi v. United States,* U.S. Court of Appeals for the Ninth Circuit, September 24, 1987.

249　　**Three widows stood**　Preliminary Statement, Petition for a Writ of Error *Coram Nobis* to Remedy Fraud Upon the Court, February 26, 2003.

251　　**. . . Judy, apologizing for her "emotional reactions"**　Copy of email provided by Judy Palya Loether.

252　　**The only journalist . . . who knew**　"Search for a Father and Truth After 50 Years," WBUR (Boston), August 29, 2002; "Truth and a Case of National Security," WBUR (Boston), August 30, 2002.

253　　**The day after Fran's train trip**　"A Case to Shake the Foundation of National Security Law," WBUR (Boston), February 27, 2003.

255　　**On Sunday, March 2, Fred Thys**　"Profile: Newly declassified records of 1948 military plane crash reopening case of Supreme Court decision allowing government to withhold information from courts to protect state secrets," NPR, *Weekend All Things Considered,* March 2, 2003.

255　　**Clayton Higgins felt obliged**　This account draws from interviews with Jeff Almeida, confirmed by Christopher Vasil, chief deputy clerk of the Supreme Court.

255　　**Immediately after talking to Vasil**　"Motion to File Petition for a Writ of Error *Coram Nobis,*" March 4, 2003.

256　　**The filing . . . sparked growing media interest**　Such as: "Unearth Military Secret Brings New Life to Old Case," by L.Stuart Ditzen, *Philadelphia Inquirer,* March 5, 2003; "Victim's Daugher Says U.S. Lied About Crash," by Marcella Bombardieri, *Boston Globe,* March 18, 2003.

257　　**On March 18, Brown received**　Copy of this message and resulting exchange of emails provided by Judy Palya Loether.

Chapter 27: A Creative Try

260　　**Clinton's declassification in 1995**　"Release of Historical Aviation Accident Reports," Sheila L. Widnall, Secretary of the Air Force, January 23, 1996.

261　　**This was the twenty-third**　Discussion here of the solicitor general's office draws from "Supreme Court Solicitations," by Tony Mauro, *Legal Times,* May 19, 2003.

262   **On May 30, almost two months after**   "Response of the United States to Motion for Leave to File a Petition for a Writ of Error *Coram Nobis*," May 2003.

264   **Brown and Almeida filed their reply**   "Petitioners' Reply in Support of Their Motion to File Petition for a Writ of Error *Coram Nobis*," June 12, 2003.

266   **"This is a creative try**   "New Light on an Old Defense of 'Secrets,'" by Marcia Coyle, *National Law Review*, March 10, 2003.

266   **"That the facts**   Interview with Kate Martin, June 2003.

267   **"For the Supreme Court to address**   Interview with Jonathan Turley, June 2003.

Chapter 28: Other Types of Comfort

269   **In mid-September, everyone arrived**   I attended this clambake at Susan Brauner's home on Cape Cod, Saturday September 13 2003. I witnessed all scenes and heard directly what I report of it.

270   **Other lawyers . . . had started to study and use**   For example, Mark Zaid, managing partner at Krieger & Zaid in Washington, D.C, whose practice often focuses on national security law, reported: "I am indeed citing to the *Reynolds* petition as an example of why courts need to be extremely careful in accepting state secret privilege declarations" (email to me, September 16, 2003).

272   **In late April . . . John Ashcroft**   "U.S. Can Detain Illegal Immigrants Indefinitely, Ashcroft Rules," Associated Press/CNN.com, April 29, 2003.

272   **That same month, federal prosecutors**   "Prosecutors Appeal 'Dirty Bomber' Case Visits," CNN, April 22, 2003.

272   **In late May, the Supreme Court**   "Supreme Court Declines Secret Hearings Case," *AP/Editor & Publisher*, May 27, 2003.

272   **The next month, a federal appellate court**   U.S. Court of Appeals for the D.C. Circuit, June 17, 2003; "Court Says Detainees' IDs Can Be Kept Secret," by Steve Fainaru, *Washington Post*, June 18, 2003.

272   **One case that most directly tested**   "Terror Case Could Redraw Lines of Power," by Siobhan Roth, *Legal Times*, July 24, 2003; "Judge Rules Out Death Penalty for Moussaoui," *Los Angeles Times*, October 3, 2003; "Court Supports Legal Curbs on Moussaoui," *Houston Chronicle*, December 31, 2003; "Ban on Moussaoui Filing Motions Directly Upheld," *Chicago Tribune*, December 31, 2003.

272   **At that moment**   Interviews with Jeff Almeida.

273   **News of this conversation drew responses**   Email message to me from Susan Brauner, November 18, 2003.

273   **Fred Korematsu also stepped forward**   "Subjecting War to the Law," by Ronald J. Riccio, *New Jersey Law Journal*, July 26, 2004; "The

Courage to Be a Civil Libertarian—When It Counts," by Howard L. Simon, *Tampa Tribune*, May 17, 2004.

273 **"Mr. Korematsu, the enemy combatants** Email message to me from Susan Brauner, November 18, 2003.

273 **On September 30 . . . Brown filed** "Independent Action for Relief from Judgement to Remedy Fraud upon the Court," *Herring et al. v. United States of America*, in U.S. District Court for the Eastern District of Pennsylvania, September 30, 2003.

274 **"The Executive Branch's familiarity** "Motion to Dismiss," *Herring et al. v. United States*, January 23, 2004.

274 **The three took a taxi** This account of the hearing in U.S. District Court draws from interviews with Judy Palya Loether, Patricia Herring, and Wilson Brown, and from the official transcript of the hearing.

275 **He was fifty-two, a Princeton graduate** Federal Judicial History, at the Federal Judicial Center database (http://www.fjc.gov/).

275 **Gilligan had the floor first.** All quotes at this hearing come from "Transcript of Hearing Before the Honorable Legrome D. Davis, U.S. District Judge," *Herring et al. v. United States of America*, U.S. District Court, Eastern District of Pennsylvania, May 11, 2004, 9:30 a.m.

279 **By that spring of 2004** "Detention Cases Before Supreme Court Will Test Limits of Presidential Power," by Linda Greenhouse, *New York Times*, April 17, 2004; "High Court at Crossroads," by Tony Mauro, *Legal Times*, February 23, 2004; "Supreme Court Will Hear 3rd Detainee Case in April," by Neil A. Lewis, *NYT*, February 21, 2004; "Justices to Weigh Presidential Powers," by David Savage, *Los Angeles Times*, January 12, 2004; "The Justices Take On the President," by Anthony Lewis, *NYT*, January 16, 2004.

279 **In his brief, he complained** As quoted in Tony Mauro, "High Court at Crossroads."

279 **The executive branch, observed one attorney** David Bradford, partner at Jenner & Block and author of a brief for former federal judges opposing the government; quoted in Tony Mauro, "High Court at Crossroads."

279 **The Supreme Court acted first** "High Court Says Detainees Have Right to Hearing," by David Savage, *Los Angeles Times*, June 29, 2004; "Court Affirms Due Process Rights of Enemy Combatants," by Tony Mauro, *New York Law Journal*, June 29, 2004; "Judges Back Detainee Access to U.S. Courts," by Charles Lane, *Washington Post*, June 29, 2004; "The Supreme Court: Detainee Access to Courts," by Linda Greenhouse, *New York Times*, June 29, 2004; "High Court Backs Detainee Right to Challenge U.S.," *Wall Street Journal*, June 29, 2004; "No Blank Check," by David Cole, *The Nation*, July 19,

2004; "What the Court Really Said," by Ronald Dworkin, *New York Review of Books*, July 14, 2004.

279   **. . . in a pair of historic decisions**   *Rasul v. Bush*; *Hamdi v. Rumsfeld*

279   **"We have long since . . ."**   "High Court Says Detainees Have Right to Hearing," by David Savage, *Los Angeles Times*, June 29, 2004.

280   **Echoing the steel-seizure case**   "Court Cases Checked a President's Powers," by David Savage, *Los Angeles Times*, July 4, 2004.

280   **Days later, Theodore Olson**   "Olson's Parting Shots: Supreme Court Term Bad for Conservatives," *Associated Press/Law.com*, July 12, 2004.

281   **On September 10, in a Memorandum**   "Memorandum and Order," *Herring et al. v. United States of America*, September 10, 2004.

282   **In Indiana**   Email message to me, September 20, 2004.

282   **In Massachusetts**   Email message to me, September 19, 2004.

282   **On November 8 . . . he filed a notice**   "Notice of Appeal," *Herring et al. v. United States of America*, November 8, 2004.

Chapter 29: The Albert Maris Courtroom

283   **Then, late on the morning**   This passage about the emergence of the Cox family draws from interviews, letters, and email conversations with Judy Palya Loether, Richard A. Cox, and Gerald Cox. Copies of all email exchanges among the plaintiffs, the Cox family, and Wilson Brown were provided by Judy Palya Loether.

285   **As it happened, Gerald Cox's feeling**   Gerald Cox wrote this in a letter to me dated April 12, 2005.

285   **He thought this despite**   Phone conversation with Wilson Brown, November 2, 2006.

286   **He found Judge Davis's order maddening**   This summary of Wilson Brown's thoughts about Judge Davis's ruling comes from interviews with Brown and from his legal brief, "Appeal from the Order of the United Stated District Court dated Sept. 10 2004, Herring et al. v. United States," filed January 19, 2005.

286   **. . . although its existence was public knowledge**   "Russian Air Gain Noted by Spaatz," *New York Times*, November 18, 1947.

286   **As Charlie Biddle noted**   In a letter to Teddy Mattern, July 25, 1950.

287   **. . . "we've been having . . . engine fires"**   "U.S. Grounds B-29s as Another Crash Kills 5 in Florida," *New York Times*, November 18, 1949.

287   **Indeed, the Soviets**   "Made in the U.S.S.R.," *Air & Space Magazine*, February–March 2001: "Operational deployment of the Tu-4 brought a series of breakdowns and near disasters as the airplane

encountered teething problems such as engine overheating, a glitch that mirrored the U.S. experience with the first generation of B-29s."

287 . . . **"the plane was on a special mission** "Nine Killed as B-29 Explodes Over City," *Waycross Journal-Herald*, October 7, 1948.

287 **He worked on his brief** "Appeal from the Order of the United Stated District Court dated September 10, 2004, *Herring et al. v. United States*," filed January 19, 2005.

287 **"I feel like we have** Email message to me, January 28, 2005.

288 **"If any of you wish to speak** Copy of email provided by Judy Palya Loether.

288 **It was exceedingly hot** This description of the DBR reception draws from interviews with Judy Palya Loether, Wilson Brown, and Patricia Herring.

288 **Down below was Logan Square** Also known as Logan Circle.

290 **When the Third Circuit** Dedication Ceremony for the Albert Branson Maris Courtroom, June 27, 1988; printed program of speakers and their remarks.

290 **The Albert Maris Courtroom was modern** The following description of the Third Circuit hearing derives from interviews with Judy Palya Loether, Wilson Brown, and Patricia Herring, and from a transcript of the hearing.

291 **Of the three, Aldisert . . . had seniority** Biographical sketches from "Federal Judicial History," Federal Judicial Center database (http://www.fjc.gov). Additional background on Aldisert, including his thoughts on Albert Maris, comes from an interview with him posted by Howard Bashman on the "How Appealing" Web log, July 7, 2003 (http://howappealing.law.com/20q/2003_07_01_20q- appellate-blog_archive.html).

292 **Wilson Brown rose to speak** Although there is no official transcript, I ordered an audiotape of this hearing from the Clerk of Court and had it transcribed. Wilson Brown then reviewed the transcript for errors and inaudible moments, and identified which judge was speaking when. The account here draws from this annotated transcript.

294 **How wise and prescient Maris had been** "Opinion of the Court" in U.S. Court of Appeals for the Third Circuit, *Reynolds v. United States; Brauner and Palya v. United States;* filed December 11, 1951.

295 **Aldisert and Van Antwerpen had attended** In the program, Aldisert and Van Antwerpen are listed among those being present at "Proceedings in Memory of Honorable Albert Branson Maris, March 9, 1989."

297   **After the others had gone** Interviews with Judy Palya Loether and Michael Stowe.

Chapter 30: The Finality of Judgment

299   **By the best available count** This tabulation provided to me in October 2007 by William Weaver. The Reagan administration, with twenty-five reported assertions, comes in a distant second.

299   **. . . the CIA successfully moved** *Tilden v. Tenet,* U.S. District Court, E.D. Virginia, Alexandria Division, November 27, 2000.

299   **In 2003, a month before** This lawsuit was filed by former TRW senior engineer Nina Schwartz, who—essentially charging fraud on behalf of the government—claimed that TRW had submitted false test results during development of an antimissile vehicle. Not Schwartz but TRW sought classified documents in this matter—an effective move, for after the government predictably intervened with a claim of privilege, TRW was able to argue that it couldn't properly defend itself without the disputed documents. A U.S. District judge dismissed Nina Schwartz's lawsuit at a hearing on February 24. See Inside Missile Defense, (www.InsideDefense.com), Feb. 14 2003.

299   **That same month, the government** *Stillman v. Dept. of Defense,* U.S. District Court for the D.C. Circuit, February 25, 2003.

300   **A group of contractors** *McDonnell Douglas and General Dynamics v. United States,* U.S. Court of Appeals for the Federal Circuit, March 17, 2003.

300   **A former Department of Energy official** *Trulock v. Lee,* U.S. Court of Appeals for the Fourth Circuit, June 3, 2003.

300   **A CIA agent found** *Sterling v. Tenet,* U.S. Court of Appeals for the Fourth Circuit, August 3, 2005.

300   **An FBI translator** *Sibel Edmunds v. U.S. Dept. of Justice,* U.S. District Court for the District of Columbia, July 6, 2004.

300   **Filed on September 22, 2005** "Opinion of the Court," U.S. Court of Appeals for the Third Circuit, *Herring et al. v. United States of America,* No. 04-4270, filed September 22, 2005.

304   **Among the most revealing** "In Legal Shift, U.S. Charges Detainee in Terrorism Case," *New York Times,* November 23, 2005.

304   **Then came the *New York Times*'s revelation** "Bush Lets U.S. Spy on Callers Without Courts," by James Risen and Eric Lichtblau, *New York Times,* December 16, 2005.

304   **During a Saturday radio talk** "Bush Insists on Tools to Fight Terror," *Los Angeles Times,* December 20, 2005; "Editor-in-Chief," *Los Angeles Times,* December 20, 2005.

304   **The *New York Times* . . . punched back**   "On the Subject of
        Leaks," *New York Times*, January 4, 2006.

304   **On December 21 . . . Brown filed**   "Petition for a Writ of Certio-
        rari," Supreme Court of the United States, *Herring et al. v. United
        States of America,* December 21, 2005.

304   **"It ain't over**   Email message to me, December 21, 2005.

305   **"There do not appear**   Email message to me, May 3, 2006.

305   **Yes, the government's claims**   "Invoking Secrets Privilege Be-
        comes a More Popular Legal Tactic by U.S.," by Scott Shane, *New York
        Times,* June 4, 2006.

305   **In February 2006 . . . Trager**   *Arar v. Ashcroft,* U.S. District Court,
        Brooklyn; "U.S. Judge Dismisses Suit by Canadian Deported to
        Syria," *New York Times,* February 17, 2006.

305   **On May 12 . . . Ellis**   *Khaled El-Masri v. George Tenet,* U.S. District
        Court for the Eastern District of Virginia, Alexandria Division, filed
        May 12, 2006.

306   **Then came three more claims**   *Hepting v. AT&T; ACLU et al. v.
        National Security Agency; Center for Constitutional Rights et al v. George
        W. Bush et al.*

306   **. . . "born with a lie on its lips."**   As quoted by John W. Dean
        in "ACLU v National Security Agency: Why the 'State Secrets
        Privilege' Shouldn't Stop the Lawsuit Challenging Warrantless Tele-
        phone Surveillance of Americans," *FindLaw,* June 16, 2006.

306   **Another believed**   Mark Zaid, managing partner at Krieger & Zaid.

306   **. . . "judicially mishandled**   William G. Weaver and Robert
        M. Pallitto, "State Secrets and Executive Privilege," *Political Science
        Quarterly,* Vol. 120 Number 1, Spring 2005.

306   **There were proposals for change**   "Who Will Guard the
        Guardians? Revisiting the State Secrets Privilege of United States v.
        Reynolds," by David A. Churchill and Elaine J. Goldenberg, *Federal
        Contracts Report,* Vol. 80 Number 11, September 30, 2003.

306   **There were even a couple of occasions**   "Court Denies State Secrets
        Claim in Wiretapping Case," *Secrecy News,* July 21, 2006; "Wiretap
        Project Ruled Illegal," *Los Angeles Times,* August 18, 2006; "U.S. Judge
        Finds Wiretapping Plan Violates the Law," *New York Times,* August 18,
        2006.

306   **In the summer of 2006**   *Hepting et al. v. AT&T Corp,* in San Fran-
        cisco; *ACLU et al. v. National Security Agency,* in Detroit.

306   **"It is important to note"**   *Hepting et al. v. AT&T Corp,* U.S. District
        Court for the Northern District of California, No. C-06-672 VRW,
        July 20, 2006.

307   **When Judge Walker's decision**   Brief of *Amici Curiae* in Support of
        Affirmance and Hepting and Al-Haramain, May 2, 2007.

307   **In late May 2007**   Reforming the State Secrets Privilege—Statement
of the Constitution Project's Liberty and Security Committee &
Coalition to Defend Checks and Balances, May 31, 2007.

307   **In mid-August**   Report to the House of Delegates, Section of Individual Rights and Responsibilities, Association of the Bar of the
City of New York, August 2007; "ABA Targets CIA Methods,
Secrets Law," by Henry Weinstein, *Los Angeles Times,* August 14,
2007.

307   **"The Reynolds decision was based**   As quoted in "ABA Targets CIA Methods, Secrets Law," by Henry Weinstein, *Los Angeles
Times,* August 14, 2007.

Chapter 31: Just One More Mission

308   **Just one more mission**   This description of the January 2007 visit
to Waycross draws from interviews, detailed written reports, and photographs provided by Judy Palya Loether, Michael Stowe, Gerald
Cox, Richard A. Cox, and David Pope.

ACKNOWLEDGMENTS

ASSEMBLING A NONFICTION CHRONICLE SUCH AS THIS REQUIRES the cooperation of a great many people, to whom I am forever indebted. Most particularly, I thank those who populate this story. Without the assistance of Judy Palya Loether, Patricia Herring, Susan Brauner, and Cathy Brauner, my task would have been impossible. Each, at varying times during my research, shared with me her memories and insights. Judy Loether—the guiding light—provided a wealth of documents, everything from family histories to Charles Biddle's letters, and proved to be a supportive, enthusiastic, indefatigable reporter. Patricia Herring welcomed me to her home and willingly explored a painful past. At her clambake on Cape Cod, during an early stage of my project, Susan Brauner served up delicious lobster rolls along with resonant memories. In the editor's office at the *Wellesley Townsman*, Cathy Brauner shared photos, impressions, and her deeply moving column "This Is What the Terrorists Took."

I began researching this narrative early one morning in April 2003, in the law offices of Drinker Biddle & Reath in downtown Philadelphia. There Wilson Brown and Jeff Almeida spent a day introducing me to the full arc of the B-29 litigation, walking me through the sequence and meaning from Cold War days to the present. Then, over a span of four years, Wilson Brown delivered a steady flow of reports, analyses, and—much to my appreciation—a carefully annotated transcript of the hearing before the Third Circuit Court of Appeals.

I am, as well, greatly indebted to Michael Stowe, who gave me a properly ordered and divided set of the two accident reports after realizing the pages from his microfilm source were muddled. He also deciphered the classification markings on the reports, explained the arcane nature of the accident forms, and generally helped translate the language of the military aviation investigator.

For my analysis of the fatal B-29 flight, I owe a considerable debt to Rinker Buck, a journalist, author, pilot, and accident analyst who welcomed me to his home in West Cornwall, Connecticut, pored over the accident reports for hours with me, wrote extended memos, and escorted me to the New England Air Museum, where we crawled through a rebuilt B-29. In Oceanside, California, I spent invaluable hours examining the accident reports with Raymond Toliver, who at age ninety-one displayed all the wit and energy that made him an accomplished Air Force colonel, B-29 test pilot, accident investigator, aviation historian, and Pentagon administrator.

For my understanding of Charles Biddle, I thank his son, James Biddle, who welcomed me to Andalusia, where we spent an afternoon touring the estate and talking of his father. For my grasp of events in Waycross, I thank the Zachry family—particularly Bernard and Michael—who met me for lunch and took me to the crash site, showing me the tree stump where Judy sat in January 2002. For educating me about the state secrets privilege, I thank Jonathan Turley, Peter Raven-Hansen, Stephen Dycus, Kate Martin, William Weaver, Mark Zaid, and Steven Aftergood. For a careful, comprehensive tabulation of state secret claims, I owe a special debt to William Weaver.

Thanks also to David Pope, Gerald Cox, Jean Perryman, Viola Ergen, William Palya, William O'Brien, and Ed Mitrani for guiding me back to the past with such grace and precision. At the Air Force Historical Research Agency in Alabama, archivist Joseph D. Caver went beyond the call of duty to help me track down microfilm records about the Banshee Project. At the Frank Folsom Papers in the University Archives of Notre Dame University, archivist Kevin Cawley rolled out dozens of boxes of Folsom memorabilia. At the federal courthouse in Philadelphia, Michael Kunz, the clerk of court for the U.S. District Court, guided my research into Judge Maris and Judge Kirkpatrick, locating documents, making introductions, and arranging appointments. I owe a debt there also to all involved in the Historical Society of the U.S. District Court and the Third Circuit, to Judith Ambler at the U.S. Couthouse's law library, and to U.S. District Judge Stewart Dalzell.

It is not possible to acknowledge here all the historians' books and articles I consulted for my grasp of the Cold War era, but I have listed their works in my notes and sources and warmly thank them. The interested reader should note that another book about the Reynolds case has been published, *In the Name of National Security,* by Louis Fisher (Lawrence: University Press of Kansas, 2006). Fisher, a senior scholar in the Law Library at the Library of Congress, provides a useful if different approach and perspective.

I offer a most special thanks to Lane Demas, who during my work on this book was my graduate student research assistant and a doctoral candidate in the history department at UC Irvine. He is now a visiting instructor at Scripps College in Claremont, California, and is due to receive his Ph.D. in United States history in June 2008. I admire his insight, dedication, and energy, all of which promise a lustrous future for the soon-to-be Professor Demas. Nona Yates, a researcher at the *Los Angeles Times,* generously provided additional help in finding obscure documents and calculating dollar equivalencies. Patricia Pierson assistant director of the literary journalism program at UC Irvine, did her best to keep me propped up.

Once the research is completed, the writing begins. I thank David Hirshey, executive editor at HarperCollins, for all his editing advice as well as his initial belief in this project. I owe a big debt also to Kate Hamill, associate editor at HarperCollins, who shepherded the manuscript through the thickets of production with unflappable grace. Susan Squire provided invaluable counsel when I struggled over an early draft. Rick Meyer, a premier editor of nonfiction narrative, gave my working draft a wise, rigorous line edit. So did Ed Cohen, a gifted copyeditor. Then came Kit Rachlis, the primary manuscript editor for this chronicle, who proved yet again what all literary journalists know—he is the best.

Many years ago, I wrote that I had no words to express properly my regard and appreciation for Kathy Robbins, who is my agent, friend, mentor, cheerleader, and scold. I must repeat myself: Her passionate support knows no bounds. Then as now, I can only say that this book would not exist but for her.

My wife, Marti Devore, and daughter, Ally Siegel, put up with me, as always. Their love, support, and toleration make it all possible.

INDEX